The Research Process

What's yo~~~~~~~~~~~~~~
guide to h~~~~~~~~~~~~~~

D0342236

9100

The Bedford
RESEARCHER

FOURTH EDITION

The Bedford
RESEARCHER

Mike Palmquist

Colorado State University

Bedford/St. Martin's   Boston ◆ New York

For Bedford/St. Martin's
Executive Editor: Leasa Buton
Developmental Editor: Sarah Macomber
Production Editor: Kendra LeFleur
Assistant Production Manager: Joe Ford
Senior Marketing Manager: Molly Parke
Editorial Assistant: Allie Goldstein
Copy Editor: Lisa Wehrle
Indexer: Jake Kawatski
Photo Researcher: Susan McDermott Barlow
Permissions Manager: Kalina K. Ingham
Senior Art Director: Anna Palchik
Text Design: Claire Seng-Niemoeller
Cover Design: Billy Boardman. Topographical map courtesy of istock
Composition: NK Graphics
Printing and Binding: RR Donnelley and Sons

President: Joan E. Feinberg
Editorial Director: Denise B. Wydra
Editor in Chief: Karen S. Henry
Director of Marketing: Karen R. Soeltz
Director of Production: Susan W. Brown
Associate Director, Editorial Production: Elise S. Kaiser
Managing Editor: Elizabeth M. Schaaf

Library of Congress Control Number: 2011921708

For information, write: Bedford/St. Martin's, 75 Arlington Street, Boston, MA 02116 (617-399-4000)

ISBN-13: 978–0–312–67512–7

Acknowledgments

Figure 1.2: © Joel Gordon.
Figure 1.3: This figure was prepared by the National Renewable Energy Laboratory for the U.S. Department of Energy.
Figures 2.3, 8.3, 8.5, 8.8, 8.17, page 143, and page 380: Reprinted with the permission of EBSCO Publishing.
Figure 2.5: Courtesy of DMOZ.org.

Acknowledgments and copyrights are continued at the back of the book on pages 438–39, which constitute an extension of the copyright page. It is a violation of the law to reproduce these selections by any means whatsoever without the written permission of the copyright holder.

Preface for Instructors

When I wrote the first edition of *The Bedford Researcher*, I focused on both enduring challenges facing writers who work with information and a new set of challenges brought about by what was then a relatively recent revolution in information technology. Those new challenges included the explosive growth in the amount of information available to writers, the rapidly expanding variety of media and genres used by writers to share their work, the critical importance of evaluating sources that—at first glance—appear to be "just like" the sources in a library, and the demands of managing information effectively and efficiently.

In the decade that has passed since I reflected on those challenges, much has changed. Google has become far more than a search engine. Handheld devices, among them iPhones and iPads, Androids and BlackBerries, Nooks and Kindles and Galaxy Tabs, have created a world in which information is available at the swipe of a finger. And librarians have become far more concerned with maintaining digital access to journals and databases than with expanding their collections of print materials.

Today, writers live and work in a complex and rapidly evolving information ecology. They connect via wire, wifi, and cellular networks. They keep in touch with each other through social media. And they wonder where the boundary lies between the personal and the public. As they work with information, however, they find that not everything has changed. As was the case in the mid-twentieth century—and, for that matter, in the centuries that preceded it—writers must still consider their purpose and the needs and interests of their readers; they must still make choices about genres and design; they are still shaped by the social, cultural, and historical contexts in which they work; and they must still grapple with limitations and take advantage of opportunities they encounter as they work on their research writing projects.

Meeting these new challenges while maintaining a focus on the fundamental relationships among writers, readers, genres, and contexts can tax even the most experienced writers. Our students, then, face a doubly difficult task: learning the core principles of research writing and mastering the technological context that has vastly complicated the rhetorical situations in which they find themselves. As I've reflected on the challenges facing our students, I've become convinced that students can be most successful if we help them understand research writing both conceptually and practically, combining a rhetorical framework with the accessible guidance students need to help them navigate the world of academic research writing. In this edition of *The Bedford Researcher*, I've expanded my treatment of the rhetorical nature of research writing, refined and deepened the discussions of the writing process, increased the number of activities students can use to make progress on their research writing projects, and provided additional strategies for managing their projects. I've also strengthened the book's focus on genre and design, critical reading, plagiarism and research ethics, argumentation, information literacy and fluency, digital tools in field research, and more.

This edition also continues the practice of offering writers and instructors a rich set of instructional technology resources on its companion Web site, **bedfordresearcher.com**. These tools are relevant, easy to use, and focused on the needs of research writers.

FEATURES

The Bedford Researcher is based on the premise that the decisions good research writers make are shaped primarily by rhetorical concerns—the writer's purposes and interests; the readers' needs, interests, values, and beliefs; the setting in which a document is written and read; and the requirements and limitations associated with an assignment. To illustrate this premise, the book presents research writing as a process of choosing, learning about, and contributing to a conversation among readers and writers.

Complete Coverage of the Research Writing Process   As in the previous editions, the text is divided into five parts. The first four parts correspond to the stages of an idealized research writing process, although the book stresses the recursive nature of research writing. The fifth part focuses on documentation systems. Part 1, Joining the Conversation, introduces the concept of research writing as a social act. It helps students understand that research writing involves exploring conversations among writers and readers, narrowing their focus to a single conversation, and developing a research question to guide their inquiry into that conversation. Part 2, Working with Sources, establishes the importance of reading critically (with a new focus on recognizing and assessing the arguments in sources), evaluating sources, managing information, taking notes, and avoiding plagiarism. Part 3, Collecting Information, helps students search for information using digital resources, print resources, and field research methods. Part 4, Writing Your Document, guides students as they develop their thesis, organize their information and ideas, frame their argument, develop an outline, draft their document, integrate source material, revise and edit their drafts, and design their document. Finally, Part 5, Documenting Sources, provides comprehensive and up-to-date chapters on MLA, APA, *Chicago*, and CSE styles.

Engaging and Useful Apparatus   The book is designed so that students can find information easily and work competently through each stage of their projects. Each chapter is structured around a set of *Key Questions* that enables students to find information quickly and ends with *Quick Reference* boxes to stress the chapter's main points. The *What's My Purpose?* boxes throughout the text remind students to constantly reflect on — and reconsider — their writing situation. The design employs clear and accessible illustrations, annotations, checklists, activities, and documentation guidelines — the parts of the text students will return to as they write.

A Conversational, Student-Friendly Tone   I've written *The Bedford Researcher* in an accessible, easy-to-follow style that treats students with respect. I want students to gain confidence in their ability to write well, conduct research effectively, and think critically. Clear, relevant examples address students' questions about research writing by concretely illustrating writing, research, and critical reading strategies.

Detailed Case Studies of Real Student Researchers   Six featured writers, real students who undertook a variety of research writing projects, including traditional research essays, Web sites, and multimodal essays, provide accessible models for your students as they conduct their own research and draft their own documents.

A Cross-Curricular Companion   Because students need a research text suitable for a variety of academic purposes, *The Bedford Researcher* and its companion Web site feature examples and models that span the disciplines, providing research writing help for composition courses and beyond. Guidelines for writing papers and detailed citation models are provided for a multitude of source types in MLA style, APA style, *Chicago* style, and CSE style. Each style is further illustrated on *The Bedford Researcher* Web site through sample documents created by the featured writers.

NEW TO THIS EDITION

This edition of *The Bedford Researcher* features the following updates:

Increased Emphasis on Project Management   Throughout this edition, you'll find improvements and expansions of a key feature of previous editions. Chapter 6, Managing Information and Taking Notes, builds on previous coverage of project and information management by calling attention not only to fundamental project management principles but also to new tools for putting those principles into practice. In addition, throughout the book, new and improved *My Research Project* activities and tutorials, along with treatments of information literacy issues, help students learn how to keep their projects on track.

Stronger Attention to Analyzing and Developing Arguments   I've added extensive coverage of the argumentative strategies and techniques students usually find in their sources. The new coverage includes significantly enhanced treatment of how to establish a position on an issue, how to develop a line of argument, and how to support an argument with reasons and evidence. I've revised Part 4,

Writing Your Document, to help students understand the role that argument can play in a wide range of research writing documents. A new argumentative student essay on a timely topic, the growing reliance of the U.S. government on private military corporations, shows how to put these argumentation strategies to work.

Expanded Treatment of Research Presentations   In a new chapter on designing documents, you'll find detailed discussions, examples, and checklists that will help students make effective oral, multimedia, and poster presentations. Along with expanded treatment of designing essays, articles, multimodal essays, and Web sites, this new focus on presentations will help students understand the distinctive challenges and opportunities involved in talking about their work with an audience.

Extensive and Up-to-Date Coverage of Digital Sources and Tools   The text offers relevant, hands-on advice for searching for and evaluating audio, video, and other digital sources; searching for e-books; saving and organizing sources with personal and social bookmarking sites and Web capture tools; integrating images, audio, and video into multimodal documents and multimedia presentations; and revising and editing with digital tools.

VALUABLE ONLINE RESOURCES

The Bedford Researcher Web site (**bedfordresearcher.com**) provides an extensive collection of free and premium materials, including tools and content designed specifically for the needs of research writers:

Free Resources
Interactive Research and Writing Exercises   These exercises extend the tutorials in the book with step-by-step prompts for the toughest research writing tasks in each chapter.

Research Project Activities   Each *My Research Project* activity in the text can be downloaded or printed from the companion Web site, for individual or class work.

Featured Student Writer Portfolios   Readers can view notes, outlines, completed activities, rough drafts, and final research documents of the six student writers featured in the book. They can also view edited transcripts of interviews in which the featured writers discuss their research writing processes.

Research Writing "How-To" Guides   These guides offer specific advice for using online library catalogs, databases, Web search sites and directories, and other digital resources. They also offer up-to-date support for designing documents and creating Web sites.

Annotated Links for Research Writing   The companion Web site gives students access to a wealth of Web-based resources for research writing and document design. Diana Hacker's *Research and Documentation Online* offers an extensive list of databases and indexes, Web resources, and reference books for more than thirty disciplines.

The Bedford Bibliographer   A straightforward, easy-to-use bibliography tool helps students keep track of sources and create bibliographies in MLA, APA, *Chicago*, or CSE style.

Premium Resources
The Bedford Researcher e-Book   Bedford/St. Martin's e-books let students do more and pay less. For about half the price of a print book, the online e-book for *The Bedford Researcher* offers the complete text of the print book combined with convenient digital tools such as highlighting, note taking, and search. The online interactive e-book can be packaged with the print book for free. To order *The Bedford Researcher* packaged free with e-book, use ISBN-13: 978-1-4576-01026.

Other Popular e-Book Formats   Students can purchase *The Bedford Researcher* in other popular e-book formats that can be downloaded to computers, tablets, and e-readers.

Premium Video Research Tutorials   These engaging video tutorials illustrate each research task and guide students through a hands-on activity, from refining a research question to performing an online search.

Other Premium Resources for Teaching Research
i-series on CD-ROM   Add more value to your text by choosing one of the following CD-ROMs, free when packaged with *The Bedford Researcher*. This popular series presents multimedia tutorials in a flexible format—because there are things you can't do in a book. To learn more about package options or any of the products below, contact your Bedford/St. Martin's sales representative or visit **bedfordstmartins.com**.

- **i · claim: visualizing argument** offers a new way to see argument—with six tutorials, an illustrated glossary, and over seventy multimedia arguments. To order *The Bedford Researcher* packaged with *i·claim*, use ISBN-13: 978-1-4576-11025.
- **i · cite: visualizing sources** brings research to life through an animated introduction, four tutorials, and hands-on source practice. To order *The Bedford Researcher* packaged with *i·cite*, use ISBN-13: 978-1-4576-11049.

Bedford/St. Martin's Research Pack includes two laminated quick-reference cards for using MLA and APA styles with brief checklists and model citations and a comprehensive suite of online research resources. To order *The Bedford Researcher* packaged free with the Research Pack, use ISBN-13: 978-1-4576-11018.

VideoCentral is a growing collection of videos for the writing class that captures real-world, academic, and student writers talking about how and why they write. *VideoCentral* can be packaged with *The Bedford Researcher* at a significant discount. An activation code is required. To order *VideoCentral* packaged with the print book, use ISBN-13: 978-1-4576-11032.

Re:Writing Plus gathers all of Bedford/St. Martin's' premium digital content for composition into one online collection. It includes hundreds of model documents, the first ever peer review game, the *i·cite visualizing sources* CD-ROM, and *VideoCentral. Re:Writing Plus* can be purchased separately or packaged with the print book at a significant discount. To order *The Bedford Researcher* with an access card for *Re:Writing Plus*, use ISBN-13: 978-1-4576-11056.

To order any of these ancillaries, please contact your Bedford/St. Martin's sales representative, email sales support (sales_support@bfwpub.com), or visit our Web site at **bedfordstmartins.com**. Activation codes are required for the e-book, *VideoCentral*, and *Re:Writing Plus*. Codes can be purchased separately or packaged with the print book at a significant discount.

Instructor Resources

Teaching with *The Bedford Researcher* can be downloaded from **bedfordresearcher .com**. In addition to chapter overviews and teaching goals and tips, the manual directs you to specific resources for each skill that you'll teach (for example, refining a thesis statement or integrating sources) and illustrates how the book's content aligns with content on the companion Web site.

Teaching Central (**bedfordstmartins.com/teachingcentral**) offers the entire list of Bedford/St. Martin's print and online professional resources in one place. You'll find landmark reference works, sourcebooks on pedagogical issues, award-winning collections, and practical advice for the classroom—all free for instructors.

Bits (**bedfordbits.com**) collects creative ideas for teaching a range of composition topics in an easily searchable blog. A community of teachers—leading scholars, authors, and editors—discuss revision, research, grammar and style, technology, peer review, and much more. Take, use, adapt, and pass the ideas around. Then, come back to the site to comment or share your own suggestion.

Content cartridges for the most common course management systems—Blackboard, WebCT, Angel, and Desire2Learn—allow you to easily download digital resources for your course. To find the cartridges available with *The Bedford Researcher*, visit **bedfordstmartins.com/catalog/bedfordresearcher**.

ACKNOWLEDGMENTS

Once again, I offer my thanks to my family—my wife Jessica, my daughter Ellen, and my son Reid—for their support as I worked on this edition of *The Bedford Researcher*. I continue to be grateful for the guidance and support I received from David Kaufer, Chris Neuwirth, and Richard Young, who have helped me, in graduate school and in the many years since, to think critically and carefully about the relationships among rhetoric, pedagogy, and technology. I offer my thanks as well to my colleagues Sue Doe, Will Hochman, Lynda Haas, and Nick Carbone for their willingness to share ideas and offer support as I worked on this book. I am also grateful to Liz Jackson, for her thoughtful and thorough revision of the instructor's manual.

I am grateful for the opportunity to work with reviewers who provided thoughtful advice and suggestions for revising this book: Valerie Balester, Texas A&M University; Patricia Brock, Pace University; April Carothers, Linn-Benton Community College; Brian Cope, Slippery Rock University; Lesa Dill, Western Kentucky University; Mike Donnelly, Ball State University; Deborah A. Eckberg, Metropolitan State University; Christopher Ervin, Western Kentucky University; Alison Ganze, Western Kentucky University; Lauri Bohanan Goodling, Georgia Perimeter College; Sarah Klontz, Arizona State University; Jennifer Merrifield, Potomac State College of WVU; Joan Nizalowski, Mesa State College; Caroline Nobile, Edinboro University of Pennsylvania; Matt Omasta, University of Rhode Island; Eugene Richie, Pace University NYC; Rene Scheys, Fullerton College; Nancy L. Schultz, Salem State College; Andrew Scott, Ball State University; Nancy A. Shaffer, University of Texas–El Paso; Andrea Silva, Wayne State University; Karyn L. Smith, Housatonic Community College; Lance Sparks, Lane Community College; Maria Staton, Ball State University; Trey Stecker, Ball State University; Richard C. Taylor, East Carolina University; Dawn Terrick, Missouri Western State University; Reginald Watson, East Carolina University; Stephanie West-Puckett, East Carolina University; Jamie White-Farnham, University of Rhode Island; Marc Wilson, Treasure Valley Community College; Stacey Wright, Syracuse University; and three anonymous reviewers. Their reactions, observations, and suggestions led to many of the improvements in this edition.

I have once again been impressed by the extraordinary support offered by the editors at Bedford/St. Martin's. Development editor Sarah Macomber's strong analysis of the reviewers' reactions to the third edition, careful edits, and timely advice helped me maintain my focus on the key issues facing students as they work in a complex and quickly changing technological context. Nick Carbone's good humor, patience, and generosity of spirit has once again made the revisions of the Web site pleasant and rewarding. I am indebted to Kendra LeFleur, who directed the production of the book, and Lisa Wehrle, who copyedited the manuscript. I am grateful, once again, for the extraordinary design work of Claire Seng-Niemoeller, and for the careful work of Mary Ellen Smith, who updated the documentation models. My thanks are offered as well to editor in chief Karen Henry for her good advice and able leadership of the editorial team. And I am grateful for the hard work and good ideas of editorial assistant Allie Goldstein. I offer my thanks once again to Rory Baruth, regional sales manager for Bedford, Freeman, and Worth Publishers, who introduced me to the editors at Bedford/St. Martin's many years ago and who has continued to support and offer suggestions for improving *The Bedford Researcher*. I am grateful as well to Joan Feinberg, Denise Wydra, and Leasa Burton for their support of *The Bedford Researcher* and for their thoughtful suggestions about the directions this new edition might take.

Finally, I offer my thanks to the six student writers who shared their work, their time, and their insights into their research writing processes with the readers of this book: Alexis Alvarez, Nicholas Brothers, Pete Jacquez, Elizabeth Leontiev, Chris Norris, and Cori Schmidtbauer. As I worked on this edition, their work served as a constant reminder that research writing is a process of continuous discovery and reflection.

Mike Palmquist
Colorado State University

Introduction for Writers

You live in the information age. You surf the Web, text your friends, download music and videos, use email, send instant messages, carry a mobile phone, watch television, read magazines and newspapers, listen to podcasts, view advertisements, attend public events, and meet and talk with others. Understanding how to work with information is among the most important writing skills you can have. In fact, most of the writing that you'll do in your lifetime — in college courses or for a career or community project — requires this skill. Take as examples the following types of documents — all of which require a writer to use information from sources:

- college research essays
- informative Web sites
- feature articles in a newspaper or magazine
- product brochures or promotional literature
- market research analysis to help start a new business or launch a new product
- proposals to a school board or community group
- PowerPoint presentations at business meetings
- letters of complaint about a product or service
- restaurant reviews or travel guides

Because such a wide range of documents relies heavily on a writer's ability to work with information, *The Bedford Researcher* is not so much about research papers as about research writing. What I hope you'll take from this text is a way of thinking about how to conduct research and write a document based on the sources of information you find.

The primary goals of *The Bedford Researcher* are to help you learn how to:

- choose and learn about a topic
- read critically, evaluate, and take notes
- develop a research question, thesis statement, and line of argument
- collect and manage information
- develop, write, revise, and design an effective document
- document sources of information

Meeting these goals requires thinking about research writing in a new way. Research writing is more than simply searching for and reporting information;

it is a process of inquiry—of asking and responding to key questions. Instead of thinking of research writing as an isolated activity, think of it as a social act—a conversation in which writers and readers exchange information and ideas about a topic.

The research writing process you'll follow in this book consists of five main activities, which correspond to the five parts of this book:

Part 1: Joining the Conversation ❯	Chapters 1, 2, and 3 focus on getting started, exploring and narrowing your topic, and developing your research question and proposal.
Part 2: Working with Sources ❯	Chapters 4 through 7 address reading critically, evaluating sources, managing information, taking notes, and avoiding plagiarism.
Part 3: Collecting Information ❯	Chapters 8 through 10 discuss searching for information with digital resources, print resources, and field research methods.
Part 4: Writing Your Document ❯	Chapters 11 through 19 focus on developing your thesis statement and line of argument; organizing and drafting your document; integrating sources; writing with style; and revising, editing, and designing your document.
Part 5: Documenting Sources ❯	Chapters 20 through 24 discuss the reasons for documenting sources and provide detailed guidance on four of the most commonly used documentation systems—MLA, APA, *Chicago*, and CSE.

As you read about these activities and carry them out in your own research project, keep in mind that they reflect a typical writing process—not a step-by-step recipe. Also keep in mind that the writing process seldom follows a straight line from choosing a topic to producing a polished document; most writers move back and forth among writing processes, rethinking their steps and revising their ideas as they work on their writing projects. Whatever your process turns out to be, remember that the order you follow is far less important than adapting these processes to the needs of your particular project.

SUPPORT THROUGHOUT YOUR RESEARCH WRITING PROCESS

The Bedford Researcher offers a wealth of support—in the book and on the companion Web site—to help you complete a research project.

In the Text

The textbook you are holding provides step-by-step guidance for writing research documents. It includes clear descriptions of research writing strategies, examples, activities, documentation guidelines, and model citations.

Color-coded tabs help you find information quickly.

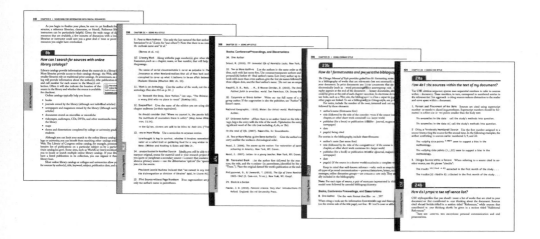

Key Questions begin each chapter and enable you to match your research writing needs to the material in the chapter.

Checklists offer at-a-glance views of a specific research or writing process. They can help you make sure that you've completed the process thoroughly and thoughtfully.

***What's My Purpose?* Boxes** help you consider—and reconsider—your purpose at every stage of the research writing process. Whether you are writing to inform or trying to persuade your readers to take action on an issue, the questions and guidance in the *What's My Purpose?* boxes help keep your project focused and manageable.

***Framing My Argument* Boxes** help you construct your argument one step at a time and use evidence skillfully. They show how your argument is developed over the course of the entire research writing process, not just at the moment you compose your thesis statement.

Information Literacy **Boxes** offer suggestions and identify opportunities as you find, evaluate, and integrate information from print, electronic, and field sources. They address important, but lesser-known facts about research and provide tips for using advanced resources.

Annotated Examples make it easier for you to learn from the many illustrations and screen shots throughout the text. Annotations point out the features and processes at work in a document or tool to help you get the most out of the resources at hand.

My Research Project **Activities** connect what's in the text with your own research writing. They show you how to put the text's practical advice to work and learn more about your own writing process.

Tutorials in the book provide you with extra help for important research writing issues, such as developing a research question, evaluating Web sites, and integrating quotations. They break each process down into steps and use examples to demonstrate a research writer's approach.

Quick Reference **Boxes** at the end of every chapter give you a brief overview of steps to take before you move on.

Cross-references to the companion Web site help you extend your knowledge online at **bedfordresearcher.com.**

On the Web Site

The Bedford Researcher Web site at **bedfordresearcher.com** offers tools and resources to aid you with the most challenging parts of the research writing process.

The Bedford Bibliographer   Use the online tools to evaluate your sources and generate an annotated bibliography in MLA, APA, *Chicago*, or CSE style.

Interactive Research and Writing Exercises   Online exercises break down the most pressing research-related challenges into manageable steps.

Research Project Activities   *My Research Project* activities throughout the text allow you to make progress on your own projects. The activities can be downloaded or printed from the Web site.

Featured Student Writer Portfolios   Take a tour of the research writing process by following six students featured in the text. View their notes and drafts, and read interviews in which the students explain how they tackled their research writing projects.

Research Writing "How-To" Guides   You'll find advice for online searching, designing documents, and using other digital research and writing tools in our easy-to-follow guides.

Annotated Links for Research Writing   Access Web-based resources for research writing and document design, along with an extensive list of specialized research sources for more than thirty disciplines.

Brief Contents

Contents

Working with Sources   59

The Bedford Researcher

I	Joining the Conversation
II	Working with Sources
III	Collecting Information
IV	Writing Your Document
V	Documenting Sources

PART I

Joining the Conversation

1 Getting Started 3

2 Exploring and Focusing 23

3 Developing Your Research Question and Proposal 40

Working on a research writing project is similar to joining a conversation. Before you contribute to the conversation, listen carefully to what others are saying. By reading widely, talking with knowledgeable people, and making firsthand observations, you can gain the knowledge you need to add your voice to the discussion.

In Part I you'll read about how to get started, how to choose an appropriate topic, how to explore and refine your topic, and how to develop a clearly stated research question and research proposal.

Part I
Joining the Conversation

> 1   Getting Started
> 2   Exploring and Focusing
> 3   Developing Your Research Question
>   and Proposal

1

Getting Started

> **Key Questions**

Getting started can be the hardest part of a research writing project. You'll likely find yourself staring at a blank computer screen or twirling a pen in your fingers as you ask, "Is this project really necessary?" or "What in the world should I write about?"

This chapter helps you get started. It provides an overview of research writing processes and project management strategies and discusses how to select, reflect on, and take a position on an appropriate topic.

1a

How can I research and write with confidence?

Even writers who are new to research writing can approach it confidently. All that's needed is a personal investment in your research writing project, an understanding of the processes involved in research writing, a willingness to learn how to work with sources, and an interest in taking a position on an issue. You can also enhance your confidence about undertaking a research writing project by learning about genre and design, understanding the importance of the contexts surrounding your writing project, paying attention to changes brought about by new information technologies, and learning how to manage your time.

Take Ownership of Your Project

Confident research writers have a strong personal investment in their research writing project. Sometimes this investment comes naturally. You might be interested in your topic, committed to achieving your purposes as a writer, intrigued by the demands of writing for a particular audience, or looking forward to the challenges of writing a new type of document, such as a Web site or a magazine article. At times, however, you need to create a sense of personal investment by looking for connections between your interests and your writing project. This can be a challenge, particularly when you've been assigned a project that wouldn't normally interest you.

The key to investing yourself in a project you wouldn't normally care about is taking ownership of the project. To take ownership, ask yourself how your project might help you pursue your personal, professional, or academic interests. Think about how the project might help you meet new people or learn new writing or research strategies. Or look for unique challenges associated with a project, such as learning how to develop arguments or use document design techniques more effectively. Your goal is to feel that you have a stake in your research writing project by finding something that appeals to your interests and helps you grow as a researcher and writer.

Understand Research Writing Processes

Research writing involves learning about a topic, taking a position on that topic, and sharing your position with your readers. Many factors affect how you will accomplish your goals. If you are writing an argument, your overall process will be somewhat different than it would be if you are writing to inform your readers. If you are writing about a topic that is new to you, you'll search for and work with sources in a way that differs from how you'd work with information about a topic you know well. Understanding the research writing processes you can draw on will help you accomplish your purposes as a writer and consider the needs, interests, values, and beliefs of your readers. You'll find a description of these processes in Figure 1.1.

Learn How to Work with Sources

Almost every writing project you'll encounter in college and the workplace involves working with information. To bring these projects to a successful conclusion, you'll need to learn how to identify and locate promising sources, and then how to read, evaluate, take notes on, and decide how to use the information, ideas, and arguments you encounter in them. From your initial exploration of a topic to your decisions about how to use quotations or video clips to make a point, you'll be engaged with sources—the work of other writers who share your interest in an issue.

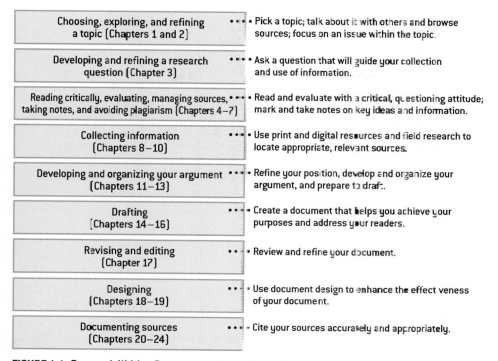

FIGURE 1.1 Research Writing Processes *As you learn about your topic and reflect on your progress, you'll move back and forth among these processes.*

Working with sources also includes managing them so that you can easily locate information when you need it. If you've ever forgotten a phone number or misplaced tickets to a concert, you know how frustrating it can be to lose something. It can be just as frustrating to lose your interview notes or forget where you found a quotation or fact. As you begin your research writing project, decide how you'll keep track of what you'll learn. You might want to start a research log—a place where you can keep the sources you collect and record your thoughts and progress. A research log can take many forms.

- a notebook
- a word processing file or a folder on your computer
- a folder or binder
- a set of note cards
- notes taken on a smartphone or a tablet, such as a Droid, a BlackBerry, an iPhone, or an iPad
- a tape recorder or voice recorder

Although it might seem like extra work now, creating a research log as you begin your project will save time in the long run.

My Research Project

CREATE A RESEARCH LOG

Create your research log now so you'll be prepared to face the challenges of planning and carrying out your project.

   The *Bedford Researcher* Web site at **bedfordresearcher.com** can help you create your research log. You'll find digital versions of the "My Research Project" activities in this book and Interactive Exercises, which extend the book's tutorials. You'll also find bibliography tools that allow you to save bibliographic information and brief annotations for your sources as you work on your project. You can use these Web resources to make progress on your research writing project, keep track of sources, and decide how to use sources to develop and present your argument.

Learn How to Develop a Position

Good research writers inevitably develop a position about their topic. This position can be thought of as the main point they want to convey to their readers. It is the single most important idea, insight, or argument that their readers will gain by reading their document.

   Writers' positions are based on a careful analysis of the conclusions they've drawn about their topic throughout the process of working with sources. Writers draw conclusions about a topic by analyzing the information, ideas, and arguments in those sources, by drawing on their personal experiences and observations, and by reflecting on the topic over the course of a research writing project. In many cases, writers will change and refine their conclusions as they learn more about the topic, as their experiences change, or as they consider their purpose and their readers' needs, interests, values, and beliefs.

   To convey your position to your readers, you will need to determine how to express your main point so that your readers are likely to accept it, identify support for your point, choose a type of document that is appropriate for your writing situation, and plan and draft your document. You'll find guidance on how to draw conclusions about the information, ideas, and arguments you find in your sources, how to develop your position, and how to plan and draft your document in Parts 3 and 4.

Understand Genre and Design

As you work on your research writing project, you can draw on two powerful tools: genre and design. Genre (types of documents) and design (the appearance of those documents) are closely related. In fact, the characteristic design of a particular type of document—for example, the use of columns, headings, and photographs in a newspaper article—can help you distinguish one type of document from another.

   To understand genre, you can turn to personal experience. You're probably familiar with "generic drugs." Imagine you have a headache and want to take

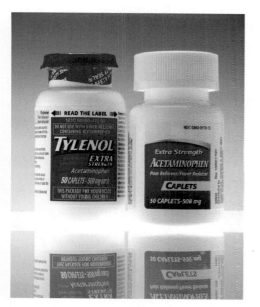

FIGURE 1.2 Brand name or generic?

a pain reliever. You might choose a name-brand drug based on the chemical compound acetaminophen, such as Tylerol or Anacin III. Or you might choose a less-expensive "generic" equivalent based on the same compound. If you're allergic to acetaminophen, you might turn to pain relievers based on aspirin or ibuprofen. Again, you'd have a choice between brand-name drugs, such as Bufferin or Motrin, and their generic equivalents.

Genre, like *generic*, is based on the Latin word *genus*, which means *kind* or *type*. In the same way that generic drugs refer to general categories of pharmaceuticals, genres refer to general categories of documents. The word *novel*, for example, refers to a general category of long fiction. When you say you like reading novels, you aren't talking about reading a particular book; instead, you're expressing a preference for a general type of document. Opinion columns, academic essays, scholarly articles, and Facebook pages are all genres. So are personal journals, thank-you letters, and blog entries. In fact, the number of genres seems to grow every year. Many of today's important genres — for instance, home pages, blogs, and phone-based text messaging — didn't even exist in 1990.

You can think of design as a writing tool as well. Document design is the use of visual elements — such as fonts, colors, page layouts, and illustrations — to enhance the effectiveness of written documents. A well-designed chart, for example, can be far more effective at conveying complex information to a reader than even the most clearly written paragraph (see Figure 1.3). Similarly, the emotional impact of a well-chosen illustration, such as a photograph of a starving child or a video clip of aid workers rushing to help victims of a natural disaster, can do far more than words alone to persuade a reader to take action. By understanding and applying the principles of document design, you can increase the likelihood that you'll achieve your purposes as a research writer and address

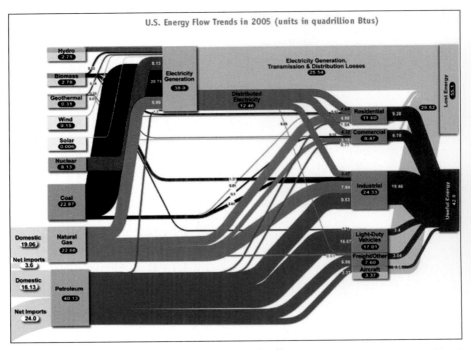

FIGURE 1.3 Conveying Complex Information through a Chart   *Source:* This figure was prepared by the National Renewable Energy Laboratory for the U.S. Department of Energy.

the needs and interests of your readers. Throughout this book, you'll find design treated as a central writing strategy, and you'll find numerous examples of the design characteristics of the genres discussed in each chapter. You'll also find in-depth discussions of design in Chapters 18 and 19.

You can tell genres apart by focusing on why they are written, how they are written, and what they look like. When you read a document, chances are good that you'll recognize it as a particular genre. The style in which it is written, its organization and use of sources, and its design work together to help you understand that a document is a scholarly journal article, a blog entry, a letter to the editor, or a brochure. On the basis of design alone, for example, it's fairly easy to tell the difference between an academic essay and an article in a popular magazine. As you read a document—and without really thinking about it—you'll notice characteristic features of a genre, such as the use of boldface headlines or detailed footnotes. And once you've identified the genre, you'll find the document easier to read. For example, understanding how a document is organized can make it easier to locate information. Similarly, if you recognize a document as an advertisement, you'll be less likely to be swayed by questionable reasoning. Genre and design can serve as powerful tools for addressing the needs, interests, values, and beliefs of your readers—and, ultimately, of achieving your purposes as a research writer.

Understand the Importance of Readers and Context

Writing seldom occurs in a vacuum. When used as a form of communication, it inevitably involves at least one writer and one reader. In this kind of context, the social relationships and experiences between you and your reader will influence your choice of genre, your decisions about what is written and how it is written, and your decisions about design. Writing can also take place in contexts that involve far more people—for example, within classrooms, workplace settings, communities, and academic or professional disciplines. Finally, writing takes place in historical, cultural, and physical contexts. Understanding these various writing contexts will help you gain insights into how best to create effective, well-designed documents.

Think about how social and historical contexts might affect how you would write a letter to a supervisor about problems you've had with a coworker. You would be likely to consider whether your supervisor was a friend or relative of your coworker. You would probably be influenced by your knowledge of problems your coworker has had with other people at your workplace. You might write the letter in one way if you were on a first-name basis with your supervisor and in another way if you were not. Your understanding of the social and historical contexts shaping how your letter would be read—the relationships among people at your workplace, official policies regarding workplace conduct, and past behaviors in the workplace—will affect your efforts to make your letter as effective as possible.

Larger cultural, historical, and disciplinary contexts will also affect what and how you write. The attack on the World Trade Center on September 11, 2001 is one example of a historical event that has strongly affected—and continues to affect—the people of the United States, influencing much of what has been written not only in newspaper and magazine articles, but also on Web sites, in professional journals, and in political blogs. Similarly, the shared experiences of members of particular disciplines, such as biology or sociology, strongly affect what is written by members of those disciplines. As disciplines develop over time, members of a discipline develop consensus about the kinds of documents, such as journal articles or grant proposals, that are best used to share information, ideas, and arguments. Agreements also develop about how to document sources of information, how to report new findings, and how to offer criticism of previous work in the field. In fact, academic disciplines—and U.S. and Canadian ones in particular—are the product of hundreds of years of arguments, decisions, revisions, and reinventions of a way of thinking and behaving. Finally, physical context affects what and how you write. If you know that your readers will give your document undivided attention over a lengthy period of time (as might be the case with a report written for a class), you're likely to choose a type of document that allows you to present your position in enough detail to get your point across—an academic essay or a journal article perhaps. If, on the other hand, you know that your readers will devote limited time to your document or will be reading it in a noisy room (perhaps on a commuter train or in an airport terminal), you might write a document that can be read quickly, such as a magazine article or blog post. Similarly, if you know that your document will be read on a phone screen, you might make different design choices than if you know it will be read in print or on a large computer monitor.

Be Aware of New Technological Opportunities and Challenges

The technological landscape that shapes the work of research writers has undergone more change in the past three decades than at any other time in recorded history. Not even the innovations in printing technologies that brought about the Gutenberg Bible, despite their undeniably important contributions to the growth of literacy, had such immediate and far-reaching effects on reading, writing, and learning. The emergence of the World Wide Web, the development of blogs and wikis, the growing use of social networking sites, the move to digital music and video, the growth in wireless access, the increasing power and sophistication of mobile phones, and the changes to libraries brought about by online library catalogs, databases, digital books, and online journals have significantly changed how research writers locate, manage, and work with sources.

For the foreseeable future, we can expect even more changes in how we access and work with information. Ten years ago, who would have thought that a telephone could help us browse the Web and take notes on sources? Yet the latest smartphones not only connect us to the Web, they allow us to listen to music at the same time—and take photos, capture video, schedule appointments, and record voice memos. Consider as well what digital book readers such as the Kindle and Nook have done for reading and what tablet computers such as the iPad have done for viewing video, surfing the Web, and communicating with others. What will the next year bring? And how will it affect our work as writers?

Prepare to Manage Your Time

Time management should be a high priority as you begin your research writing project. If you don't schedule your time well, for example, you might spend far too much time collecting information and far too little working with it.

As you begin thinking about your research writing project, consider creating a project timeline. A timeline can help you identify important milestones in your project and determine when you need to meet them.

Information Literacy

You can increase your ability to write with confidence by paying attention to the choices you make as you search for and use information. Throughout this book, you'll find Information Literacy boxes that indicate an important opportunity or challenge associated with information and information technology. The advice you find will help you improve your ability to work with technology, and as a result will help you become a better writer.

My Research Project

CREATE A PROJECT TIMELINE

In your research log, start a project timeline like the one shown here. The steps in your process might be slightly different, but most research writing projects follow this general process. As you create your timeline, keep in mind any specific requirements of your assignment, such as handing in a first draft, revised drafts, and so on.

PROJECT TIMELINE		
ACTIVITY	**START DATE**	**COMPLETION DATE**
Select your topic		
Explore your topic		
Refine your topic		
Develop your research question		
Read and evaluate information		
Begin to take a position		
Take notes		
Plan your search for information		
Collect information		
Organize your information		
Draw conclusions about your topic		
Develop your thesis statement		
Identify reasons and evidence		
Organize your document		
Write the first draft of your document		
Review and revise your first draft		
Write and revise additional drafts		
Edit your draft		
Design your document		
Finalize in-text and end-of-text citations		
Publish and submit your document		

You can download or print this activity at **bedfordresearcher.com**. Click on Activities.

FEATURED WRITERS

Discussions throughout this book are illustrated by six featured writers — real students who crafted a variety of research projects, including traditional essays, a multimodal essay, and a Web site. You can learn from these real-life examples as you plan and conduct your own research, and draft and revise your own document.

Alexis Alvarez • Writing about the Impact of Competitive Sports on Adolescent Girls
Alexis wrote a research essay about the effects competitive sports can have on adolescent girls. She explored the general topic of competitive sports and women before refining her topic to the use of steroids by female teenaged athletes. You can read her essay on p. 382.

Nicholas Brothers • Writing about Private Military Corporations and the War on Terror
Nicholas wrote an argumentative research essay about the growing importance of private military corporations in U.S. wars. He supported his argument with published sources and interviews. You can read his essay on p. 411.

Pete Jacquez • Creating a Web site about the Benefits of Wind Power
Pete created a Web site about the benefits of wind-generated electrical power. His site provides both information about wind power and an argument in favor of increasing reliance on wind power. You can view his Web site at **bedfordresearcher.com**.

Elizabeth Leontiev • Writing about the Impact of the U.S. War on Drugs on Coca Farmers in South America
Elizabeth wrote an argumentative research essay for her composition course. She explored the general topic of the war on drugs and then joined a conversation about the effects of U.S. efforts to eradicate coca farming in South America. You can read her research essay on p. 357.

Chris Norris • Writing a Multimodal Essay about Metal Music
Chris wrote a multimodal essay — an essay created in PowerPoint that used text, images, audio, and video to convey his argument — about the resurgence in popularity of metal music. Chris conducted research into the history of metal music, interviewed a local metal band, and created a complex and engaging essay that has to be seen (and heard) to be fully appreciated. You can read his multimodal essay at **bedfordresearcher.com**.

Cori Schmidtbauer • Writing about Portia's Unconventional Role in *The Merchant of Venice*
Cori wrote an analytic research essay that addressed whether Portia fits the ideal of the Renaissance woman. She used sources from literary theorists to debate whether Shakespeare's play was ahead of its time. You can read her essay at **bedfordresearcher.com**.

You can follow the featured writers' research writing process by visiting the *Bedford Researcher* Web site at **bedfordresearcher.com** and clicking on Featured Writers. Here you'll find interviews in which the writers discuss their work, and you can read their assignments, the notes they took as they worked on their projects, and drafts of their documents.

1b

How can I choose an appropriate topic?

In the most general sense, your topic is what you will research and write about—it is the foundation on which your research writing project is built. An appropriate topic, however, is much more than a simple subject heading in an almanac or encyclopedia. It is a subject of debate, discussion, and discovery.

Thinking of your topic as a topic of conversation is critical to your success as a research writer. Research writing goes beyond merely locating and reporting information. Instead, it is an ongoing process of inquiry in which you must consider your purposes, your readers, and the conventions associated with the type of document you plan to write. Ultimately, research writing is about taking and sharing a position on your topic. In some cases, this will involve sharing your understanding or evaluation of a topic with your readers. In other cases, it will involve attempting to convince them to accept your argument about a topic. In still other cases, it will involve sharing your interpretation or analysis of a topic with your readers. Sharing your position—and the information, ideas, and arguments you draw on to support it—allows you to contribute to and advance a conversation about your topic.

Although locating a topic is as easy as visiting your library, reading the newspaper, or browsing the Web, choosing a topic that is well suited to your research writing project requires additional work. It involves reflecting on your assignment, your interests, and your readers.

To choose a suitable topic, analyze your assignment, generate ideas about appropriate topics, and consider the level of interest you and your readers might have in each topic.

Step 1: Analyze Your Assignment

Research writers in academic and professional settings usually work in response to an assignment. You might be given general guidelines, such as "choose a topic in your major"; you might be asked to choose a topic within a general subject area, such as race relations; or you might be given complete freedom in your choice of topic.

Be aware, however, that no matter how much freedom you have, your assignment will provide important clues about what your instructor and your other readers will expect. To analyze your assignment, ask yourself the following questions about your research writing situation.

Who Are My Readers and Why Would They Read My Document?   Your assignment might identify your readers, or audience, for you. If you are writing a research project for a class, one of your most important readers will be your instructor. You are also likely to have additional readers, such as your classmates, people who have a professional or personal interest in your topic, or, if your project will be published in print or online, the readers of a particular newspaper,

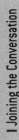

? WHAT'S MY PURPOSE?

Every writer has a purpose, or reason, for writing. In fact, most writers have multiple purposes. If you are writing a research project for a class, your purposes might include completing the assignment as required, learning something new, improving your writing skills, informing readers about an important topic, convincing them to adopt your position on an issue, and getting a good grade. If you are an employee working on a project status report, your purposes might include conveying key information to your superiors, performing well enough to earn a promotion, and gaining valuable experience in project management. Whatever your purposes for conducting a research project, your topic should help you accomplish them.

"What's My Purpose?" boxes like this one, located throughout this book, will help you consider and reconsider your purpose throughout your research writing process.

magazine, or Web site. If you are writing in a business or professional setting, your readers might include supervisors, customers, or other people associated with the organization. In some cases, you might be asked to define your own audience. As you consider possible topics, ask yourself which subjects these readers would be most interested in learning about. Featured writer Cori Schmidtbauer, for example, would probably not have written about the work of William Shakespeare if her target audience had been the readers of a magazine such as *PC World* or *Street Rod*.

Regardless of who your readers are, remember that they aren't empty vessels waiting to be filled with information or told what to think about a topic. They will have their own purposes for reading your document. If the topic you select doesn't fit those purposes, they're likely to stop reading.

What Will Influence Me and What Will Influence My Readers?   Research writers aren't mindless robots who churn through sources and create documents without emotion or conviction—or at least they shouldn't be. Your topic should interest you. An appropriate topic will keep you motivated as you carry out the work needed to complete your research project successfully. Your project should also be your own, even if it's been assigned to you. One of the most important things you can do as a research writer is to make a personal connection with the topic. To make that connection, look for topics that can help you pursue your personal, professional, and academic interests.

Readers are influenced by their interest in a particular topic, their knowledge of the topic, and their values and beliefs. If your readers have no interest in your topic, know little about it, or are offended by it, you aren't likely to meet with much success.

What Type of Document Am I Writing?   Assignments often specify the type of document—or *genre*—you will be writing. You might be asked to write essays, reports, or Web sites. You might be asked to write articles, opinion columns, letters to the editor, multimedia presentations, brochures, or flyers. The genre

TUTORIAL

How do I analyze the audience for a research writing assignment?

Learn about your readers by looking for clues about their needs, interests, and expectations.

COMP 150: College Composition Portfolio 3: Engaging in a Public Issue
Due Date: May 2nd at the beginning of class

1 Analyze the assignment's purpose for clues about your audience.

2 Look for terms such as *reader* and *audience*. Then examine the text near those terms for clues about your readers' expectations.

3 Identify clues about the assignment's genre; look for terms such as *essay, report, argument, article*, or *Web site*.

In this essay, you will write a public response — an article or essay directed to a specific publication — for readers who are interested in the issue you analyzed in your last portfolio. To accomplish this goal, you will: (1) assess the writing situation surrounding the issue; (2) collect information from a variety of sources, including written texts, personal experience, and, if appropriate, field research; (3) evaluate your sources to choose those that best support your argument; and (4) make a sufficiently narrow argumentative claim and support that claim with sound reasoning and evidence.

You should address your article or essay to readers of a publication that has published work about your issue. You will need to analyze the publication, its readers (specifically, their needs, interests, experiences, assumptions, and values), and the writing situation that has shaped discourse about this issue. In general, your audience is likely to expect you to thoroughly explain the points you are making and to support your argument using appropriate forms of evidence. In addition, it is likely that your audience will expect you to use a reasonable tone, to respect your readers and sources, and to avoid slang. Your readers are also likely to expect you to acknowledge and cite your sources in a manner consistent with other sources published by your target publication.

Review another example and work on analyzing your own research writing assignment at **bedfordresearcher.com**. Click on Interactive Exercises.

of your document will have an impact on the kinds of topics you choose. For example, consider the differences among the topics addressed in articles in news magazines such as *Time* and *Newsweek*, the topics addressed in scholarly journals in biology, and the topics addressed on Web sites published by the U.S. Department of Education. Genre will also affect your decisions about the design of your document. To better understand the relationships among genre, design, and topic, review the research essay written by featured writer Alexis Alvarez, the Web site developed by featured writer Pete Jacquez, and the multimodal essay written by featured writer Chris Norris. As you reflect on potential topics for your research writing project, keep in mind the type of document specified in your assignment.

What Contexts Will Affect My Work on the Document?   Assignments often give important clues about the contexts—or settings—in which a document will be read. Contexts range from the immediate shared experiences of readers and writers, to shared cultures, histories, and disciplines, to the physical settings in which documents are written and read.

- *Social context* affects how writers and readers understand each other. Readers familiar with topics such as violence in U.S. secondary schools, for example, will not need to be educated about them—they will already know the key points. This reduces the amount of time and effort writers need to devote to providing background information.

- *Cultural and historical contexts* refer to a larger set of similarities and differences among readers. For instance, readers from the midwestern region of the United States might find it easier to understand the allusions and metaphors used in a document written by someone from Oregon than those in a document written by someone from Peru or Sri Lanka. Similarly, modern teenagers might find it easier to follow what's being said in a document written one month ago by a high school senior in Milwaukee than a document written in 1897 by a retired railroad engineer from Saskatchewan.

- *Disciplinary context* refers to the similar writing practices, general agreements about appropriate types of documents, and shared assumptions about what is worth writing about common to disciplines such as history, construction management, or chemistry. The way that a historian writes a journal article is shaped strongly by disciplinary context and is likely to differ in important ways from how a chemist writes a journal article.

- *Physical context* affects how you read and write (on paper or on a computer screen) and how well you can concentrate (consider the differences between trying to read in a noisy, crowded, jolting bus and a quiet, well-lit room).

For students, one of the most important social and cultural contexts shaping their written work is academic life itself, that complex mix of instructors, fellow students, classes, tests, labs, and writing assignments that you negotiate on a daily basis. As you analyze an assignment, ask whether it will require you to consider particular disciplinary contexts, whether you'll be asked to consider your class as a community, whether you'll be asked to address readers outside of your class setting, and what physical settings might be involved in the writing and reading of your document.

What Role Will I Adopt Toward My Readers?   A role is a way of relating to your readers. The roles you take on will reflect your purpose, your understanding of your readers, and the type of document you plan to write. If you hope to convince or persuade your readers, for example, you would take on the role of an advocate. Advocates are likely to write documents such as argumentative essays, blogs, opinion columns, editorials, funding proposals, and sales plans. If you hope to help your readers understand the significance of a particular work of art or to understand the workings of a complex organization such as the stock market, you would take on the role of interpreter.

Other roles involve activities such as reflecting on a subject, analyzing, evaluating, defining and solving problems, informing your readers, and making arguments, among others. As you consider which topics might interest you, think about how you plan to relate to your readers. Some topics will be more appropriate for an assignment that asks you to interpret an object, event, or process to your readers, while others will be more appropriate for assignments that ask you to inform or persuade or solve problems.

What Will Affect My Ability to Work on This Project?   The requirements of your assignment, the limitations you will face as you work, and the opportunities you can capitalize upon will affect your ability to work on your research project.

Requirements and Limitations   If you are writing your research project for a class, examine the requirements of your assignment:

- the type of document — or *genre*
- the required length or page count
- the project due date
- the number and type of sources you can use (digital, print, and field)
- any suggested or required resources, such as a library catalog or database
- specific requirements about the organization and structure of your document (a title page, introduction, body, conclusion, works cited list, and so on)
- expected documentation format (such as MLA, APA, *Chicago*, or CSE)
- any intermediate reports or activities due before you turn in the final project document (such as thesis statements, notes, outlines, and rough drafts)

You might also face limitations, such as lack of access to information or lack of time to work.

Determining your requirements and limitations will help you weigh the potential drawbacks of a topic. You might find that you need to narrow the scope of your topic significantly given your time and page limit.

Opportunities   Sometimes writers get so wrapped up in the requirements and limitations of the assignment that they overlook their opportunities. As you think about your topic, ask yourself whether you can take advantage of opportunities such as:

- access to a specialized or particularly good library
- personal experience with and knowledge about a topic
- access to people who are experts on a topic

For example, Alexis Alvarez thought about her personal experiences and those of her friends before deciding to focus on the impact of competitive sports programs on adolescent girls.

Step 2: Generate Ideas about Appropriate Topics

By now you might have some ideas of topics that interest you and that fit your research writing situation. Your next step is to think more carefully about potential topics by using prewriting activities such as brainstorming, freewriting, looping, and clustering. You can use these activities to generate possible topics and narrow your focus from broad, general topics to those that would be more appropriate for a research project.

Brainstorming   Brainstorming involves listing ideas as they occur to you. This list should not consist of complete sentences—in fact, brainstorming lists are meant to record the many ideas that come into your head as you think of them. Brainstorming is most successful when you avoid censoring yourself. Although you'll end up using only a few of the ideas you generate during brainstorming, don't worry until later about weeding out the useful ideas from the less promising ones.

Brainstorming sessions are usually conducted in response to a specific question. Featured writer Chris Norris generated the following list in response to the question, "What interests me personally about this project?"

> *I already know a lot about metal music and I have some friends in bands and working on crews, so I could get some useful ideas from them.*
>
> *I like the social consciousness of metal music.*
>
> *Good concerts: I could really get into this kind of research.*
>
> *Learning more about the history (and future) of metal music.*

Freewriting   When freewriting, you write full sentences quickly, without stopping and—most important—without editing what you write. You might want to start with one of the ideas you generated in your brainstorming activity, or you can begin your freewriting session with a phrase such as "I am interested in my topic because. . . ." After brainstorming about the general topic of metal music, Chris Norris focused his freewriting on his readers' purposes and interest. The following is an excerpt from Chris's freewriting:

> People love music and metal music fans are passionate about it. My readers probably want to know about the reasons why metal is becoming popular again, and probably about what happened to make it lose popularity in the past. My readers might want to know whether metal is actually relevant, or just a fad appealing to teens and adults who miss the excitement of their teenage years. My readers will probably want to know about the messages behind metal music and whether those messages are actually worth listening to. And they'll want to know if the music is actually any good.

Chris did not edit his work or worry about spelling, grammar, or style.

Some writers set a timer and freewrite for five, ten, or fifteen minutes; others set a goal of a certain number of pages and keep writing until they have met that goal. (Hint: If you find it difficult to write without editing, try blindwriting— freewriting on a computer with the monitor turned off.)

Looping   Looping is an alternative form of freewriting. During a looping session, you write for a set amount of time (say five minutes) and then read what you've written. As you read, identify one key idea in what you've written and then write for five minutes with the new key idea as your starting point. Chris Norris, for example, wrote in response to a sentence he had generated during freewriting, "My readers will probably want to know about the messages behind metal music and whether those messages are actually worth listening to."

> My readers will be both my professor, who I'm not sure would know a lot about metal music, although you never know, and my fellow students, who probably grew up with at least some exposure to heavy metal. Either way, they'll want to know what metal is about and whether it's relevant to their lives, or is just another way for music companies to make money.

Clustering   Clustering involves presenting your ideas about a potential topic in graphical form. Clustering can help you gain a different perspective on a topic by helping you map out the relationships among your ideas. It can also help you generate new ideas. Featured writer Nicholas Brothers used clustering to map out his ideas and further refine his topic (see Figure 1.4).

When you have completed your brainstorming, freewriting, looping, and clustering activities, review what you've written. You'll most likely find that these prewriting techniques have generated a useful list of ideas for a topic.

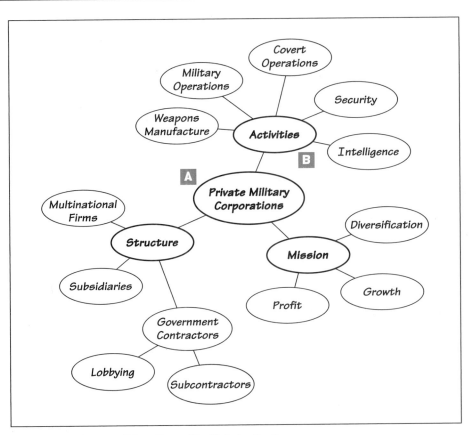

FIGURE 1.4 A Cluster of Ideas Created by Nicholas Brothers

A Nicholas listed a central idea and three key areas to explore.

B Key areas are also linked to related ideas.

My Research Project

GENERATE IDEAS ABOUT A TOPIC

In your research log, use brainstorming, freewriting, looping, and clustering to generate ideas for a topic.

Brainstorm responses to the following questions.

- What do I want to accomplish with this project?
- What interests me personally about this project?
- What interests me academically about this project?
- Who are my readers?
- What topics do my readers need to read about?
- What topics would my readers like to read about?

Freewrite in response to one of the following prompts, replacing the X's with the ideas for topics that you generated during your brainstorming session. Before you begin, set a goal of a certain number of minutes or a set amount of pages you will write.

- Writing about *X* will help me accomplish the following purposes:
- I am personally interested in *X* because . . .
- I am academically interested in *X* because . . .
- My readers need or would like to know about *X* because . . .

Select a response from your freewriting activity and carry out the following **looping** exercise.

1. Paste the response at the top of your word processing file or write it at the top of a page in your notebook. Then freewrite for five minutes about the response.
2. Identify the best idea in this freewriting.
3. Freewrite for five more minutes about the idea you've identified.
4. Repeat the process until you've refined your idea into a potential topic.

Generate additional ideas about your potential topic by using a **clustering** exercise.

1. In the middle of a sheet of paper, or in the center of a digital document (word processing file or graphics file), write your potential topic.
2. Identify ideas that are related to your central topic and list them near it. Think about the importance and relevance of each related idea, and draw lines and circles to show the relationships among your ideas.
3. Write additional ideas related to the ideas in Step 2. In turn, draw lines and circles to show their relationships to the other ideas in your cluster.
4. Repeat the process until you've created a cluster of ideas that represents your current understanding of the topic you are considering.

You can download or print this activity at **bedfordresearcher.com**.

Step 3: Consider Your Writing Situation   [FRAMING MY ARGUMENT]

After you've spent time thinking and prewriting about potential topics for your research project, you should select the strongest candidate.

As you make your choice, think carefully again about the level of interest you and your readers might have in the topic. Some topics, such as government use of private military corporations, which is addressed by Nicholas Brothers, will appeal to a large number of people, including those who have friends or family serving overseas and individuals who are concerned about the growth of government spending. Other topics, such as the unconventional role of Portia in William Shakespeare's *The Merchant of Venice*, which was addressed by Cori Schmidtbauer, will appeal to a smaller group of readers—in this case, literary scholars or devoted fans of Shakespeare's dramas. The key concern when

A search for *private military corporations*, for example, produces more than 100 times as many results as a search for *Portia, unconventional role,* and *"Merchant of Venice."* Both topics, however, resulted in successful research projects.

FIGURE 1.5 Gauging Reader Interest by Searching the Web

choosing a topic is not the size of your potential audience, but rather your interest in the topic and its compatibility with your writing situation.

In addition, remember that your topic is subject to change. It's a starting point, not a final destination. As you explore your topic, you'll begin to focus on a specific issue — a point of disagreement, uncertainty, concern, or curiosity — that is being discussed by a community of readers and writers.

> **QUICK REFERENCE**

Getting Started

✔ Gain confidence about research writing by becoming acquainted with the research writing process. (p. 3)

✔ Create a research log to manage information and ideas as you work. (p. 6)

✔ Develop a project timeline to help manage your time. (p. 11)

✔ Analyze your assignment by reflecting on your research writing situation — purposes, readers, type of document (genre), contexts, requirements, limitations, and opportunities. (p. 13)

✔ Generate ideas about appropriate topics by brainstorming, freewriting, looping, and clustering. (p. 18)

✔ Choose the most promising and appropriate topic. (p. 21)

2

Exploring and Focusing

> **Key Questions**
>

Exploring involves gaining a general understanding of the issues—points of disagreement, uncertainty, concern, or curiosity—within a topic. Focusing on a single issue lays the groundwork for developing the research question that will frame your thinking about that issue and guides your efforts to gain a comprehensive understanding of it.

2a

How can I explore my topic?

Beginning to explore your topic is similar to attending a public meeting on a controversial issue. Imagine yourself at a meeting about a proposed development in your neighborhood. You're uncertain about whether to support or oppose its construction, but it seems as though all the others at the meeting have made up their minds. After an hour of people shouting back and forth, the moderator suggests a break to allow tempers to cool.

During the break, you wander from one group of people to another. Everyone is talking about the same topic, but the conversations are radically different. In one group, four people who bitterly oppose the development are talking about how to stop it. In another group, a developer is explaining the steps that will be taken to minimize the project's impact on the neighborhood. Yet another group is discussing alternative uses of the building site. As you walk around the room, you listen for information to help you decide which conversation you want to join. Eventually, you join the group discussing alternatives to development because this issue interests you most.

This process is similar to the strategies you'll use to explore your topic and focus on an issue within it. At this early stage in your research project, you are listening in on conversations about several issues so that you can choose the one that intrigues you most.

To explore your topic, create a plan, discuss your topic with others, conduct preliminary observations, and find and review sources.

Step 1: Create a Plan to Explore Your Topic

Before you start exploring your topic, create an informal research plan.

The most common elements of a research plan include:

- a list of people with whom you can discuss your topic, including people who know a great deal about or have been involved with the topic, and people, such as librarians, who can help you locate information about your topic
- a list of questions to ask people who can help you explore your topic
- a list of settings you might observe to learn more about your topic
- a list of resources to search and browse, such as library catalogs, databases, Web search sites, and Web directories
- a system for keeping track of the information you collect

After you create your plan, use it to guide your work and to remind yourself of steps you might overlook. A note such as "talk to Professor Chapman about recent clinical studies" can come in handy if you've become so busy searching the Web or your library's catalog that you forget about your other plans for exploring your topic. After you've drafted your plan, share it with your instructor, your supervisor, or a librarian, who might suggest additional resources, shortcuts, and alternative strategies. Take notes on the feedback you receive and, if necessary, revise your plan.

?   **WHAT'S MY PURPOSE?**

Review your purpose in your research log. As you develop your research plan, remember that it should reflect your purpose for working on the project and provide directions for locating, collecting, and managing information.

Step 2: Discuss Your Topic with Others

Talking about your topic with people who know about it or have been affected by it can provide you with insights that are not available through other sources. An instructor, a supervisor, or a librarian can also help you identify additional resources.

My Research Project

CREATE A PLAN TO EXPLORE YOUR TOPIC

In your research log, answer the following questions.

- Who can help me learn more about my topic?
- What questions should I ask people on my list?
- What settings can I observe to learn more about my topic?
- What resources can I search or browse to learn more about my topic?
- How can I keep track of information I collect as I explore my topic?

Using your responses, write your plan as a series of steps and ask your instructor, your supervisor, or a librarian to review it.

　　You can download or print this activity at **bedfordresearcher.com.**

Featured writer Alexis Alvarez explored her topic—women and competitive sports—in part by talking with family members and friends who had competed in organized sports. These discussions helped Alexis better see the many different issues she could pursue within her topic.

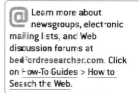

Learn more about newsgroups, electronic mailing lists, and Web discussion forums at bedfordresearcher.com. Click on How-To Guides > How to Search the Web.

　　You can also explore a topic by conducting formal interviews (see p. 183) or by writing letters and email messages (see p. 197). If you are uncertain about how to find people you can interview about your topic, you might start by visiting a Web discussion forum or blog devoted to discussion of serious issues. (For an example, visit the *New York Times* political blog, The Caucus, at **thecaucus.blogs.nytimes.com.**)

Step 3: Conduct Preliminary Observations

Observation is a powerful tool, especially when you are just getting started on a research project. Like discussing your topic with others, observing can provide you with valuable information that isn't available from other sources.

　　Featured writer Chris Norris used observation to help explore his topic, the growing interest among young adults in metal music. Chris observed shows featuring local metal bands, which provided him with a different perspective than he could have gained through other information-gathering techniques.

Step 4: Find and Review Sources

After you've talked with others about your topic and observed relevant settings, take advantage of the work other writers have done on the topic by finding and reviewing sources.

Search Your Library's Online Catalog.   Online library catalogs allow you to search for sources by keyword, title, and author. Before you begin your search, generate a list of words and phrases associated with your topic. If you already know the names of authors or the titles of books or periodicals related to your topic, search for them. At this point, however, you'll usually conduct a keyword search on your topic.

Featured writer Nicholas Brothers wrote a research essay about U. S. reliance on private military corporations. He began exploring his topic by conducting a keyword search in his library's online catalog on the broad topic of *private military corporations* (see Figure 2.1). For more about searching online library catalogs, see p. 148.

Browse Your Library's Shelves.   Once you've located a relevant book or periodical through your library's online catalog, you can usually find other sources about your topic on the same or nearby shelves (see Figure 2.2). Scan the titles of those works to locate additional sources you might not have found in your online catalog search.

As you browse your library, be aware of differences in the types of sources you find. Depending on your topic, some types of sources will be more appropriate than others. For example, if you are interested in a topic such as featured

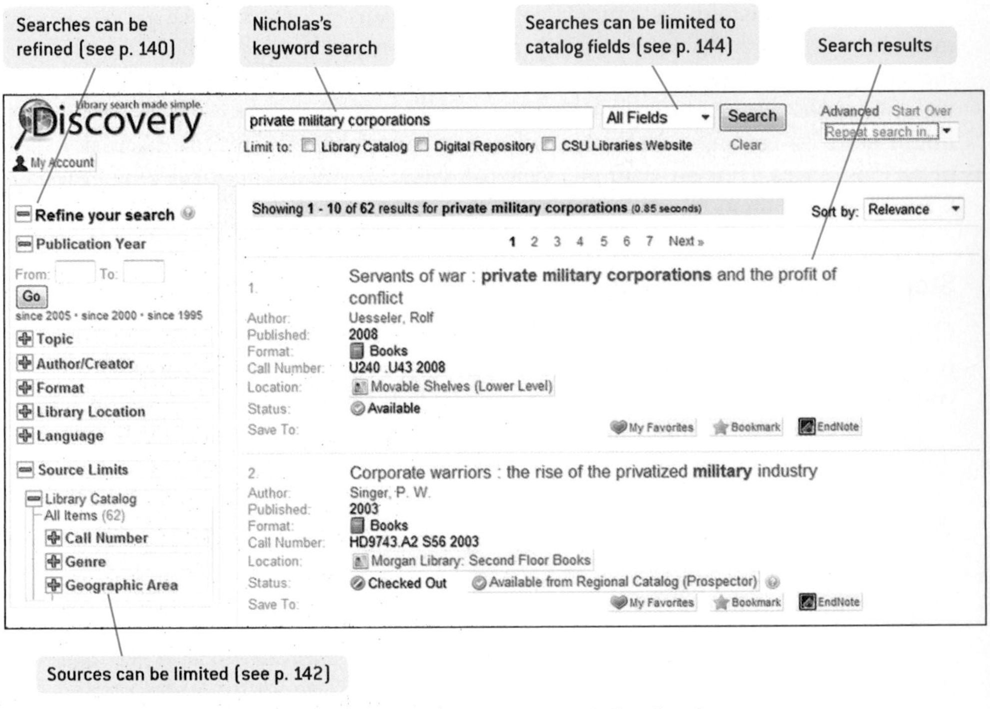

FIGURE 2.1 **Nicholas Brothers' Initial Search in His Library's Online Catalog**

FIGURE 2.2 Browsing the Shelves in a Library

A   If you located the book *Bolivia & Coca* . . .

B   . . . browse the shelves to find related works such as *The Coca Boom and Rural Social Change in Bolivia*.

writer Pete Jacquez's (wind-generated electrical power), and want to learn about the latest developments in wind turbine design, you might focus on trade and professional journals, newspapers, and magazines. If you are interested in a topic such as Shakespearean drama, as featured writer Cori Schmidtbauer was, you would focus on books and articles in scholarly journals. Note the following characteristics of sources you might find as you browse the shelves at your library.

- **Books** undergo a lengthy editorial process before they are published, and librarians evaluate them before adding them to the library collection.

- **Articles in scholarly journals** also undergo a lengthy editorial process before they are published. Most are reviewed — evaluated for accuracy, completeness, and methodological soundness — by experts in the field before they are accepted for publication. You can usually recognize a scholarly journal by its listing of an editorial board, the use of works cited lists and in-text citation in articles found in the journal, and the presence of the words *peer reviewed, blind reviewed,* or *refereed.*

- **Articles in trade and other professional journals** do not always go through a strict review process. You can find out whether articles are reviewed by looking at the submission policies printed in the journal.

- **Articles in magazines and newspapers** are usually reviewed only by the editors of the publication. Editorials typically represent an editor's or editorial board's opinion on an issue and are not subject to review. Similarly, opinion columns and letters to the editor seldom go through a review process.

- **Theses and dissertations** are final projects for students in graduate programs. Theses and dissertations vary in quality and reliability, although they have been reviewed and approved by committees of professors.

- **Microfilm and microfiche** are methods of storing documents such as older issues of newspapers and magazines or government documents and reports.

- **Other sources** include maps, videotapes, audiotapes, and multimedia items such as CD-ROMs and DVDs.

When you locate a source that seems particularly useful, read its works cited list, footnotes, endnotes, or in-text citations for related sources and then find and evaluate them.

Browse Newsstands and Bookstores.   If your topic is a current one, browse at a newsstand for specialty newspapers and magazines to which your library doesn't subscribe. If your topic has a broad, popular appeal, you might look at the books in a large bookstore or on a bookseller's Web site.

Search Available Databases.   Databases organize information as records (or entries) on a particular topic. Most databases provide publication information about articles in journals, magazines, and newspapers. You can search databases in much the same way that you can search an online library catalog (see Figure 2.3). If you have difficulty locating databases or aren't sure which databases are appropriate for your topic, ask a reference librarian for assistance. To learn more about searching databases, see p. 152.

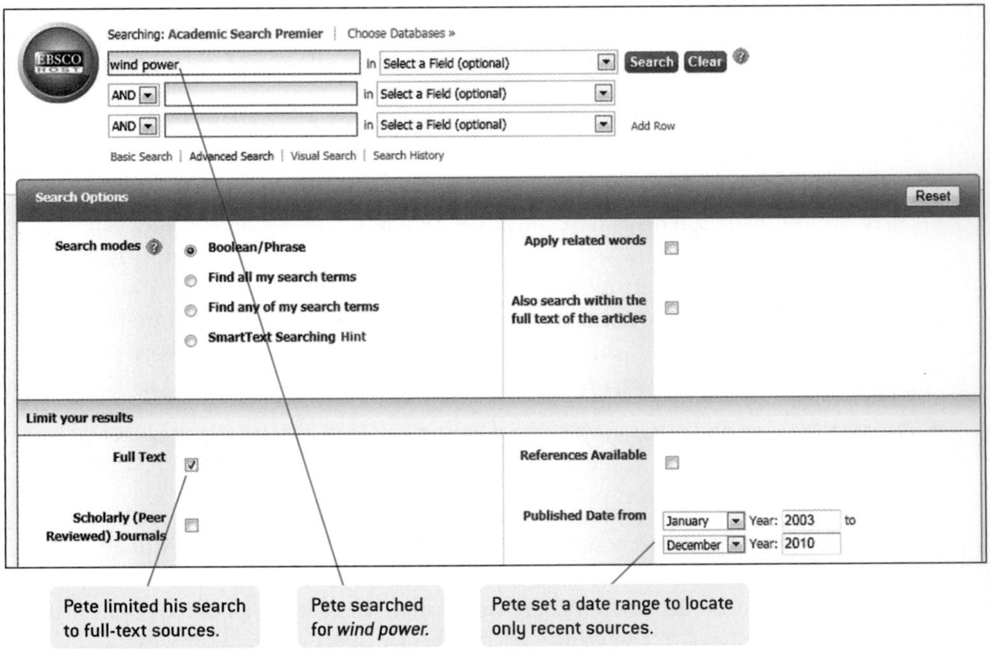

FIGURE 2.3 **Pete Jacquez's Initial Search in the Academic Search Premier Database**

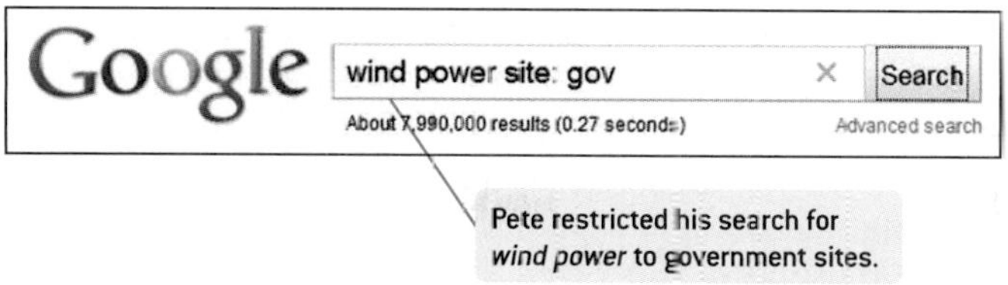

Google   wind power site: gov   ✕   Search

About 7,990,000 results (0.27 seconds)   Advanced search

FIGURE 2.4
Pete Jacquez's Initial
Search on Google

Pete restricted his search for
wind power to government sites.

Search the Web and Consult Web Directories.   Web searches allow you to locate quickly a great deal of information about your topic—although not all of it will be as reliable as the sources you locate through a library catalog or database. To start searching the Web, visit one of the leading search sites (see Figure 2.4), such as Ask (ask.com), Bing (bing.com), Google (google.com), or Yahoo! (yahoo.com).

You can also use Web directories, which employ editors—real people—to organize links to Web sites in categories and subcategories (see p. 160 to learn more about Web directories). Leading Web directories include Open Directory (dmoz.org) and Google Directory (directory.google.com). When Pete Jacquez visited Open Directory, he found information on his topic by clicking on the general category Science and then by clicking in succession on the subcategories Energy and Wind Power (see Figure 2.5).

d m o z   open directory project   In partnership with **Aol Search.**

about dmoz | dmoz blog | suggest URL | help | link | editor login

Categories of information   Search *advanced*

Arts
Movies, Television, Music...

Business
Jobs, Real Estate, Investing...

Computers
Internet, Software, Hardware...

Games
Video Games, RPGs, Gambling...

Health
Fitness, Medicine, Alternative...

Home
Family, Consumers, Cooking...

Kids and Teens
Arts, School Time, Teen Life...

News
Media, Newspapers, Weather...

Recreation
Travel, Food, Outdoors, Humor...

Reference
Maps, Education, Libraries...

Regional
US, Canada, UK, Europe...

Science
Biology, Psychology, Physics...

Shopping
Clothing, Food, Gifts...

Society
People, Religion, Issues...

Sports
Baseball, Soccer, Basketball...

World
Català, Dansk, Deutsch, Español, Français, Italiano, 日本語, Nederlands, Polski, Русский, Svenska...

Become an Editor   Help build the largest human-edited directory of the web

Copyright © 1998-2010 Netscape

4,740,471 sites - 87,562 editors - over 999,620 categories

FIGURE 2.5 Searching the Open Directory

Browse Electronic Mailing Lists, Newsgroups, Web Discussion Forums, Blogs, and Wikis. Electronic mailing lists, newsgroups, Web discussion forums, blogs, and wikis can be excellent sources of information, but they can also contain some outrageous misinformation. Because most of these resources are unmoderated—that is, anything sent to them is published—you'll find everything from expert opinions to the musings of folks who know little or nothing about your topic. When read with a bit of skepticism, however, the messages can help you identify issues within your topic. For more on these online resources, see Chapter 8.

Information Literacy

Once you visit a site, you can begin to browse the Web. Browsing the Web is similar to browsing the shelves in the library. That is, once you've located a Web site that is relevant to your research question, you can usually follow links from that site to related sites. For instance, one of the Web sites Pete Jacquez visited as a result of his initial search on Google (see Figure 2.4) was the National Renewable Energy Laboratory's National Wind Technology Center Web site, which contains a list of Web-based resources related to wind power (see Figure 2.6). For more on Web searches, see Chapter 8.

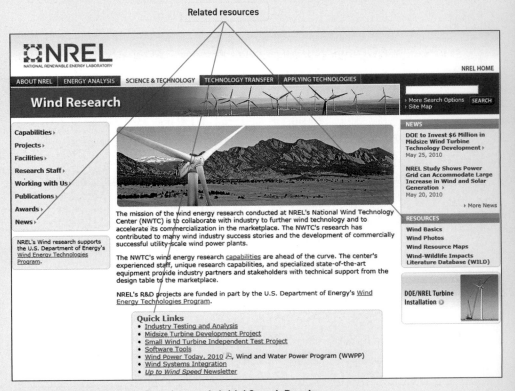

FIGURE 2.6 A Site Listed in Pete Jacquez's Initial Search Results

Record Your Search Results. As you explore your topic, record your searches: Identify the library catalogs, databases, and Web sites you search; list the words and phrases you use in your searches; and note the quality and quantity of results produced by each search. This information will be useful if, later on, you want to conduct these searches again or conduct the same searches on different search sites or databases.

> @ Learn more about locating information on the Web at bedfordresearcher.com. Click on How-To Guides

Skim Your Sources. Skimming—reading just enough to get a general idea of what a document is about—enables you to gather information quickly from the sources you've located as you've explored your topic. You can skim books, articles, Web pages, newsgroups, chat transcripts, interview notes, observation notes, or anything else in written form. Figures 2.7 and 2.8 illustrate strategies for skimming brief print documents and Web pages. Key strategies include identifying the type of document—or genre—you are skimming; scanning titles, headings and subheadings, and figure captions; reading the first and last sentences of paragraphs; scanning menus and other navigation aids; and looking for information

Check the title for cues about content.

Skim opening paragraphs for the purpose and scope of the document.

Skim captions of photos and figures, which often highlight important information, ideas, and arguments.

Check headings and subheadings to learn about content and organization.

Read the first and last sentences of paragraphs to find key information.

FIGURE 2.7 Skimming a Print Document

Check the page title in the tab or title bar of the browser for the purpose and content of the page.

Check the URL to learn about the purpose of a Web page. Look for cues such as .edu for education, .gov for government, and .com for commercial and business sites.

Read the navigation headers and menus to learn about the content and organization of the site.

Scan for boldface, colored, or italic text. Important information is often highlighted in some way on the page.

Read the title.

Check for links to other sites to learn more about the issue.

Read the first and last sentences of paragraphs to find key information.

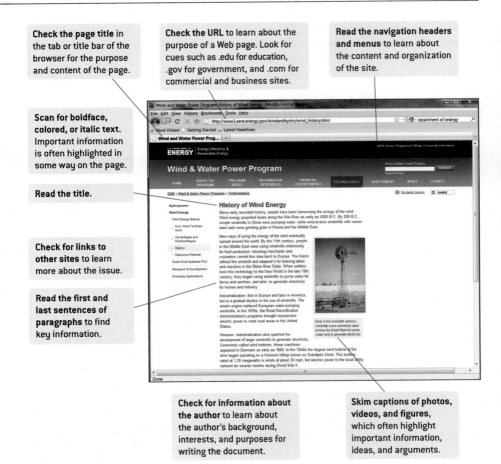

Check for information about the author to learn about the author's background, interests, and purposes for writing the document.

Skim captions of photos, videos, and figures, which often highlight important information, ideas, and arguments.

FIGURE 2.8 Skimming a Web Page

about authors and publishers. If you are reading a longer document, such as a book or report, consider these additional strategies.

- **Check the table of contents,** if one is provided. This provides a useful overview of the document's content and organization.

- **Check the index,** if one is provided, to learn more about the content of the document.

- **Check the glossary,** if one is provided. The terms that are defined can provide clues about the focus of the document.

- **Check the works cited list,** if one is provided, to learn about the types of evidence used in the document.

- **Check for pull quotes** (quotations or brief passages pulled out of the text and set in larger type elsewhere on the page), which often call attention to important information, ideas, and arguments in a document.

- **Check for information about the author** to learn about the writer's background, interests, and purposes for writing the document.

Mark, Annotate, and Take Brief Notes on Your Sources.   As you skim your sources, do the following:

- Mark them by highlighting or underlining important passages so that you'll be able to locate key passages easily later in your research writing process (see Figure 2.9).
- Annotate them by briefly recording in the margins your initial reactions to a source.
- Take brief notes in your research log. For example, you might note similarities or differences among your sources, such as different proposals for solving a problem or different interpretations of an issue. These notes allow you to start to pull together the information, ideas, and arguments that several of your sources touch on.

Learn more about annotating, marking, and taking notes on sources in Chapter 4 and Chapter 6.

Figure 1-3. Status of offshore wind energy technology

In shallow water, the substructure extends to the sea floor and includes monopoles, gravity bases, and suction buckets. In the transitional depth, new technologies are being created, or adapted from the oil and gas industry, including jacket substructures and multi-pile foundations, which also extend to the sea floor. At some depth it is no longer economically feasible to have a rigid structure fixed to the sea floor, and floating platforms may be required. Three idealized concepts have arisen for floating platform designs, including the semisubmersible, the spar buoy, and the tension-leg platform, each of which use a different method for achieving static stability.

Although it is not yet known which of these designs will deliver the best system performance, designers seek platforms that are easy to install and minimize overall turbine loads. To determine this optimized design point, advanced computer simulation models need to be developed and validated. As shown in the figure, most of the projects now reside in shallow water, and only two

← same technology used for the oil and gas industries can be adapted for wind

still in the development stage for wind power ₅

FIGURE 2.9 Pete Jacquez's Annotations and Highlighting on a Printout of a Page from an Online Magazine

TUTORIAL

How can I identify conversations in my sources?

You can identify conversations taking place in your sources by looking for patterns. Creating a four-column table like the one below can help you sort things out. In this example, Elizabeth Leontiev notes that three of her sources talk about the effectiveness of the U.S. war on drugs. She used this conversation as the basis for her research on the impact of U.S. drug policy on South American coca farmers.

1 Record the source. Here, the writer uses the authors' last names.

2 Record concepts that are repeated in your sources.

3 Record other broad themes that you've noticed in your sources.

4 Note points on which the sources disagree.

5 Note the sources that these sources are citing. (You might use them later.)

Source	Gordon	Forero	Logan
Repeated Concepts	"zero cocaine, not zero coca"	"zero cocaine, not zero coca"	
Broad Themes	Overall effectiveness of U.S. war on drugs	Overall effectiveness of U.S. war on drugs	U.S. interference in affairs of other countries
Disagreements	U.S. policy of coca extermination — argues it has failed	U.S. policy of coca extermination — focuses on political issues	U.S. policy of coca extermination — argues policy is likely to change
Key Voices	Forero, Chipana, Morales	Morales	Morales, Reinicke

Review another example and work on identifying conversations in your sources at **bedfordresearcher.com**. Click on Interactive Exercises.

My Research Project

EXPLORE YOUR TOPIC

As you work through the strategies discussed in this chapter, use the following activity to keep track of your topic exploration in your research log.

1. What is my topic?

2. Have I discussed my topic with others? If so, what have I learned? If not, who are likely candidates for interviews — such as librarians, instructors, and people involved with or affected by my topic — and what questions should I ask them?

3. Are there any preliminary observations I should conduct? Have I done so? If so, what have I learned?

4. Have I found and reviewed sources? Have I searched the library catalog and browsed the shelves? Have I searched databases and the Web? Have I skimmed, marked, annotated, and taken brief notes on the sources I've found? If so, what have I learned about my topic?

You can download or print this activity at **bedfordresearcher.com**.

2b

How can I focus on an issue?

Once you've explored your topic, your most important goal is to focus on a specific issue. Issues are points of disagreement, uncertainty, concern, or curiosity that are being discussed by communities of readers and writers.

As he explored the general topic of metal music, Chris Norris read sources, listened to music, talked with his professor about his topic, and kept a running list of ideas and information that interested him. Chris started to make connections among the wide range of information, ideas, and arguments he encountered, and he was ultimately able to focus on the single issue that interested him most: the rebirth of the popularity of metal music.

Moving from your topic to a single issue about that topic involves identifying conversations about issues in your topic, assessing your interest in the issues, and asking whether writing about this issue will allow you to achieve your purposes as a writer.

Step 1: Identify Conversations about Issues in Your Topic

Identifying conversations about issues in your topic is the first step in determining which issue is most appropriate for your research project. As you work through this process, look for patterns in the information, ideas, and arguments you encounter in your sources.

Find Central Concepts Repeated in Your Sources.   When several sources refer to the same idea, you can assume that this information is central to the topic. For instance, as Alexis Alvarez looked at articles and Web sites about the impact of competitive athletics on adolescent girls, she found repeated references to self-esteem, confidence, and performance-enhancing drugs. Noticing this repetition enabled Alexis to identify some of the important conversations about her topic.

Find Broad Themes Discussed in Your Sources.   Sources that discuss the same general theme are most likely involved in the same conversation. Featured writer Elizabeth Leontiev found that some of the sources she explored focused on the history of the U.S. war on drugs, some focused on its cost, others focused on its effectiveness, and still others focused on the impact of the war on drugs both in Central and South America. By noting these broad themes, Elizabeth was able to identify some of the key conversations taking place about her topic.

Find Disagreements among Your Sources.   Some sources will explicitly indicate that they disagree with arguments, ideas, or information in other sources. For example, Pete Jacquez found that some sources reported on the cost effectiveness of wind-generated electrical power, while others argued that electricity generated from burning gas, coal, or oil is more cost-effective. Looking for such explicit statements of disagreement helped Pete identify a group of sources that were engaged in conversation with one another.

Find Recurring Voices in Your Sources.   As you read sources, you might find that some authors write frequently about your topic or that some authors are referred to frequently by other writers. These authors might have significant experience or expertise related to the topic, or they might represent particular perspectives on the topic. Stay alert for these recurring voices.

Step 2: Assess Your Interest in the Issues

Once you've identified issues that are being discussed in your sources, you are ready to assess the importance and relevance of those issues. Determine your personal interest in each issue by asking what interests you most about each one. Identifying personal connections between your sources and your own interests will help you focus on an issue that will sustain your interest throughout the course of your research project.

Step 3: Choose an Issue   [FRAMING MY ARGUMENT]

After you've assessed the issues you've found during your exploration of your topic, select the strongest candidate and the one that interests you most. Think, too, about the level of interest your readers might have in the issue and whether writing about it will help you achieve your purposes as a writer.

Evaluate each issue by asking yourself the following questions.

- **Will selecting this issue help me achieve my purposes as a writer?** Review your purpose and examine how each of the issues you have identified will help you best accomplish it.

- **Will my readers want or need to read about this issue?** Ask yourself which issue your readers would be most interested in or would most need to know about.

- **Is this issue appropriate for my project's context?** Consider the social and disciplinary contexts in which you are writing. If you are writing for a science class, for example, ask whether the issue will meet the expectations of your instructor and other readers.

- **Is this issue appropriate for the type of document I plan to write?** Some issues that are well suited for editorials and opinion columns in your school newspaper, for example, might not be suitable for an academic or professional paper.

- **Is this issue compatible with my requirements and limitations?** Determine whether you can address an issue reasonably, given your assignment due date.

- **What opportunities do I have if I choose this issue?** Identify any special resources that might be available to you, such as access to a special collection in a library, experts on an issue, or individuals who have been affected by it.

To assess the importance and relevance of issues discussed in his sources, Pete Jacquez brainstormed about one of the issues that interested him most, strategies for increasing U.S. use of wind-generated electrical power. He listed six aspects of his writing situation and generated ideas about each one (see Figure 2.10).

Table 2.1 shows the topics explored by the featured writers and the issues they addressed.

TABLE 2.1 THE PROGRESSION FROM TOPIC TO CONVERSATION

FEATURED WRITER	TOPIC	ISSUE
Alexis Alvarez	Women and competitive sports	Steroid use among adolescent girls involved in competitive sports
Nicholas Brothers	Private military corporations	Use of private military corporations to support the U.S. war on terror
Pete Jacquez	Wind-generated electrical power	Best strategies for increasing U.S. use of wind-generated electrical power
Elizabeth Leontiev	The war on drugs	Impact of U.S. war on drugs on South American coca farmers
Chris Norris	Contemporary music	Resurgence in popularity of metal music
Cori Schmidtbauer	William Shakespeare's dramas	Portia's unconventional role in *The Merchant of Venice*

Purpose:

Seems to fit. I want to figure out how we can use wind power, so I'm focusing on strategies would help us increase use. It would be good to look at how new laws (fed? state?) might encourage development of wind farms. Look at tax breaks, new technologies, research and development funding.

Readers:

Lots of folks are worried about global warming, so even if they think "environmentalist" is a bad word, they probably won't see wind power as some ridiculous scheme. And it's getting almost as cheap as coal, and with gas prices getting so high maybe we'll be moving to electric cars, so maybe they'll see the value of having more, eco-friendly power sources (well, aside from the birds).

Context/Discipline:

Seems to be a good fit, both for CSU and for my class. Doesn't matter for the assignment in terms of discipline, but there's been a lot of discussion across campus about increased costs and how alternative energy might help us reduce costs.

Type of Document:

People can find a Web site a lot easier than an essay, and if they read what I write, that's a good thing. I shouldn't have too much trouble putting up a small site. I can probably just use Word to make the pages.

Requirements/Limitations:

I might need to focus this more. Maybe look only at Colorado.

Opportunities:

CSU is the first school to give students an option of paying for wind power, and there are some profs here who were involved in that. I could interview one of them.

FIGURE 2.10 Pete Jacquez's Brainstorming about Issues

My Research Project

CHOOSE AN ISSUE WITHIN YOUR TOPIC

In your research log, complete the following activity to focus your topic on a single issue.

1. What are the three most important issues I have identified so far?

2. Of these issues, which one will best help me sustain my interest in this project?

3. Which one will best help me achieve my purposes as a writer?

4. Which one will best address my readers' needs, interests, values, and beliefs?

5. Which one is best suited to my context (social, cultural, historical, disciplinary, physical)?

6. Which one is most appropriate for the type of document I plan to write?

7. Which one best fits the requirements of my assignment?

8. Which one has the fewest limitations?

9. Which one allows me to best take advantage of opportunities?

10. Based on these answers, the issue I want to choose is:

You can download or print this activity at **bedfordresearcher.com**.

QUICK REFERENCE

Exploring and Focusing

- ☑ Get organized by creating a plan to explore your topic. (p. 24)
- ☑ Discuss your topic with people who know about or have been affected by it. (p. 24)
- ☑ Conduct preliminary observations. (p 25)
- ☑ Find and review written sources by searching your library catalog, browsing its shelves, searching databases, searching the Web, and skimming your sources. (p. 25)
- ☑ Identify issues related to your topic. (p. 34)
- ☑ Evaluate the issues in light of your research writing situation. (p. 35)
- ☑ Choose an issue. (p. 36)

3

Developing Your Research Question and Proposal

Your research question directs your efforts to develop a research proposal, create a search plan, and collect information. It also provides the foundation for developing your position—the main point you will make about your issue.

3a

How can I develop my research question?

A research question is a brief question that directs your efforts to collect, critically read, evaluate, and take notes on your sources. An effective research question focuses on a specific issue, reflects your writing situation, and is narrow enough to allow you to collect information in time to meet your deadlines. Most research questions begin with the word *what, why, when, where, who,* or *how.* Some research questions use the word *would* or *could* to ask whether something is possible. Still others use the word *should* to analyze the appropriateness of a particular action, policy, procedure, or decision. Since your research question may change as you learn more about your issue, it's best to think of it as a flexible guide. By revising your research question to reflect your growing understanding of the issue you've decided to address, you will build a solid foundation for developing your position on the issue.

Developing your research question involves reflecting on your writing situation, generating potential research questions, crafting questions that reflect your writing situation, and choosing and refining your question.

Step 1: Reflect on Your Writing Situation

As you've explored your topic and focused on your issue, you've learned more about the conversation you've decided to join. The sources you've read have almost certainly helped you gain an understanding of some of the most important information, ideas, and arguments shaping the conversation. You might also have had the opportunity to talk with others about your issue and perhaps even to conduct observations. If you're like most research writers, your initial thoughts about your topic and issue have changed as you've carried out your investigations.

Ask yourself whether what you've learned has changed your understanding of your writing situation. Then ask yourself what you'd like to learn next. Finally, ask yourself how strongly your initial understanding of the issue has shaped your exploration of your topic and issue. Every writer begins a project with a particular set of interests, beliefs, and prior knowledge of an issue — that is, a set of biases. Consider how your biases might have shaped your interpretation of what you've learned about the conversation you've decided to join.

My Research Project

REFLECT ON YOUR WRITING SITUATION

Use the following questions to see whether your understanding of your writing situation has changed since you started working on your project.

1. What has changed, if anything, about what you want to accomplish with your project?

2. Have you changed the role you want to adopt? Do you want to inform your readers, reflect on your issue, conduct an analysis, carry out an evaluation, define or solve a problem, convince your readers to accept an argument, mediate a disagreement, or persuade readers to take action? Do you want to adopt multiple roles?

3. What have you learned about your readers? What insights have you gained about their needs and interests; their attitudes, values, and beliefs; or their knowledge of the issue?

4. What kinds of sources would be best to rely on as you carry out your project?

5. What kind of document do you think you'll write?

6. What new opportunities and limitations will affect your work on your project?

↓

7. How have your biases — your interests, beliefs, and prior knowledge of the issue — affected your ability to learn about the issue you'll address in your project?

You can download or print this activity at **bedfordresearcher.com**.

Step 2: Generate Potential Research Questions

Your next step is to generate a list of questions about the issue you've decided to address. Questions can focus on the following.

- **Information.** What is known—and not known—about an issue?
- **History.** What has occurred in the past that is relevant to an issue?
- **Assumptions.** What conclusions—merited or not—have writers and readers already made about an issue?
- **Goals.** What do the writers and readers involved in conversation about this issue want to see happen (or not happen)?
- **Outcomes.** What has happened so far? What is likely to happen?
- **Policies.** What are the best procedures for carrying out actions? For making decisions?

Questions can lead you to engage in the following kinds of thinking processes.

- **Definition.** Describing specific aspects of an issue.
- **Evaluation.** Asking about strengths and weaknesses or appropriateness.
- **Comparison/Contrast.** Asking about distinctions between aspects of an issue.
- **Cause/Effect Analysis.** Asking what leads to a specific result.
- **Problem/Solution Analysis or Advocacy.** Defining problems, considering outcomes of a problem, assessing potential solutions, and/or offering solutions.
- **Sequential Analysis.** Asking about step-by-step series of events.
- **Inquiry.** Seeking new information; conducting original research.
- **Reporting.** Conveying what is known about an event, idea, or phenomenon.

By combining a specific focus, such as assumptions, with a specific type of thinking process, such as definition, you can create carefully tailored research questions.

> What assumptions have shaped debate about this issue?
> What assumptions have worked against a resolution of this issue?

In Table 3.1 (p. 44), different focuses and types of thinking processes are used to generate questions about Pete Jacquez's issue, *best strategies for increasing U.S. use of wind-generated electrical power.*

My Research Project

GENERATE POTENTIAL RESEARCH QUESTIONS

Use the following table to generate potential research questions. Create at least one potential question for each cell in the table.

	Definition	Evaluation	Comparison/ Contrast	Cause/ Effect	Problem/ Solution	Sequence	Inquiry	Reporting
Information								
History								
Assumptions								
Goals								
Outcomes								
Policies								

You can download or print this activity at **bedfordresearcher.com**.

Step 3: Craft Questions that Reflect Your Writing Situation   [FRAMING MY ARGUMENT]

Review your potential research questions and select a question that interests you and is appropriate for your research writing situation. Then consider how the research question might help you accomplish your purpose. Ask yourself whether you are interested in focusing on such concerns as the current state of knowledge about your issue, its history, the assumptions informing the conversation about the issue, the goals of writers involved in the conversation, the likely outcomes of the issue, or policies associated with the issue. Then reflect on the range of options you have for thinking about these concerns. Are you interested, for example, in defining or evaluating? Are you interested in conducting such analyses as comparing alternatives, looking for cause/effect relationships, defining or solving problems, or tracing a sequence of events? Are you interested in conducting your own study? Are you interested in reporting what others have done or are doing?

Specific question words can help you craft an effective research question. If you are interested in conducting an analysis, for example, you might use the words *what, why, when, where, who,* and *how.* If you are interested in exploring goals and outcomes, you might use the words *would* or *could.* If the conversation focuses on determining an appropriate course of action, generate questions using the word *should.* Consider the differences in the following questions.

- **What** are the benefits of wind power?
- **Would** it be feasible to require electrical companies to generate 20 percent of their power through wind turbines?
- **Should** the federal government pursue legislation to support wind power?

TABLE 3.1 GENERATING RESEARCH QUESTIONS

	DEFINITION	EVALUATION	COMPARISON/CONTRAST	CAUSE/EFFECT	PROBLEM/SOLUTION	SEQUENCE	INQUIRY	REPORTING
Information	Where are the best locations for generating wind power?	How effective are current strategies for increasing use of wind power?	What are the similarities and differences among strategies to increase use of wind power?	What will lead to increased use of wind power?	What are the primary obstacles to increasing use of wind power?	What process is likely to be most effective at increasing use of wind power?	How could we increase U.S. use of wind power?	What strategies are now being tried to increase use of wind power?
History	Which strategies have been used to increase use of wind power?	Which strategies have been most effective at increasing use of wind power?	When will the costs of wind-generated electrical power rival that of power generated by natural gas, coal, and oil?	What has led to efforts to increase use of wind power?	How have obstacles to increased use of wind power been overcome?	What process has been followed to successfully implement wind power in other countries?	What can we learn from the past to increase use of wind power?	How are people using lessons from the past to increase current use of wind power?
Assumptions	Which values drive efforts to increase use of wind power?	Which assumptions have proven most damaging in efforts to increase use of wind power?	Which assumptions are driving efforts to increase use of wind power?	What faulty assumptions have led to failures in the wind power industry?	What can be done to rescue efforts to increase reliance on wind power?	What has led to current assumptions about wind power?	How can we change assumptions about use of wind power?	What are the focuses of the debate about use of wind power?

	DEFINITION	EVALUATION	COMPARISON/CONTRAST	CAUSE/EFFECT	PROBLEM/SOLUTION	SEQUENCE	INQUIRY	REPORTING
Goals	What are the goals of wind power advocates?	Which goals are most likely to be realized by advocates of wind power?	What are the differences among the goals pursued by different groups of wind power advocates?	What is likely to occur if current goals of wind power advocates are realized?	What are the primary obstacles to wind power and how can they be overcome?	How have the goals pursued by wind power advocates developed over time?	Would advocates of wind power respond positively to a shift in short-term goals?	How is the goal of greater use of wind power being pursued by its advocates?
Outcomes	What is likely to result from efforts to increase use of wind power?	What are the best outcomes that can be expected from efforts to increase use of wind power?	Compared to the use of coal-based power plants, what are the advantages of outcomes from efforts to increase use of wind power?	Could advertising campaigns increase the likelihood of widespread adoption of wind power?	What undesirable consequences are likely to result from efforts to increase use of wind power?	When will wind power be an economically viable alternative to power from coal?	Why are legislators hesitant about supporting increased use of wind power?	Who are the most likely users of wind power?
Policies	What policies should the government implement to support wind power?	What are the advantages of pursuing a policy of increased use of wind power?	How do policy initiatives led by wind-power advocates differ from those led by the coal industry?	What are the likely results of government support for wind power?	To what extent can a policy of greater reliance on wind power reduce reliance on petroleum imports?	How will the energy industry respond to passage of a national energy policy favoring wind power?	How do consumers respond to "extra-cost" wind power initiatives?	Would it be feasible to require electrical companies to generate 20% of their power through wind turbines?

My Research Project

CRAFT FOCUSED RESEARCH QUESTIONS

Review your list of potential research questions and identify those that interest you most. Then focus your most interesting questions by using the following prompts.

1. Which of the questions seem most likely to help you accomplish your purpose and address the needs and interests of your readers?

2. List each of the remaining questions, then revise each one using question words that don't appear in the question:

   - Question 1 . . .
     - Who
     - What
     - Where
     - When
     - How
     - Why
     - Could
     - Would
     - Should
   - Question 2 . . .
     - Who
     - What
     - Etc.

3. Highlight the most promising research questions. Then choose the one that best addresses your interests, purpose, and readers.

You can download or print this activity at **bedfordresearcher.com**.

Each question would lead to differences in how to search for sources of information, which sources to use in a project document, what role to adopt as a writer, and how to organize and draft the document.

Step 4: Select and Refine Your Research Question

Choose the research question that seems most likely to help you achieve your purpose as a writer and address the needs and interests of your readers. Then refine your question by referring to shared assumptions and existing conditions, narrowing its scope, and conducting preliminary searches.

Refer to Shared Assumptions and Existing Conditions. You can refine your research question by using qualifying words and phrases to narrow its scope, by calling attention to assumptions that have been made by the community of writers and readers who are addressing your issue, or by referring to existing conditions relevant to your issue. Note the difference between the following three versions of featured writer Alexis Alvarez's research question.

Original Question

What should be done about steroid use by adolescent girls involved in competitive sports?

Alternative 1

Even though we know that widespread drug testing of all athletes, younger and older, is impossible, what should be done about steroid use by adolescent girls involved in competitive sports?

Alternative 2

Given the lack of knowledge among athletes and their parents about the health consequences of steroid use, what should be done about steroid use by adolescent girls involved in competitive sports?

As you refine your research question, you might use conditional words and phrases such as the following:

Mix . . .	and Match
Although	we know that . . .
Because	it is uncertain . . .
Even though	it is clear that . . .
Given that	studies indicate . . .
In light of	recent events . . .
Now that	it has been shown . . .
Since	the lack of . . .
While	we cannot . . .

Narrow the Scope of Your Research Question. Early research questions typically suffer from lack of focus. You can narrow the scope of your question by looking for vague words and phrases and replacing them with more specific words or phrases. The process of moving from a broad research question to one that might be addressed effectively in a research essay might produce the following sequence.

Original Research Question

What is behind the increased popularity in women's sports?

Refined

What has led to the increased popularity of women's sports in colleges and universities?

Further Refined

How has Title IX increased opportunities for women athletes in American colleges and universities?

In this example, the writer has narrowed the scope of the research question in two ways. First, the writer has shifted its focus from women's sports in general to women's sports in American colleges and universities. Second, the writer has moved from a general focus on increased popularity of women's sports to a more specific focus on opportunities brought about by Title IX, federal legislation that mandated equal opportunities for women athletes. Table 3.2 shows the featured writers' progress from a general topic to a focused issue to a refined research question.

Conduct Preliminary Searches.   One of the best ways to test your research question is to conduct some preliminary searches in an online library catalog or database or on the Web. If you locate a vast amount of information in your searches, you might need to revise your question so that it focuses on a more manageable aspect of the issue. In contrast, if you find almost nothing in your search, you might need to expand the scope of your research question.

TABLE 3.2 THE FEATURED WRITERS' RESEARCH QUESTIONS

FEATURED WRITER	TOPIC	ISSUE	RESEARCH QUESTION
Alexis Alvarez	Women and competitive sports	Steroid use among adolescent girls involved in competitive sports	What should be done about steroid use by adolescent girls involved in competitive sports?
Nicholas Brothers	Private military corporations	Use of private military corporations to support the U.S. war on terror	What roles do private military corporations play in the U.S. military's war on terror?
Pete Jacquez	Wind-generated electrical power	Best strategies for increasing U.S. use of wind-generated electrical power	What strategies, if any, should Coloradoans use to encourage local, state, and federal governments to increase U.S. use of wind-generated electrical power?
Elizabeth Leontiev	The war on drugs	Impact of U.S. war on drugs on South American coca farmers	How can we reduce the economic impact of the war on drugs on South American coca farmers?
Chris Norris	Contemporary music	Resurgence in popularity of metal music	What accounts for the resurgence in popularity of metal music?
Cori Schmidtbauer	William Shakespeare's dramas	Portia's unconventional role in *The Merchant of Venice*	How does Portia's character in *The Merchant of Venice* fit the ideal of an Elizabethan woman?

TUTORIAL

How do I refine my research question?

The first draft of your research question might be too broad, which can make it difficult for you to focus your research efforts. Refine your initial research question so that you can collect information efficiently.

In this example, Pete Jacquez refines his research question about the use of wind-generated electrical power. He used his research question as he collected and worked with sources, and later, he developed his thesis statement to answer his question.

Preliminary Research Question:
How can we increase our reliance on alternative energy?

1 Refer to shared assumptions and existing conditions by using phrases such as *although it is clear that ...*, *because we cannot ...*, and *given that studies have shown....*

In light of consumer demand for low-cost electricity, how can we increase our reliance on alternative energy?

2 Identify vague words and phrases, such as *alternative* and *reliance on*, and replace them with more specific language.

In light of consumer demand for low-cost electricity what steps can U.S. citizens take to encourage local, state, and federal governments to support increased use of wind-generated electrical energy?

3 Using these specific terms, conduct preliminary searches in your library catalog, databases, and on the Web. If you get too many results, narrow your focus even further. (Here, Pete narrows his target audience from *U.S. citizens* to *Colorado citizens* and focuses on passing a statewide referendum.)

In light of consumer demand for low-cost electricity, what steps can Colorado citizens take to pass a statewide referendum requiring increased use of reliance on wind-generated electrical energy?

Review another example and work on narrowing your own research question at **bedfordresearcher.com**. Click on Interactive Exercises.

3b

How can I create a research proposal?

A research proposal—sometimes called a prospectus—is a formal presentation of your plan for your research writing project. A proposal helps you pull together the planning you've done on your project, identify areas where you need additional planning, and assess the progress you've made so far.

Unlike a research plan (see p. 24), which is designed primarily to help *you* decide how to collect information, a research proposal is addressed to someone else, usually an instructor, a supervisor, or a funding agency. Although the specific format for research proposals can vary widely across disciplines, a research proposal typically includes the following parts.

- A title page
- An introduction that identifies your topic issue, and/or research question
- A review of literature
- An explanation of how you will collect information
- A project timeline
- A working bibliography

In addition to these core elements, you can also provide an abstract or executive summary, offer an overview of key challenges, and include a funding request. You can read about how to develop each of these core and optional elements below.

Identify Your Topic, Issue, and Research Question

A title page and introduction offer your readers an overview of the topic and issue you'll address in your project document. Your title page should include the working title of your research writing project, your name and contact information, and the date. Your introduction should identify the topic you've chosen and the issue you've decided to address; state your research question and, if you have created one, your position on the issue (see p. 63); describe your purpose; and identify and describe your readers. It should also identify the type of document you'll create and explain how your choice of genre reflects your purpose, your understanding of your readers, and the contexts that will shape your work on your research project.

Provide a Review of Literature

A review of literature presents an overview of the key information, ideas, and arguments in the sources you've collected so far. You should identify the most useful sources you found during your exploration of your topic and explain why you found them useful. Keep in mind, however, that a review of literature goes beyond the simple list of sources that are typically found in a working bibliography by offering a discussion of important approaches to your issue. That is, a review of literature focuses not so much on individual sources as on groups of sources and the shared ideas or positions taken by groups of sources. Focusing on general approaches to an issue, as opposed to the individual positions adopted in particular sources, can help you understand the major ideas that are being considered in the conversation you are planning to join. By understanding existing approaches to an issue, you can determine whether you agree with any of those approaches or whether you want to introduce a completely new approach. In turn, this will help you develop your own individual position on the issue.

For an example that illustrates how key approaches to an issue can be discussed, see featured writer Nicholas Brothers's review of literature on p. 54.

Explain How You'll Collect Information

Your research proposal should help your reader understand how you will collect information. Your plan should identify:

- the types of sources you intend to collect (such as books, journal articles, or opinion columns)
- the types of search tools (such as library catalogs, databases, and Web search sites) and research methods (such as browsing library shelves, consulting librarians, or conducting surveys) you want to use
- the types of strategies (such as simple and advanced database searches or field research) that you intend to use in your searches
- the schedule you will follow as you carry out your searches

Your research question will influence your decisions about how you will collect information. For example, you can use your research question — and, if you've developed one, your position on your issue (see p. 63) — to help identify keywords and phrases that might be used in database, catalog, and Web searches.

Identify Relevant Types of Sources. To identify relevant sources for your writing project, consider the nature of the conversation you are joining, the scope and timeliness of your subject, the information you'll need to develop your ideas, and the evidence you'll need to support your points. Ask yourself, for example, about the conversation you've decided to join. Does it focus on a highly specialized issue within a scholarly discipline, such as a discussion of gene splicing in biochemistry? If so, you're likely to find that the best sources will be scholarly books and journal articles. Does it address a subject that has broad appeal, such as transportation problems in your state or region? If so, you'll find it helpful to draw on a much wider range of sources, including newspaper and magazine articles, editorials and opinion columns, blogs, and Web sites.

You should also ask whether the issue you've decided to address is relatively broad or highly focused, and whether it is of enduring interest. Some issues, such as funding for higher education or reducing alcohol consumption by college students, tend to be discussed over an extended period of time in a wide range of sources. If your subject focuses on a recent event, however, it might be best to turn to magazine and newspaper articles, the Web, blogs, observation, surveys, or interviews—that is, sources that are published or updated recently enough that they are likely to contain current information or observations about the event.

Consider what you need to learn about your topic and issue. If your topic or issue is relatively unfamiliar to you, look for sources that offer general overviews or discuss important aspects of the topic or issue. The introductory chapter of a scholarly book, for example, often provides a general overview of a topic, even when the rest of the book focuses on a specific issue. You can also look for overviews of a topic in magazine articles, in professional journal articles, and on the Web.

Finally, ask yourself about the evidence you'll need. As you reflect on what you want to say about your issue, think about the kind of evidence other writers have used to make their points. If you've found, for example, that most of the sources you explored use numerical data found in scholarly research reports, be sure to search for those kinds of reports. Similarly, if you notice that several writers tend to refer to expert opinion, search for sources written by recognized experts in a field.

Identify Appropriate Search Tools and Research Methods.   Once you've identified the types of sources that seem most relevant, determine which search tools and research methods you might use to locate those sources. In general, you can use three sets of resources to locate information.

- Online search tools, such as online library catalogs, databases, and Web search sites, allow you to search and browse for sources using a computer, tablet, or smartphone. Online search tools provide access to publication information about—and in some cases to the complete text of—print and digital sources. You can read about online search tools in Chapter 8.

- Print resources, such as bibliographies, indexes, encyclopedias, dictionaries, handbooks, almanacs, and atlases, can be found in library reference and periodical rooms. Unlike online search tools, which typically cover recent publications, many print resources provide information about publications over several decades—and in some cases over more than a century. You can read about print resources in Chapter 9.

- Field research methods, such as interviews and observations, allow you to collect information firsthand. In addition to conducting observations and interviews, you can correspond with experts, attend public events and performances, and view or listen to television and radio programs. You can read about field research methods in Chapter 10.

Featured writer Nicholas Brothers knew that his project would require the use of recent sources. As he thought about how to collect information, he decided to search databases for recent scholarly articles and to look for Web sites that provided access to recent reports and debates about the issue. To obtain the most up-to-date information, he also scheduled an interview with a professor at his university who was knowledgeable about the issue.

Develop a Project Timeline

A project timeline will give your reader an indication of the range of days, weeks, or months over which you will be completing your research and writing your document. Your timeline can range from a general description of the number of days or weeks you'll devote to your project to a detailed list of key project activities and the amount of time devoted to completing them. If you are working on a group project, a project timeline can be especially useful, since it will require discussion of individual responsibilities for completing tasks and deadlines for completing them.

Compile a Working or Annotated Bibliography

A working bibliography lists the sources you've collected so far. Sometimes you will be asked to create an annotated bibliography, which contains a brief description of each source. Your working or annotated bibliography should conform to the documentation system (such as MLA, APA, *Chicago*, or CSE) specified by your instructor, supervisor, or funding agency. For more information on bibliographies, see p. 113.

Clarify and Elaborate on Your Core Proposal

Depending on your purpose, your reader and the scope of your research writing project, you can choose to include several optional elements.

- **An abstract or executive summary** provides a brief summary — usually fifty to two hundred words — of your project. It should allow your reader to gain a general understanding of your project and your plans for completing it.

- **An overview of key challenges** allows you to share your thoughts about potential problems you'll need to address as you work on your project. This section of your research proposal might discuss difficulties you're likely to encounter, such as locating or collecting specific types of sources, gaining enough knowledge about an issue to develop a credible position, or finding enough respondents for a survey. It also provides an opportunity for your instructor, supervisor, or potential funder to respond by suggesting strategies for meeting specific challenges.

- **A funding request and rationale** provides a budget that identifies costs for key project activities, such as conducting your search, reviewing the sources you collect, writing and designing the document, and publishing or distributing the document.

Writing a formal research proposal allows you to reflect on the work you've done so far and get feedback on your plans to carry out your project. Perhaps more important, it requires you to make decisions about the best strategies for completing your project.

Brothers 1

Nicholas Brothers

English 108: College Writing and Research

Dawn Terrick

September 17, 2010

Research Proposal: Private Military

Corporations and the War on Terror

Introduction: For my research project, I would like to explore the world of the modern private military corporation (PMC). Mercenaries have been used throughout history by countries all over the world. With few exceptions, they have suffered a poor reputation; seen as unprofessional and unreliable, they went unused by many first-world nations in the age of standing professional armies. Yet, in recent years, PMCs have morphed into corporate entities and gained new respect. But is this respect deserved? Throughout the Afghanistan and Iraq conflicts, the United States' use of private military corporations has increased to what I consider startling levels.

While I will strive to be as objective as possible when conducting my research, my prior personal interest in this issue has always put me at odds with the supporters of PMCs. Fundamentally, I believe that overreliance on contractors is a danger to national and international security. However, it is entirely possible that, with further study, I will gain a new appreciation for PMCs and their personnel.

> Position statement is clear and concise.

My purpose is ultimately to build an argument about the United States' continued use of PMCs. To present my position on the issue, I will need to inform my readers about the history of PMCs and analyze the corporations' evolving role in our country's military engagements. My readers are my class peers (from many different backgrounds and studying different subjects) and my instructor. Although there is a wide range of scholarship and reportage on this topic, I believe the general public remains unaware of the pervasiveness of these corporations. It's my hope that upon reading my paper, the layperson will have a better understanding of how and why PMCs are involved in the wars in Iraq and Afghanistan. I will be creating an academic essay and a brief presentation to convey my research and argument to my readers. The print format of the essay will allow readers to follow my logic at their own pace and reread sections of the essay as needed, and it will also provide them an easy way to look up the sources I use if they want to explore the topic further — which I hope they will. The presentation will allow me to explain a complicated issue in a more conversational format and answer any questions.

> Discussion of purpose addresses the writer's intent and the readers' needs.

I plan to begin my paper with background information — mostly recent history unless I find something compelling from the distant past that I feel readers must know to better understand the present. I would like to explore the practical and moral costs of using PMCs. In doing so, I will likely focus on specific companies and incidents during the "War on Terror" years.

Research Question: What roles do private military corporations play in the U.S. military's war on terror?

Review of Literature: The book that originally piqued my interest in this topic was Jeremy Scahill's *Blackwater: The Rise of the World's Most Powerful Mercenary Army*, which depicts PMCs as very dangerous entities. Articles I've come across in publications such as *Salon.com* and *Mother Jones* also strongly criticize PMCs. On the complete opposite end of the spectrum are the corporate Web sites of the PMCs, which of course paint their contractors in only the most positive light. I found a more evenhanded approach to the topic in P. W. Singer's *Corporate Warriors: The Rise of the Privatized Military Industry*, which provides a solid overview of the history of PMCs and explains their structure and functions.

Search Plan and Relevant Sources: I will need to continue to seek out a range of perspectives on PMCs as I develop my own argument. I plan to conduct some field research by interviewing people who have firsthand experience with or expertise on PMCs. My brother, Michael Brothers, is in the military and might agree to an interview, and I plan to look at the research interests of the political science professors at Missouri Western to see if anyone might be able to provide me with insight on the war from an academic perspective.

I have already located three books on the subject through the library's online catalog, and by reading through the citations and sources used by the authors of these books, I have identified several other books that I might explore. In addition, I have used simple keyword and advanced searches on EBSCOhost, LexisNexis, and *NYTimes.com* to find several magazine, newspaper, and scholarly journal articles that provide contrasting viewpoints on the use of PMCs. They range from first-person accounts of PMC operations to academic articles analyzing the history and current use of PMCs.

I'd also like to take a look at some official government reports and read the actual language of some of the laws that surround PMCs. The Department of Defense Web site as well as senators' and representatives' Web sites might be good places to start. Once my first draft is complete, I might conduct another round of research to help answer any new questions or expand on new supporting points that I've developed.

I Joining the Conversation

The research question is open-ended but focuses on a specific time and place.

The literature review helps Nicholas think about his sources' different positions.

Nicholas identifies both a general search idea and a specific plan to carry out the search.

Brothers 3

Project Timeline: I have a little more than one month to complete this project. I already have several solid sources and plan to have my first assignment (the background paper based on what I know so far) completed one week from today. The next week, I'll conduct my interviews and write an interview paper based on my conversations. From there, I will combine the background paper and the interview paper, synthesizing these two drafts along with any new sources I've found. I will receive feedback on my first draft from my classmates and instructor. Then, I'll conduct any additional research needed and revise the draft by the due date of Oct. 20th. After the final draft is submitted, I'll create a reverse outline and summarize my paper's most important points for a brief in-class presentation the following week.

> A general project timeline indicates the time devoted to each stage of the process.

Key Challenges: Finding knowledgeable first-hand sources will be the main problem I will encounter, but I have some candidates in mind in helping me to understand the perceptions of U.S. military personnel, the history of mercenaries, and the political ramifications of their present-day use by the United States. I will contact them soon to inquire about their willingness and availability. I feel that I have already amassed a good deal of research material and plans, but I am wary that my sources so far might be geared toward my inherent bias toward the subject. I would like to make sure I have real opposing views to explore and not just straw men; this is a goal I will continually have to work toward.

> Writing down key challenges helps Nicholas avoid potential problems.

Time is another challenge. I have to conduct field research quickly and synthesize the results of the interview paper with the rest of my research in a short amount of time to create a first draft. I'm also concerned about focusing my topic enough for the paper to make sense — there are a lot of issues related to my topic that are intriguing, from the history of mercenaries to the legal status of PMCs and their lack of culpability for their crimes. Limiting the scope of my project could be difficult given the many aspects of the topic that seem worth addressing.

Brothers 4

Working Bibliography

Scahill, Jeremy. *Blackwater: The Rise of the World's Most Powerful Mercenary Army.* 2nd ed. New York: Nation Books, 2007. Print.

This book details the history of the private military corporation formerly known as Blackwater, with a focus on its controversial operations in Iraq and Afghanistan. Scahill is a reporter for *The Nation* and has reported extensively on Blackwater. I will use this book throughout my research project, as Blackwater (now Xe Services) remains one of the most powerful, visible, and divisive PMCs in the world.

Singer, P. W. *Corporate Warriors: The Rise of the Privatized Military Industry.* 2nd ed. Ithaca: Cornell UP, 2008. Print.

This scholarly look at the issue takes a balanced view: Singer is able to see the opportunities that PMCs provide while casting a critical eye at the potentials for abuse. I believe this will be an essential resource due to its balanced viewpoint and thoroughness.

The working bibliography summarizes sources and evaluates their usefulness.

Smith, Eugene B. "The New Condottieri and US Policy: The Privatization of Conflict and Its Implications." *Parameters: US Army War College* 32.4 (2002): 104. *Academic Search Premier.* EBSCO. Web. 11 Feb. 2010.

Written before the invasion of Iraq, this academic article briefly outlines the history of the privatization of warfare and concludes that the United States should employ PMCs due to their track record. At the time of this article's writing, Eugene B. Smith was a lieutenant colonel in the United States Army and served in the United States Central Command area of operations. This article might be useful in understanding the mindset of the military command that has increasingly employed private contractors in the last decade.

My Research Project

CREATE A RESEARCH PROPOSAL

Use the following activity to create a formal research proposal.

1. Provide the working title for your project.

2. Describe your issue.

3. Describe your purpose for working on this project.

4. Describe your readers' needs, interests, values, and beliefs.

5. State your research question.

6. Briefly review key findings about your issue from the sources you found as you explored your topic.

7. Indicate how you'll locate additional information, ideas, and arguments about your issue.

8. Include your project timeline.

9. Include your working bibliography.

10. Discuss the key challenges you face (optional).

11. Identify specific funding requests (optional).

You can download or print this activity at **bedfordresearcher.com**.

> **QUICK REFERENCE**

Developing Your Research Question and Proposal

- ☑ Reflect on your writing situation. (p. 41)
- ☑ Generate potential research questions. (p. 42)
- ☑ Craft questions that reflect your writing situation. (p. 43)
- ☑ Choose and refine your research question. (p. 46)
- ☑ If necessary, develop a research proposal. (p. 50)

The Bedford Researcher

I	Joining the Conversation
II	**Working with Sources**
III	Collecting Information
IV	Writing Your Document
V	Documenting Sources

PART II

Working with Sources

As you collect information, you'll read critically, evaluate sources, take notes, and guard against unintentional plagiarism. The next four chapters lead you through the process of engaging with the information, ideas, and arguments you will encounter as you work on your research writing project.

4

Reading Critically

> **Key Questions**

Critical readers read actively and with an attitude. Reading actively means working with a text as you read: skimming, reading for meaning, and rereading passages that leave you with questions. It means underlining and highlighting text, noting your reactions in the margins, and taking notes carefully and systematically. Reading with an attitude means never taking what you read at face value. It means asking questions, looking for implications, making inferences, and making connections to other sources.

4a

How does reading critically differ from evaluating?

At first glance, reading critically might seem to be the same as evaluating, which is discussed in detail in the next chapter. Although the two processes are related, they're not identical. Critically reading a source — questioning what it says and thinking about what it means — focuses your attention on making sense of the source. In contrast, evaluation focuses your attention on determining how reliably a source presents its information and how well it meets your needs as a research writer.

4b

How can I use my research question to read critically?

Your research question focuses your attention on your issue, provides the foundation for your search plan, and directs you to specific sources as you collect information. Your research question also provides the basis for developing a position on your issue, which you can also use to guide your critical reading.

The position you develop on your issue serves as an answer to your research question. At this point in your research writing process, your position on your issue is likely to be tentative and incomplete. As you learn more about your issue by reading critically, however, you'll develop and refine your position. Your position, in turn, will provide a foundation for your thesis statement — a formal statement of the main point you want to make about your issue. Figure 4.1 shows the progression from research question to position statement to thesis statement in the context of the research writing process.

As a response to your research question, your position can help you decide whether you agree or disagree with an author — and, thus, whether you want to

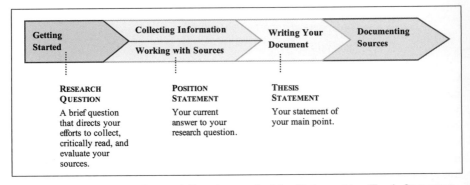

FIGURE 4.1 Moving from a Research Question to a Position Statement to a Thesis Statement

align yourself with his or her position on the issue. It will also help you judge whether the evidence provided in a source might be of use to you as you develop your argument—either to support your own argument or to illustrate an alternative approach to the issue. As you read critically, always keep your position in mind and test it against the information, ideas, and arguments you encounter in your sources. Remember, however, that your position might change as you learn more about your issue. Be flexible, as a result, and be willing to change your position in response to new and compelling information, ideas, and arguments.

Develop a Position Statement

To develop a statement about your position on your issue, brainstorm or freewrite in response to your research question. After reviewing your response, draft a brief statement of your position and use it to guide your critical reading.

Featured Writer Alexis Alvarez's Research Question:

What should be done about steroid use by adolescent girls involved in competitive sports?

Responses:

The typical response to steroid use in sports, such as the Olympics or professional football, seems to be some sort of punishment—losing a medal or being banned from competition for a period of time. But will this work with kids—especially kids who don't seem to have the same level of maturity as older athletes? And what about parents who encourage kids—and most likely provide the funds—to use steroids to get ahead (parents with college scholarship dollars in their eyes, no doubt)? So . . . maybe punishment isn't the answer—or at least it's only part of the answer. It seems from my reading so far that most kids don't understand the negative consequences of using steroids. They only see the potential benefits (making a team, performing at a higher level, getting famous, getting a scholarship, etc.). And parents might not understand those consequences as well. And then some coaches might even get into the act, "helping" kids compete at a higher level, and getting the wins they "need." If kids don't understand the consequences, then education might be useful. And most kids don't like to cheat, so maybe part of the answer is putting more of an emphasis on fair play. And you need to get parents and coaches into some sort of solution too.

Initial Position Statement:

Steroid use by adolescent girls involved in competitive sports might be addressed by educating athletes, parents, and coaches about health consequences and emphasizing fair play.

This statement is too vague to use as a thesis statement, but it would serve as an effective guide for critically reading sources. For example, if you read a source that argues for a solution to the problem of steroid use by young athletes, you could ask whether that solution makes sense in light of what you had read in other sources or whether it is based on a different set of assumptions.

Table 4.1 presents the movement from research question to position statement in the featured writers' projects. Note how each position statement attempts to answer the research question and thus lets readers know what the writer thinks an answer to the research question might be. The development of their position statements marked a significant step for the featured writers in their progress toward writing their final documents. By offering a preliminary answer to their research questions, they began to take ownership of their work: They shifted their focus from learning about the conversations they had decided to join to beginning to develop their contributions to the conversations.

> @ Read more about the Featured Writers at bedfordresearcher.com.

TABLE 4.1 THE FEATURED WRITERS' POSITION STATEMENTS

FEATURED WRITER	RESEARCH QUESTION	POSITION STATEMENT
Alexis Alvarez	What should be done about steroid use by adolescent girls involved in competitive sports?	Steroid use by adolescent girls involved in competitive sports should be addressed by educating athletes, parents, and coaches about health consequences and emphasizing fair play.
Nicholas Brothers	What dangers are associated with U.S. reliance on private military corporations in its war on terror?	The overreliance of the United States on private military corporations is a danger to national and international security.
Pete Jacquez	What strategies, if any, should Coloradoans use to encourage local, state, and federal governments to increase U.S. use of wind-generated electrical power?	Coloradoans should encourage local, state, and federal governments to increase reliance on wind-generated electrical power through a mix of tax incentives and reduced regulation.
Elizabeth Leontiev	How can we reduce the economic impact of the war on drugs on South American coca farmers?	The U.S. and South American governments should adopt the "zero cocaine, not zero coca" policy.
Chris Norris	What accounts for the resurgence in popularity of metal music?	Metal music has a political message, musical diversity, and a strong fan base.
Cori Schmidtbauer	How does Portia's character in *The Merchant of Venice* fit in with Elizabethan ideas of women?	Portia appears to rebel against the expectations of Elizabethan culture.

My Research Project

DRAFT A POSITION STATEMENT

In your research log, complete the following activity to draft your position statement.

1. Write your current research question.

2. Brainstorm or freewrite in response to your research question.

3. Select the response that best reflects your current understanding of the conversation you have decided to join. If appropriate, combine responses into one position statement.

4. Write your position statement.

You can print or download this activity at **bedfordresearcher.com**.

4c

How can I read with an attitude?

Reading critically means reading with an attitude. Your attitude will change during your research writing process. As you begin to read your sources critically, your attitude might be one of curiosity. You'll note new information and mark key passages that provide you with insights into the conversation you're joining. You'll adopt a more questioning attitude as you try to determine whether sources fit in your project or are reliable. Later, after you begin to draw conclusions about the conversation, you might take on a more skeptical attitude, becoming more aggressive in challenging arguments made in sources than you were at first.

Regardless of where you are in your research writing process, you should always adopt a critical attitude. Accept nothing at face value; ask questions; look for similarities and differences among the sources you read; examine the implications of what you read for your research project; be on the alert for unusual information; and note relevant sources and information. Most important, be open to ideas and arguments, even if you don't agree with them. Give them a chance to affect how you think about the conversation you've decided to join.

Approach a Source with Your Writing Situation in Mind

One way to get into the habit of reading critically is to approach a source with your writing situation in mind. To do so, think about your research question and position statement; your purpose and role; your readers' needs, interests, values, and beliefs; the type of document you've decided to write; the design of your document and the context in which it will be read; your requirements and limitations; and your opportunities.

Your Research Question and Position Statement As you critically read your sources, answer the following questions.

- Are the information, ideas, and arguments in this source relevant to my research question and position statement?
- Does this source present information, ideas, and arguments that make me reconsider my research question or position statement?
- Does this source provide any new information, ideas, or arguments?
- Does this source offer a new perspective on the conversation?

 WHAT'S MY PURPOSE?

Return to your research log and review your purpose. Keeping your purpose in mind as you read will make it easier to recognize useful information when you come across it. As you read, ask yourself the following questions:

- Will the information in this source help me accomplish my purpose? Can I use the information in this source as support for points I want to make? Can I use it to illustrate ideas that differ from mine?
- Is the information in this source more useful for my purpose than what I've found in other sources?
- Does the source provide a good model of a convincing argument or an effective presentation of information? Can I learn anything from the presentation of the points and evidence in this source?

Your Readers' Needs, Interests, Values, and Beliefs Keep in mind your readers' needs, interests, values, and beliefs by asking the following questions as you read.

- Would my readers want to know about the information, ideas, and arguments found in this source?
- Would my readers find the source's information convincing or compelling?
- Would my readers benefit from a review of the argument and evidence presented in this source?
- What are my readers likely to think about the argument and evidence presented in this source? How will they respond to them?

The Type of Document You Will Write Consider the conventions associated with the type of document, or genre, you've decided to write. Ask yourself:

- What type of evidence is usually provided in this type of document?
- Will I be expected to provide charts, graphics, photographs, or other types of illustrations? If so, can I learn anything from how illustrations are used in the source?
- How are documents of this type typically organized? Can I find examples of effective organizational strategies in the sources I read?

The Design of Your Document and the Context in Which It Will Be Read Research documents are presented in a variety of formats—for example, as printed texts, Web pages, or multimedia presentations. They're also read in a wide range of settings: in an office by someone sitting at a desk; on a bus or train by someone commuting to or from work; on a computer with a large, high-resolution monitor or a cramped screen; on a tablet or smartphone. As you read your sources, be alert to what you can learn about organizing and formatting your document effectively. Answer the following questions about your document and the context in which it will be read.

- Does this source provide a useful model for designing my document?
- Does this source help me understand how I might address the context in which my document will be read?

Your Requirements and Limitations As you read, keep your requirements and limitations in mind. Ask yourself:

- If I find useful information in a source, will I be able to follow up on it with additional research? Will I have enough time to follow up on that information?
- How much information can I include in my document? Will my readers be looking for a general overview or a detailed report?

Your Opportunities Instead of limiting your options, take advantage of them. As you read, ask yourself whether a source presents any possibilities or opportunities you have not yet discovered.

As you read a source, remember that you are working on your research writing project to make a contribution, to shape your readers' thinking about your issue. Don't hesitate to question the authors who have written before you. You should respect their work, but you shouldn't assume that their conclusions are the last word. Be prepared to challenge their ideas and arguments. If you don't do this, you'll simply repeat the ideas of others instead of advancing your own.

4d

What strategies can I use to read actively?

Once you have drafted your position statement, thought about your writing situation, and decided what to focus on, you're ready to start reading actively. Reading actively means interacting with sources and considering them in light of the conversation you've decided to join. When you read actively, you might do one or more of the following.

- identify key information, ideas, and arguments
- write questions in the margins

- jot down reactions to information, ideas, and arguments
- record quotations, paraphrases, and summaries in the form of notes
- take notes about how you might use information, ideas, and arguments in your project document
- link one part of the source to another visually
- identify important passages for later rereading

As you read sources, use three active-reading strategies: marking a source, annotating a source, and taking notes.

Mark Sources

Marking a source to identify key information, ideas, and arguments is a simple yet powerful active-reading strategy. Common marking techniques include:

- using a highlighter, a pen, or a pencil to identify key passages in a print source
- attaching notes or flags to printed pages
- highlighting passages in digital texts

Annotate Sources

You can further engage with your sources by writing brief annotations, or notes, in the margins of print sources and by using commenting tools for digital sources. Many research writers use annotations in combination with marking (see Figure 4.2). If you have highlighted a passage (marking) with which you disagree, as might happen as you read a source with your position in mind, you can write a brief note about why you disagree with the passage (annotating). You might make note of another source you've read that could support your argument, or you might write a reminder about the need to look for information that will help you argue against the passage.

> @ Learn more about digitally highlighting text at bedfordresearcher.com. Click on How-To Guides.

Take Notes

Notes provide a compact, easy-to-review record of the most important information, ideas, and arguments you've found in your sources. Notes can help you keep track of your ideas about significant patterns you've seen in your sources, such as similarities and differences, repeated ideas and arguments, and frequently cited information. Notes can also help you keep track of your thoughts about planning your document. Equally important, careful note taking helps you avoid plagiarism. For these reasons, note taking is one of the most important research writing skills you can draw on as you work on your research writing project.

46   THE RISE

The second implication is that this new private military actor is driven by business profit rather than individual profit. PMFs function as registered trade units, not as personal black-market ventures for individual profit or adventure. As firms, they can make use of complex corporate financing, ranging from sale of stock shares to intra-firm trade, meaning that a wider variety of deals and contracts can be worked out. For good reason, individual mercenaries tend only to trust payments in cash and, in turn, cannot be trusted for anything beyond the short-term.

This is possibly the thesis of Singer's argument on this issue. We recognize these corporations as legal where we have not recognized an individual mercenary as legal, despite the similar jobs they might do.

The key is that it is not the person that matters, but the structure that they are within. Many PMF employees have been mercenaries both before and after their employ, but their processes, relationships, and impacts within local conflicts were completely different.

The third distinguishing characteristic of the privatized military industry is that the arena they compete on is the open global market. That is, unlike the activities of the White Legion or similar mercenary units, PMFs are considered legal entities bound to their employers by recognized contracts and in many cases at least nominally to their home states by laws requiring registration, periodic reporting, and licensing of foreign contracts.[17] Rather than denying their existence, private military firms are registered businesses and, in fact, often publicly advertise their services—including many even having corporate websites on the Internet.[18] This status differentiates them not only from mercenaries, who had to hide from the law, but also from past entities, such as the charter companies, that did not coexist with any state law, but rather made their own laws.

I think it's better to focus on the crimes and abuses these corporations commit than quibble about what we should call them.

New military firms also provide a much wider offering of services and, importantly, to a much wider variety of clients. As the head of Sandline was proud to note, firms in the privatized military industry are 'structured organizations with professional and corporate hierarchies . . . We cover the full spectrum—training, logistics, support, operational support, post-conflict resolution.'[19] This provides another differentiation from past private military organizations. The goal of PMFs is service provision rather than the exchange of goods—a key distinction from the charter companies. Although one sector exclusively focuses on combat services like contract units and military entrepreneurs, another distinctive development is that PMFs provide military services outside the tactical sphere. Moreover, many are diversified enough to work for multiple (and a wider variety of) clients, in multiple markets and theatres at once—something none of the prior private military actors could do. As previously noted, those that have hired PMFs include other multinational corporations; state regimes—both foreign and the home bases of the firms; international organizations; and even nongovernmental organizations.

The corporate approach and the openness of this market also create more proficient recruitment patterns. Unlike the black market word-of-

II Working with Sources

FIGURE 4.2 A Source Highlighted and Annotated by Nicholas Brothers

Notes can include direct quotations, paraphrases, and summaries, as well as your thoughts about your sources as a group and your plans for your document. You can read more about taking notes in Chapter 6. You can read about avoiding plagiarism in Chapter 7.

TUTORIAL

How can I read actively?

Marking and annotating allow you to identify key information, ideas, and arguments, record your reactions to a source, question the source, connect the source to other sources, and note how you might use information, ideas, and arguments.

In this example, featured writer Chris Norris marks and annotates an article from msnbc.com about current trends in contemporary music. Later, he will use passages from the article to support his argument about the resurgence of metal music.

 Identify key information, ideas, and arguments.

 Write questions in the margins.

 Record your reactions to information, ideas, and arguments in the margins.

 Note how you might use information, ideas, and arguments in your project document.

 Link parts of the text visually.

 Identify important passages for later rereading.

Source: Used with permission of the Associated Press. Copyright © 2011. All rights reserved.

Review another example and read one of your sources actively by viewing this tutorial at **bedfordresearcher.com**. Click on Interactive Exercises.

4e

What should I pay attention to as I read?

Different research writing projects will require you to pay attention to different things as you read. In general, however, you should pay attention to the following.

- the type of source—or genre—you are reading
- whether the source is a primary or secondary source
- the author's main point
- reasons and evidence offered to support the point
- new information (information you haven't read before)
- ideas and information that you find difficult to understand
- ideas and information that are similar to or different from those you have found in other sources

Noting these aspects of a source during your active reading will help you better understand the source, its role in the conversation you've decided to join, and how you might use it in your document.

Identify the Type of Source You Are Reading

One of the most important things to pay attention to as you read is the type of source—or genre—you are reading. If a source is an opinion column rather than an objective summary of an argument, for example, you'll be less likely to be taken in by a questionable use of logic or analysis. If you are reading an annual corporate report for stockholders in a company, you'll recognize that the primary concern of the writers is to present the company in as positive a light as possible. If an article comes from a peer-reviewed scholarly journal, you'll be sure that it's been judged by experts in the field as well founded and worthy of publishing.

Recognizing the type of source you are reading will help you create a context for understanding and questioning the information, ideas, and arguments presented in the source.

Identify Primary and Secondary Sources

Primary sources are either original works or evidence provided directly by an observer of an event. Primary sources include

- poems, short stories, novels, essays, paintings, musical scores and recordings, sculpture, and other works of art or literature
- diaries, journals, memoirs, and autobiographies
- interviews, speeches, government and business records, letters, and memos
- reports, drawings, photographs, films, or video and audio recordings of an event

II Working with Sources

- physical artifacts associated with an event, such as a weapon used in a crime or a piece of pottery found in an archaeological dig

Secondary sources comment on or interpret an event, often using primary sources as evidence (see Table 4.2).

As a research writer, you should attempt to obtain as many primary sources as possible so that you can come to your own conclusions about your issue. Remember that your goal is to develop your own ideas about an issue, so that you can create an original, well-supported contribution to the conversation you've decided to join. If you rely entirely or mostly on secondary sources, you'll be viewing the issue through the eyes of other researchers. Be sure to ask yourself, when you read a secondary source, what factors might have affected the author's argument, presentation, or analysis.

Identify Main Points

Most sources, whether they are informative or argumentative, make a main point that you should pay attention to as you read critically. For example:

- An editorial in a local newspaper urges voters to approve financing of a new school.
- An article reports a new advance in automobile emissions testing.
- A Web page provides information about the benefits of a new technique for treating a sports injury.

Usually, but not always, the main point will be expressed in the form of a thesis statement (see p. 205). As you read critically, make sure you understand what the author of the source wants readers to know, accept, believe, or do as a result of reading the document.

Identify Reasons

Once you've identified a main point, look for key points that support it. If an author is arguing, for instance, that English should be the only language used for official government business in the United States, that author might support his or her argument with the following additional points.

| TABLE 4.2 EXAMPLES OF PRIMARY AND SECONDARY SOURCES | |
PRIMARY SOURCES	SECONDARY SOURCES
A play by William Shakespeare	An article that presents an analysis of the play
A transcript of the statement made by President George W. Bush on September 11, 2001	A recording of an interview in which a historian discusses the significance of the statement
A report of a laboratory study concerning the benefits of strength training for women with osteoporosis	A Web site that presents a review of recent research about prevention and treatment of osteoporosis

- Use of multiple languages erodes patriotism.
- Use of multiple languages keeps people apart — if they can't talk to each other they won't learn to respect each other.
- Use of multiple languages in government business costs taxpayers money because so many alternative forms need to be printed.

Consider the Use of Evidence

Authors typically use *appeals* to connect a reason to supporting evidence. Appeals can take many forms, including the following.

- **Appeals to authority.** Appeals to authority ask a reader to accept a reason because someone in a position of authority supports it. The evidence used to support this kind of appeal typically takes the form of quotations, paraphrases, or summaries of the ideas of experts on an issue. As you read a source, ask yourself which authorities the writer has identified and how the writer has used information from those authorities to support a point. Ask whether the authority is an appropriate choice, and whether information from the authority is presented fairly and effectively.

- **Appeals to emotion.** Writers frequently use emotional appeals to frame an argument. A writer might introduce an article with a brief description of a situation that affects one or more people, for example, in the hope that readers will be more sympathetic to the argument that follows. As you read sources, be aware of the uses to which emotional appeals can be put and consider whether you might accept the writer's argument if the emotional appeal were not made.

- **Appeals to principles, values, and beliefs.** Writers frequently rely on the assumption that their readers share with them particular principles, values, and beliefs. Religious and ethical arguments are often based on this kind of appeal, such as the belief that you should treat others as you would have them treat you, that men and women should be treated equally, or that every vote should count. When you encounter an appeal to principles, values, or beliefs, ask yourself what you can learn about the writer's principles, values, and beliefs, and then decide whether you share them.

- **Appeals to character.** Appeals to character might be referred to as the "trust me" strategy. This kind of appeal asks readers to consider the writer's character as a basis for accepting an argument. It can also ask readers to consider their own characters — to trust, as it were, in themselves.

- **Appeals to logic.** When writers make logical appeals, they present a set of propositions in the hope that you will accept them and agree with their conclusion. Appeals to logic often occur in the form of if/then reasoning, as in, "If this is true, then we can expect such and such to happen." As you read a source, identify the assumptions that lie behind a writer's logical appeals about an issue. You might find that, despite a well-reasoned argument, you can't accept the argument because you don't share the writer's assumptions.

II Working with Sources

- **Reasoning based on empirical evidence.** Many of us think of empirical evidence as information presented in numerical form. We think of it as "data." In fact, empirical evidence is any sort of information obtained through observation. A firsthand account of an event should be thought of as empirical evidence. So should results from surveys. So should measurements from an experiment. So should observation notes and transcripts of interviews.

As persuasive as these appeals and forms of reasoning might seem, keep in mind that they are only as good as the evidence offered to support them. In some cases, evidence is offered in the form of statements from experts on a subject or people in positions of authority. In other cases, evidence might include personal experience. In still other cases, evidence might include firsthand observations, excerpts from an interview, or statistical data.

In many cases writers will present general conclusions based on evidence rather than a detailed discussion of the evidence. For example, a writer is much more likely to point out that more than half of the respondents to a survey agreed with a particular solution to a problem, rather than explain that 11 percent strongly disagreed, 22 percent disagreed, 7 percent had no opinion, 42 percent agreed, and 18 percent strongly agreed. When you find empirical evidence used in a source, consider where the evidence comes from and how it is being used. If the information appears to be presented fairly, ask whether you might be able to use it to support your own ideas, and attempt to verify its accuracy by consulting additional sources.

Identify Interpretive Frameworks

Writers frequently analyze and interpret the evidence they've presented. As you read a source, keep in mind that any analysis or interpretation, no matter how well grounded in evidence, is subject to the writer's purpose, interests, values, beliefs, and background. To do this, try to understand what sort of interpretive framework is being used to analyze and make claims about the evidence the writer presents in the document.

An interpretive framework is a set of strategies for identifying patterns. Typically, these frameworks have been used successfully and refined over time by writers interested in a given subject area or working in a particular field. Writers can choose from hundreds (perhaps thousands) of specialized frameworks used in disciplines across the arts, sciences, social sciences, humanities, engineering, and business. A historian, for example, might apply a feminist, social, political, or cultural analysis to interpret diaries written by women who worked in defense plants during World War II, while a sociologist might conduct correlational tests to interpret the results of a survey. As you read sources, pay particular attention to writers who use four broad interpretive frameworks: trend analysis, causal analysis, data analysis, and text analysis.

- **Trend analysis.** Trends are patterns that hold up over time. Trend analysis, as a result, focuses on sequences of events and the relationships among them. It is based on the assumption that understanding what has happened in the past will allow us to make sense of what is happening in the present and to draw inferences about what is likely to happen in the future.

Trends can be identified and analyzed in nearly every field, from politics to consumer affairs to the arts. Economists interested in rising fuel prices, for example, often turn to historical accounts of similar fuel crises in the 1970s to understand recent increases. Sports and entertainment analysts, as well, frequently turn to trend analysis—in attempts to forecast the next NBA champion, for instance, or to explain the reemergence of superheroes in popular culture during the last decade.

As you read sources that use trend analysis, keep in mind that claims based on this form of analysis typically present historical information (sometimes in the form of statistics), argue that a trend exists, and then draw conclusions based on the existence of that trend. Ask yourself, as you read sources using this form of analysis, whether sufficient evidence exists to establish a trend, whether appropriate evidence has been used, and whether alternative conclusions might be drawn from the same evidence.

- **Causal analysis.** Causal analysis focuses on the factors that bring about a particular situation, such as the dot-com collapse in the late 1990s, the rise of terrorist groups, or the impact of calorie restriction on longevity. Writers use causal analysis when they believe that understanding the underlying reasons for a situation will help people address the situation, influence the likelihood of it happening again, or appreciate its potential consequences.

  As you read sources that use causal analysis, ask whether the writer has identified multiple causes (since most effects are the result of more than a single cause), whether the writer has identified important causes (since some causes are far more important than others), and whether the writer has confused correlation with causation. Correlation is the observation that two things are related. It's been shown, for example, that people who own large, expensive homes often drive luxury cars. Most people would agree, however, that it would be foolish to think that the best way to get a nice new home is to buy an expensive car. Instead, they'd point out that there are other factors—such as a high income combined with a desire to live in a nice home and drive an expensive car—that are the likely causes.

- **Data analysis.** Data is any type of information, such as facts and observations. When data is available in the form of numerical information, such as a collection of measurements or a set of test scores, it can be used to make claims about an issue.

  Data analysis is something most people do on a regular basis. If you've looked at the percentage of people who favor a particular political candidate over another, for example, you've engaged in data analysis. Similarly, if you've checked your bank account to determine whether you have enough money for a new coat, you've carried out a form of data analysis. Writers typically analyze numerical information to help readers better understand an issue, to look for differences, and to explore relationships.

As you read sources that use this form of analysis, ask whether the writer has presented sufficient evidence to support his or her analysis and whether the reasoning presented by the writer is rigorous and fair. For example, if someone is arguing that a recent survey provides enough evidence for the adoption of a new policy, ask how many people were surveyed and whether they represent a broad cross section of the population. You should also ask whether the writer has described the statistical methods used to make the claim and, if so, whether the methods are appropriate.

Keep in mind as well the common problems that sources relying on data analysis can suffer from, such as base-rate fallacies and cherry picking. An example of a base-rate fallacy would be a claim that drinking a particular drink, such as coffee, can double your risk of coming down with cancer. If the initial risk was one in ten million, this means that the new risk is two in ten million—far less than the chance of getting in a car accident as you drive to the coffee shop. Cherry picking involves selecting only those findings that support a writer's conclusions, rather than reporting all of the relevant findings.

- **Text analysis.** Today, the word *text* can refer to a wide range of printed or digital works—and even some forms of artistic expression that we'd be hard pressed to think of as documents. Texts open to interpretation include novels, poems, plays, essays, articles, movies, speeches, blogs, songs, paintings, photographs, sculptures, performances, Web pages, videos, television shows, and computer games.

  Many writers use the elements of literary analysis to analyze texts. In this form of analysis, interpreters focus on theme, plot, setting, characterization, imagery, style, and structure as well as the contexts—social, cultural, political, and historical—that shape a work. Writers who use this form of analysis focus both on what is actually presented in the text and what is implied or conveyed "between the lines." They rely heavily on close reading of the text to discern meaning, critique a writer's technique, and search for patterns that will help them understand the text as fully as possible. They also tend to consider and include in their analysis other elements of the wider writing situation in which the text was produced—in particular, the writer's purpose, intended audience, use of sources, and choice of genre.

  As you read sources that use text analysis, ask whether the claims made about the text are supported by evidence drawn from the text itself. Be wary of situations in which the writer simply uses the text as a point of departure, rather than offering evidence in the form of quotations, paraphrases, and summaries. Ask as well whether the writer is considering the text in its entirety. In some cases, writers pick and choose from a text and ignore its overall meaning.

Identify New Information

As you read, mark and annotate passages that contain information that is new to you. Keep track of new information in your research log in the form of a list or as a series of brief descriptions of what you've learned and where you learned it.

Identify Hard-to-Understand Information

As you read, you might be tempted to ignore information that's hard to understand. If you skip over this information, you might miss something that is critical to the success of your research project. When you encounter information that's difficult to understand, mark it and make a brief annotation reminding yourself to check it out later.

Sometimes you'll learn enough from your reading of other sources that the passage won't seem as difficult when you come back to it later. And sometimes you'll still be faced with a passage that's impossible to figure out on your own. In this case, turn to someone else for advice.

- Search a database, library catalog, or the Web using words you didn't understand in the source.
- Ask your instructor or a librarian for help.
- Ask a question about the passage on a newsgroup or electronic mailing list.
- Interview an expert in the area.

Identify Similarities and Differences

You can learn a lot by looking for similarities and differences among the sources you read. For example, you might identify a group of authors who take a similar approach to an issue, such as favoring increased government support for wind energy. You could then contrast this group with other groups of authors, such as those who believe that market forces should be the primary factor encouraging wind power and those who believe we should focus on other forms of energy. Similarly, you can make note of information in one source that agrees or disagrees with information in another. These notes can help you build your own argument or identify information that will allow you (and potentially your readers) to better understand the issue.

II Working with Sources

My Research Project

NOTE CONNECTIONS AMONG SOURCES

In your research log, identify connections among your sources.

1. Do your sources tend to fall into one or more genres, such as scholarly articles, books, blog entries, or Web pages? If so, identify the most common genres.

2. Do your sources tend to be primary or secondary sources, or a mix of the two types? Why do you think you're seeing this pattern?

↓

3. Do the authors of your sources tend to agree with each other? Disagree? Fall into various groups? Please describe the pattern you see.

4. Does the information in one or more sources contradict information in other sources? If so, where are you seeing the contradiction, and what do you think is causing it?

5. Do authors tend to rely on similar arguments and evidence? If so, describe the arguments and evidence.

6. Are any sources cited frequently by the authors of your sources? If so, identify the source.

7. What interpretive frameworks are found in your sources? Are any of them used in more than one source? If so, why do you think they are relying on this framework or frameworks?

You can print or download this activity at **bedfordresearcher.com**.

4f

How many times should I read a source?

As you work through your sources, you'll find that many are less relevant to your research project than you'd hoped when you collected them. When you come across one of these sources, move on to the next source. Other sources are worth reading more carefully. When a source offers what seems like good information, ideas, or arguments, use a three-pass approach.

1. Skim the source to get a general idea of its organization and content.
2. Read actively, marking and annotating relevant passages in the text and taking notes on important information, ideas, and arguments.
3. Reread passages that are either particularly promising or difficult to understand.

First Pass: Skim for Organization and Content

Before investing too much time in a source, skim it. Skimming — reading just enough to get a general idea of what a source is about — can tell you a great deal in a minimal amount of time.

Skimming is an important first step in reading a source critically. Skimming helps you understand how a source is organized, which can help you more quickly assess its usefulness and relevance. If the source uses a familiar organizational pattern, you'll find it easier to locate key information.

You can also learn a great deal about the content of a source through skimming. Skimming is most effective when you approach your sources with your writing situation and specific questions in mind. Before you skim a source, write a list of questions about the source in your research log. As you skim, add questions to your list. When you're finished, write answers to your questions. Your questions might include the following.

- What is the main point of this source?
- What reasons are offered to support the main point?
- What evidence is offered to support reasons?
- Who is it written for?
- Why was it written?

CHECKLIST FOR SKIMMING SOURCES

✔ Identify the type of document — for example, book, magazine article, opinion column, scholarly journal article, personal Web site, blog entry.

✔ Check the title.

✔ Look at the table of contents, if one is provided.

✔ Read the abstract, if one is provided, or the introduction.

✔ Check major headings and subheadings.

✔ Read the titles or captions of any figures and tables.

✔ Look for pull quotes (quotations or brief passages pulled out into the margins or set somewhere on the page in larger type).

✔ Scan the first sentences and last sentences of paragraphs for key information.

✔ Check the works cited list, if one is provided.

My Research Project

USE QUESTIONS TO GUIDE CRITICAL READING

Before you read a source, generate a list of questions about it. As you read, keep those questions in mind and ask additional questions. After you've read the source, use this activity to keep track of the answers to your questions. In your research log, create a table like the one shown here. For each source, write the name of the source and questions you would like to answer as you read the source. After you read the source, write your responses to your questions in the appropriate column.

SOURCE	
Question 1:	Response:
Question 2:	Response:
Question 3:	Response:
Question 4:	Response:

You can print or download this activity at **bedfordresearcher.com**.

Second Pass: Read Actively

After you've skimmed the source and identified promising sections, read those sections actively—highlighting or underlining key passages, making annotations in the margin, or taking notes in your research log. You should read either the entire source or at least enough to know that you don't need to read any more.

Third Pass: Reread Important Passages   [FRAMING MY ARGUMENT]

If you decide that a source is valuable—or if you still have questions about the source—reread passages that you've identified as important. Again, read actively, continuing to note your reactions and ideas as you read. Rereading key passages in this way can help you gain a better understanding of the source, which can make a tremendous difference as you begin writing. Rereading passages—indeed, even an entire source—can also be useful as you plan, draft, and revise your document. As you refine your argument, return to your sources to determine whether you are presenting information, ideas, and arguments from them fairly and accurately and whether you might find additional material to support your argument.

Mark and Annotate Sources with Your Argument in Mind.   As you read critically, remember that you'll need to advance and support an argument in your project document. You'll need to understand what others have written so that you can fairly represent the issue to your readers, differentiate your argument from those made by other writers, and identify evidence to support your argument. As you read, mark key passages by highlighting or underlining, and make annotations to remind yourself of the importance or potential uses of the information, ideas, and arguments in the passage (see Figure 4.3). Keep your writing situation in mind as you make your annotations. Consider your purpose and role as a writer, and think about your readers' needs, interests, values, and beliefs. Use your annotations to call attention to how you might use the information in each marked or highlighted passage to accomplish your goals as a writer.

> ## QUICK REFERENCE

Reading Critically

☑ Draft a position statement. (p. 63)

☑ Read with an attitude, keeping in mind the following: your research question and position statement; your purpose; your readers' needs, interests, values, and beliefs; the type of document you will write and the context in which it will be read; your requirements and limitations; and your opportunities. (p. 65)

☑ Mark, annotate, and take notes on your sources. (p. 68)

☑ Identify primary and secondary sources, main points, evidence, interpretive frameworks, new and hard-to-understand information, and similarities and differences among sources. (p. 71)

☑ Read the source multiple times, first skimming, then reading actively, then rereading important passages. (p. 78)

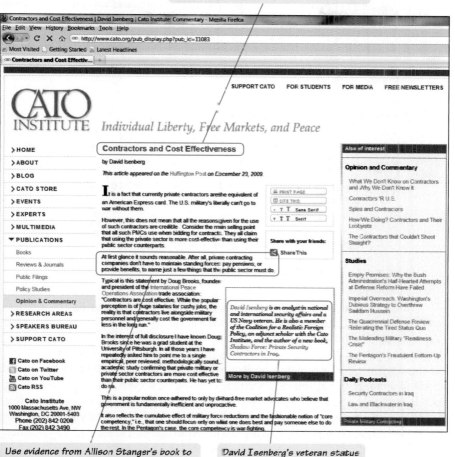

FIGURE 4.3 Marking and Annotating Sources with Your Argument in Mind

5

Evaluating Sources

 Key Questions

At the beginning of a research project, you'll most likely make quick judgments about your sources. Skimming an article, a book, or a Web site might be enough to tell you that spending more time with the source would be wasted effort. As you encounter a new source, determine how well it meets your needs as a research writer and how reliably it presents information, ideas, and arguments.

5a

What factors should I use to evaluate a source?

Evaluating a source means examining its relevance, evidence, author, publisher, timeliness, comprehensiveness, and genre.

Evaluate Relevance

Relevance is the extent to which a source provides information you can use in your research writing project. The most important questions you should ask to determine the relevance of a source are about your purpose and audience.

> **?** **WHAT'S MY PURPOSE?**
>
> Determine if the information in a source will help you accomplish your purpose. In the course of your research, you might find a number of information-filled sources. If the information is not relevant, however, it won't help you fulfill your purpose. For example, an analysis of the new user interface in the latest iPod might contain accurate and up-to-date information, but if you're writing about the monopolistic practices of leading digital music publishers, this source probably won't be of much use to you.

Determine if the Information in a Source Will Help You Address Your Readers' Needs, Interests, Values, and Beliefs. The information in a source should be useful to your readers. You might be tempted to include a beautifully worded quotation, but if your readers won't see how it contributes to your document, don't use it. Your readers will expect information that meets their needs. If they want to read about downloading music online, for instance, pass up sources that focus only on traditional music publishers.

Evaluate Evidence

Evidence is information offered to support an author's reasoning about an issue (see p. 72). Evidence is connected to reasons through appeals to authority, emotion, principles, values, beliefs, character, and logic. It can also include measurements and observations, typically referred to as empirical evidence. An argument in favor of charging local sales tax on Web-based purchases might use statistics—a form of empirical evidence. It could calculate the revenue a town of fifty thousand might lose if 5 percent of its citizens made fifteen online purchases in a given year. As a research writer, you can evaluate not only the kind of information used in a source but also the quality, amount, and appropriateness of that evidence. Ask the following questions about each source.

- **Is enough evidence offered?** A lack of evidence might indicate fundamental flaws in the author's argument.

- **Is the right kind of evidence offered?** More evidence isn't always better evidence. As you evaluate a source, ask yourself whether the evidence is appropriate for the points being made. Ask as well whether more than one type of evidence is being used. Many sources rely far too heavily on a single type, such as personal experience or anecdotal evidence.

- **Is the evidence used fairly?** Look for reasonable alternative interpretations, questionable or inappropriate use of evidence, and evidence that seems to contradict points made elsewhere in a source. If statistics are offered as evidence, ask yourself whether they are interpreted fairly or presented clearly. If a quotation is used to support a point, try to determine whether it is used appropriately.

- **Is the source of the evidence provided?** Knowing the origins of evidence can make a significant difference in your evaluation of a source. For example, if a source quotes a political poll but doesn't indicate which organization conducted the poll, you might question the reliability of the source.

Evaluate the Author

In addition to relevance and evidence, you can evaluate a source based on who wrote it. Take, for example, two editorials published in your local newspaper that make similar arguments and offer similar evidence. One is written by a fourteen-year-old middle school student, the other by a U.S. senator. You would certainly favor an editorial written by the senator if the subject was U.S. foreign policy. If the subject was student perceptions about drug abuse prevention in schools, however, you might value the middle school student's opinion more highly.

The importance of authorship as an evaluation criterion varies from source to source. In some cases, including many Web sites, you won't even know who the author is. In other cases, such as signed opinion columns in a newspaper or magazine, your evaluation could be affected by knowing that the author is politically conservative, liberal, or moderate. Similarly, you might find it useful to know that a message published on a Web discussion forum was written by someone who is recognized as an expert in the field.

Ask the following questions about the author of a source.

- **Is the author knowledgeable about the topic?** It can be difficult to judge an author because expertise can be gained in many ways. An author might be an acknowledged expert in a field; he or she might be a reporter who has written extensively about a topic; or he or she might be recounting first-hand experiences. Then again, an author might have little or no experience with a topic beyond a desire to say something about it. How can you tell the difference? Look for a description of the author in the source. If none is provided, the source might give a URL for the author's home page, and you can check out his or her credentials there. Or perhaps you can locate information about the author on the Web or in a biographical reference such as *Who's Who*.

- **What is the author's affiliation?** Knowing the institution, agency, or organization that employs the author or the political party or organizations to which the author belongs can help you evaluate the assumptions that inform a source.

- **How do the author's biases affect the information, ideas, and arguments in the source?** We all have a bias—a set of interests that shapes our perceptions of a topic. As you evaluate a source, consider the extent to which the author's biases affect the presentation of information, ideas, and arguments in the source. To uncover an author's biases, try to learn more about his or her affiliations. You might infer a bias, for instance, if you learn that an author writes frequently about gun control regulations and works for the National Firearms Association.

Evaluate the Publisher

A publisher is a person or group that prints or produces the documents written by authors. Publishers provide access to print or digital sources, including books, newspapers, journals, Web sites, sound and video files, and databases. Some documents — such as messages posted to newsgroups or sources obtained through field research — have no publisher.

You can make informed judgments about publishers in much the same way that you can evaluate authors. Ask the following questions about the publisher of a source.

- **How can I locate information about the publisher?** If a publisher is listed in a print document, search for information about the publisher on the Web. You can often tell whether a publisher is reputable by looking at the types of material it publishes. If you are viewing a document on the Web, search for a link to the site's home page.

- **How do the publisher's biases affect the information, ideas, and arguments in the source?** Like authors, publishers have biases. Unlike authors, they often advertise them. Many publishers have a mission statement on their Web sites, while others present information on their Web pages that can help you figure out their bias. You might already know a fair amount about the biases of a publisher, particularly if the publisher is a major newspaper or magazine, such as the *New York Times* (regarded as liberal) or the *Wall Street Journal* (regarded as conservative). If the publisher is a scholarly or professional journal, you can often gain an understanding of its biases by looking over the contents of several issues or by reading a few of its articles.

Evaluate Timeliness

The importance of timeliness — a source's publication date — varies according to your writing situation. If your research project would benefit from sources that have recently been published, then evaluate recent sources more favorably than dated ones. If you're writing an article on the use of superconducting materials in new mass transportation projects, you probably won't want to spend a lot of time with articles published in 1968. On the other hand, if you're writing about the 1968 presidential contest between Hubert Humphrey and Richard Nixon, sources published during that time period will take on greater importance.

Print sources usually list a publication date. It can be more difficult, however, to tell when Web sources were created. When in doubt, back up undated information found on the Web with a dated source.

II Working with Sources

Evaluate Comprehensiveness

Comprehensiveness is the extent to which a source provides a complete and balanced view of a topic. Like timeliness, the importance of comprehensiveness varies according to the demands of your writing situation. If you are working on a narrowly focused project, such as the role played by shifts in Pacific Ocean currents on snowfall patterns in Colorado in the winter of 2008, you might not find this evaluation criterion as useful as the others. However, if you are considering a broader issue, such as the potential effects of global climate change on agricultural production in North America, or if you are still learning as much as you can about your issue, give preference to sources that provide full treatment.

Evaluate Genre   [FRAMING MY ARGUMENT]

Identifying the genre—or document type—of the source you are evaluating can help you understand a great deal about its intended readers, the kind of appeals and evidence it is likely to use, and the kind of argument it is likely to make. An article in a professional journal, for example, will almost certainly rely on published sources or original research, and it will carefully document its sources so that its readers can locate related documents easily. In contrast, a blog entry is more likely to rely on personal observation and reflection or on responding to events or arguments made in other blogs and is far less likely, as a result, to contain extensive documentation of sources.

By understanding the conventions of a particular genre, you can understand whether the information, ideas, and arguments found in it might be of use to you as you work on your research writing project. To evaluate a genre, ask the following questions.

- **What style of writing does the genre use?** Ask how formally (or informally) the document is written. Check for the use of specialized terms that might be unfamiliar to general readers. Try to understand how the writer views himself or herself in relation to readers.

- **How is evidence used?** Identify numerical information; quotations and paraphrases; summaries of other documents; charts, graphs, and tables; and images and other illustrations. Ask yourself why the writer would choose the types of evidence you've found in the document.

- **How is the genre organized?** Try to break the document into major sections. Ask whether you've seen this type of organization used in other documents and think about the purposes of those documents. You'll often find that documents within a genre are organized in similar ways.

- **What citation style is used?** Determine whether the sources of information, ideas, and arguments are identified in the document.

- **How is the document designed?** A document's appearance can tell you a great deal about its purpose, intended readers, and likely means of distribution. Ask about its medium—print or digital. Ask whether it uses color,

CHECKLIST FOR EVALUATING SOURCES

☑ **Determine whether the source is relevant.** Will the source help you accomplish your purpose and address your readers' needs, interests, values, and beliefs?

☑ **Determine whether the source provides evidence and uses it appropriately.** Is enough evidence of the right kind offered? Is evidence used fairly, is it convincing, and is its source provided?

☑ **Learn about the author of the source.** Ask whether the author is knowledgeable. Try to determine the author's affiliation and consider how the author's biases affect the information, ideas, and arguments in the source.

☑ **Learn about the publisher of the source.** Try to locate information about the publisher, and reflect on how the publisher's biases affect the information, ideas, and arguments in the source.

☑ **Think about the timeliness of the source** and its impact on and relevance to your project.

☑ **Consider the comprehensiveness of the source** and its impact on and relevance to your project.

☑ **Consider the genre of the source** and its impact on the kind of information included in the source, the manner in which information is used by the author, and the likely audience for which the source was written.

columns of text, images, and other illustrations. Ask what types of readers might appreciate the use of these design elements; then ask what effects these elements might have on potential readers.

Consider Genre in Your Decisions about Sources for Your Writing Project. As you consider which sources are best suited for your writing project, keep in mind the importance of referring to sources that your readers will recognize as relevant, reliable, and authoritative. An important part of your purpose as a writer is to influence your readers, and the types of sources you use to support your argument will have an impact on them. Featured writer Pete Jacquez, for example, might have drawn supporting evidence for his argument about wind-generated electrical power from a wide range of blogs, personal Web sites, discussion forums, and magazine articles. Instead, he chose to rely primarily on government reports, such as the National Renewable Energy Laboratory's *Wind Power: Today and Tomorrow*, because he knew government reports are generally recognized as credible, reliable, and authoritative (see Figure 5.1).

> @ The bibliography tools at bedfordresearcher.com can help you evaluate and keep track of bibliographic information for your sources. As you collect new sources, enter the bibliographic information and evaluate each source.

By choosing sources that your readers will recognize as appropriate and reasonable, you can increase the chances that your project will be successful. Understanding the types of documents that are typically used in the genre you've selected for your project document can help you make an effective argument.

**FIGURE 5.1 Pete Jacquez Relied
Heavily on Government Reports**

II Working with Sources

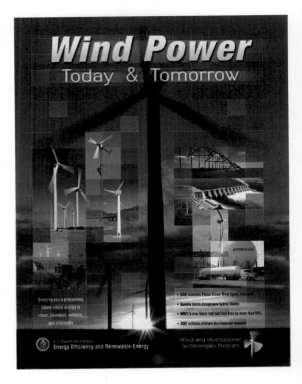

My Research Project

CONDUCT A SOURCE EVALUATION

A source evaluation applies the evaluation criteria you've read about in this chapter to a single source. You should consider each criterion in light of your writing situation and then determine the suitability of the source for your research writing project. To carry out a source evaluation, respond to the following prompts.

1. Provide the complete citation for the source.

2. In what ways are the information, ideas, and arguments in the source relevant to your research writing project?

3. Is the line of argument in the source sound and well supported? In what ways can you use it in your project?

4. What have you learned about the author and publisher that would lead you to accept, question, or reject the line of argument presented in the source?

5. In what ways does the publication date of the source affect your judgment of its usefulness for your project?

6. In what ways does the comprehensiveness of the source affect your judgment of its usefulness for your project?

7. In what ways does the genre of the source affect your judgment of its usefulness for your project?

8. In what ways could this source help you achieve your purpose and address the needs and interests of your readers?

9. How are you likely to use this source in your project?

You can print or download this activity at **bedfordresearcher.com**.

5b

Should I evaluate all types of sources in the same way?

You can apply the general evaluative criteria discussed in the previous section to most types of sources. However, two sets of sources—digital and field sources—can pose challenges during evaluation. The following discussion highlights additional factors to keep in mind as you evaluate digital and field sources.

Evaluate the Relevance and Credibility of Digital Sources

Because anyone can create a Web site, start a blog, contribute to a wiki, or post a message to a social networking site, email list, or Web discussion forum, approach these sources with more caution than you would reserve for print sources such as books and journal articles, which are typically published only after a lengthy editorial review process.

Web Sites and Blogs   To assess the relevance and credibility of a Web site or a blog, examine its domain (.edu, .com, and so on) and look for information about the site (often available through an About This Site or Site Information page). The following tutorial provides information about evaluating Web sites.

Social Networking Sites, Newsgroups, Email Lists, Discussion Forums   To assess the relevance and credibility of a message on one of these online forums, try to learn something about the author. On social networking sites, you can usually link back to authors' personal pages. In newsgroups, email lists, and discussion forums, check for a "signature" at the end of the message and try to locate a Frequently Asked Questions (FAQ) list. A signature can provide information about the sender, such as a professional title, and the URL for a personal home page where you can learn more about the author. An FAQ can tell you about the purpose of a newsgroup, email list, or discussion forum; whether messages are moderated (reviewed prior to posting); and whether membership is open to all or restricted to a particular group. You can use the information you uncover to evaluate the information and ideas you find on the site, group, list, or forum. It can be useful, for example, to

> Learn more at
> bedfordresearcher.com.
> Click on How-To Guides.

TUTORIAL

How do I evaluate a Web site?

Because Web sites can be published without having gone through a rigorous review process, you'll want to evaluate them carefully. Evaluate a Web site by learning about its author, publisher, purpose, publication date, use of evidence, relevance, timeliness, and credibility. This example shows how you can evaluate a Web page that featured writer Alexis Alvarez found as she explored her topic: steroid use by adolescent girls involved in competitive sports.

1 Check its domain (.com, .edu, .gov, and so on) to learn about its purpose and publisher:

.biz, .com, .coop	business	**.name**	personal
.edu	higher education	**.net**	network organization
.gov	government	**.org**	nonprofit organization
.mil	military	**.pro**	professional

2 Check the title bar, page header, and page titles to learn about the site's purpose, publisher (p. 85), and relevance (p. 82).

3 Search for information — on the site or through a separate Web search — about the author (p. 84) or publisher (p. 85), if identified.

4 Check timeliness (p. 85) by looking for a publication or a "last modified" date.

5 Read the body text and review illustrations to evaluate relevance (p. 82), evidence (p. 83), and comprehensiveness (p. 86).

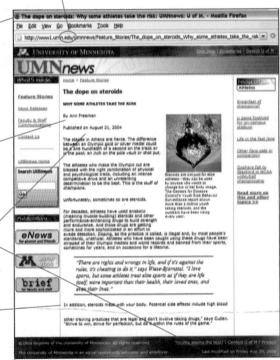

6 Check page footers for information about the publisher and author. Look for *About This Site* or *Contact* links.

Review another example and evaluate your Web sources at **bedfordresearcher.com**. Click on Interactive Exercises.

know that the moderator of a discussion forum is a member of an organization frequently discussed in the group. Similarly, it can help to know that a Facebook fan page is run by a corporation whose staff members might delete negative comments or provide potentially misleading responses.

Wikis   Wikis are Web sites that can be added to or edited by visitors to the site. Wikis such as Wikipedia (en.wikipedia.org) have grown in importance on the Web, and many Wikipedia pages are highly ranked by Web search sites such as Ask, Bing, Google, and Yahoo! Wikis can be good resources as you start a research writing project. In some cases, people who are experts on an issue contribute to wikis and provide information and analyses that can help you gain an initial understanding of an issue. They also often provide links to other resources that can help you learn about the issue. Unfortunately, it can be difficult to evaluate the credibility of wiki pages because their creators and editors are often difficult to identify and because changes to wiki pages can occur quickly. Susan Kruglinski, in an article in *Discover* magazine (discovermagazine .com/2006/jul/evolutionmap/), reports that the Wikipedia entry for evolution was changed more than 2,000 times by sixty-eight editors over a five-year period. Her discussion of those changes calls attention to the difficulty of treating wiki pages as authoritative and stable.

In most cases, it is best to use wikis when you are beginning to learn about an issue. Avoid citing them as the "last word" on a topic because those last words might change before you submit your final draft.

Evaluate the Relevance and Accuracy of Field Sources

With some adjustment, most of the criteria discussed in this chapter can be applied to field sources such as interviews, correspondence, observations, and surveys. Relevance and the accuracy of the information you collect deserve additional attention. Ask the following questions as you evaluate information collected through field research.

- Are the questions you asked in an interview, a survey, or correspondence still relevant to your research project?

- Is the information you collected in an observation still relevant? Are your observation notes as complete as you had hoped they would be?

- Are the individuals you interviewed or corresponded with as qualified and knowledgeable as you expected?

Information Literacy

If you remain uncertain about the credibility of a source, consider using a citation database (see p. 157). Citation databases identify sources that have cited a particular source, allowing you to locate the citing source and determine how other writers have responded to it. Although these databases seldom identify all sources that have cited a source, they can help you understand the role the source is playing in a larger conversation about an issue. Leading citation databases include the Web of Science, available through many university and college libraries, and Google Scholar, available at scholar.google.com.

- Were questions in interviews, surveys, and correspondence answered fully and honestly?
- Did survey respondents have adequate time to complete the survey? Did they appear to believe their privacy would be respected?

My Research Project

USE EVALUATION TO TRIM A WORKING BIBLIOGRAPHY

Use the bibliography tools at **bedfordresearcher.com** to evaluate sources on the criteria defined in this chapter, enter publication information, create annotations, save text from digital sources, and generate a bibliography.

You can use your evaluations to determine which sources should be added to or removed from your working bibliography. If you decide that a source is no longer relevant to your project, however, don't throw it away. There's always a chance that you'll decide you need it later. Instead of deleting it, put it in a category named "irrelevant," or move it into a new bibliography named "other sources" or "unused sources."

 QUICK REFERENCE

Evaluating Your Sources

☑ Evaluate the relevance, evidence, author, publisher, timeliness, comprehensiveness, and genre of your sources. (p. 82)

☑ Evaluate Web sources for relevance and credibility. (p. 89)

☑ Evaluate field research for relevance and accuracy. (p. 91)

Part II
Working with Sources

4	Reading Critically
5	Evaluating Sources
6	**Managing Information and Taking Notes**
7	Avoiding Plagiarism

6

Managing Information and Taking Notes

Even with a narrowly defined research question, it's likely that your searches will produce a large number of relevant sources. To use those sources most effectively, you should decide how to save and organize the information you collect, take notes carefully, and keep track of your sources.

Saving and organizing information will help you work with your sources more easily as you plan and draft your document. Taking notes allows you to focus more closely on what your sources tell you about your topic and issue and helps you learn how each source can help you answer your research question. Working and annotated bibliographies provide a detailed record of the sources you've consulted. Together, these strategies help you avoid plagiarism and lay the foundation for drafting your document, making them some of the most important research writing skills you can develop.

6a

How can I save and organize the information I find?

As you begin to collect information, spend some time reflecting on how you will save and keep track of it.

Decide How to Save and Organize Print Information

During your research project, you'll accumulate a great deal of print information, such as:

- your written notes (in a notebook, on loose pieces of paper, on Post-It Notes, and so on)
- printouts from Web pages and databases
- articles sent through a library's fax-on-demand service
- printed word processing documents, such as various drafts of your research question and position statement
- books, magazines, newspapers, brochures, pamphlets, and government documents
- photocopies of articles, book chapters, and other documents
- letters, printed email messages, survey results, and so on

Rather than letting all this information build up in messy piles on your desk or stuffing it into folders in your backpack, create a filing system to keep track of your print documents. Filing systems can range from well-organized piles of paper labeled with Post-It Notes to three-ring binders to file cabinets filled with neatly labeled files and folders.

Regardless of the approach you take, keep the following principles in mind.

- **Create an organizational scheme that allows you to locate your print materials.** Decide whether you want to group material by topic, by date, by pro versus con, by type of material (Web pages, photocopies, original documents, field sources, and so on), or by author.

- **Stick with your organizational scheme.** You'll find it difficult to locate materials if you use different approaches at different points in your research project.

- **Make sure printed documents provide complete publication information.** If a source doesn't contain publication information, write it on the document yourself.

- **Date your notes.** Indicating dates when you recorded information can help you reconstruct what you might have been doing while you took the notes. Dates are also essential for documenting Web sources and other sources obtained online.

- **Write a brief note on each of your print materials.** Indicate how it might contribute to your project.

Decide How to Save and Organize Digital Information

As you save digital information, keep it organized. The simplest organizational strategy is to save your work in a single folder (see Figure 6.1). As you save your work, use descriptive file names. Rather than naming a file "Notes 1," for instance, name it "Interview Notes from John Garcia, April 22." Keep in mind that the single-folder approach might not work well for larger projects. At some point, the sheer number of files in the folder makes it difficult to find a single file easily. Rather than scrolling through several screens of files, you might find it more efficient to create multiple folders to hold related files (see Figure 6.2).

Copying and Pasting   You can use the COPY and PASTE commands in your browser and word processor to save digital documents and graphics. Remember to copy and paste the URL and record the date on which you accessed the page so that you can return to it if necessary and cite it appropriately.

Downloading   Toward the end of your research writing project, particularly when you are drafting your document, you might find yourself wishing that you'd saved all of your digital sources on a hard drive, flash drive, or smartphone.

FIGURE 6.1 A Project Workspace Using a Single Folder

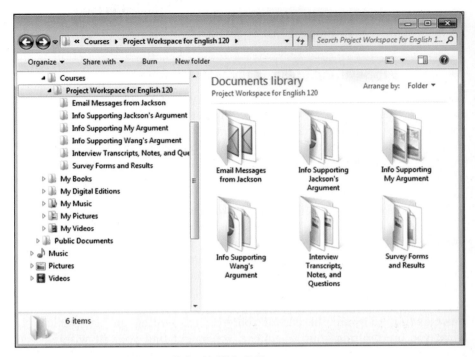

FIGURE 6.2 A Project Workspace Using Multiple Folders

Saving sources allows you to open them in a Web browser or word processor at a later time.

How you save your sources will vary according to the type of digital source you're viewing.

- Web pages can be saved using the SAVE AS or SAVE PAGE AS menu command in your browser, which is usually located in the File or Page menus in your browser. In many browsers, you can open this menu by clicking on a page or tool icon near the upper right corner of the page.

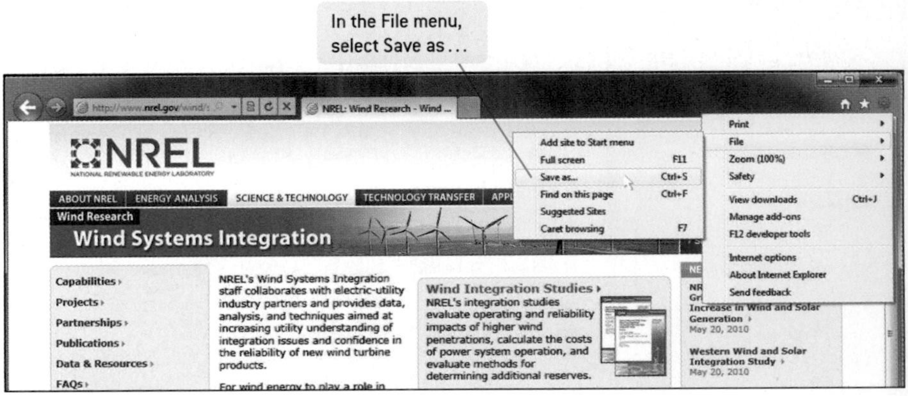

FIGURE 6.3 Saving a Web Page

- Images and other media materials from the Web can be saved by right-clicking (in Windows) or control-clicking (on the Macintosh) on the item you want to save and selecting SAVE IMAGE AS . . . or SAVE PICTURE AS . . . or some variation of that command from the pop-up menu.
- Databases often allow you to mark and save records returned by a search.

Remember that downloading a source does not automatically record the URL or the date on which you viewed the source for the first time. Be sure to record that information in your research log, your working bibliography (see p. 114), or in a document in the folder where you've saved your files.

Using Email   You can email yourself messages containing digital documents you've found in your research. Some databases, such as those from EBSCO and OCLC/FirstSearch, allow you to email the text of selected records directly from the database (see Figure 6.4). You can also use email as a form of file folder by sending messages to yourself that include copies of documents in the form of pasted text or attached files. If you use a subject line such as "My Comp 110 Research Project," you can view your messages by subject line and easily view all of the information you've collected or you could simply search for messages containing the phrase *research project*.

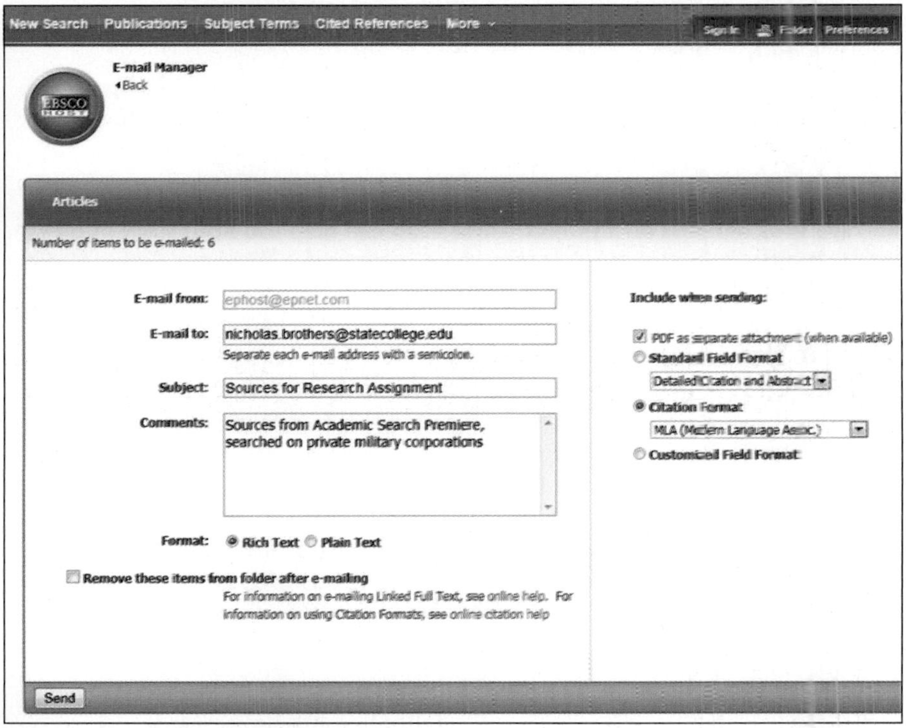

FIGURE 6.4 Sending Email from a Database

Using Your Phone If you have a smartphone, such as a BlackBerry, a Droid, or an iPhone, you can record conversations with others, record voice messages that contain ideas about your project, save videos, take photos of sources you find in the periodical room (see p. 171), and surf the Web to locate sources. You can save the information on your phone or send it to your email account using the methods discussed above.

Most smartphones allow you to run "apps" (or applications) in the same way you can run programs on a computer. Many of these apps are available at no or low cost. Some of the most useful apps you can use to save and organize information include:

- **Notes Apps,** such as Evernote, OneNote, Note Everything, Simplenote, and Springnote, allow you to take and organize notes on your phone. Many notes apps allow you to tag, sort, and share your notes. Some will also record spoken notes.

- **Voice Recorder Apps,** such as Jott, OI Notepad, and VR Voice Recorder, as well as the voice tools built into many phone operating systems, allow you to record spoken memos. Some of these apps will also attempt to convert speech to text.

- **Bookmarking Apps,** such as Bookmarks, MyBookmarks, and Web Shortcuts, allow you to save the URLs for sites you've found as you browse the Web with your phone. Some of these apps also allow you to import or export Bookmarks and Favorites from your computer.

- **File Manager Apps,** such as AndExplorer, Download, and File Manager Pro, allow you to download files from the Web, save them on your phone, and copy them to memory cards or send them via email as attachments.

- **To-Do Lists,** such as Astrid, Tag ToDo List, and TaskJot, allow you to manage your progress on a project. These tools can help you keep track of important activities and dates. They can also be useful for planning your project.

Saving Bookmarks and Favorites in Your Browser You can use a Bookmarks or Favorites list in your Web browser to keep track of your sources (see Figure 6.5). Be aware that there are drawbacks to relying on a Bookmarks or Favorites list as a place to "store" your sources. First, pages on the Web can and do change. If you suspect that the page you want to mark might change before you complete your research writing project, download or print it so that you won't lose its content. Second, some Web pages are generated by database programs. In such cases, you might not be able to return to the page using a Bookmarks or Favorites list. A URL like the following usually indicates that a Web page is generated by a database program:

http://firstsearch.oclc.org/FUNC/QUERY:%7Fnext=NEXTCMD%7F%22/
FUNC/SRCH_RESULTS%22%7FentityListType=0%7Fentitycntr=
1%7FentityItemCount=0%7F%3Asessionid=1265726%7F4%7F/fsres4.txt

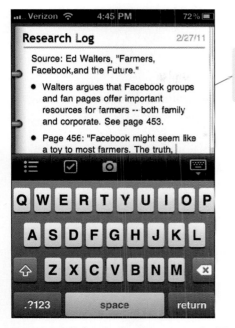

Smartphone apps like OneNote allow you to store digital notes and photos for easy access.

FIGURE 6.5 Using the OneNote app on the iPhone

Although this long string of characters starts out looking like a normal URL, the majority of the characters are used by the database program to determine which records to display on a page. In many cases, the URL works only while you are conducting your search. If you add such a URL to your Bookmarks or Favorites list, there's a good chance it won't work later. To avoid this problem, consider downloading Web pages (see p. 95) or using Web capture and clipping tools (see p. 100).

Keep in mind that Bookmarks and Favorites lists can become disorganized. To avoid this problem, put related items into folders, and give the items on your list descriptive names.

Using Bookmarking Web Sites   Bookmarking Web sites allow you to save your bookmarks online. The advantages of these sites for research writers include (1) the ability to view bookmarks at any time from any computer, smartphone, or tablet with a Web connection; (2) the ability to use tagging (labeling of sources in your own words as opposed to using predefined lists of categories); and (3) the ability to browse collections of bookmarks created by others who share your interest in a subject. To use these sites, you must create an account. To access your bookmarks, you must either visit the site or, if one is available, install the site's browser toolbar or button. Many of these sites also offer apps for use on smartphones. Leading bookmarking Web sites include:

BlinkList:	blinklist.com
Delicious:	delicious.com
Diigo:	diigo.com
Faves:	faves.com
Google Bookmarks:	google.com/bookmarks/
Pearltrees:	pearltrees.com
Yahoo! Bookmarks:	bookmarks.yahoo.com

Using Web Capture and Clipping Tools   A wide range of programs are available to help you keep track of the information you find online. Some of these programs work with your browser as toolbars or "add-ons" (a term used for programs that work within the Firefox browser). Most leading social bookmarking sites, for example, have created free tools that can be added to your Web browser (see Figure 6.6). By clicking on the ClipMark button, for instance, you

FIGURE 6.6 Zotero Firefox Add-on

can add a Web page—or portions of a page—to your collection of materials on ClipMarks. Some add-ons in Firefox offer powerful sets of tools for managing information. Zotero and ScrapBook both allow you to save entire pages or parts of pages to your local computer, while Zotero also provides support for citing sources. In addition, some of these tools, such as Evernote, offer apps that you can use on a smartphone.

Leading no-fee Web capture tools include:

Clipmarks Toolbar:	clipmarks.com/install/
Diigo:	diigo.com
Evernote:	evernote.com
ScrapBook Firefox Add-on:	addons.mozilla.org/en-US/firefox/addon/427/
Zotero Firefox Add-on:	zotero.org

Using bedfordresearcher.com   Use the bibliography tools at **bedfordresearcher .com** to save bibliographic information about each of your sources, write a brief note or annotation about each source, evaluate each source, and save text from digital sources. You can also create a bibliography formatted in MLA, APA, *Chicago*, or CSE style. Read more about bibliographies later in this chapter on p. 113.

Using Web Document Sites   As you work on your research writing project, you might find yourself using more than one computer. If so, consider using Web-based productivity tools, such as those offered by Google, Microsoft, and Zoho, to save your work (see Figure 6.7). Access to these sites requires a network connection, but you will be able to use them with any computer, phone, or tablet

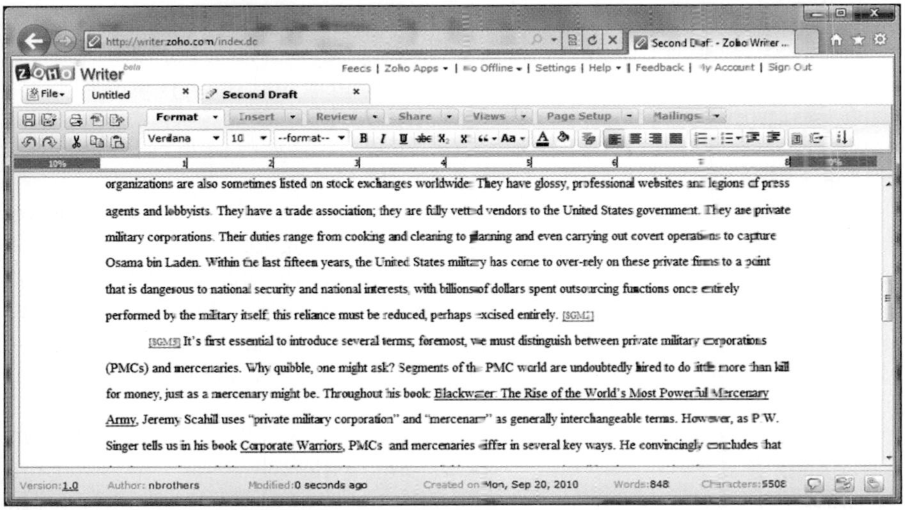

FIGURE 6.7 Zoho's document editor, Writer

that can connect to the Web. You can use the tools on these sites to save copies of sources, create lists of links, and plan your document.

In addition to offering applications such as word processing, presentation tools, spreadsheet tools, and file uploads, these sites usually support collaborative work. Typically, you can share documents and files, use project management tools such as calendars, and engage in various forms of Web-based discussion. In addition to free tools, many of these sites also offer premium services for a monthly or yearly fee. Leading, no-fee Web document sites include:

Acrobat.com:	acrobat.com
Google Docs:	docs.google.com
Windows Live Office:	office.live.com
Writing@CSU:	writing.colostate.edu
Zoho:	zoho.com

Backing Up Your Files   Whatever strategies you use to save and organize digital materials, replacing lost information takes time and effort. Avoid the risk of lost information by taking the time to make copies of your digital files and downloads, email messages, saved Web pages and clippings, and Bookmarks or Favorites list.

6b

Why should I take notes?

Taking notes benefits research writers in two ways. First, it helps you keep track of the most important information, ideas, and arguments you've encountered in your sources. Although you can also do this by saving copies of each of your sources, notes help you zero in on the passages, images, tables, and other parts of your sources that you'll find most useful as you plan and draft your document. If you are working on a project that involves more than a few sources, taking notes will save you a great deal of time searching across your sources for a specific passage.

Second, and more important, taking notes helps you understand your sources more thoroughly than if you simply saved and highlighted copies of them. By paraphrasing or summarizing a source, for example, you force yourself to present passages from the source in your own words (see p. 105). This process of putting things into your own words requires you to connect the source to what you already know, which can help you learn more about the issue you're addressing in your research writing project.

Taking notes, as a result, plays a much more vital role in your research writing project than simply keeping track of information. It helps you better understand the issue and lays the groundwork for your own contribution to the conversation you've decided to join.

6c

How should I take notes?

Your decisions about how to take notes will affect not only the methods you use but also what you'll focus on as you take them. Your methods—such as using note cards, a paper notebook, a word processing program, Web-based tools, or a smartphone, for example—should reflect how you like to work with information. If you're uncertain about what might work best for you, talk to other writers, your instructor, or a librarian and then try a few of the most promising methods. You'll find that each method has its own advantages and disadvantages and that no single method is always better than another.

What you choose to focus on as you take notes will vary as you work through your project. Early on in your note-taking process, you might find yourself looking for a general understanding of your issue. Later, you might find yourself taking note of similarities and differences among the arguments made in your sources. Still later, you might use your notes to critique those arguments and begin planning your document.

Choose a Method and Use It Consistently

Some research writers take notes by hand, on note cards, on photocopies of sources, in a notebook, on loose sheets of paper, on the transcript of an interview, or on correspondence. Others choose to take notes digitally, in a word processing program, in a database program, in a bibliographic citation program such as EndNote or Reference Manager, in email messages, or in a blog.

Still other research writers have turned to Web-based tools, such as Diigo and Evernote (see p. 101), which allow you to create notes, save Web-based materials (including images) for later viewing, and organize notes with folders and labels. Using these kinds of tools, you can save "clips" (all or part of a page) for later viewing, annotate your clips, and create notes to manage your project.

Your notes will be most useful if you take them systematically and consistently. For example, instead of taking some notes on Post-It Notes, some on note cards, and the rest in a word processing file, take all of your notes in one form. This will make it easier to find information later and reduce the time and effort required to organize and draft your document. It will also reduce the chances that you'll plagiarize unintentionally (see p. 121).

Quote Directly

A direct quotation is an exact copy of words found in a source. When you quote directly in your notes, you should enclose the passage in quotation marks, identify the source, and list the number of the page (or paragraph, if you are using a digital source that does not indicate page numbers) where the quotation can be found. Proofread what you have written to make sure it matches the original source exactly—including wording, punctuation, and spelling.

You should take direct-quotation notes in the following cases.

- when a passage in a source features an idea that you want to argue for or against
- when a passage in a source provides a clear and concise statement that would enhance your project document
- when you want to use the exact words of an authority or expert
- when you want to use the exact words of someone who has firsthand experience with the issue you are researching

Be sure to place quotation marks around a quoted passage when you take a note. If you don't use quotation marks, you might later think the passage is a paraphrase or summary and unintentionally plagiarize it when you draft your document. To learn more about avoiding plagiarism, see Chapter 7 (p. 120). In some cases, it makes sense to modify a direct quotation while you're taking notes. You might want to quote only parts of a passage, add clarifying information to a note, or correct an error in the original text.

Modifying a Direct Quotation Using an Ellipsis   When only part of a passage relates to your project, you might want to quote only that part in your notes. To indicate that you have changed a quotation by deleting words, use three spaced periods, called an ellipsis (...). If you don't use an ellipsis, your readers will assume that a quotation you are presenting is identical to the text found in the source.

Original Passage

Anderson is convinced that this is the right way to do it because he's seen all of the ways that aren't. A girls' basketball coach for more than two decades, he'd already experienced firsthand all that modern youth sports had to offer. It wasn't pretty: Screaming, red-faced parents who shuffle their children from program to program because Junior or Jane doesn't get enough court time. Elite squads that serve as showcases for a few superstar players trying to attract the attention of a Division 1 program. Eight-year-old prima donnas factory-installed with a sense of entitlement simply because they know their way around a ball and a pair of high-tops.

Source: Eric Dexheimer, "Nothing to Lose," retrieved from http://www .westword.com/issues/2004-05-13/news/sports_print.html, paragraph 15.

Quotation Modified Correctly Using an Ellipsis

"Anderson is convinced that this is the right way to do it because he's seen all of the ways that aren't. A girls' basketball coach for more than two decades, he'd already experienced firsthand all that modern youth sports had to offer. . . . Screaming, red-faced parents who shuffle their children from program to program because Junior or Jane doesn't get enough court time. Elite squads that serve as showcases for a few superstar players. . . . Eight-year-old prima donnas . . . with a sense of entitlement simply because they know their way around a ball and a pair of high-tops" (paragraph 15).

Three periods indicate material deleted from a sentence.

Four periods indicate the deletion of a full sentence or more.

Modifying a Direct Quotation Using Brackets   To modify a direct quotation by changing or adding words, use brackets: [ ]. If you don't use brackets when you change or add words, readers will assume the quotation you are presenting is identical to the text found in the source.

Quotation Modified Correctly Using Brackets

"The [Corporation for National Service] is an independent agency with a 15-member board of directors that is appointed by the president and confirmed by the Senate" (Lenkowsky and Perry 299).

[Corporation for National Service] replaces the original text's use of the acronym CNS.

Remember that using brackets and ellipses does not entitle you to change the meaning of a quotation. Check your notes against the original passages to be sure you aren't misrepresenting the source.

Modifying Quotations Using "Sic"   If a passage you are quoting contains a misspelled word or an incorrect fact, use the word "sic" in brackets to indicate that the error occurred in the original passage. If you don't use "sic," your readers will think that the mistake is yours.

Quotation Modified Correctly Using "Sic"

"George W. Brush's [sic] interest in faith-based initiatives strongly shaped his national service agenda" (Vincent 221).

To avoid unintentional plagiarism when quoting from sources, take careful notes by using the following checklist. Be aware, however, that mistakes can happen, particularly if you are taking notes in a hurry. As you draft your document, remember to look for notes that differ from your usual style of writing. More often than not, if a note doesn't sound like your own writing, it isn't.

CHECKLIST FOR QUOTING

To quote accurately when taking notes, follow these guidelines.

✔ Identify the author, title, and the page or paragraph where the passage can be found.

✔ Avoid unintentional plagiarism by using quotation marks.

✔ Use ellipses, brackets, and "sic" as necessary.

✔ Check your note against the original passage to be sure you aren't introducing errors or misrepresenting the source.

Paraphrase

When you restate a passage from a source in your own words, you are paraphrasing the source. Typically, a paraphrase is roughly as long as the original passage. You can use paraphrases to illustrate or support points you make in your document or to refer to ideas with which you disagree. Even though you are using your own words when you paraphrase, you must still cite the source because the paraphrase presents ideas and information that are not your own.

One of the most common problems with using source material is paraphrasing too closely—that is, making such minor changes to the words of a source that your paraphrase remains nearly identical to the original passage. Another common problem is distorting the meaning of the source.

Consider the differences among the original passage below and the appropriate and inappropriate paraphrases that follow it.

Original Passage

"High school grades and test scores are not the only factors considered by colleges and universities in the admissions process. Other factors that influence college admissions decisions include high school rank, being an athlete, alumni connection, extracurricular activities, special talents, and other personal characteristics of applicants."

Source: William H. Gray III, "In the Best Interest of America, Affirmative Action Is a Must," p. 144.

Appropriate Paraphrase

William H. Gray III notes that, in addition to high school grades and standardized test scores, most colleges and universities make admissions decisions based on an applicant's participation in sports, involvement in extracurricular activities, personal qualities, talents, relations to alumni, and class rank (144).

Preserves the meaning of the original passage without replicating sentence structure and wording

Inappropriate Paraphrase

William H. Gray III notes that high school grades and test scores are not the only issues weighed by colleges and universities during college admissions decisions. Other factors that influence those decisions are high school rank, participating in athletics, connections to alumni, out-of-school activities, unique talents, and other personal qualities of applicants (144).

Does not differ sufficiently from original; uses the same sentence structure and changes only some key words

Inappropriate Paraphrase

William H. Gray III notes that participation in sports and involvement in extracurricular activities are among the most important factors affecting college admissions decisions (144).

Distorts the meaning of the original passage

When paraphrasing, focus on understanding the key ideas in the passage and then restate them in your own words. Begin a paraphrase with the phrase "In other words." This strategy reminds you that it's important to do more than simply change a few words in the passage. You might also want to set the original source aside while you paraphrase so that you won't be tempted to copy sentences directly from it. After you've completed your paraphrase, check it for accuracy.

TUTORIAL

How do I paraphrase a source?

Paraphrasing a source involves restating the ideas and information in a passage in your own words. Use different words and sentence structure to help ensure that your paraphrase isn't too close to the original passage. In this example, Alexis Alvarez identifies a relevant passage in one of her sources and creates a note that paraphrases the passage.

1 Select the passage you want to paraphrase.

Original Passage: Why do athletes risk chronic debilitating diseases and death by taking steroids? Because these drugs work. In very short order, they pack on pounds of muscle and increase strength dramatically. Weight training while using steroids maximizes your gains.

Source: Kendrick, C. (n.d.) *Seduced by steroids.* Retrieved from http://www.familyeducation.com/drugs-and-alcohol/sports/36182.htm .

2 Identify relevant information and ideas in the passage.

Why do athletes risk chronic debilitating diseases and death by taking steroids? Because these drugs work. In very short order, they pack on pounds of muscle and increase strength dramatically. Weight training while using steroids maximizes your gains.

3 Draft a paraphrase that identifies the source and includes the information.

Kendrick (n.d.) asks why athletes use steroids, which can lead to serious illness and death. He responds to his own question by noting that steroids increase muscle mass and strength and are particularly effective when used with weight training.

4 Revise the paraphrase so that it uses wording and sentence structure that differs from the original passage.

Kendrick (n.d.) notes that, despite long-term and potentially lethal health risks, athletes use steroids because, in combination with weight training, they can dramatically increase strength and muscle mass.

Review another example and work on creating your own paraphrases at **bedfordresearcher.com**. Click on Interactive Exercises.

II Working with Sources

CHECKLIST FOR PARAPHRASING

To paraphrase, follow these guidelines.

✔ Be sure that you understand the passage by reading it and the surrounding text carefully.

✔ Restate the passage in your own words. Make sure that you do more than simply change a few key words.

✔ Compare the original passage with your paraphrase. Make sure that you've conveyed the meaning of the passage but that the wording and sentence structure differ from those in the original passage.

✔ Note the author, title, and the page or paragraph where the passage can be found.

Summarize

A summary is a concise statement of information in a source. Research writers often summarize an entire source, but they can also summarize lengthy passages. You can write summaries to capture the overall argument and information in a source, and to record a writer's argument so that you can later refute it. Keep in mind that summaries must include a citation of the source.

Here is an original passage from *Scientific American*, a source one might consult while researching television addiction. Two notes containing summaries of the passage, the first showing an appropriate summary and the second an inappropriate one, follow the original.

Original Passage

What is more surprising is that the sense of relaxation ends when the set is turned off, but the feelings of passivity and lowered alertness continue. Survey participants commonly reflect that television has somehow absorbed or sucked out their energy, leaving them depleted. They say they have more difficulty concentrating after viewing than before. In contrast, they rarely indicate such difficulty after reading. After playing sports or engaging in hobbies, people report improvements in mood. After watching TV, people's moods are about the same or worse than before.

Source: Robert Kubey and Mihaly Csikszentmihalyi, "Television Addiction," p. 76

Appropriate Summary

Kubey and Csikszentmihalyi, "Television Addiction," p. 76

Kubey and Csikszentmihalyi report that although watching television may relax a viewer, studies have shown it does little to improve a viewer's alertness, energy level, or mood. (summary)

The summary conveys the main point of the article and clearly identifies its authors.

Inappropriate Summary

Although watching television may relax a viewer, viewers report that turning off the television set makes them feel moody and depressed. (summary)

> The summary misrepresents the main point of the article and does not identify the authors.

To avoid unintentional plagiarism when summarizing a source begin your summary with "The author argues that" or "The author found that." Set the original source aside while you write your summary so that you won't be tempted to copy sentences directly from it. After you've completed your summary, check it for accuracy.

CHECKLIST FOR SUMMARIZING

To summarize, follow these guidelines.

✔ Be sure that you understand the source by reading it carefully.

✔ Summarize main points and reasons in your own words. Make sure that you do more than string together a series of close paraphrases of key passages.

✔ Check for unintentional plagiarism by comparing the original source with your summary.

✔ Note the author, title, and, if you are summarizing only part of a source, the page or paragraphs where the information can be found.

Record Your Reactions and Impressions

You can use your notes to keep track of your reactions and impressions (see Figure 6.8). If you've read a source before and jotted down brief notes in the margins or added comments using a word processor, look for those now and use them as the basis for a more substantial reflection on the information, ideas, or arguments in a source. For example, you might have written, "This makes sense" in the margin. If so, take some time to create a note that explains why it makes sense and what the source adds to your understanding of the issue. Learn more about annotating sources during critical reading on p. 68.

If you are reading or viewing a source for the first time, use your notes to record your initial impressions, ask questions, and respond to claims made by the author. Then review your notes and expand them by reflecting in more detail on the points raised in your first set of notes

Compare Sources

Your notes can indicate connections among your sources by identifying relationships among information, ideas, and arguments. Paying attention to your sources as a group—not just to individual sources—helps you gain a more complete understanding of your issue. It also can be useful when you begin planning and

The title of the source is listed at the top of the note. — Notes on *Blackwater: The Rise of the World's Most Powerful Mercenary Army* **by Jeremy Scahill**

Quotes	Notes and Reactions
"On April 28, 2004, the Abu Ghraib prison scandal was blown into the open when CBS's *60 Minutes II* broadcast graphic images depicting U.S. soldiers torturing and humiliating Iraqi prisoners. It soon emerged that private contractors from two U.S. corporations—the San Diego–based firm Titan Corporation and the Virginia-based CACI—were allegedly involved in the torture, having provided interrogators for use at the prison during the period of alleged abuse." (p. 157)	This is a key event in the Iraq War and this passage will surely be a linchpin in the section of my paper regarding PMC malfeasance and crimes.
"The full magnitude of the industry-wide profits is difficult to gauge because many of the firms, like Blackwater, are ultra-secretive and not publicly traded. But some experts began estimating the value of the industry at $100 billion a year." (p. 158)	A key fact here. This is something I'd like to have another citation to back up, though.
"In late 2006, Senator Lindsey Graham quietly inserted language into the 2007 defense authorization bill, which Bush subsequently signed, that sought to place contractors under the Pentagon's UCMJ [Uniform Code of Military Justice], but what effective impact—if any—this could have remains unclear, with experts predicting resistance from the private war industry." (p. 360)	I'd like to do some more research to see if the UCMJ has been effectively applied to a contractor in the years between the publication of this book and now. Personally, I'd doubt it. This is a powerful industry with plenty of lawyers to challenge this language.

The quotation is surrounded by quotation marks.

Nicholas writes down his reactions to the quotations.

Page numbers follow quotations.

FIGURE 6.8 An Example from Nicholas Brothers's Notes and Reactions

organizing your document, since those connections can help you frame your argument. To compare sources, use the following techniques.

- **Look for similarities.** As you gain more familiarity with your issue, you'll start to notice that some sources share the same general approach to the issue. As you take notes, identify similarities among your sources. Later, it can help you define groups of authors that you can use to support your argument, point to as misguided for the same general reason, or use to illustrate a particular point. Featured writer Chris Norris reviewed his notes and identified connections he saw between what he'd observed at shows and what he'd learned from his interviews with the musicians in Last Word, a local metal band. In his observation notes, Chris added a comparison note: "This ties in with Adler's interview."

- **Look for disagreements.** As you learn more about a conversation, you'll begin to understand how writers align themselves. As a result, you'll be prepared to decide which sources might provide support for your argument and which sources will serve best to illustrate alternative approaches to the issue (see Figure 6.9). Taking note of disagreements among your sources can help you determine the sticking points in the conversation you've

---

46   THE RISE

The second implication is that this new private military actor is driven by business profit rather than individual profit. PMFs function as registered trade units, not as personal black-market ventures for individual profit or adventure. As firms, they can make use of complex corporate financing, ranging from sale of stock shares to intra-firm trade, meaning that a wider variety of deals and contracts can be worked out. For good reason, individual mercenaries tend only to trust payments in cash and, in turn, cannot be trusted for anything beyond the short-term.

The key is that it is not the person that matters, but the structure that they are within. Many PMF employees have been mercenaries both before and after their employ, but their processes, relationships, and impacts within local conflicts were completely different.

The third distinguishing characteristic of the privatized military industry is that the arena they compete on is the open global market. That is, unlike the activities of the White Legion or similar mercenary units, PMFs are considered legal entities bound to their employers by recognized contracts and in many cases at least nominally to their home states by laws requiring registration, periodic reporting, and licensing of foreign contracts.[17] Rather than denying their existence, private military firms are registered businesses and, in fact, often publicly advertise their services—including many even having corporate websites on the Internet.[18] This status differentiates them not only from mercenaries, who had to hide from the law, but also from past entities, such as the charter companies, that did not coexist with any state law, but rather made their own laws.

New military firms also provide a much wider offering of services and, importantly, to a much wider variety of clients. As the head of Sandline was proud to note, firms in the privatized military industry are "structured organizations with professional and corporate hierarchies . . . We cover the full spectrum—training, logistics, support, operational support, post-conflict resolution."[19] This provides another differentiation from past private military organizations. The goal of PMFs is service provision rather than the exchange of goods—a key distinction from the charter companies. Although one sector exclusively focuses on combat services like contract units and military entrepreneurs, another distinctive development is that PMFs provide military services outside the tactical sphere. Moreover, many are diversified enough to work for multiple (and a wider variety of) clients, in multiple markets and theatres at once—something none of the prior private military actors could do. As previously noted, those that have hired PMFs include other multinational corporations; state regimes—both foreign and the home bases of the firms; international organizations; and even nongovernmental organizations.

Line up this argument against Scahill's virtually interchangeable use of the terms "private military corporation" and "mercenary"

FIGURE 6.9 An Annotation about a Disagreement among Sources. *Nicholas Brothers reminds himself about the differences among his sources.*

II Working with Sources

My Research Project

RESPOND TO SOURCES

As you take notes, you'll gain a deeper understanding of your sources, both individually and as a group. Use your knowledge of your sources to create a response. Your response can be useful later as you plan and draft your project document. Use one or more of the following prompts as the basis for your response.

- What do you agree with in one or more of your sources? Briefly summarize the idea or argument with which you agree and then explain why you agree.

- What do you disagree with in one or more of your sources? Briefly summarize the idea or argument with which you disagree and then explain why you disagree.

- What do you see as the most important idea emerging from your research so far? Briefly summarize the idea and then explain its importance.

- Why do you think one or more of the authors you've taken notes on so far approach the issue as they have? Briefly describe their approach and then explain why they are taking it.

- What approach do you think should be taken on this issue? Briefly describe the approach and then explain its importance.

You can print or download this activity at **bedfordresearcher.com**.

decided to join. In turn, understanding where your sources disagree can help you decide where to make your contribution to the conversation.

- **Look for common citations.** As your read your sources, pay attention to the sources they cite. If the majority of your sources refer to a source that you haven't yet consulted, do so. Any source that is being referenced frequently is likely to contain important information, ideas, or arguments. Take note of frequently cited sources and consult them later.

Classify Sources

As you take notes, use them to classify your sources. Among other purposes, you can keep track of sources that might be used to support particular points in your document, that represent various approaches to your issue, and that include important information or ideas. Strategies for classifying sources include tagging, labeling, grouping, listing, and visualizing.

- **Tagging and labeling.** Tags are words or phrases that can be associated with digital notes. When tags are used, it is common to apply more than one tag to a note. Labels, in turn, can be applied to print notes. You can use tags and labels to remind yourself about the purpose or content of a note or to help you remember something about the source. You might tag a note with one of the reasons you're planning to use in your document, for example, or you might label a note as useful for your introduction. Later, as you're working on your introduction or fleshing out that reason, you can quickly call up all of your relevant tagged notes. Similarly, you might label a note to remind yourself about the approach taken in the source to which it refers and later, as you draft, look for notes with that label.

- **Grouping.** As you read and take notes on your sources, you can begin to classify them into groups — organized, perhaps, by the part of the document in which you plan to refer to the source, the approach advanced in the source, or the kind of evidence contained in the source. If you are working with print notes, you can put them in piles, envelopes, or folders. If you are working with digital notes, you might drag each note into a group (within, for example, a word processing file) or into a folder (if you are saving each note as a distinct file).

- **Listing.** Listing is similar to grouping, but it does not require you to move your notes into a particular location. Instead, you can create notes that list your sources. You might, for example, list all of the sources that contain information that might be used to support your position and then list sources that contain information that contradicts your position.

- **Visualizing.** You can use the same mapping and clustering techniques as you take notes that you use as you generate ideas and organize your document (see p. 18 and p. 201). For example, you can create notes that contain a sketch of the relationships among the sources you've read so far. Or you could draw clusters of sources that support or illustrate a particular approach to your issue and then write brief notes about what they have in common, how the clusters of sources differ from each other, and so on. Similarly, you can draw maps showing the relationships among important ideas addressed in your sources and identify which sources are associated with each idea.

Plan Your Document

Planning notes are directions to yourself about how you might use a source in your project document, how you might organize the document, or ideas you should remember later. You can use planning notes to keep track of your ideas about the role that might be played in your document by the information, ideas, and arguments you encounter. Featured writer Chris Norris wrote planning notes — such as, "How will this tie in? Use on opening screen?" — as he prepared to write his multimodal essay.

6d

How can I create a bibliography to organize information?

A bibliography is a list of sources with complete publication information, usually formatted according to the rules of a documentation system such as those created by the Modern Language Association (see Chapter 21), the American Psychological Association (see Chapter 22), or the Council of Science Editors (see Chapter 24), or found in books such as the *Chicago Manual of Style* (see Chapter 23). As you take notes on your sources, use a working bibliography or an annotated bibliography to keep track of the sources you've consulted.

Create a Working Bibliography

A working bibliography is a running list of the sources you've explored and plan to use as you work on your research writing project. Publication information is provided for each source. The organization of your working bibliography can vary according to your needs and preferences. You can organize your sources in any of the following ways.

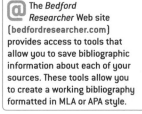

The *Bedford Researcher* Web site (bedfordresearcher.com) provides access to tools that allow you to save bibliographic information about each of your sources. These tools allow you to create a working bibliography formatted in MLA or APA style.

- in the order in which you collected your sources
- in categories
- by author
- by publication title
- according to how the information, ideas, and arguments in the source align with your position on your issue
- according to an outline of your project document

The entries in a working bibliography should include as much publication information about a source as you can gather (see Table 6.1).

Your working bibliography will change significantly as you work on your research writing project. As you explore your topic and choose an issue, collect sources, read them critically, evaluate them, and take notes, you will add potentially useful sources and delete sources that are no longer relevant. Eventually, your working bibliography will become one of the following.

- a *works cited* or *reference list*—a formal list of the sources you have referred to in a document
- a *bibliography* or *works consulted list*—a formal list of the sources that contributed to your thinking about an issue, even if those sources were not referred to explicitly in the text of the document

Keeping your working bibliography up-to-date is a critical part of your research writing process. It helps you keep track of your sources and increases the likelihood that you will cite all the sources you use in your document—an important contribution to your efforts to avoid plagiarism.

The first five sources from Elizabeth Leontiev's working bibliography are found in Figure 6.10.

Create an Annotated Bibliography   [FRAMING MY ARGUMENT]

An *annotated bibliography* provides a brief note about each of the sources you've listed, in addition to its complete citation information. These notes, or annotations, are typically no longer than two or three sentences. The content, focus, and

TABLE 6.1 INFORMATION YOU SHOULD LIST IN A WORKING BIBLIOGRAPHY	
TYPE OF SOURCE	**INFORMATION YOU SHOULD LIST**
All Sources	Author(s) Title Publication year Medium consulted
Book	Editor(s) of book (if applicable) Publication city Publisher Series and series editor (if applicable) Translator (if applicable) Volume (if applicable) Edition (if applicable)
Chapter in an Edited Book	Publication city Publisher Editor(s) of book Book title Page numbers
Journal, Magazine, or Newspaper Article	Journal title Volume number or date Issue number or date Page numbers
Web Page, Blog Entry or Reply, Discussion Forum or Newsgroup Post, Email Message, or Chat Transcript	URL Access date (the date you read the source) Sponsoring organization (if listed)
Field Research	Title (usually a description of the source, such as "Personal Interview with Jessica Lynn Richards" or "Observation of June Allison's Class at Tavelli Elementary School") Date (usually the date on which the field research was conducted)

length of your annotations will reflect your purposes for creating an annotated bibliography.

- In some research writing projects, you will submit an annotated bibliography to an instructor for review and comment. In this situation, your instructor will most likely expect a clear description of the content of each source and some indication of how you might use the source.

- In other research writing projects, the annotated bibliography might serve simply as a planning tool—a more detailed version of a working bibliography. As a result, your annotations might call your attention to key passages or information in a source, suggest where you might use information or ideas from the source in your project document, or emphasize relationships between this source and others you've collected.

Entries follow MLA style
(see p. 331).

Borwick, Phoebe, and Amy Donohue. "Drugs: Nobody's Winning the
  War." *Just Focus*. Global Education Centre, 10 Oct. 2006. Web. 5
  June 2007.

Forero, Juan. "Coca Advocate Wins Election for President in Bolivia."
  New York Times. New York Times, 19 Dec. 2005. Web. 3 June 2007.

Gordon, Gretchen. "The United States, Bolivia, and the Political
  Economy of Coca." *Multinational Monitor* 27.1 (2006): 15-20.
  Expanded Academic ASAP. Web. 15 May 2007.

Harman, Danna. "In Bolivia, a Setback for US Anti-Coca Drive."
  Christian Science Monitor. Christian Science Monitor, 22 Dec. 2005.
  Web. 12 May 2007.

United States. Office of National Drug Control Policy. "Drug
  Facts: Cocaine." *Office of National Drug Control Policy*.
  Executive Office of the President of the United States,
  n.d. Web. 8 June 2007.

When authors are not listed, the sponsoring organization is listed as the author.

FIGURE 6.10 Part of Elizabeth Leontiev's Working Bibliography

- In still other research writing projects, the annotated bibliography might
  be the end product of your research efforts. In this case, you will write your
  annotations for your readers, keeping their needs, interests, values, and beliefs in mind.

An annotated bibliography is a useful tool even if it's not something you'll
be expected to submit for a grade. By turning your working bibliography into
an annotated bibliography, you can remind yourself of the information, ideas,
and arguments in your sources and how each source might be used in your
document.

Alexis Alvarez created an annotated bibliography that she used to record
her ideas about how to use her sources and that her instructor used to assess
her progress on her research writing project (see Figure 6.11). In contrast, Pete
Jacquez created an annotated bibliography that he included on his Web site
about wind-generated electrical power. Because his bibliography was intended
for readers who were interested in learning more about wind power, his annotations focused primarily on describing the information, ideas, and arguments in
each source. The first four entries in his annotated bibliography are found in
Figure 6.12.

Costello, B. (2004, July 4). Too late? Survey suggests millions
of kids could be juicing. *New York Post*. Retrieved from
http://www.nypost.com

This article discusses steroid and other performance-enhancing drugs
used by eighth- through twelfth-grade boys and girls and provides a
number of relevant statistics. I'll use this source to support statements
about steroid use among young female athletes.

Davies, D., & Armstrong, M. (1989). *Psychological factors in
competitive sport*. New York, NY: Falmer Press.

This book addresses various psychological factors in sports including
learning, motivation, anxiety, stress, and performance. I'll use it to
support my discussion of why sports can have negative effects on girls.

DeNoon, D. (2004, August 4). *Steroid use: Hitting closer to home*.
Retrieved from http://webmd.com/fitness-exercise/features/
steroid-use-hitting-closer-to-home

This Web page provides information about increasing steroid use in
America as well as the latest statistical figures regarding this use. I'll
use it for statistical evidence and to drive home the point that this
problem needs to be addressed.

Dexheimer, E. (2004, May 13). Nothing to lose: The Colorado
Impact teaches girls about life — then hoops. *Denver Westword*.
Retrieved from http://www.westword.com

Article about a different way of coaching club basketball focusing
mainly on the Colorado Impact club and their policies on practice
and community service. I'll use it to provide the basketball coach's
viewpoint of club basketball and the effects of it on parents,
athletes, etc.

Entries follow APA style (see p. 362).

Annotations provide brief summaries of the purpose and content of the sources.

Annotations are intended for Alexis and her teacher. They indicate how and where Alexis will use the sources in her document.

II Working with Sources

FIGURE 6.11 Part of Alexis Alvarez's Annotated Bibliography

Refine Your Argument by Turning Your Working Bibliography into an Annotated Bibliography. Your working bibliography is simply a list of sources. If you've forgotten what the source is about, you'll need to consult your notes or review the source before you can think about how to use it in your project document. By turning your working bibliography into an annotated bibliography, however, you can remind yourself of the role each source might play in your document. Create annotations that (1) remind you of the information, ideas, and arguments in the source and (2) record your ideas about how the source might be used to advance your position on your issue.

Entries follow APA style (see p. 362).

Bisbee, D. W. (2004). NEPA review of offshore wind farms. *Boston College Environmental Affairs Law Review, 31*(2), 349–385. **Retrieved from http://www.bc.edu/schools/law/lawreviews/ environmental.html**

This review focuses on offshore wind farms and their efficiency at producing electricity. The article notes that offshore wind farms can sometimes be inconsistent in their output of electrical power due to variable winds. The article speculates about the extent to which this inefficiency resulting from inconsistent winds reduces the viability of offshore wind farms as an alternative to fossil fuel plants.

Bohlander, B. (2004, April 26). *Colorado State first university in the United States to offer choice of wind power to campus residents.* **Retrieved from http://www.newsinfo. colostate.edu/index.asp?page=news_item_display&news_ item_id=627126272**

Annotations provide brief summaries of the purpose and content of the sources.

This news release announces that Colorado State University is the first university to offer students the option of purchasing wind-generated electrical power for their use in dormitories and other campus housing. The news release discusses the future of wind power and provides information about the specific costs for students who choose to utilize wind power while living on campus.

Brown, L. R. (2003). Wind power is set to become world's leading energy source. *Humanist, 63*(5), 5. **Retrieved from http://www .thehumanist.org**

This article addresses advancements in wind power technology and how further advancements will help in the push for wind-generated electricity. This article supports the idea that wind power can and should be utilized as an alternative to fossil fuels.

Annotations are intended for visitors to Pete's Web site, rather than for his instructor or himself.

Chasteen, S. (2004). Who owns wind? *Science and Spirit, 15*(1), 12–15.

This article focuses on the economic aspect of implementing wind power. The author identifies the issue of economic motives behind wind power, which has become more relevant as large firms look to move into the wind power market.

FIGURE 6.12 Part of Pete Jacquez's Annotated Bibliography

My Research Project

CREATE A WORKING OR ANNOTATED BIBLIOGRAPHY

Create a bibliography to keep track of your sources as you work on your research writing project. Your bibliography should include complete citation information for the sources you are considering for use in your project. You may also include annotations that contain source descriptions, source evaluations, reflections on the source, and plans for using the source in your project.

You can create a bibliography in print form (such as in a notebook) or in digital form (for example, in a word processing file). You can also use the bibliography tools at **bedfordresearcher.com**, which allow you to create entries for new sources, annotate sources, evaluate sources, copy and save some or all of the text from a source, and display your working bibliography in various citation styles (see Part V).

You can print or download this activity at **bedfordresearcher.com**.

> **QUICK REFERENCE**

Managing Information and Taking Notes

- ☑ Decide how you will save and organize print information. (p. 94)
- ☑ Decide how you will save and organize digital information. (p. 95)
- ☑ Decide how you will record your notes; then take notes systematically and consistently. (p. 103)
- ☑ Take notes to quote passages directly. (p. 103)
- ☑ Take notes to paraphrase key ideas. (p. 105)
- ☑ Take notes to summarize whole sources or lengthy passages. (p. 103)
- ☑ Take notes to record your reactions and impressions. (p. 109)
- ☑ Take notes to compare the information, ideas, and arguments in sources. (p. 109)
- ☑ Take notes to classify sources. (p. 112)
- ☑ Take notes to help plan your document. (p. 113)
- ☑ Create a working bibliography (p. 114) or an annotated bibliography (p. 114).

Part II
Working with Sources

4   Reading Critically
5   Evaluating Sources
6   Managing Information
     and Taking Notes
7   Avoiding Plagiarism

7

Avoiding Plagiarism

Few writers intentionally try to pass off the work of others as their own. However, deadlines and other pressures can lead writers to take notes poorly and cite sources improperly. In addition, easy access to documents through the Web and full-text databases has made it all too easy to copy and paste work from other writers without acknowledging its source.

Failing to cite your sources can lead to serious problems. Your readers will not be able to determine which ideas and information in your text are your own or which are drawn from your sources. If they suspect you are failing to acknowledge your sources, they are likely to doubt your credibility and suspect your competence, and they might even stop reading your document. More seriously, submitting academic work that does not include proper identification of sources might result in failure in a course or some other disciplinary action.

7a

What is plagiarism?

Plagiarism is a form of intellectual dishonesty. It involves either unintentionally using someone else's work without properly acknowledging where the ideas or information came from (the most common form of plagiarism) or intentionally passing off someone else's work as your own (the most serious form of plagiarism).

Plagiarism is based on the notion of "copyright," or ownership of a document or idea. Like a patent, which protects an invention, a copyright protects an author's investment of time and energy in the creation of a document. Essentially, it assures authors that, when they create a document, someone else won't be able to steal ideas from it and profit from that theft without penalty.

In this sense, plagiarism in academic writing differs in important ways from the kind of mixing and remixing that can take place in popular culture. The expectations of readers of source-based documents differ, for instance, from people who listen to music. While listeners enjoying a song on the radio might not be surprised to hear part of another song added to a mix, readers of an article in *Time* magazine or an academic journal might be alarmed to read an unattributed passage that they recognize as the work of another writer. Context matters, and in this case the context of academic writing differs significantly from that of popular culture.

Unintentional Plagiarism

In most cases, plagiarism is unintentional, and most cases of unintentional plagiarism result from taking poor notes or failing to use notes properly. You are plagiarizing if you:

- quote a passage in a note but neglect to include quotation marks and then later insert the quotation into your document without remembering that it is a direct quotation
- include a paraphrase that differs so slightly from the original passage that it might as well be a direct quotation
- don't clearly distinguish between your ideas and ideas that come from your sources
- neglect to list the source of a paraphrase, quotation, or summary in your text or in your works cited list

Although unintentional plagiarism is, by definition, something that the writer hasn't planned to do, it is nonetheless a serious issue and, when detected, is likely to have consequences. Some instructors might require that an assignment be rewritten; others might impose a penalty, such as a lowered grade or failure on the assignment.

Intentional Plagiarism

Intentional plagiarism, although less common than unintentional plagiarism, can lead to academic penalties ranging from a reduced grade on an assignment to failure of a course to expulsion. Intentional plagiarism includes:

- engaging in "patchwork writing," which involves piecing together passages from two or more sources without acknowledging the sources and without properly quoting or paraphrasing.
- creating fake citations to mislead a reader about the sources of information used in a document.
- copying or closely paraphrasing extended passages from another document and passing them off as the writer's original work.
- copying an entire document and passing it off as the writer's original work.
- purchasing a document and passing it off as the writer's original work.

> @ For additional help, consult the St. Martin's Tutorial on Avoiding Plagiarism at bedfordstmartins.com/ plagiarismtutorial.

Plagiarism in Group Projects

Peer review and other collaborative activities raise important, and confusing, questions.

- If another writer suggests changes to your document and you subsequently incorporate them into your document, are you plagiarizing?
- What if those suggestions significantly change your document?
- If you work with a group of writers on a project, do you need to identify the parts that each of you wrote?
- Is it okay to list yourself as a coauthor if another writer does most of the work on a collaborative writing project?

The answers to these questions will vary from situation to situation. In general, it's appropriate to use comments from reviewers in your document without citing them. If a reviewer's comments are particularly helpful, you might acknowledge his or her contributions in your document; writers often thank reviewers in a footnote or endnote or in an acknowledgments section. It is usually appropriate to list coauthors on a collaboratively written document without individually identifying the text that was written by each coauthor, although some instructors ask that individual contributions be noted in the document or on a cover page. If you are uncertain about what is appropriate, ask your instructor.

TUTORIAL

How can I avoid unintentional plagiarism?

Unintentional plagiarism is the use of another writer's work without properly acknowledging the source of the ideas or information. Unintentional plagiarism is often the result of rushed work on a project. It can sometimes result from inadequate research writing skills or honest mistakes. In this example, Cori Schmidtbauer checks her rough draft for unintentional plagiarism.

To avoid unintentional plagiarism, follow these steps:

1 Check for a works cited or reference list.

2 Identify each quotation, paraphrase, and summary.

3 Check for appropriate attributions.

4 Check for appropriate in-text citation.

5 Ensure that each source is included in your works cited or reference list.

6 Check for changes in writing style. If you find changes, check your notes to identify the source of the passage and ensure that you haven't neglected to include quotation marks or paraphrased too closely.

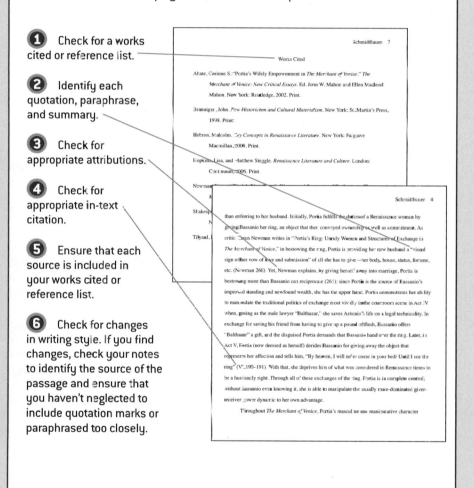

Schmidtbauer 7

Works Cited

Abate, Corinne S. "Portia's Wifely Empowerment in *The Merchant of Venice.*" *The Merchant of Venice: New Critical Essays.* Ed. John W. Mahon and Ellen Macleod Mahon. New York: Routledge, 2002. Print.

Brannigar, John. *New Historicism and Cultural Materialism.* New York: St. Martin's Press, 1998. Print.

Hebron, Malcolm. *Key Concepts in Renaissance Literature.* New York: Palgrave Macmillan, 2008. Print.

Hopkins, Lisa, and Matthew Steggle. *Renaissance Literature and Culture.* London: Continuum, 2005. Print.

Newman

Shakesp

Tilyard,

Schmidtbauer 4

than referring to her husband. Initially, Portia fulfills the duties of a Renaissance woman by giving Bassanio her ring, an object that their conveyed ownership as well as commitment. As critic Karen Newman writes in "Portia's Ring: Unruly Women and Structures of Exchange in *The Merchant of Venice,*" in bestowing the ring, Portia is providing her new husband a "visual sign of her vow of love and submission" of all she has to give—her body, house, status, fortune, etc. (Newman 260) Yet, Newman explains, by giving herself away into marriage, Portia is bestowing more than Bassanio can reciprocate (261): since Portia is the source of Bassanio's improved standing and newfound wealth, she has the upper hand. Portia demonstrates her ability to manipulate the traditional politics of exchange most vividly in the courtroom scene in Act IV when, posing as the male lawyer "Balthazar," she saves Antonio's life on a legal technicality. In exchange for saving his friend from having to give up a pound of flesh, Bassanio offers "Balthazar" a ring, and the disguised Portia demands that Bassanio hand over the ring. Later, in Act V, Portia (now dressed as herself) derides Bassanio for giving away the object that represents her affection and tells him, "By heaven, I will ne'er come in your bed/ Until I see the ring" (V.190–191). With that, she deprives him of what was considered in Renaissance times to be a husbandly right. Through all of these exchanges of the ring, Portia is in complete control; without Bassanio even knowing it, she is able to manipulate the usually male-dominated giver-receiver power dynamic to her own advantage.

Throughout *The Merchant of Venice,* Portia's masculine and manipulative character

Review another example and assess your own draft for unintentional plagiarism at **bedfordresearcher.com**. Click on Interactive Exercises.

7b

What are research ethics?

Research ethics are based on the notion that writing—and in particular research writing—is an honest exchange of information, ideas, and arguments among writers and readers who share an interest in an issue. As a research writer, you'll want to behave honestly and ethically. In general, you should:

- acknowledge the sources of the information, ideas, and arguments used in your document. By doing so, you show respect for the work that others have done before you.
- accurately and fairly represent the information, ideas, and arguments—to ensure that you do not misrepresent that work to your readers.
- provide citation information for your sources. These citations help your readers understand how you have drawn your conclusions and where they can locate those sources should they want to consult them.

These three rules are the essence of research ethics. Ultimately, failing to act ethically—even when the failure is unintentional—can reflect poorly on you and your document. If your readers suspect that you have acted unethically, they will question the accuracy and credibility of the information, ideas, and arguments in your document. If they suspect you've sacrificed research ethics altogether, they'll probably stop reading your document.

Use Ethical Research Practices   [**FRAMING MY ARGUMENT**]   Few readers will give you credit for being a good researcher. If they notice that you've cut a few corners, however, they'll start to question your credibility. If they suspect you've sacrificed research ethics altogether, they'll probably stop reading your document. By attending to research ethics—by acknowledging your sources, representing them fairly, and citing them accurately—you can safeguard the trust of your readers and increase the chances that they'll pay attention to your argument. Figure 7.1 shows how Cori Schmidtbauer attended to research ethics in her essay about Portia's role in *The Merchant of Venice*.

7c

What is common knowledge?

Although crediting other authors for their work is important, you almost certainly won't need to document every fact and idea used in your document, because some of the information you'll use falls under the category of common knowledge. Common knowledge is information that is widely known, such as the fact that the Declaration of Independence was signed in 1776. Or it might be the

> than deferring to her husband. Initially, Portia fulfills the duties of a Renaissance woman by giving Bassanio her ring, an object that then conveyed ownership as well as commitment. As critic Karen Newman writes in "Portia's Ring: Unruly Women and Structures of Exchange in *The Merchant of Venice*," in bestowing the ring, Portia is providing her new husband a "visual sign of her vow of love and submission" of all she has to give—her body, house, status, fortune, etc. (Newman 260). Yet, Newman explains, by giving herself away into marriage, Portia is bestowing more than Bassanio can reciprocate (261): since Portia is the source of Bassanio's improved standing and newfound wealth, she has the upper hand. Portia demonstrates her ability to manipulate the traditional politics of exchange most vividly in the courtroom scene in Act IV.

An attribution is used to identify the source of a paraphrase and subsequent quotation.

Quotation marks and parenthetical source citation indicate partial quotation.

Brannigan, John. *New Historicism and Cultural Materialism.* New York: St. Martin's Press, 1998. Print.

Hebron, Malcolm. *Key Concepts in Renaissance Literature.* New York: Palgrave Macmillan, 2008. Print.

Hopkins, Lisa, and Matthew Steggle. *Renaissance Literature and Culture.* London: Continuum, 2006. Print.

Newman, Karen. "Portia's Ring: Unruly Women and Structures of Exchange in *The Merchant of Venice*." *Shakespeare Quarterly* 38.1 (1987): 19–33. Print.

Sources are cited in MLA style.

Complete source information is included in the works cited list.

FIGURE 7.1 Attending to Research Ethics

II Working with Sources

kind of knowledge that people working in a particular field, such as petroleum engineering, use on a regular basis.

If you're relatively new to your topic, it can be difficult to determine whether information in a source is common knowledge. As you explore your topic, however, you will begin to identify what is generally known. For instance, if three or more sources use the same information without citing its source, you can assume that the information is common knowledge. If those sources use the information and cite the source, however, make sure you cite it as well.

7d

What is fair use and when should I ask permission to use a source?

The concept of fair use deals with how much of a source you can borrow or quote. According to Section 107 of the Copyright Act of 1976—the fair use provision, available at copyright.gov/title17/—writers can use copyrighted materials for purposes of "criticism, comment, news reporting, teaching (including multiple copies for classroom use), scholarship, or research." In other words, writers generally don't need to seek permission to make brief quotations from a source or to summarize or paraphrase a source.

If you are working on an assignment for a course—and do not plan to publish the assignment on the Web or in print—you generally can use material from another source without seeking permission. Remember, however, that in all cases you must still cite the source of the material you use.

Writers who plan to publish their work should seek permission to use material from a source if they want to quote a lengthy passage or, in the case of shorter works such as poems and song lyrics, if they want to quote a significant percentage of the source.

If you seek permission to use a source, explain why and how you want to use it. Many authors and publishers allow academic use of their work but frown on commercial uses. When you contact an author or a publisher, include your name and contact information, the source you wish to use, the purpose for which you will use the source, and the time during which it will be used (see Figure 7.2).

If you contact an author or a publisher by mail, include a self-addressed, stamped envelope. It saves the author or publisher the cost of responding by mail, indicates that you are serious, and, perhaps most important, shows good manners.

7e

How can I avoid plagiarism?

In most cases, writers who plagiarize do so unintentionally. You can avoid unintentional plagiarism by learning how to:

- conduct a knowledge inventory
- take notes carefully
- distinguish between your ideas and those drawn from your sources
- cite sources in the text and in a works cited or reference list
- recognize misconceptions about intentional plagiarism

Information Literacy

Writers who wish to use multimedia sources, such as images, audio, or video, should consider either seeking permission to use the source or linking directly to it. Be cautious about linking directly to multimedia sources, however, since some Web sites specifically ask that you not link to content on their site (typically because doing so increases the demand on Web servers). Although sites such as YouTube have a large number of servers set up to handle multiple links to the materials on their sites, smaller sites often lack the resources to handle the demand.

Dear Ms. Jackson:

I am a student and am completing a research project for my writing class, English Composition 200, at Colorado State University. The research project will be used only for educational purposes and will be distributed only to my instructor and members of my class for a period of three weeks during April and May of this year.   **A**

B I would like to include in my project the following image, which is displayed on your site at www.westernliving.org/images/2302a.jpg, and would greatly appreciate your permission to do so:

C If you are able to grant me the requested permission, please respond to this email message. My deadline for completing my project is April 22nd. I appreciate your quick response.

If you are not the copyright holder or do not have authority to grant this request, I would appreciate any information you can provide concerning the current copyright holder.

Thank you for considering this request.

Sincerely,

Glenn Choi   **D**

GlennChoi@students.colostate.edu

(970) 555-1515

FIGURE 7.2 Sample Permission Request

A Or "... on the Web at www.myschool.edu."

B Insert or describe passage or image. For example: "paragraphs 3 through 5 of the article," a thumbnail of the image, the URL of a document or image on the Web.

C Or "... sign the enclosed copy of this letter and return it to me."

D Provide contact information, such as name, address, email address, phone number, fax number.

Gaining control over these five sets of research writing skills can reduce the risk of plagiarizing unintentionally. Conducting a knowledge inventory will help you determine what you know—and need to learn—about your subject. Taking notes carefully will reduce the chance that, during drafting, you'll think a direct quotation from a source is a paraphrase or summary written in your own words. Learning how to distinguish between your ideas and those from your sources will help you ensure that the information and ideas from a source don't mistakenly read as if they are your own work. Citing sources in your text and in a list at the end of your document will let your readers know that you want to give credit to the sources from which you've drawn information, ideas, and arguments. And understanding the most common excuses for intentional plagiarism will help you resist the kinds of shortcuts that get writers into trouble.

Conduct a Knowledge Inventory

You can avoid unintentional plagiarism by ensuring that you have a clear understanding of your issue. When you are just beginning to learn about an issue, you might find it difficult not only to express your own ideas clearly and effectively, but also to restate or reframe the information, ideas, and arguments you've encountered in your sources. The result might be a document composed of passages that have been copied without attribution or paraphrased too closely. To address difficulties understanding an issue, conduct a knowledge inventory to gain insights into what you do and don't understand about the issue. Conducting a knowledge inventory involves answering three questions.

1. What do you already know about the issue?
2. What don't you know?
3. What do you want to know?

Your answers can provide a starting point for brainstorming, collecting and working with sources, and planning. They can also serve as a guide for discussing the issue with others. Once you've completed your knowledge inventory, meet with your instructor, consult a librarian, or talk with people who are knowledgeable about the issue. Ideally, your discussions will help you determine the most productive way to learn more about your issue. You might, for example, identify key concepts that, if you understood them more fully, would help you write about your issue more effectively.

My Research Project

CONDUCT A KNOWLEDGE INVENTORY

In your research log, answer the following questions about the issue you've decided to address in your project document.

1. What do I already know about the issue?

2. What don't I know?

3. What do I want to know?

Review your answers, then identify the concepts that, if you understood them more fully, would allow you to work on your assignment more effectively. Learn about those concepts by discussing them with your instructor, a librarian, or someone who knows about or has been affected by the issue.

You can print or download this activity at **bedfordresearcher.com**.

Take Notes Carefully

Unintentional plagiarism occurs most often when a writer takes poor notes and then uses information from their notes in a document. Notes might contain direct quotations that are not surrounded with quotation marks, paraphrases that differ in only minor ways from the original passage, and summaries that contain original passages from a source. Taking notes accurately and appropriately is the first—and arguably the most important—step in avoiding unintentional plagiarism. For guidance on quoting, paraphrasing, and summarizing during note taking, see Chapter 6. For guidance on integrating quotations, paraphrases, summaries, numerical information, and illustrations into your document, see Chapter 15.

To avoid plagiarizing as you take notes, keep the following guidelines in mind.

- Surround every quotation with quotation marks.
- Ensure that every paraphrase differs in both wording and sentence structure from the original passage.
- Avoid creating summaries that are little more than a patchwork of sentences pulled from the original source.
- Include publication information—in particular, author information and the location of passages that are quoted or paraphrased—about the source on every note.
- Double-check your notes to be sure that they are accurate and do not include problems that might lead to unintentional plagiarism when you integrate source information into your project document.

The following tutorial illustrates some of the problems that can arise as you take notes on your sources.

As You Draft, Distinguish between Your Ideas and Ideas in Your Sources

To distinguish between your ideas and those obtained through your sources, use attributions—words and phrases that alert your readers to the source of the information or ideas you are using. To avoid plagiarizing as you integrate information from your notes into your document, use these guidelines.

- Look for notes that differ from your usual style of writing. More often than not, if a note doesn't sound like your own writing, it isn't. If you find a note that might be a direct quotation, a close paraphrase, or a patchwork summary, double-check the note against the original source.
- Use author attributions to clearly distinguish information, ideas, and arguments drawn from your sources. Failing to do so is likely to lead your readers to think the information, ideas, and arguments are your own. To avoid this problem, attribute source information using phrases such as "according to Jessica Richards" and "Sandra Chapman argues."

You can learn more about using attributions to identify the origin of quotations, paraphrases, and summaries in Chapter 15.

II Working with Sources

TUTORIAL

How do I avoid plagiarism as I take notes?

You can avoid plagiarism at the earliest stage of research by taking notes that quote, paraphrase, and summarize sources accurately and by recording the source of the information.

Original Passage: This study examines patterns of attendance at four-year and selective four-year colleges across students from single- and two-parent families. In particular, we examine whether these students differ in their choice of colleges to which they apply, are admitted, and which they attend. . . . Differences in access might arise from two possible sources. First, disrupted and intact families may differ in the resources they can bring to bear to prepare their children for college. Second, the impact of these resources on college choices of children from disrupted and intact families may differ. Our results suggest that although both influences are present, differences in the levels of resources account for the largest proportion of the difference in the college choices between children from disrupted and intact families.

Source: Dean Lillard and Jennifer Gerner, "Getting to the Ivy League: How Family Composition Affects College Choice," p. 709.

1 Quote appropriately by identifying your source, using quotation marks around quoted material, and providing a page number for the quotation

2 Avoid quoting inappropriately by checking your notes for quotation marks and proper citation of the source's information. Be sure that you've quoted the source accurately, using ellipses and brackets to show any deletions (see p. 000).

3 When you paraphrase information from a source in your notes, be sure to use your own words to record the meaning of the passage, and provide a page number to help you locate the information (and create a full citation) later on.

Quotation

Appropriate

Family structure can also be a significant factor in college choice; as Lillard and Gerner note, "disrupted and intact families may differ in the resources they can bring to bear to prepare their children for college" (709).

Inappropriate

Family structure can also be a significant factor in college choice, as disrupted and intact families may differ in the resources they can bring to bear to prepare their children for college.

Paraphrase

Appropriate

According to Dean Lillard and Jennifer Gerner, when it comes to the college admissions process, two-parent families may be able to provide more for their children than single-parent families. Students from two-parent families are also better able to take advantage of the resources available to them (709).

II Working with Sources

4 Avoid inappropriate paraphrases by reviewing your notes against the source's wording to make sure they aren't a close match. If the source's wording is compelling and you want to capture it, consider using a quotation instead.

Inappropriate

Different family structures may differ in the resources they can bring to bear to prepare students for college. Second, the impact of these resources can also be affected.

5 When summarizing, use your own words to create an overview of the source's line of argument. Make sure you record the author and title of the source in your notes alongside the summary.

Summary

Appropriate

In the article "Getting to the Ivy League: How Family Composition Affects College Choice," Dean Lillard and Jennifer Gerner stress that a student's family structure is one of the factors that affects college admissions choices. They find that students who grow up single-parent households are at a disadvantage compared to students from two-parent families and are less likely to be given the resources they need to help them with the college application process.

6 Avoid inappropriate summaries by citing the source of your information. Review your notes to be sure you haven't used the source's wording in your summary.

Inappropriate

Patterns of attendance were studied at four-year and selective four-year colleges across college applicants from single- and two-parent families, focusing in particular on differences in decisions about which college to apply to, admissions decision, and colleges attended. Researchers found that differences in resources accounted for the primary difference in college choices between children from single- and two-parent families.

Review another example and work on creating accurate notes at **bedfordresearcher.com**. Click on Interactive Exercises.

Identify Sources in Your Document

Include a complete citation for each source you refer to in your document. The citation should appear both in the text of the document (as an in-text citation) and in a works cited or references list.

In the following examples, the writer includes MLA-style parenthetical citations that refer readers to a list of works cited at the end of the document. Note that MLA style, as well as APA, *Chicago*, and CSE styles, allow for a combination of attributions and parenthetical information to refer to sources (see Chapters 21–24).

> Jessica Richards argues, "We need to develop an efficient, cost-effective means of distributing hydrogen fuels before we can move to a hydrogen economy. If we don't we'll be operating in crisis mode when the next serious oil shortage arrives." (322).

> "We need to develop an efficient, cost-effective means of distributing hydrogen fuels before we can move to a hydrogen economy" (Richards 322).

Be sure to cite page or paragraph numbers for paraphrased and summarized information as well as for direct quotations. The following paraphrase of Jessica Richards's comments about energy needs includes the page number of the original passage in parentheses.

> Jessica Richards argues that we need to create an "efficient, cost-effective" system for delivering hydrogen fuel now, instead of while we are facing a critical oil shortage (322).

To learn more about identifying sources in your document, see pp. 251–59 in Chapter 15. To learn how to document sources using the MLA, APA, *Chicago* and CSE documentation systems, see Chapters 21–24.

Understand Why Writers Plagiarize

Although most plagiarism is unintentional, some students do plagiarize deliberately. The causes of intentional plagiarism range from running out of time to seeing little value in a course. The most common reasons offered to explain intentional plagiarism—and steps you can take to avoid falling victim to its temptation—are listed below.

"It's easier to plagiarize."　Some people believe it takes less work to cheat than to create an original document. That's probably true—but only in the short term. If you are pursuing a college degree, the odds are high that your profession will require writing ability or an understanding of how to work with information. When you're assigned a report or a proposal down the road, you might regret not taking the time to hone your writing and research skills.

"I ran out of time."　Most writers occasionally find themselves wondering where all the time has gone and how they can possibly complete an assignment on schedule. If you find yourself in this situation, contact your instructor about a revised deadline. You might find that you'll face a penalty for turning in work late, but that penalty will almost certainly be less severe than a penalty for intentional plagiarism.

"I couldn't care less about this assignment." It's not unusual to put off assignments that don't interest you. Rather than avoiding the work, try to approach the assignment in a way that interests you (see p. 4). If that fails, contact your instructor to see if you can customize the assignment so that it better aligns with your interests.

"I'm no good at writing." A lot of people have doubts about their ability to earn a good grade in a writing course. Occasionally, however, some students convince themselves that plagiarizing is a reasonable alternative to writing their own documents. If you lack confidence, seek assistance from your instructor, a campus writing center, a tutoring center, one of the many online writing centers on the Web (such as the Writing@CSU Web site at writing.colostate.edu), or a friend or family member. You're likely to find that, even with only modest support, you'll be able to do well.

"I didn't think I'd get caught." Some students believe—and might even have experiences to support their belief—that they won't get caught plagiarizing. Most writing instructors, however, become familiar with their students' writing styles. If they notice a sudden change in style, or encounter varying styles in the same document, they might become suspicious. The availability of plagiarism detection software also increases the likelihood that plagiarism will be detected.

"Everybody cheats." Some people plagiarize because they believe that many of their classmates are doing so. They fear that, if they don't plagiarize, they'll be at a competitive disadvantage. In fact, however, the number of students who plagiarize is quite low. Don't be persuaded by dramatic statistics that plagiarism is the norm in writing classes. The reality is that few students plagiarize intentionally, and those who do still tend to earn lower grades than their peers.

"This course is a waste of my time." If you view a course as little more than a box that needs to be checked, it might seem reasonable to check that box with as little effort as possible. Turning in work that isn't your own, however, can backfire. If you are caught plagiarizing, you'll most likely receive a reduced—or failing—grade for the assignment or the course. Instead of plagiarizing, talk with the instructor or an academic advisor about your lack of interest. You might find that the course actually has some relevance to your interests and career plans.

7f

What should I do if I'm accused of plagiarism?

If your instructor expresses concerns about the originality of your work or the manner in which you've documented your use of information, ideas, and arguments from sources, ask for a meeting to discuss the situation. To prepare for the meeting:

- review your document to identify passages that might have raised suspicions.
- collect the materials you've used in your writing project, such as copies of your sources, responses to surveys, interview transcripts, and so on.
- collect materials you've written during the project, such as the results of brainstorming and freewriting sessions; organizational materials you've created, such as clusters, maps, and outlines; and rough and final drafts of your document.
- reflect on your research writing process.

During the meeting, listen to the concerns of your instructor before responding. It will be natural to feel defensive about the situation, but you'll probably be more comfortable if you take notes and try to understand why your instructor has concerns about your document. Once your instructor is finished expressing his or her concerns, think carefully about what has been said and respond as clearly as possible. You'll probably find that your instructor will have follow-up questions, most likely about the sources you've used, your research writing process, and the document you've written.

If you find that you have engaged in unintentional plagiarism, ask your instructor for guidance about how to avoid it in the future and ask what sort of penalty you will face for doing so. Ask, as well, what consequences you might face should it be determined that you have plagiarized intentionally.

If you and your instructor are unable to resolve the situation, you might face a disciplinary process. To prepare for that process, learn as much as you can about the academic integrity policies at your institution.

> **QUICK REFERENCE**

Avoiding Plagiarism

- ✔ Understand the definition of plagiarism and the concept of copyright. (p. 121)
- ✔ Understand the meaning of research ethics. (p. 124)
- ✔ Understand the concept of common knowledge. (p. 124)
- ✔ Understand the concept of fair use and, if necessary, seek permission to use sources. (p. 125)
- ✔ Understand how to reduce the chance that you'll plagiarize unintentionally. (p. 126)
- ✔ Understand why you might be tempted to plagiarize intentionally and reflect on strategies for avoiding temptation. (p. 132)
- ✔ Understand what to do if you are accused of plagiarism. (p. 133)

The Bedford Researcher

I	Joining the Conversation
II	Working with Sources
III	**Collecting Information**
IV	Writing Your Document
V	Documenting Sources

PART III

Collecting Information

(8) Searching for Information with Digital Resources 137

(9) Searching for Information with Print Resources 170

(10) Searching for Information with Field Research Methods 181

Learning how to collect information provides the foundation for a successful research project. As you begin to answer your research question, you'll want to know more about how and where to look for useful sources of information. In this section you'll learn how to search for information using digital resources, print resources, and field research methods.

8

Searching for Information with Digital Resources

Part II
Collecting Information

8   Searching for Information with
    Digital Resources

9   Searching for Information with
    Print Resources

10 Searching for Information with
    Field Research Methods

> **Key Questions**

Since the computer became a research tool, the primary challenge associated with collecting information has changed. Research writers no longer worry about locating *enough* sources; instead, they worry about finding the *right* sources. This chapter addresses the important differences among online library catalogs, databases, Web search sites, and media search sites that you can use to locate information, and explains how to use these resources to locate the best sources for your research writing project.

8a

How can I prepare to search?

To increase your chances of obtaining good results from searches of digital resources, reflect on the work you've done so far, identify search terms related to your issue, learn about the types of searches you might conduct, and get feedback on your plans to carry out those searches.

Review Your Research Plan and Proposal

As you prepared to explore your topic, you might have created an informal research plan. Later, after you identified your issue, you might have created a research proposal (sometimes called a prospectus). If either of these documents is available, review them. You're likely to find that they'll provide useful guidance for planning your search of digital resources.

You should also spend time reflecting on the progress you've made so far in identifying useful sources. If you searched library catalogs, databases, or the Web, you probably noticed that one or more of these resources produced better results than others. You might also have noticed that some search terms produced better results than others. Be sure to consider what you've learned so far about useful digital resources and promising search terms.

Identify Keywords and Phrases

You can identify useful search terms by using a range of idea-generating techniques, such as brainstorming and clustering, and by building on your research question (see p. 40), position statement (see p. 63), or thesis statement (see p. 203). Brainstorming, freewriting, looping, and clustering (see p. 18) can help you come up with words and phrases that you can use in your searches. Elizabeth Leontiev, for example, used freewriting to generate ideas for her searches. When she completed her freewriting session, she highlighted promising words and phrases.

> The best source I've read so far is Gutierrez, who said that the best way to improve quality of life for coca farmers is planting alternative crops, like bananas, or even going into dairy farming. There are probably a lot of alternatives—maybe coffee is an option. But there are a lot of obstacles, such as FARC, which is heavily involved in the drug trade, and they prevent farmers from shifting to alternative crops. These groups don't want to lose money by reducing the amount of coca produced. So the farmers find themselves and their families caught between the drug cartels and the government.

You can also generate search terms by using your research question, position statement, or thesis statement as a starting point. Alexis Alvarez, for example, typed her research question in a word processor, formatted the most important words and phrases in the question in boldface, and then brainstormed a list of related words and phrases.

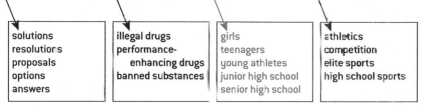

What should be done about **steroid use** by **adolescent girls** involved in **competitive sports?**

solutions	illegal drugs	girls	athletics
resolutions	performance-	teenagers	competition
proposals	enhancing drugs	young athletes	elite sports
options	banned substances	junior high school	high school sports
answers		senior high school	

III Collecting Information

My Research Project

IDENTIFY SEARCH TERMS

To generate keywords for your searches, review your research question, position statement, thesis statement, and working bibliography and highlight important words and phrases, the names of important authors, and titles of important sources. If you want to generate additional search terms, use brainstorming, freewriting, looping, or clustering (see p. 18) to do so. Highlight important words and phrases in what you write and add them to your list.

You can download or print this activity at **bedfordresearcher.com**.

Plan Basic Searches

Basic searches consist of entering one or more keywords or phrases in a search field and clicking on the search button. A basic search allows to you look for documents that contain a single word or phrase in the subject, title, text, or, in the case of databases, other parts of a database record (see p. 152 for more information about databases). When you enter one or two words in the search field on Google or your library catalog, for example, you are conducting a basic search.

Basic searches can return large sets of results. To increase the odds that your results will be relevant to your subject, consider adding keywords, using exact phrases, and using wildcards.

Adding Keywords   In most cases, using several keywords together will limit the number of results returned by your search. This strategy is especially helpful when searching the Web, which tends to produce thousands (sometimes millions) of hits for individual words or phrases. For example, adding *competitive* to a search for the keyword *sports* on Google will reduce the number of results by more than 95 percent. Adding *adolescent* to a search for *competitive* and *sports* (see Figure 8.1) will reduce it a further 80 percent. You can find out how the search tool you are using treats multiple keywords by consulting its help page or by conducting some test searches and reviewing your results.

Searching for Exact Phrases   Sometimes the best way to locate information is to search for an exact phrase. To further refine your search, you might use the phrases *adolescent girls* and *competitive sports* (see Figure 8.2). This would eliminate sources in which the words *adolescent* and *girls* appear, but are separated by other words. The basic search forms in many catalogs, databases, and Web search sites permit you to specify phrases using quotation marks.

Using Wildcards   Sometimes you're not sure what form of a word is most likely to occur. Rather than conducting several searches for *compete, competes, competitive, competition,* and *competitions,* for example, you can combine keywords into a single wildcard search. Wildcards are symbols that take the place of letters or strings of letters. By standing in for multiple letters, they allow you to expand the scope of your search.

FIGURE 8.1 A Simple Search with Keywords on Google

FIGURE 8.2 A Simple Search with Phrases on Bing

Quotation marks indicate that the words between them should be treated as a phrase.

The most commonly used wildcard symbols are:

* usually takes the place of one or more characters, such as *compet**

? usually takes the place of a single character, such as *wom?n*

Other wildcard symbols include !, +, #, and $. Consult the help section in a catalog or database or the advanced search page of a Web search engine to learn whether wildcard symbols are supported.

Plan Advanced Searches

In addition to simple searches, most library catalogs, databases, and Web search sites provide an advanced search page. These pages allow you to focus your searches in powerful ways using Boolean operators (which are used to search for all, some, or none of the words in a search box), special symbols (which are used primarily in Web searches), and search limits (such as publication date and document characteristics).

Focusing Searches with Boolean Operators   Boolean operators let you focus a search by specifying whether keywords or phrases *can, must,* or *must not* appear in the results. Some Boolean operators also allow you to search for keywords or phrases that appear next to, before or after, or within a certain distance from one another within a document. Table 8.1 lists commonly used Boolean operators and their functions.

III Collecting Information

TABLE 8.1   COMMONLY USED BOOLEAN OPERATORS

BOOLEAN OPERATOR	FUNCTION	EXAMPLE
AND/&/+	Finds sources that include both terms (either keywords or phrases)	adolescent AND girls adolescent & girls +adolescent +girls
OR/I	Finds sources that include either term	sports OR athletics sports I athletics
NOT/−	Finds sources that include one term but not the other	girls NOT boys girls −boys
ADJ (adjacent)	Finds sources in which the keywords appear next to each other	competitive ADJ athletics
NEAR	Finds sources in which the keywords appear within a certain number of words of each other (usually twenty-five; depending on the database, you may be able to change the default setting)	adolescent NEAR athlete
BEFORE	Finds sources in which keywords appear in a particular order	competitive BEFORE athletics
Parentheses ( )	Although not strictly a Boolean search term, parentheses are used to group keywords and Boolean operators	competitive AND (athletics OR sports) AND (girls NOT boys)

Many databases, online catalogs, and Web search sites include the use of Boolean search terms—typically AND, OR, and NOT or plus (+) and minus (–) signs—in their advanced search forms (see Figure 8.3) or in expert search forms (see Figure 8.4).

Limiting Searches   Advanced search forms allow you to limit your searches to documents that have particular characteristics, such as publication date and document type (see Figures 8.5 and 8.6). Search limits allow you to narrow your search in ways that are not available in simple searches. Although the specific limits that are available in an advanced search form vary across databases, library catalogs, and Web search sites, common limits include publication date (or, in the case of Web pages, the date on which a page was last updated), type of document, and the availability of full text (for databases).

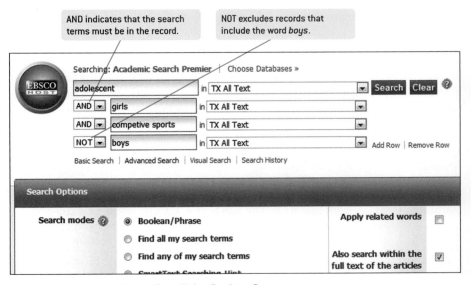

FIGURE 8.3 Advanced Search Form Using Boolean Operators

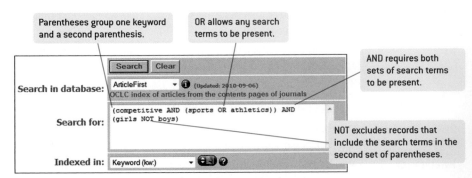

FIGURE 8.4 Expert Search Form Using Boolean Operators

TUTORIAL

How do I conduct a Boolean search in a database?

Use the advanced search in a database to conduct a Boolean search. In this example, Pete Jacquez conducted a Boolean search with limits on the Academic Search Premier database.

1. Use Boolean operators to specify which terms **must** be in the source (AND), **can** be in the source (OR), or **must not** be in the source (NOT).

2. Enter your keywords and phrases. This search looks for articles about wind power and legislation in Colorado that do not involve discussions of lobbying.

3. Choose the database fields that should be searched. Here, the author field is chosen to exclude authors named Owens since he already has that source.

New Search | Publications | Subject Terms | Cited References | More ∨

Sign In | Folder | Preferences | New Features! | Help

Searching: Academic Search Premier | Choose Databases »

Ask a librarian

"wind power" in TX All Text | Search | Clear

AND ∨ legislation in TX All Text

AND ∨ Colorado in TX All Text

NOT ∨ Owens in AU Author

NOT ∨ lobbying in TX All Text | Add Row | Remove Row

Basic Search | Advanced Search | Visual Search | Search History

Search Options | Reset

Search modes ⊙ Boolean/Phrase
○ Find all my search terms
○ Find any of my search terms
○ SmartText Searching Hint

Apply related words ☐

Also search within the full text of the articles ☐

Limit your results

Full Text ☐

Scholarly (Peer Reviewed) Journals ☐

Publication [   ]

References Available ☐

Published Date from January ∨ Year: 2007 to
December ∨ Year: 2011

Publication Type | All / Periodical / Newspaper / Book

4. Set additional limits on your search, such as availability of full text, scholarly journals, and publication date range.

Review another example and work on conducting Boolean searches in a database at **bedfordresearcher.com**. Click on Interactive Exercises.

III Collecting Information

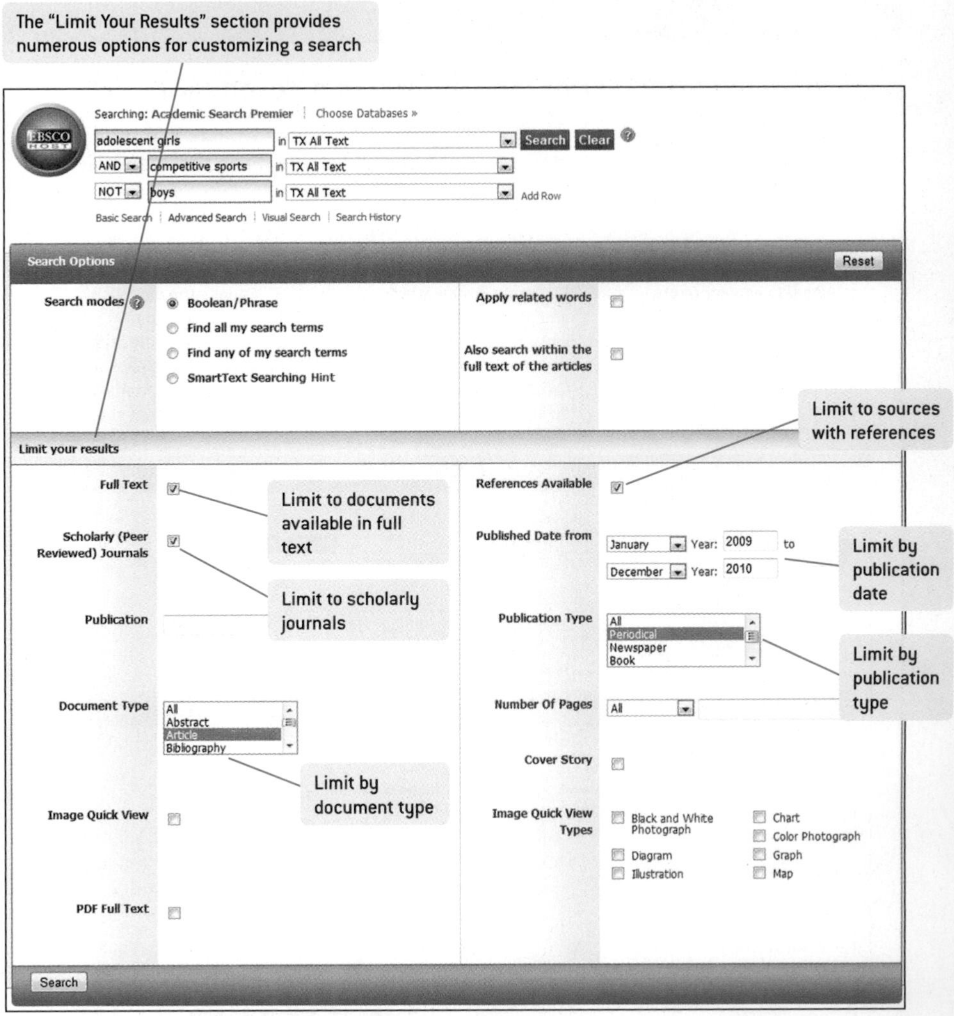

The "Limit Your Results" section provides numerous options for customizing a search

FIGURE 8.5 Advanced Search Using Limits in a Database

Information Literacy

Many advanced search pages allow you to search for pages or documents that have been modified within a specific period of time. Others allow you to identify pages or documents that were found by the search site during a specific period of time. These options differ in important ways and are subject to critical limitations.

- Modification date is not the same as publication date. Adding an image or changing a single word on a page constitutes a modification. A page created in 1997 will be included in search results for recent sources if a spelling error was corrected last week.

- The "found on date" is not the same as the publication date. It takes a while for a search site to locate new pages — sometimes as little as an hour after the page is released and sometimes as long as two weeks. In addition, some pages and documents might have been created several years ago but have been found only recently because they have just been made public on a Web site.

Google **Advanced Search**   Advanced Search Tips

Boolean AND

adolescent girls "competitive sports" steroids OR drugs OR HGH –boys filetype:pdf site:.gov

Phrase required with Boolean AND

Find web pages that have...
all these words: adolescent girls
this exact wording or phrase: competitive sports   tip

Boolean OR

one or more of these words: steroids   OR drugs   OR HGH   tip

Boolean NOT

But don't show pages that have...
any of these unwanted words: boys   tip

Need more tools?

Language specified

Results per page: 20 results
Language: English
File type: Adobe Acrobat PDF (.pdf)

Limited to results from government Web sites

Document saved in a specific format

Search within a site or domain: .gov
                                   (e.g. youtube.com, .edu)
⊞ Date, usage rights, numeric range, and more

Other limits include dates document last changed and filtering for sexual content

Advanced Search

©2010 Google

FIGURE 8.6 Advanced Search Using Limits on a Web Search Site

Many databases and library catalogs also allow you to search within a set of results. This allows you to narrow your results further by adding search terms and setting additional limits.

Using Special Operators in Web Searches   A number of leading Web sites, such as Google, Yahoo!, Ask, and Bing offer special operators that allow you to fine-tune a Web search (see Figure 8.7). These special operators can be used in combination with keyword, phrase, wildcard, and Boolean searches. Table 8.2 lists several special operators in Web searches.

Conducting Visual Searches   Some database companies have begun offering "visual searches," which allow you to view topics and sources relevant to your search (see Figure 8.8). To take advantage of this kind of search, start with a general topic and then successively narrow it. The related topics suggested by the visual search tool can call your attention to aspects of your issue that you might

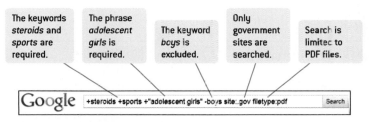

The keywords *steroids* and *sports* are required.

The phrase *adolescent girls* is required.

The keyword *boys* is excluded.

Only government sites are searched.

Search is limited to PDF files.

Google +steroids +sports +"adolescent girls" -boys site:.gov filetype:pdf   Search

FIGURE 8.7 Searching with Special Operators

TABLE 8.2 SPECIAL OPERATORS				
FUNCTION	ASK	BING	GOOGLE	YAHOO!
Words in Body Text		Inbody:steroid	intext:steroid	
Words in Page Title	Intitle:steroid	Title:steroid	intitle:steroid	intitle:steroid
Words in URL	Inurl:steroids	Inanchor: steroids	Inurl:steroids	inurl:steroids
Search a Single Domain	site:www.the antidrug.com	site:www.the antidrug.com	site:www.the antidrug.com	site:www.the antidrug.com
Locate Pages Linking to a Page	Inlink:www.the antidrug.com	Inbody:www.the antidrug.com	link:www.the antidrug.com	link:www.the antidrug.com
Find Documents in a Specific Format	filetype:pdf	filetype:pdf	filetype:pdf	filetype:pdf
Find Synonyms		define:steroid	define:steroid	

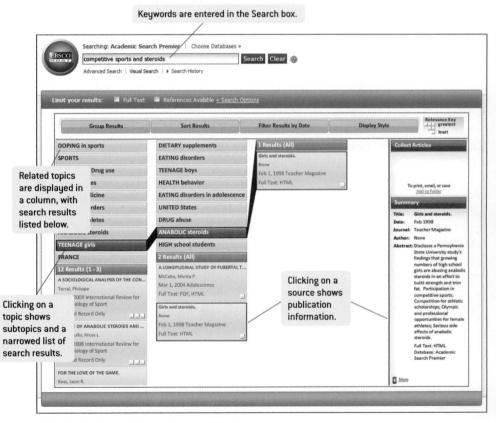

FIGURE 8.8 A Visual Search in an EBSCO Database

My Research Project

PLAN ADVANCED SEARCHES

If basic searches are likely to result in large sets of results, plan to conduct advanced searches. To get started, review your research plan or research proposal. Then, with your list of potential search terms in mind, consider the following questions.

1. Should I limit my searches to particular types of documents, such as scholarly journals or recent newspaper articles, magazine articles, and blog posts? Should I focus on scholarly books? Should I focus on trade and professional journals? Should I focus on Web discussion forums and email discussion lists? Should I focus on images and video?

2. Should I limit my searches to sources published during a certain time period, such as the past two years or between 1960 and 1963?

3. How can I focus my searches by using Boolean search terms?

4. How can I focus my searches of the Web by using special search symbols?

5. What could I gain from using visual search tools?

You can download or print this activity at **bedfordresearcher.com**.

III Collecting Information

not have considered and indicate relative differences in the numbers of sources associated with each related topic.

Similarly, you'll find specialized Web search sites that allow you to view search results in a visual form. Some sites, such as the Bing Visual Search page (bing.com/visualsearch) and Spezify (spezify.com), allow you to enter search terms and then view information associated with images returned by the search. Others, such as Snap (snap.com), allow you to preview sites found in a search or use clustering and mapping to explore the results of a search. By viewing the visual representations of the relationships among your search results, you can gain a more complete understanding of the scope and nature of your issue. In addition, the different representations of the kinds of sources returned by visual search sites—some are shown as video clips, others as thumbnails of Web pages, and still others as files or documents, for example—can help you focus on the kinds of sources that are likely to be of greatest value to your research writing project.

Review and Get Feedback on Your Plans   [FRAMING MY ARGUMENT]

As you develop your plans, keep your writing situation in mind. The keywords and phrases you use in your searches should help you accomplish your purposes and address the needs, interests, values, and beliefs of your readers, while the resources you choose—library catalogs, particular databases, and specific Web search sites and directories—should reflect the type of document you plan to write.

As you begin to finalize your plans, be sure to get feedback from your instructor, a reference librarian, classmates, or friends. Reference librarians and instructors can be particularly helpful. Given the wide range of digital search resources that are available, a few minutes of discussion with a knowledgeable librarian or instructor could save you a great deal of time or point you to key resources you might have overlooked.

How can I search for sources with online library catalogs?

Library catalogs provide information about the materials in a library's collection. Most libraries provide access to their catalogs through the Web, although some smaller libraries rely on traditional print catalogs. At a minimum, an online catalog will provide information about the author(s), title, publication date, subject, and call number for each source in the library's collection. Often it will also indicate the location of the source in the library and whether the source is available for checkout.

Find other sites that list online library catalogs at bedfordresearcher.com. Click on Annotated Links.

Online catalogs typically help you locate:

- books
- journals owned by the library (although not individual articles)
- newspapers and magazines owned by the library (although not individual articles)
- documents stored on microfilm or microfiche
- videotapes, audiotapes, CDs, DVDs, and other multimedia items owned by the library
- maps
- theses and dissertations completed by college or university graduate students

Although you can limit your search to the online library catalog at your college or university, you can benefit from searching other catalogs available on the Web. The Library of Congress online catalog, for example, presents a comprehensive list of publications on a particular subject or by a particular author (visit catalog.loc.gov). Some sites, such as WorldCat (www.worldcat.org), allow you to locate or search multiple online library catalogs. If your library doesn't have a listed publication in its collection, you can request it through interlibrary loan.

Most online library catalogs at colleges and universities allow you to search for sources by author(s), title, keyword, subject, publication date, and call number.

Search by Keyword

You can search for a specific word or phrase. In many online library catalogs, you can decide whether to search in all or only some parts (or fields) of a catalog record, such as title or subject (see Figure 8.9).

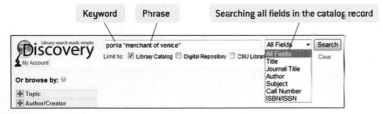

FIGURE 8.9 Searching by Keyword in an Online Library Catalog

Search by Author

If you search by author, you can find sources written by a particular person or organization. Figure 8.10 shows a search Cori Schmidtbauer conducted for sources written by John Brannigan, one of the writers she'd learned about as she explored her topic.

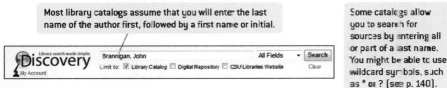

FIGURE 8.10 Searching by Author

Search by Title

If you know the exact title of a source or some of the words in the title, you can search by title to find sources (see Figure 8.11).

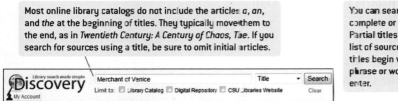

FIGURE 8.11 Searching by Title

Browse by Subject Heading or Call Number

To locate sources related to a promising result, browse by either subject heading or call number (see Figure 8.12).

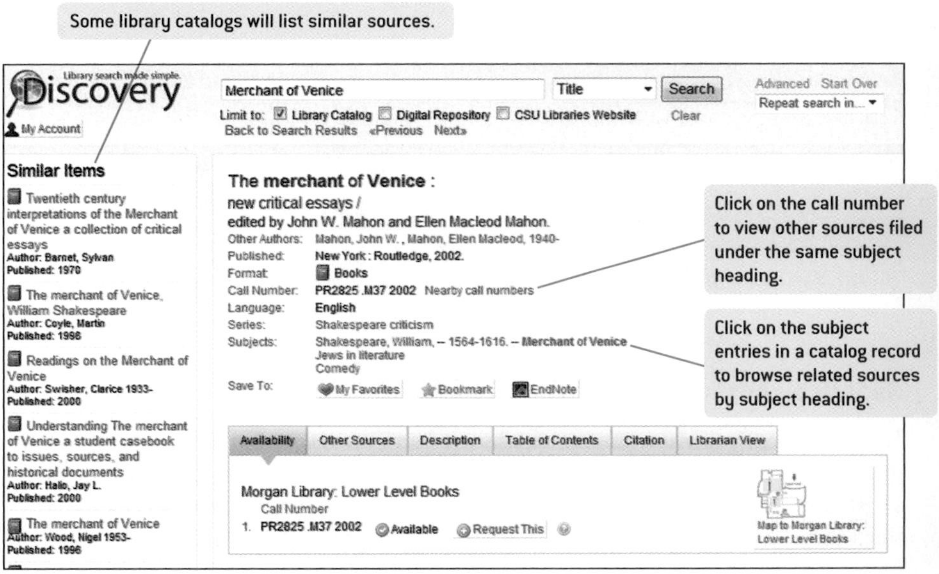

FIGURE 8.12 Browsing by Library of Congress Subject Heading

To browse directly by subject heading or call number, find out whether your library uses the Library of Congress or Dewey decimal classification systems. Then conduct a call number or subject setting search in your library catalog (the specific options for doing so vary across library catalogs) and enter a main subject heading call number.

Library of Congress Classification System

A General Works	E History: United States
B Philosophy, Psychology, Religion	F History: United States Local and America
C Auxiliary Sciences of History	G Geography, Anthropology, Recreation
D History: General and Old World	H Social Sciences

Information Literacy

Using Call Numbers and Subject Headings. Browsing by call number allows you to take a virtual stroll through your library. You can begin by entering a call number from the Library of Congress classification system or the Dewey decimal system or, if you are viewing the record for a book that you find interesting, by clicking on the call number to browse a list of sources with nearby call numbers.

III Collecting Information

J	Political Science	R	Medicine
K	Law	S	Agriculture
L	Education	T	Technology
M	Music and Books on Music	U	Military Science
N	Fine Arts	V	Naval Science
P	Language and Literature	Z	Library Science and Information Resources
Q	Science		

Dewey Decimal Classification System

000	Computers, Internet, and Systems	500	Science
100	Philosophy	600	Technology
200	Religion	700	Arts
300	Social Sciences, Sociology, and Anthropology	800	Literature, Rhetoric, and Criticism
400	Language	900	History

Search with Multiple Strategies

Online library catalogs can help you locate sources quickly, especially when you conduct simple searches, such as an author search by last name. If the last name is a common one such as Smith, Garcia, or Chen, however, your search might produce far more results than you would like. In this case, it might help to use the catalog's advanced search form to search with more than one type of strategy—such as author and keyword—at the same time (see Figure 8.13).

Search with a combination of keyword, titles, and subject.

If you're working on a topic that is time-sensitive, limit your search by publication date.

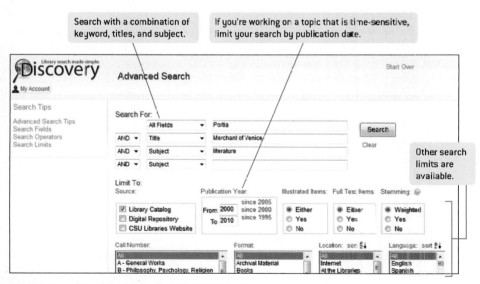

Other search limits are available.

FIGURE 8.13 Searching with a Combination of Terms

III Collecting Information

My Research Project

PREPARE TO SEARCH ONLINE LIBRARY CATALOGS

As you get ready to search online library catalogs, return to your research plan or research proposal and make a list of names, keywords, and phrases. Examine your working bibliography to identify the authors, titles, and subjects of your best sources. Then answer the following questions.

1. What are the names of authors I can use to search by author?

2. What are the titles of works that have been referred to me or that I have found in works cited pages that I can use to search by title?

3. What words and phrases can I use to search by keyword?

4. What words and phrases can I use to search by subject?

5. Does it make sense to search by date? If so, what are the dates I should search within?

6. Would call numbers in the Library of Congress or Dewey decimal classification systems be useful for me to browse? If so, what are these call numbers?

You can download or print this activity at **bedfordresearcher.com**.

8c

How can I search for sources with databases?

Databases operate much like online library catalogs, although they focus on a different collection of sources. Whereas an online catalog allows you to search for publications owned by the library, a database allows you to search for sources that have been published on a particular subject or in a particular discipline regardless of whether the library owns the sources. Although some databases can be accessed publicly through the Web, such as ERIC (eric.ed.gov), most are available only through subscription services on library computers or a library Web site.

Databases supply publication information and brief descriptions of the information in a source; some — but not all — provide digital copies of the source. Using the citation information provided by the database, you can check your library's online catalog for the title of the publication in which it appears. If your library does not own the publication, you can request it through interlibrary loan (see p. 171).

Databases fall into five general categories.

- **News and information databases** focus on recently published articles in newspapers and popular magazines.

- **Subject databases** focus on a broad subject area, such as education, business, or government.

- **Bibliographies** focus on publications in a specific discipline or profession, such as literary studies, computational linguistics, or the social sciences.

- **Citation indexes** identify sources that have referenced a specific publication, such as an article in a journal or a conference proceeding.

- **Media databases** provide access to images, video, and audio sources.

To search for sources with databases, identify databases that are relevant to the issue you are addressing in your research writing project and then carry out basic and advanced searches.

Identify Relevant Databases

To identify databases that might be relevant to your issue, review your library's list of databases or consult a reference librarian. Ask yourself the following questions.

Am I Focusing on an Issue That Is Likely to Have Been Addressed in Recent News Coverage?   If so, consider searching databases that focus on newspapers and weekly magazines, such as:

- LexisNexis Academic
- ProQuest Newspapers
- Alternative Press Index
- Newspaper Source

Am I Focusing on an Issue That Is Related to a Broad Area of Interest, Such as Business, Education, or Government?   If so, consider searching databases that focus on more general issues, such as:

- Academic Search Premier
- Article First
- Catalog of U.S. Government Publications
- WorldCat

Am I Focusing on an Issue That Is Related to a Particular Profession or Academic Discipline?   If so, consult bibliographies that focus on that area. Many libraries provide advice about databases that are relevant to a particular profession or discipline. For example, if you are interested in an issue related to sociology, you might consult the following databases.

- Family and Society Studies Worldwide
- Social Science Abstracts
- Sociological Abstracts

III Collecting Information

Have I Already Identified Sources about My Issue?   If you have already located promising sources, you can search citation indexes to identify sources that refer to your sources. Depending on your area, you might search the following databases.

- Science Citation Index
- Social Sciences Citation Index
- Arts & Humanities Citation Index

Is the Full Text of the Source Available?   Full-text databases offer the complete source for viewing or download, usually either a PDF file (a type of file that can be viewed in Adobe's Acrobat Reader) or as an HTML (Web page) or plain-text document. These databases cut out the middle step of needing to search for the specific periodical that published the article. If you are not sure that your library will own the sources provided by a database, or if you'd simply like to locate them more quickly, consider using full-text databases. Databases that offer some or all of their sources in full text include:

- Academic Search Premier
- ERIC
- IEEE Xplore
- LexisNexis Academic
- ScienceDirect

Am I Searching for Nontextual Materials?   If you are seeking photographs and other image, video, or audio sources, turn to media databases such as the following.

- ARTstor
- AccessScience
- Mountain West Digital Library

Information Literacy

Access to most databases is purchased by a library in a manner similar to subscribing to a journal or magazine. Large research libraries often subscribe to hundreds of databases, while smaller libraries might subscribe to only a handful. Because libraries must purchase subscriptions to databases, they typically restrict access to the databases to library patrons, such as students, staff, and faculty. Typically, students, faculty, and staff can access these resources from computers that are logged into the campus network. The general public cannot access these databases unless they connect to them through computers that are in the library or in a campus office or computer lab. If your library does not subscribe to databases that meet your needs, consider using Deep Web search sites such as OIAster (oiaster.worldcat.org) and CompletePlanet (aip.completeplanet .com), which offer access to Web-based databases and specialized directories (see p. 160).

Search News and Information Databases

News and information databases focus on recently published articles in newspapers, such as the *New York Times*, and popular magazines, such as *Time* and *Newsweek*. Some databases of this type, such as LexisNexis Academic, also allow you to search articles distributed by news services, such as the Associated Press, and transcripts of radio and television programs (see Figures 8.14 and 8.15).

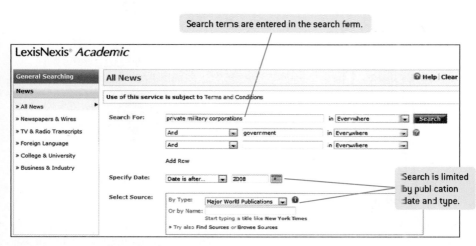

FIGURE 8.14 Searching a News and Information Database

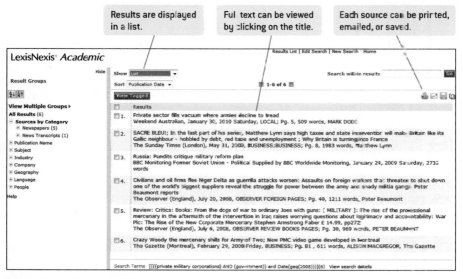

FIGURE 8.15 Search Results

III Collecting Information

Search Subject Databases

Subject databases provide information and abstracts (brief summaries) on sources about a broad subject area, such as education, business, or government. Article-First, for example, identifies sources published in a wide range of academic and professional journals (see Figure 8.16).

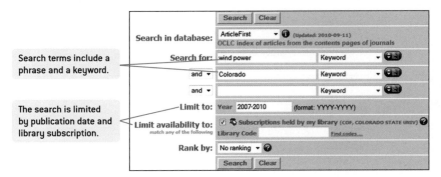

Search terms include a phrase and a keyword.

The search is limited by publication date and library subscription.

FIGURE 8.16 Searching a Subject Database

Search Bibliographies

Bibliographies provide publication information about publications in a specific discipline or profession, such as literary studies, computational linguistics, or the social sciences (see Figure 8.17). The MLA International Bibliography, for example, provides information about sources published in the field of English literature.

Searching: MLA International Bibliography | Choose Databases »

portia   in Select a Field (optional)   Search Clear

AND   Merchant of Venice   in Select a Field (optional)

AND   in Select a Field (optional)   Add Row

Search terms.   asic Search | Advanced Search | Visual Search | ▶ Search History

Page: 1   Date Descending Sort ✓   Page Options ✓   Alert / Save / Share ✓

5 Results for...
Boolean/Phrase:
portia and Merchant of Venice

1. The Currency *of* Yiddish: Ettinger's Serkele and the Reinvention *of* Shylock
   By: Quint, Alyssa Pia; Prooftexts: A Journal *of* Jewish Literary History, 2004 Winter; 24 (1): 99-115, 131. (Journal article)

Limiters
☑ Full Text

Search results are limited to full-text sources.

s: Jewish characters; Ettinger, Solomon; Yiddish language literature; Jewish characters; Sha
e: MLA International Bibliography
to folder

Clicking on the title shows citation information.

PDF Full Text

Clicking on the links opens the source.

Refine your results
☑ Full Text
☐ Exclude Dissertations
☐ Scholarly (Peer Reviewed) Journals

1967   Publication   2004
       Date

Update   Show More »

2. *Portia* and the Prince *of* Morocco
   By: Ungerer, Gustav; Shakespeare Studies, 2003; 31: 89-126. (Journal article)
   Subjects: Morocco, Prince of (character); Portia of Belmont (character); the English; slave trade; Spain; Morocco; cross-cultural relations; Moors; Jews
   Database: MLA International Bibliography
   Add to folder

   HTML Full Text   PDF Full Text

FIGURE 8.17 Searching a Bibliography

III Collecting Information

Search Citation Indexes

Citation indexes provide publication information and abstracts on sources that have referenced a specific publication. A list of these citations can lead you to other relevant sources on your issue, and they can expand your understanding of the conversation you are joining. If you have already located sources on your issue, you can search a citation database, such as the Web of Science, for articles that cite your sources (see Figure 8.18).

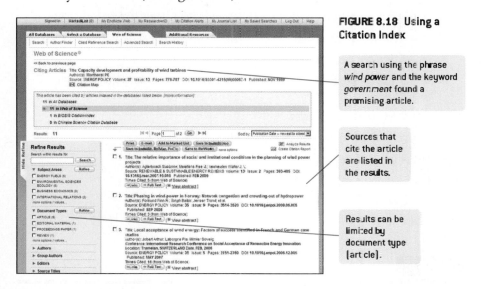

FIGURE 8.18 Using a Citation Index

A search using the phrase *wind power* and the keyword *government* found a promising article.

Sources that cite the article are listed in the results.

Results can be limited by document type (article).

Search Media Databases

Media databases provide access to images, videos, and audio sources. You can use these databases to view historical and contemporary photographs, images of works of art, television shows and movies, and audio recordings of various kinds (see Figure 8.19).

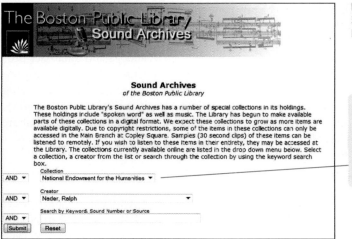

FIGURE 8.19 Searching an Audio Database

Boston Public Library's Sound Archives database allows you to search for audio footage by collection, creator, and keyword.

III Collecting Information

My Research Project

RECORD SEARCHES

One of the most important research strategies you can use as you collect information is keeping track of your searches. You should note not only the keywords or phrases and the search strategies you used with them (wildcards, Boolean search, author search, and so on) but also how many sources the search turned up and whether those sources were relevant to your research project.

In your research log, record the following information for each of your searches.

1. Resource that was searched

2. Search terms used (keywords, phrases, publication information)

3. Search strategies used (simple search, wildcard search, exact phrase search, Boolean search)

4. Date search was conducted

5. Number of results produced by the search

6. Relevance of the results

7. Notes about the search

You can download or print this activity at **bedfordresearcher.com**.

8d

How can I search for sources with Web search sites?

The Web has become the largest and most accessible "library" in the world. Its "collection" includes Web pages, blogs, reviews, social-networking sites, magazine and journal articles, books, music, photos, and video, among many other items.

Unfortunately, the Web is also the most disorganized library in the world, since it's being built by millions of people without a common plan or much communication among them. To locate sources, researchers usually turn to Web search sites. Like online library catalogs and databases, Web search sites help you locate information quickly and easily. However, while library catalogs and databases provide results that have been carefully selected by librarians and database editors, the Web pages produced by Web search sites can be uneven in quality, ranging from refereed articles in scholarly journals to home pages written by fifth graders. As you prepare to search the Web, consider the types of Web search sites that are available and the types of searches you'll conduct on them.

Identify Relevant Web Search Sites

A surprisingly large number of Web search sites can help you locate sources about the written conversation you've decided to join. Established search sites, such as Ask, Bing, Google, and Yahoo!, constantly compete with new sites, each hoping that you'll turn to them when you wish to conduct a search. To determine which search sites might be best suited to the needs of your research writing situation, consider their areas of emphasis, which range from general to such focused areas as blogs or social networking sites, and the tools they offer to support searching and working with results.

Use Web Search Engines. When you use a Web search engine (see Figure 8.20), you obtain information about Web pages and other forms of information on the Internet, including PDF files, PowerPoint files, Word files, blogs, and newsgroups (see p. 164). Web search engines keep track of these sources by locating documents on Web sites and entering them in a searchable database. Leading Web search engines include

> @ Find a list of additional Web search engines at bedfordresearcher.com. Click on Annotated Links.

AltaVista:	altavista.com
Ask:	ask.com
Bing:	bing.com
Blekko:	blekko.com
DuckDuckGo:	duckduckgo.com
Gigablast:	gigablast.com
Google:	google.com
Yahoo! Search:	search.yahoo.com

FIGURE 8.20 Google Is the Leading Web Search Engine

III Collecting Information

Information Literacy

Keep two cautions in mind as you use Web search engines. First, because most search engines index only a portion of the Web — sometimes as much as 50 percent and sometimes as little as 5 percent — you should use more than one search engine to search the Web. If you don't find what you're looking for on one, it doesn't mean you won't find it or another. Second, because Web pages can be moved, deleted, or revised, you might find that a search engine's results are inaccurate. Some search sites, such as Google, provide access to cached versions of older Web pages.

Use Web Directories. Unlike Web search sites, Web directories employ human editors to organize information about Web pages into categories and subcategories. Directories allow you to browse lists of Web sites by clicking on general topics, such as Health or Education, and then successively narrow your search by clicking on subtopics. Many directories also permit you to conduct keyword searches within specific categories (see Figure 8.21B). This enables you to search within a collection of Web sites that have already been judged by real people to be relevant to your topic. Leading Web directories include

About.com:	about.com
Best of the Web:	botw.org
Google Directory:	google.com/dirhp
ipl2:	ipl.org
Open Directory Project:	dmoz.org
WWW Virtual Library:	vlib.org
Yahoo! Directory:	dir.yahoo.com

FIGURE 8.21A **Searching a Web Directory**

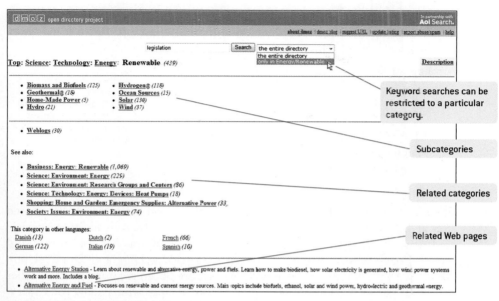

FIGURE 8.21B Searching a Web Directory

Use Deep Web Search Sites and Directories. Many specialized topics are addressed through databases or database-supported Web sites that, although accessible through the Web, are not indexed by conventional Web search sites such as Google or Bing. These sites are referred to collectively as the Deep Web or the Invisible Web because they are not easily found by the search technologies used by leading search sites. To search the Deep Web, try such search sites as Complete Planet, a directory of more than seventy thousand searchable databases and specialty search engines, and OIAster, a search site sponsored by the Online Computer Library Center (OCLC) cooperative. Leading Deep Web search sites and directories include

Complete Planet:	aip.completeplanet.com
Internet Archive:	archive.org
OAIster:	oaister.worldcat.org
Scirus:	scirus.com

Use Meta Search Sites. On a meta search site you can conduct a search on several Web search engines or Web directories at the same time. These sites typically search the major search engines and directories and then present a limited number of results on a single page.

Use a meta search site early in your search for information on the Web. You might use a meta search site to do a side-by-side comparison of various search sites and directories. When Pete Jacquez searched for the phrase *wind power* on search.com, for example, he found that the search sites Google and Yahoo! produced more useful sets of results than the Gigablast and Alexa search sites. Leading meta search sites include

Dogpile:	dogpile.com
ixquick:	ixquick.com
Mamma:	mamma.com
Metacrawler:	metacrawler.com
Search.com:	search.com
Zuula:	zuula.com

> @ Find a list of additional meta search sites at bedfordresearcher.com. Click on Annotated Links.

Use News Search Sites.   You can search for news on most major Web search sites and directories, such as Bing, Google, Ask, and Yahoo! In addition, special-ized news search sites allow you to conduct focused searches for current and archived news reports, while social news sites such as Digg and StumbleUpon allow you to view news stories and videos that have been recommended by other readers. If you own a smartphone, you can also use apps which allow you to view and search news from major newspapers and news sites. Leading news search sites include

AltaVista News:	altavista.com/news/
Ask News:	ask.com/news
Bing News:	www.bing.com/news
Digg:	digg.com
Google News:	news.google.com
StumbleUpon:	www.stumbleupon.com
World News:	wn.com
Yahoo! News:	news.yahoo.com

Use Reference Search Sites.   On a reference search site you can search for information that has been collected in encyclopedias, almanacs, atlases, dictio-naries, and other reference resources. Some reference sites, such as Encyclopedia Britannica Online, offer limited access to information from their encyclopedias for no charge and complete access for a fee. Other sites, such as Information Please and Bartleby.com allow unrestricted access to recently published reference works, including the *Columbia Encyclopedia, The Encyclopedia of World History,* and *The World Factbook.* If you own a smartphone, you can also use apps such as FactBook, WikiMobile Encyclopedia, and Wikipedia Mobile to check facts and look up information as you work on your project.

   One widely used reference site, Wikipedia (en.wikipedia.org), is collabora-tively written by its readers. Because of its comprehensiveness, Wikipedia can serve as a useful starting point for research on a topic. However, because any reader can make changes to the site, it's best to double-check the information you find there. For more information about the drawbacks of relying on wikis as authoritative sources of information, see p. 95. Leading reference search sites include

Bartleby.com Reference:	bartleby.com/reference
Encyclopedia Britannica Online:	britannica.com
Encyclopedia.com:	encyclopedia.com
GoogleKnol:	knol.google.com
Information Please:	infoplease.com
Wikipedia:	en.wikipedia.org

Use Government Documents Search Sites and Directories. Many government agencies and institutions have turned to the Web as their primary means of distributing their publications. FirstGov, sponsored by the U.S. government, allows you to search the federal government's network of online resources. GPO Access provides publication information about print documents and links to those publications when they are available online. Sites such as FecStats and FedWorld give access to a wide range of government-related materials. In addition to these specialized government Web sites, you can locate government publications through many Web directories, such as Yahoo!. Leading government documents sites include

About.com's U.S. Government Information Directory:	usgovinfo.about.com
Canadian Government Search Engines:	recherche–search.gc.ca
FedStats:	fedstats.gov
FedWorld:	www.fedworld.gov
Google U.S. Government Search:	google.com/unclesam
GPO Access:	gpoaccess.gov
GovSpot.com:	www.govspot.com
SearchGov.com:	searchgov.com
State and Local Government Directory:	statelocalgov.net
USA.gov:	usa.gov

Use e-Book Sites. Access to e-books (books in digital form) began with open-access projects such as Project Gutenberg and the Internet Archive Community Text collection. These sites offer access to historical texts that are no longer under copyright as well as to books released under various open-access licenses. The availability of e-books increased when Google launched its digital books project in partnership with leading publishers and university libraries, including Harvard, Stanford, and the University of Michigan. The project is designed

III Collecting Information

to provide digital access to millions of books originally available only in print while protecting the copyright and commercial interests of authors and publishers. The number of books available in digital form surged, however, following Amazon's launch of its Kindle e-book reader, which provided a convenient way of purchasing and reading digital books. Amazon's competitors, among them Apple, Barnes and Noble, and Sony, responded with their own e-book readers and online bookstores, as well as applications for smartphones and tablet computers.

You can locate (and often preview) e-books by visiting sites such as

Amazon:	amazon.com
Barnes and Noble:	barnesandnoble.com/ebooks
Google Books:	books.google.com
Internet Archive Community Books:	archive.org/details/texts
Online Books Page:	onlinebooks.library.upenn.edu
Project Gutenberg:	gutenberg.org
Sony:	ebookstore.sony.com
Wikibooks:	wikibooks.org

Use Blog Search Sites.   Blogs—short for Weblogs—consist of chronologically ordered entries on a Web site and most closely resemble entries in a diary or journal. Blog entries usually include a title and a text message, and can also incorporate images, audio, video, and other types of media. Many entries provide links to other pages on the Web. The purposes of blogs vary.

- Some blogs report on events and issues (see Figure 8.22). The bloggers who provided daily—sometimes hourly—reports on the 2008 political conventions offered valuable, firsthand insights into aspects of the conventions that were not addressed through the mainstream media. Similarly, the bloggers who reported on the Iraq War offered a perspective on events in Iraq and elsewhere that would not have been available otherwise.

- Some blogs alert readers to information elsewhere on the Web. These blogs cite recently published news reports and articles, the latest developments in a particular discipline, and new contributions to an ongoing debate—and provide commentary on that information.

- Some blogs serve as public relations spaces for institutions and organizations, such as corporations, government agencies, and colleges. These blogs typically focus on services or activities associated with the institution or organization.

- Some blogs serve largely as a space for personal reflection and expression. A blogger might share his or her thoughts about each day, current events, or other issues with friends and family.

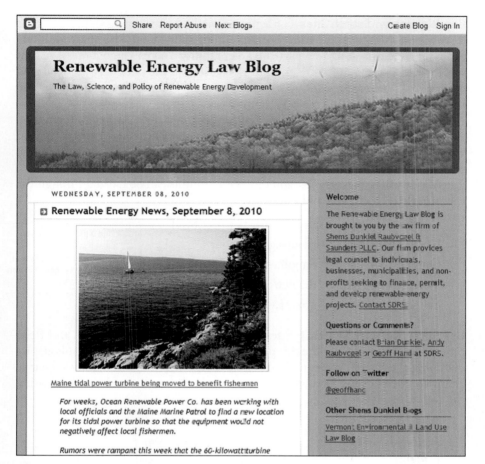

FIGURE 8.22 Blog Entry on Renewable Energy Law

Research writers can use blogs as sources of information and commentary on an issue and as sources of firsthand accounts by individuals involved in or affected by an issue. If you find blogs by experts in the field, you can begin a dialogue with people involved in or knowledgeable about your issue. To locate blogs that are relevant to your research question, use the following blog search sites and directories.

Best of the Web Blogs:	blogs.botw.org
BlogCatalog:	blogcatalog.com
Blogdigger:	blogdigger.com
Google Blogsearch:	blogsearch.google.com
IceRocket:	icerocket.com
Technorati:	technorati.com

Use Discussion Search Sites.   Electronic mailing lists, newsgroups, and Web discussion forums support conversations among individuals who share an interest in an issue or belong to a particular community. You can read a message sent to a mailing list, sometimes referred to as a listserv, in the same way that you read other email messages. Messages posted to newsgroups and Web discussion forums can be read using most Web browsers.

In addition to reading messages, you can post your own. Although there is no guarantee that you'll receive helpful responses, experts in a particular area often read and contribute to these forums. If you are fortunate enough to get into a discussion with one or more knowledgeable people, you might obtain useful information.

Mailing lists, newsgroups, and discussion forums can be located through the following search engines and directories.

CataList:	lsoft.com/lists/listref.html
Google Groups:	groups.google.com
Omgili:	omgili.com
Tile.net:	tile.net/lists
Yahoo! Groups:	groups.yahoo.com

> **@** Find a list of additional search sites for newsgroups and mailing lists at **bedfordresearcher.com**. Click on Annotated Links.

Use Social Network Search.   Sites such as MySpace, Facebook, Hi5, and Bebo provide opportunities to identify people who share your interest in an issue. By searching these sites, you can identify individuals who might be knowledgeable about an issue or have been affected by it. You can search social networks using the following sites.

Bebo Search:	bebo.com/
Facebook Search:	facebook.com/srch.php
Hi5 Search:	hi5.com/
IceRocket:	icerocket.com/
LinkedIn Search:	linkedin.com
MySpace Search:	myspace.com/
Social Mention:	socialmention.com
Social Network Search:	socialnetworksearch.com

Use Alternative Search Sites.   The Web is anything but static—it changes all the time. It shouldn't come as a surprise that search tools will change as well. The following sites approach searching the Web in new and promising ways.

Google Goggles (www.google.com/mobile/googles) allows you to use a photograph, rather than words, as the basis for a search.

Rollyo (rollyo.com) allows you to build custom search lists, which contain only the sites you want to search. You can also search sites created by Rollyo staff and users.

Snap (snap.com) shows visual previews of the Web pages returned by the search.

A search for metal music produces a collage of texts, images, videos, and music files.

Clicking on a result re-centers the results, showing additional results and moving others off the screen.

FIGURE 8.23 Spezify.com

Controls allow you to play videos or sound files, link to the item, or add it to your Bookmarks or Favorites list.

III Collecting Information

Spezify (spezify.com) uses "live" thumbnails of Web pages, images, and video to help you explore a topic (see Figure 8.23).

WebBrain (webbrain.com) creates a visual map based on your search and lists sites relevant to the part of the map you are exploring.

8e

How can I search for sources with media search sites?

The Web is home not only to textual information, such as articles and books, but also to a growing collection of other types of media, such as photographs, podcasts, and streaming video. Image search sites have been available on the Web for a number of years. More recently, search sites have turned their attention to audio and video as well. You can locate useful information about your issue by searching for recordings of radio broadcasts, television shows, documentaries, podcasts, and other media.

9

Searching for Information with Print Resources

Contrary to recent claims, there is life (and information) beyond the World Wide Web. Print resources can help you locate a wealth of information relevant to your research project.

? WHAT'S MY PURPOSE?

To make the most effective use of the print resources available in a library, ask how the information they can point you toward will help you achieve your purpose as a writer. If you're working on a research project that has a historical component, as was the case with Elizabeth Leontiev and Cori Schmidtbauer, you'll find that print bibliographies and indexes can point you toward sources that cannot be located

9a

How can I use the library stacks to locate sources?

The library stacks—or shelves—house the library's collection of bound publications. You can locate publications by browsing the stacks and checking works cited pages for related publications. Once you've decided a source is relevant to your issue, you can check it out or request it through interlibrary loan.

Browse the Stacks

One of the advantages of the classification systems used by most libraries—typically either the Library of Congress or Dewey decimal classification system—is that they are subject based. As a result, you can browse the stacks to look for sources on a topic because books on similar subjects are shelved together. For example, if your research takes you to the stacks for books about alcohol abuse, you're likely to find books about drug abuse, treatment programs, and codependency nearby.

When you find a publication that seems useful, check the works cited page for related works. The combination of browsing the stacks for sources and checking the works cited pages of those sources can lead you to publications relevant to your issue.

Check Out Books and Periodicals

In some cases, you'll discover that a publication you want is not available because it has been checked out, reserved for a course, or placed in off-site storage. If a publication is checked out, you may be able to recall it—that is, ask that it be returned to the library and held for you. If it has been placed on reserve, you may be able to photocopy or take notes on it. If it has been placed in off-site storage, you can usually request it at the circulation desk.

Use Interlibrary Loan

If you can't obtain the book or periodical you need from your library, use interlibrary loan to borrow materials from another library. Most libraries allow you to request materials in person or on the Web. Some libraries let you check the status of your interlibrary loan request or renew interlibrary loan materials through the Web. You can learn how to use interlibrary loan at your library by consulting its Web site or a librarian.

9b

How can I use a library periodicals room to locate sources?

Periodicals include newspapers, magazines, and scholarly and professional journals. A periodicals room — or journals room — contains recent issues for library visitors to browse. Many libraries also have a separate room for newspapers published in the last few weeks or months.

To ensure everyone's access to recently published issues, most libraries don't allow you to check out periodicals published within the last year, and they usually don't allow newspapers to be checked out at all. Older periodicals are sometimes placed in bound volumes in the stacks. Few libraries, however, keep back issues of newspapers in paper form. Instead, you can often find back issues of leading newspapers in full-text databases or in microforms. *Microform* is a generic name for both microfilm, a strip of film containing greatly reduced images of printed pages, and microfiche, film roughly the shape and size of an index card containing the same kinds of miniaturized images. You view these images using a microform reader, a projection unit that looks something like a large computer monitor. Many microform readers allow you to print full-size copies of the pages.

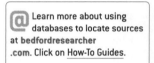
Learn more about using databases to locate sources at bedfordresearcher .com. Click on How-To Guides.

Use Works Cited Lists to Find Key Voices   [FRAMING MY ARGUMENT]

Many of the articles you'll find in your library's periodicals room will contain works cited or reference lists. When you find an article that is relevant to your argument, check the list of sources for related articles. As you find new sources, check for authors whose work is cited frequently (see Figure 9.1). This will help

Information Literacy

To help you locate articles in periodicals, most periodicals rooms provide access to online databases, which are more likely than print indexes and bibliographies to contain listings of recent publications. Once you've identified articles you want to review, you'll need to find the periodicals containing those articles. Most online library catalogs allow you to conduct a title search for a periodical, in the same way you conduct a title search for a book. The online catalog will tell you the call number of the periodical, and most online catalogs will give information about its location in the library. In addition, some libraries provide a printed list that identifies where periodicals are located. If you have difficulty finding a periodical or judging which publications are likely to contain articles relevant to your research project, ask a librarian for assistance.

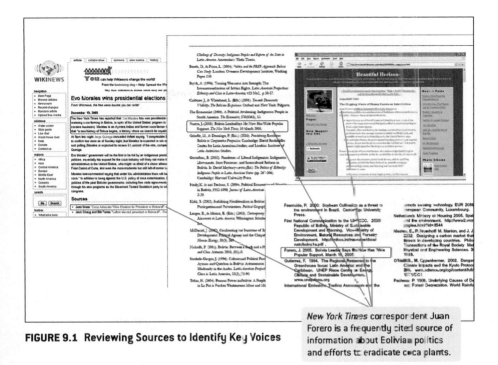

FIGURE 9.1 Reviewing Sources to Identify Key Voices

New York Times correspondent Juan Forero is a frequently cited source of information about Bolivian politics and efforts to eradicate coca plants.

III Collecting Information

identify key voices in the conversation, writers whose work is either controversial, groundbreaking, fundamental, or in some other way central to the conversation.

9c

How can I use a library reference room to locate sources?

Reference rooms contain print resources on a range of topics, from government to finance to philosophy to science. Some of the most important print resources you can consult in a reference room include bibliographies, indexes, biographies, general and specialized encyclopedias, handbooks, almanacs, and atlases.

Consult Bibliographies

Bibliographies list books, articles, and other publications that have been judged relevant to a topic. Some bibliographies provide only citations, while others include abstracts—brief descriptions—of listed sources. Complete bibliographies attempt to list all of the sources published about a topic, while selective bibliographies attempt to list only the best sources published about a topic. Some bibliographies limit their inclusion of sources by time period, often focusing on sources published during a given year.

Types of Bibliographies   You're likely to find several types of bibliographies in your library's reference room or stacks, including trade bibliographies, general bibliographies, and specialized bibliographies.

- **Trade Bibliographies** allow you to locate books published about a particular topic. Leading trade bibliographies include *The Subject Guide to Books in Print*, *Books in Print*, and *Cumulative Book Index*. Cori Schmidtbauer found a large number of books about *The Merchant of Venice* in the *Annual Bibliography of English Language and Literature* (see Figure 9.2).

- **General Bibliographies** cover a wide range of topics, usually in selective lists. For sources on humanities topics, consult *The Humanities: A Selective Guide to Information Sources*. For sources on social science topics, see *Social Science Reference Sources: A Practical Guide*. For sources on science topics, go to bibliographies such as *Information Sources in Science and Technology*, *Guide to Information Sources in the Botanical Sciences*, and *Guide to Information Sources in the Physical Sciences*.

- **Specialized Bibliographies** typically provide lists of sources — often annotated — about a topic. For example, *Art Books: A Basic Bibliography of Monographs on Artists*, edited by Wolfgang M. Freitag, focuses on sources about important artists.

Locating Bibliographies   Although most general and trade bibliographies can be found in your library reference room, specialized bibliographies are likely to be located in your library's stacks. To locate bibliographies, follow these steps.

1. *Consult a cumulative bibliography.* Cumulative bibliographies provide an index of published bibliographies. *The Bibliographic Index: A Cumulative Bibliography of Bibliographies*, for instance, identifies bibliographies on a wide range of topics and is updated annually.

III Collecting Information

Information Literacy

Although many of the reference books in library reference rooms serve the same purposes as the databases discussed in Chapter 8, others offer information not available in databases. Using reference books to locate print resources has several benefits.

- **Most databases have short memories.** Databases seldom index sources published before 1970, and typically index sources only as far back as the mid-1980s. Depending on the conversation you've decided to join, a database might not allow you to locate important sources.

- **Most databases focus on short works.** In contrast, many of the print resources in library reference rooms will refer you to books and longer publications as well as to articles in periodicals.

- **Many library reference resources are unavailable in digital form.** For instance, the *Encyclopedia of Creativity,* which offers more than two hundred articles, is available only in print form.

- **Entries in print indexes are easier to browse.** Despite efforts to aid browsing, databases support searching far better than they do browsing.

304 SIXTEENTH CENTURY [2007

The Merchant of Venice ———————————————— The subject heading

5690. BAYNHAM, MATT. Why is mercy 'twice blest'? NQ (54:3) 2007, 285.

5691. BILELLO, THOMAS C. Accomplished with what she lacks: law, equity, and Portia's con. *In* (pp. 109–26) 5221.

5692. CANTOR, PAUL A. The shores of hybridity: Shakespeare and the Mediterranean. LCom (3:4) 2006, 896–913.

5693. CHERNAIK, WARREN. *The Merchant of Venice.* (Bibl. 2006, 5957.) Rev. by Willy Maley in MLR (102:4) 2007, 1139–42.

5694. FITZPATRICK, LISA. Staging *The Merchant of Venice* in Cork: the concretization of a Shakespearean play for a new society. ModDr (50:2) 2007, 168–83.

Recently published articles

5695. FORKER, CHARLES R. Marlowe's *Edward II* and *The Merchant of Venice*. SNL (57:2) 2007, 65, 70.

5696. GROSS, KENNETH. Shylock is Shakespeare. (Bibl. 2006, 5961.) Rev. by Katharine Craik in TLS, 21 Sept. 2007, 24; by William J. Kennedy in RQ (60:2) 2007, 665–7; by Martin J. Plax in CompDr (41:2) 2007, 260–4.

Publication information

5697. HALIO, JAY L. The study of Shakespearean playbooks. *In* (pp. 38–45) 5409.

5698. HARRIS, JONATHAN GIL. The time of Shakespeare's Jewry. SStud (35) 2007, 39–46.

5699. IYENGAR, SUJATA. Moorish dancing in *The Two Noble Kinsmen* See 5885.

5700. KAPLAN, M. LINDSAY. Jessica's mother: medieval constructions of Jewish race and gender in *The Merchant of Venice*. ShQ (58:1) 2007, 1–30.

5701. KOLLMANN, JUDITH. How 'all that glisters is not gold' became 'all that is gold does not glitter': Aragorn's debt to Shakespeare. *In* (pp. 110–27) 17430.

5702. LAKE, JAMES H. The influence of primacy and recency upon audience response to Michael Radford's *The Merchant of Venice*. SNL (57:2) 2007, 61, 78.

5703. LEVIN, RICHARD. Launcelot's and Huck's moral dilemmas. SNL (56:3) 2006/07, 83.

5704. MAGNUS, LAURY. Michael Radford's *The Merchant of Venice* and the vexed question of performance. LitFQ (35:2) 2007, 108–20.

5705. MAZER, CARY M. The intentional-fallacy fallacy. *In* (pp. 99–113) 5412.

5706. ROSS, CHARLES. Avoiding the issue of fraud: 4, 5 Philip & Mary c.8 (the Heiress Protection Statute), Portia, and Desdemona. *In* (pp. 91–108) 5221.

5707. ROSTON, MURRAY. Tradition and subversion in Renaissance literature: studies in Shakespeare, Spenser, Jonson, and Donne. Pittsburgh, PA: Duquesne UP, 2007. pp. xiii, 258. Rev. by Christopher Baker in RQ (60:4) 2007, 1458–60.

5708. ROTHWELL, KENNETH S. Trevor Nunn's *The Merchant of Venice*: Portia's house of mystery, magic, and menace. *In* (pp. 204–16) 5409.

5709. WILSON, LUKE. Drama and marine insurance in Shakespeare's London. *In* (pp. 127–42) 5221.

FIGURE 9.2 An Entry from the *Annual Bibliography of English Language and Literature* on *The Merchant of Venice*

III Collecting Information

2. *Consult your library's online catalog.* When you search your library's online catalog, use keywords related to your issue plus the keyword *bibliography*. Cori Schmidtbauer searched her college's online catalog using the keywords *Shakespeare* and *bibliography*.

3. *If necessary, seek advice from a reference librarian.* Reference librarians will help you find bibliographies that are relevant to your issue.

Consult Indexes

Indexes provide citation information for sources found in a particular set of publications. Many indexes also include abstracts — brief descriptions — that can help you determine whether a source is worth locating and reviewing. The following types of indexes can be found in libraries.

Periodical Indexes   Periodical indexes list sources published in magazines, trade journals, scholarly journals, and newspapers. Some periodical indexes cover a wide range of periodicals, others focus on periodicals that address a single subject, and still others focus on a small set or even an individual periodical.

- *The Readers' Guide to Periodical Literature* indexes roughly two hundred general-interest magazines. Updated monthly, the *Readers' Guide* organizes entries by author and subject.

- *Art Index* provides information about sources published only in art magazines and journals. Updated quarterly, *Art Index* organizes entries by author and subject.

- The *New York Times Index* lists articles published only in that newspaper. Updated twice a month, the *Index* organizes entries by subject, geography, organization, and references to individuals.

A student writer used *The Readers' Guide to Periodical Literature* to locate early sources about college admission (see Figure 9.3).

Significant differences can exist between the print and digital database versions of periodical indexes. For example, while the printed *Readers' Guide to Periodical Literature* covers publications since 1900, the *Readers' Guide* database only contains information on articles published since 1983.

> @ Find an annotated list of periodical indexes at bedfordresearcher.com. Click on Annotated Links.

Indexes of Materials in Books   To locate articles in edited books, turn to resources such as the *Essay and General Literature Index,* which indexes nearly five thousand book-length collections of articles and essays in the arts, humanities, and social sciences. You might also find subject-specific indexes of materials in books. *The Cumulative Bibliography of Asian Studies,* for example, covers articles in edited books.

Pamphlet Indexes   Libraries frequently collect pamphlets of various kinds. To help patrons find these materials, many libraries create a pamphlet index. Ask

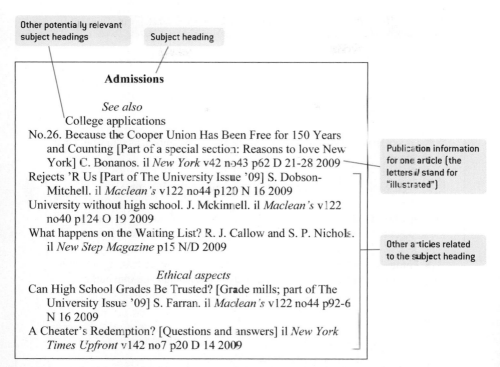

Other potentially relevant subject headings

Subject heading

Admissions

See also
College applications

No.26. Because the Cooper Union Has Been Free for 150 Years and Counting [Part of a special section: Reasons to love New York] C. Bonanos. il *New York* v42 no43 p62 D 21-28 2009

Rejects 'R Us [Part of The University Issue '09] S. Dobson-Mitchell. il *Maclean's* v122 no44 p120 N 16 2009

University without high school. J. Mckinnell. il *Maclean's* v122 no40 p124 O 19 2009

What happens on the Waiting List? R. J. Callow and S. P. Nichols. il *New Step Magazine* p15 N/D 2009

Ethical aspects
Can High School Grades Be Trusted? [Grade mills; part of The University Issue '09] S. Farran. il *Maclean's* v122 no44 p92-6 N 16 2009

A Cheater's Redemption? [Questions and answers] il *New York Times Upfront* v142 no7 p20 D 14 2009

Publication information for one article (the letters *il* stand for "illustrated")

Other articles related to the subject heading

FIGURE 9.3 A Listing in *The Readers' Guide to Periodical Literature*

a reference librarian whether your library has a pamphlet index and where it is. You can also consult the *Vertical File Index.* Updated monthly, this index lists roughly three thousand brief sources on ten to fifteen newsworthy topics each month.

Government Documents Indexes   Government documents indexes list documents published by federal, state, and local governments.

- To find documents published by the federal government, consult the *Monthly Catalog of United States Government Publications.*

- To locate documents published by the U.S. Congress, look in the *CIS Index to Publications of the United States Congress.*

- To obtain information about the daily proceedings of the House of Representatives and the Senate, consult the *Congressional Record.*

- For documents published by the Supreme Court, consult *United States Reports*, the cumulative index of the *Official Reports of the Supreme Court.*

- To locate government documents containing statistical information, including census reports, look in the *Statistical Abstract of the United States.*

Many larger college and university libraries serve as depositories of government documents. As a result, indexes to government documents might be found in

TUTORIAL

How do I use a bibliography?

Use a bibliography to locate important publications about a subject. In this example, Cori Schmidtbauer used *The Humanities: A Selective Guide to Information Sources* to locate information about William Shakespeare.

1 Locate your subject through the index or page headings, as you would in a phone book.

2 If it is provided, read background information about the subject.

3 Review the bibliography to identify sources that are judged by the author of the subject entry or the editors of the bibliography to be relevant to the subject.

4 Entries in specialized bibliographies are often written by leading scholars. If the author of an entry is identified, search for publications by that author.

Literature ■ *459*

1152. **Annual Bibliography of Victorian Studies.** Edmonton, Alberta: LITIR Database, 1977– . Ann. ISSN 0227-1400.
   The Victorian period is defined as the time period from about 1830 to the beginning of World War I in 1914. This annual bibliography contains English-language materials of various kinds, including books, periodical articles, and reviews relating to that interesting period. It is not limited to literary subjects but attempts to treat the period in its entirety. The work is composed of seven major segments or categories, beginning with general reference works, including fine arts, philosophy and religion, history, social science, and technology. Most important is the section on language and literature, with sections on individual authors. Reviews are cited after the work itself. Indexed by subject, author, title, and reviewer. There is a cumulative index issued of *Victorian Studies* (Indiana University Press, 1957–), a quarterly... lished an annual bibliography of books and periodical articles since its first... Bibliography" serves as a continuation of the list originally published in A... and was a project of a Committee on Victorian Literature of the Modern La... tion of America. Periodic cumulations of these bibliographies have been... University of Illinois Press as *Bibliographies of Studies in Victorian Litera*... (1945); *1945–1954* (1956); *1955–1964* (1967). AMS published the most recent... the periods *1965–1974* (1981), and *1975–1984* (1991).

1153. **Interviews and Conversations with 20th-Ce...** **Writing in English: An Index.** Series I–III. Stan A. Vrana... Scarecrow Press, 1982–1990. 3v. ISBN 0-8108-2352-7 (III).
   Series II of this work appeared in 1986 and augments the coverage of... by adding more personalities. In Series I and II, the interviews were publish... and 1980. Series III continues the coverage, indexing interviews published b... 1985. In all the volumes, arrangement is alphabetical by name of the autho... then listed chronologically. These interviews are taken from a variety of sou... and periodicals, both general and literary, from the United States and foreign... included, much to Vrana's credit, are African and Asian titles. Monographic... covered, but are listed separately. About 3,600 interviews are identified i... 4,500 in the second series, and 5,600 in the third series, providing an extrao... venient access tool for this important material.

1154. **Shakespeare Survey: An Annual Survey of S...** **Study and Production.** Cambridge, UK: Cambridge Un... 1948– . Ann. ISSN 0080-9152.
   This is a highly useful and highly successful annual review of studie... but foremost area of literary research. In the past, it has been under the comb... of several scholarly and cultural organizations: the University of Birmingha... Manchester, Royal Shakespeare Theatre, and the Shakespeare Birthplace... are given to specific themes that provide a focus for the articles of that year... particular element or feature of Shakespearean study. The scope is internati... are furnished by scholars from a number of countries and regions. Most impo... bibliography is the regular feature "The Year's Contribution to Shakespearea... is a critical survey of research and publication in the field.

1155. **The Wellesley Index to Victorian Periodica...** Walter E. Houghton, ed. Toronto: University of Toronto Pres... 5v. ISBN 0-4150-3054-4 (v.1).

Relevant source

Description of source

Author, publisher, and ISBN help locate the source

Literature ■ *471*

as a supplement to the entire set, furnishing excerpts written in the previous ten years and bringing the critical coverage to the 1970s. Volume 5 (1989) is another ten-year supplement. In all volumes, critical studies from both books and periodicals are used.

1188. **The Essential Shakespeare: An Annotated Bibliography of Major Modern Studies.** 2d ed. Larry S. Champion. New York: G. K. Hall, 1993. 463p. (A Reference Publication in Literature). ISBN 0-8161-7332-X.
   An especially useful tool for a student in identifying relevant and important critical studies is this annotated bibliography of more than 1,500 entries, now in its second edition. The coverage is limited to modern criticism, providing references to those studies published only in the twentieth century. Major sections or categories represented are general works, poems and sonnets, English history plays, comedies, and tragedies. Included in the general works section are bibliographies, editions, studies of sources, and film studies. Each of the specialized sections also contains an opening subsection on general studies. Annotations are detailed and furnish scope notes and dominant themes from each work. Although some oversights have been noted in the past edition, the work remains a useful source of information.

*1189. **Exploring Shakespeare.** Detroit: Gale Research, 1997. (The Gale DISCovering Program). ISBN 0-7876-0913-7. (CD-ROM).
   Another in the publisher's program (entries 1255, 1285) presenting a resource kit for teaching/learning consisting of a CD-ROM along with a guide and manual, this is a comprehensive multimedia tool for high school and college students that examines four of the most frequently studied tragedies. Treated here are "Macbeth," "Julius Caesar," "Hamlet," and "Romeo and Juliet"; full text is provided, along with detailed plot summaries with synopsis of each act, critical essays, thematic interpretations, and descriptions of historical context. There are listings of characters, related documents, and so forth. A good biography of Shakespeare is provided, as are a time line, notes, and a glossary. Hypertext links bring up relevant full-text documents as well as graphics, audio, and video clips.
   *Shakespeare (Creative Multimedia Corporation, 1989) is a CD-ROM publication offering the complete text of all plays, poems, and sonnets in both Queen's English and American English versions. A similar effort is **Complete Works of Shakespeare* (Andromeda Interactive, 1994), which provides full text of plays and sonnets along with numerous images.

1190. **The Feminist Companion to Literature in English: Women Writers from the Middle Ages to the Present.** Virginia Blain et al. New Haven, CT: Yale University Press, 1990. 1231p. ISBN 0-300-04854-8.
   This is the most comprehensive biographical dictionary of its type, covering some 2,700 female writers from the Middle Ages to the mid-1980s who have written in the English language. The work has traded depth for its great breadth, and entries are limited to no more than 500 words. Arrangement is alphabetical by name of writer, with entries providing a biographical sketch, description of important writings, and a brief list of secondary source material for additional reference. Emphasis has been given to inclusion of British writers, although there is representation from the United States, Africa, Asia, the Caribbean, the South Pacific, Australia, and Canada. Novelists, poets, and playwrights are treated along with writers of diaries, letters, biographies, nonfiction, and children's literature. Along with the biographical entries, there are about sixty on topics such as black feminist criticism and science fiction.

Review another example and work on using bibliographies at **bedfordresearcher.com.** Click on Interactive Exercises.

either the reference room or a separate government documents collection in your library. Ask a reference librarian for help.

Citation Indexes   Citation indexes allow you to determine which publications make reference to other publications, a useful strategy for finding sources that are engaged in the same conversation. To learn which sources refer to an article published in a scientific journal, for example, you could consult the *Science Citation Index.*

Consult Biographies

Biographies cover key figures in a field, time period, or geographic region. *Who's Who in America,* for instance, provides brief biographies of important figures in the United States during a given year, while *Great Lives from History* takes a broader view, offering biographies of key figures in world history.

Consult General and Specialized Encyclopedias

General encyclopedias attempt to provide a little knowledge about a lot of things. The idea behind a general encyclopedia, such as the *New Encyclopaedia Britannica,* is to present enough information about a topic to get you started on a more detailed search.

Specialized encyclopedias such as *The MIT Encyclopedia of the Cognitive Sciences,* for example, take a narrower focus than general encyclopedias, usually of a field of study or a narrow historical period. In addition, articles in specialized encyclopedias are typically longer than articles in general encyclopedias and offer more detailed coverage of topics.

Consult Handbooks

Like encyclopedias, handbooks provide useful background information about a topic in a compact form. Unlike encyclopedias, most handbooks, such as *The Engineering Handbook* and the *International Handbook of Psychology,* cover a narrow topic area. Entries in handbooks are also much shorter than the articles found in encyclopedias.

Consult Almanacs

Almanacs contain lists, charts, and tables of information of various types. You're probably familiar with *The Old Farmer's Almanac,* which is known for its accuracy in predicting weather over the course of a year. Information in almanacs can range from the average rainfall in Australia to the batting averages of the 1927 Yankees to the average income of Germans and Poles prior to World War II.

Consult Atlases

Atlases provide maps and related information about a region or country. Some atlases take a historical perspective, while others take a topical perspective.

My Research Project

DISCUSS YOUR RESEARCH PROJECT WITH OTHERS

Return to your research log and review what you've learned about your issue. Then ask whether you've taken advantage of the print resources available in your library reference room. If you're uncertain about how you might use these resources, discuss your project with a reference librarian. Given the wide range of specialized print resources that are available, a few minutes of discussion with a knowledgeable librarian could save you a great deal of time.

 QUICK REFERENCE

Searching for Information with Print Resources

☑ Use the library stacks to locate sources. (p. 171)

☑ Use the periodicals room to locate sources. (p. 172)

☑ Use the reference room to locate sources. (p. 173)

Part III
Collecting Information

8   Searching for Information with
    Digital Resources

9   Searching for Information with
    Print Resources

10 Searching for Information with
     Field Research Methods

10

Searching for Information with Field Research Methods

> **Key Questions**

Published documents aren't the only source of information for a research project. Nor are they always the best. Publications — such as books, articles, Web sites, or television reports — offer someone else's interpretation of an event or an issue. By relying on another person's interpretation, you're looking through that person's eyes rather than through your own.

Experienced research writers know that you don't have to use published reports to find out how an event or issue has affected people — you can ask the people yourself. You don't have to view television or radio coverage of an event—you can go to the event yourself. And you don't have to rely on someone else's survey of public opinion—you can conduct your own.

> **? WHAT'S MY PURPOSE?**
>
> Your preparations for using field research methods will be most effective if you clearly understand your purpose for carrying out your research project and your purpose for using field research. Before committing yourself to designing and administering a survey, for example, ask yourself what kind of results you can expect to gain and what role those results will play in your project. Ask as well whether a certain field research method is the best technique for gaining that information, or whether you might gain it more effectively and efficiently in another way.

10a

When should I use field research methods?

Some research writers think of field research as the next-best thing to learning about an issue through a published source. If they can't find anything relevant in books, articles, newspapers, blogs, Twitter, or the broadcast media, they think, then field research might be worth considering.

These writers misunderstand the value and power of field research. Far from being a good fallback position, field research is sometimes the best way to learn about an issue or collect information to support a position.

Consider using field research methods if you find yourself in one of the following situations.

- If published sources address your issue from a perspective that you don't find useful, field research can provide another way of approaching the issue. For example, most discussions of gun rights and gun control focus on constitutional arguments. If you want to consider the issue from another perspective, such as differences in how people from rural areas and urban or suburban areas understand the issue, you might find it useful to collect information through interviews, surveys, or correspondence.

- If you are interested in an issue that most people think of as settled, published sources are unlikely to include information, ideas, and arguments that might help you challenge the conventional wisdom about the issue. Field research, in contrast, can bring new voices, experiences, and ideas into the conversation.

- In some cases, you'll find yourself considering an aspect of an issue that hasn't been addressed so far in your sources. If you come up with a new idea or argument that seems reasonable and obvious, field research can provide a useful reality check, allowing you to explore your idea or argument through interviews, observation, surveys, or correspondence.

- Sometimes you'll find that your line of argument can be strengthened by including primary sources in your document. Information from interviews, correspondence, or observation notes can bring a document to life, providing your readers with firsthand reports from people who know about or have been affected by an issue. Similarly, information from a survey can allow your readers to see trends and differences among groups that might not otherwise be clear.

Whether you rely primarily on field research or use it in combination with information from published sources, remember that field research methods can be powerful tools for exploring your issue and developing your position. As you conduct field research, keep in mind the strategies discussed in Chapter 6 for managing print and digital information. Using those strategies will help you save and organize the information you collect so that you can locate it quickly and easily.

10b

How can I use interviews to collect information?

Interviews — in which one person seeks information from another — can provide firsthand accounts of an event, authoritative interpretations of events and issues, and reactions to an event or issue from the people who have been affected by it. Most interviews follow a question-and-answer format, but some more closely resemble a free-flowing discussion. You can conduct interviews face to face, over the telephone, via email, and even through an instant messaging program.

Decide Whether to Conduct an Interview

Thinking carefully about the role an interview might play in your research project can help you decide whether and how to conduct it. Sometimes the decision to interview is a natural extension of the kind of work you're doing. For example, although Alexis Alvarez was able to find plenty of information from other sources about the pressures that would lead adolescent female athletes to use performance-enhancing drugs, she decided to interview friends and family members who had played competitive sports because she knew that firsthand reports would strengthen her argument. Sometimes interviews are conducted because an issue is so current that little authoritative information is available to a writer. Conducting an interview can provide needed information about the issue.

Sometimes the decision to conduct an interview isn't so much the result of careful planning as it is the recognition of an available opportunity. Pete Jacquez, who created a Web site about wind-generated electrical power, learned that one of his friends had recently signed up for a wind power program offered by his university. His interview produced a personal perspective about wind power that he wouldn't have been able to find through print or digital sources. Similarly, Nicholas Brothers had the opportunity to interview a professor who provided him with valuable insights about his issue, the growing use of private military corporations by the U.S. government.

> @ Read more about Nicholas Brothers and Pete Jacquez at bedfordresearcher.com. Click on Featured Writers.

Plan Your Interview

The most important things to consider as you plan your interview are whom to interview, what to ask, and how to conduct your interview.

Deciding Whom to Interview   Your decisions about whom to interview should be based on the kind of information you want for your research project.

- If you're trying to better understand a specific aspect of a conversation, interview an expert in the field such as a professor, government official, or member of the business community.
- If you want to learn what people in general think about an issue, interview a number of people who are affected by the issue in different ways.
- If you're hoping to collect quotations from people who are authorities on a subject, interview someone who will be recognized as knowledgeable by your readers.

Once you've decided what sorts of people you want to interview, you'll need to identify and contact interview candidates. If you're working on a research project for a class, ask your instructor and classmates for suggestions. Then ask whether they can introduce you to the people they suggest. Before you call to set up an interview, make some preparations.

1. Write a script to help you remember what to say.
2. Prepare a list of dates and times that work for you.
3. Estimate how much time you'll need to complete the interview.
4. Be ready to suggest a location for the interview.
5. Leave your phone number or email address so that your interview candidate can get in touch with you if a conflict arises.

> @ Find a list of Web sites about conducting interviews at bedfordresearcher .com. Click on Annotated Links.

Decide What You Should Ask   [FRAMING MY ARGUMENT]

Your interview questions should focus on the issue you want to address in your project. As you prepare your questions, keep the following principles in mind.

1. *Consider your research question, the role you are adopting, and the kind of information you want to collect.* Are you seeking background information,

or do you want someone's opinion? An answer to the question, "How did this situation come about?" will be quite different from an answer to the question, "What do you think about this situation?"

2. *Ask questions that require more than a yes or no answer.* You'll learn much more from an answer to a question such as, "What factors will affect your vote on referendum X?" than from an answer to, "Will you vote for referendum X?"

3. *Prepare a limited number of main questions and many follow-up questions.* Good interviews seldom involve more than eight to ten main questions, but experienced interviewers know that each question can lead to several follow-up questions, such as "Why do you think this has happened?" or "How did your coworkers react to the new policy?"

4. *Be flexible.* Be prepared to tailor your follow-up questions to the interviewee's responses.

Deciding How to Conduct Your Interview   You can conduct interviews face to face, over the telephone, and through a wide range of computer-based tools, such as email, chat, and video communication programs. Each method has advantages and disadvantages.

- **Face to Face** Interviews conducted in person or through a computer-based video tool such as Skype or Google Voice allow you to carry out a nearly normal conversation with the person you are interviewing. You can rely on your experiences in other conversations to determine whether the interview is effective, whether the person you are interviewing is comfortable, and whether he or she understands your questions. Most interviewees will answer your questions directly, and most will elaborate by giving examples, suggestions about related resources, and so on. If you can see the person you interview, pay close attention to nonverbal cues, such as facial expressions, body positions, and eye contact. Nonverbal cues can help you understand whether your questions are clear, welcome, or surprising, and can alert you to opportunities to ask useful follow-up questions.

- **Telephone** Interviews conducted over the phone also let you hold a fairly normal conversation, but it's important to ensure that you can carry out your side of the conversation in relative peace and without distractions. You won't have visual cues to help you connect with the person you are interviewing, so be sure to pay attention to pauses, tone of voice, and changes in speaking volume that might indicate surprise, discomfort, or confusion. As in face-to-face interviews, you'll receive fairly direct responses and elaboration to questions.

- **Written** Interviews conducted by email, chat, text messaging, or letter can be a good option if the person you'd like to interview is difficult to reach because of distance or a busy schedule. Written responses to interview questions are generally more precise than spoken responses. Written responses can be reviewed and revised by the person being interviewed to ensure that statements are clear and accurate, while spoken responses are usually more spontaneous.

Deciding Whether to Share Questions in Advance   Sharing questions in advance can have benefits and drawbacks. It can allow the person you'll interview to reflect on your questions and prepare a response. If you are interested in seeing candid reactions to a question, however, or if you worry that seeing the questions might make the interviewee reluctant to go through with the interview, don't share them. Ultimately, the decision about whether to share questions in advance depends on your purpose.

Deciding How to Record and Take Notes on Your Interview   Recording or saving a transcript of an interview, along with taking notes, provide you with a complete record of what was said, which helps you ensure the accuracy of quotations, paraphrases, and summaries.

- **Recordings** If you plan to record a face-to-face, telephone, or video-based interview, seek permission in advance or at the start of the interview. Remember that some people might be nervous about being recorded, and be prepared to explain how you'll use a recording. If you think someone might be nervous about being recorded, be sure that your initial questions will allow them to become comfortable about the interview process.

- **Transcripts** If you are conducting an interview via email (or even via a series of text messages), you'll have a written record of all the responses to your questions. Similarly, you can save a transcript from most chat sessions and even Google Voice conversations, either by saving a file from the chat program or copying and pasting the transcript into a word processing file. Transcripts can be used to create accurate quotations, and they make it relatively easy to review responses to your questions.

- **Taking Notes** You should always take notes during an interview. Recordings and transcripts can be lost through everything from running out of file space on a recorder to computer crashes. More important, taking notes allows you to record your reactions to new information and ideas, to save your thoughts about how you might use all or part of an interview in your document, and to identify important parts of the interview for later review.

Conduct Your Interview

Consult the following checklist before you conduct your interview.

CHECKLIST FOR CONDUCTING INTERVIEWS

☑ **Arrive early and review your questions.** If you are conducting your interview over the phone or a computer, set time aside before the interview to review your questions and then contact the person you are interviewing at the agreed-upon time.

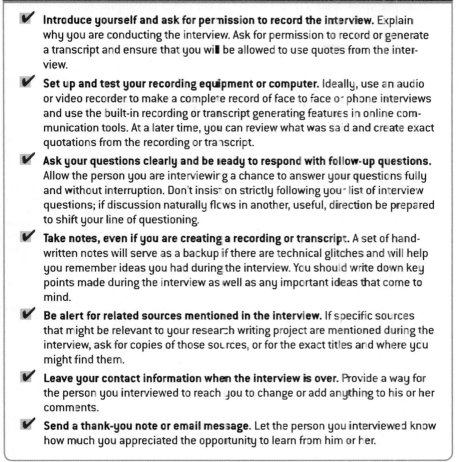

CHECKLIST FOR CONDUCTING INTERVIEWS (continued)

✔ **Introduce yourself and ask for permission to record the interview.** Explain why you are conducting the interview. Ask for permission to record or generate a transcript and ensure that you will be allowed to use quotes from the interview.

✔ **Set up and test your recording equipment or computer.** Ideally, use an audio or video recorder to make a complete record of face to face or phone interviews and use the built-in recording or transcript generating features in online communication tools. At a later time, you can review what was said and create exact quotations from the recording or transcript.

✔ **Ask your questions clearly and be ready to respond with follow-up questions.** Allow the person you are interviewing a chance to answer your questions fully and without interruption. Don't insist on strictly following your list of interview questions; if discussion naturally flows in another, useful, direction be prepared to shift your line of questioning.

✔ **Take notes, even if you are creating a recording or transcript.** A set of handwritten notes will serve as a backup if there are technical glitches and will help you remember ideas you had during the interview. You should write down key points made during the interview as well as any important ideas that come to mind.

✔ **Be alert for related sources mentioned in the interview.** If specific sources that might be relevant to your research writing project are mentioned during the interview, ask for copies of those sources, or for the exact titles and where you might find them.

✔ **Leave your contact information when the interview is over.** Provide a way for the person you interviewed to reach you to change or add anything to his or her comments.

✔ **Send a thank-you note or email message.** Let the person you interviewed know how much you appreciated the opportunity to learn from him or her.

III Collecting Information

Analyze Your Results

Treat your interview recording or transcript as you would any other source. Read it, listen to it, or view it critically.

- Look for new information, ideas, and arguments.
- Look for statements that confirm or contradict information from your other sources.
- Look for inconsistencies and contradictions within the interview as a whole.
- Ask whether the information, ideas, and arguments are relevant and credible.
- Ask whether you consider the person you interviewed as qualified as you'd expected when you planned the interview.
- Look for statements that might be useful in providing context about the issue.

Nicholas Brothers's notes on his interview with Dr. Jonathan Euchner, assistant professor of political science at Missouri Western State University

Privatization movement began in 1978

- not just military: airline industry too
- privatization gained momentum over Reagan, Bush-41, and Clinton administrations

Use for section on history of PMCs

PMC contractors mean less bureaucracy and fewer regulations; this is attractive to U.S. military leadership

Said "accountability is key" when it comes to abuses by contractors

This accountability seems intangible— discuss the continuity issue and the difficulty of terminating contracts with PMCs

Thinks the burden of war in Iraq and Afghanistan has been pushed to relatively few military families

- "The wars are almost an abstraction."
- wars have been paid for with borrowed money
- doesn't think citizens will pay attention to PMCs unless there is a tragic catalyst (like contractors directly responsible for American deaths)

Good quote to use in conclusion

Stop Outsourcing Security Act

- Missouri's junior senator Claire McCaskill could be a key ally for this bill

Look up who else supports this Act and whether it has gone through Congress

FIGURE 10.1 Annotated Transcript of Nicholas Brothers's Interview with Jonathan Euchner

- Look for statements that might help your readers better understand the issue or that would help them view the issue in a particular way.

Then ask whether you can use the information, ideas, and arguments from the interview in your project document. If not, ask whether it is useful for helping you understand the issue more fully or raises questions that you could investigate in other ways.

10c

How can I use observation to collect information?

Like interviewing, observing a setting can provide you with valuable information you would not be able to find in other sources. Although some observations
can involve a significant amount of time and effort, an observation need not be
complicated to be useful.

Decide Whether to Conduct an Observation

The most important decision you'll make regarding an observation is whether
to conduct it in the first place. Some topics are more suited to observation than
others. For example, before writing his multimodal essay on the resurgence of
metal music, Chris Norris observed musicians and fans at two concerts. Observing gave Chris insights about the relationship among metal musicians and their
fans and the contexts in which the concerts took place that he couldn't have
gained simply by reading about metal music or interviewing musicians and fans.

Plan Your Observation

As you plan your observation, determine the following.

What You Should Observe and How Often You Should Observe It   If, for example, you've decided to observe children in a day-care center, you'll quickly
learn that there are not only many day-care providers in your community but
also several different kinds of providers. Clearly, observing a large day-care center won't tell you much about what happens in a small center operated out of a
home. In addition, there's no guarantee that what you'll see in one day-care center on any given day will be typical. Should you conduct multiple observations?
Should you observe multiple types of day-care providers?

The answers to these questions will depend largely on what role the information you collect during your observations will play in your research writing
project. If you want to learn more about the topic but don't plan to use anything
you observe as a source of evidence in your project, then you might want to
conduct a fairly limited observation. If you decide to use evidence from your
observations throughout your project, then you will need to conduct multiple
observations, possibly in more than one setting. In this case, as you prepare for
each observation, review your notes from previous sessions so that you can focus
on the most important aspects of what you've observed so far.

What to Look For   The biggest limitation of observation is that you can see only
one thing at a time. Experienced observers focus their observations on activities
that are most relevant to their research projects. As a result, their observations are
somewhat selective. Spreading yourself too thin will result in fairly "thin" results.

Then again, narrowing in too quickly can mean that you miss important aspects of the setting. Your reasons for conducting an observation and what you hope to gain from it are probably your best guide to what to focus on.

Whether You Need Permission to Observe   Seeking permission to observe someone can be complicated. People have expectations about privacy, but people can (and often do) change their behavior when they know they are being observed. As you consider whether to ask for permission, imagine yourself in the position of someone who is being observed. If you are still uncertain, ask your instructor for advice.

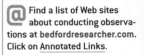 Find a list of Web sites about conducting observations at bedfordresearcher.com. Click on Annotated Links.

If you decide to seek permission to conduct your observations, consider how best to approach the person you'll ask for permission. If you decide to send a letter or an email message, be sure to include a clear description of your research writing project and explanations of why you believe observation will enhance your work on the project, how the observations will be used in your project, and how you will ensure the privacy of the individuals, groups, or organization you observe. If you decide to contact the person by telephone, jot down some notes before you call.

In some cases, you might find it useful to use a permission form (see Figure 10.2).

Current School / Program Information

Name _____

Address _____

City _____ State _____

Zip Code _____

Phone _____

Email _____

I, the undersigned, hereby authorize [*observer name*] to observe [*the setting*] for the purposes of completing work on [*name of the research writing project*]. I understand that I may revoke this authorization, in writing, at any time.

Signature: _____

Date: _____

FIGURE 10.2 Sample Permission Form for Observation Sessions

Conduct Your Observation

You'll find a number of similarities between collecting information in an interview and collecting information during an observation. The checklist that follows will help you conduct your observation.

CHECKLIST FOR CONDUCTING OBSERVATIONS

✔ **Arrive early.** Give yourself time to get prepared.

✔ **Review your planning notes.** Remind yourself what you're looking for and how you will record your observations.

✔ **Introduce yourself.** If you have asked for permission to observe a setting (such as a class or a day-care center), introduce yourself before you begin your observation. Use your introduction as an opportunity to obtain signatures or consent forms if you need them.

✔ **Set up your recording equipment.** You'll certainly want to make sure you've got a notepad and pens or pencils. You might also have an audio or a video recorder, a laptop computer, or a smartphone or tablet. Test whatever you've brought with you to make sure it's working properly.

✔ **Take notes.** As with interviews, take notes during your observation even if you're using an audio or a video recorder. Noting your impressions and ideas while conducting an observation can help you keep track of critical events. In addition, if your recorder doesn't work as expected, a set of notes can mean the difference between salvaging something from the observation and having to do it all over again. If you find yourself in a situation where you can't take notes — such as at a swimming lesson, when you're taking part in the lesson — try to write down your thoughts about what you've observed immediately after the session.

✔ **Leave contact information and send thank-you notes.** If you have asked someone for permission to observe the setting, give the person a way to contact you, and send a thank-you note after you have completed the observation.

Analyze Your Results

Treat your observation notes or recording as you would any other source. Ask whether you observed the setting thoroughly enough to feel confident about moving forward with an analysis. If so, do the following.

- Identify key features and patterns of behavior.
- Identify key individuals and describe their actions.
- Look for unusual and surprising patterns and actions.
- Ask what you've learned about the issue through observation.
- Look for patterns and actions that might be useful in providing context about the issue.
- Look for patterns and actions that, if described, might help your readers better understand the issue or lead them to view the issue in a particular way.

Then ask whether you are confident enough about the results of your analysis to use what you've learned in your project document. If not, ask whether it is useful for helping you understand the issue more fully or raises questions that you could investigate in other ways.

10d

How can I use surveys to collect information?

Surveys allow you to collect information about beliefs, attitudes, and behaviors from a group of people. Typically, surveys help you answer *what* or *who* questions — such as "Who will you vote for in the next election?" Surveys are less useful in obtaining the answers to *why* questions. In an interview, for instance, you can ask, "Why did you vote the way you did in the last election?" and expect to get a reasonably well-thought-out answer. In a survey, however, people often neglect to write lengthy, careful responses. If you conduct a survey, remember to include a copy of your survey questions in an appendix to your project document.

Decide Whether to Conduct a Survey

Your decision about whether to conduct a survey should be based on the role it will play in your research project, the amount of work required to do a good job, and the kind of information you are seeking. In many cases, you'll find that other field research methods are more appropriate than surveys. Surveys are useful if you want to collect information about the attitudes and behaviors of a large group of people (more than five or ten). If you simply want opinions from a handful of people, you can gain that information more efficiently by interviewing or corresponding with them.

Plan Your Survey

As you plan your survey, determine the following.

Whom to Survey   You must decide whom and how many people to survey. For instance, if you're interested in what students in a specific class think about an issue, survey all of them. Even if the class is fairly large (say, one hundred students), you probably won't have too much trouble tabulating the results of a brief survey. Keep in mind, however, that most surveys aren't given to everyone in a group. National polls, for instance, seldom survey more than one thousand people, yet they are used to assess the opinions of everyone in the country. So how will you select your representative sample? One way is to choose people from the group at random. You could open your

> @ Find a list of Web sites about conducting surveys at bedfordresearcher.com. Click on Annotated Links.

school's directory and then pick, say, every twentieth name. Another option is to stratify your sample. For example, you could randomly select a specific number of first-year, second-year, third-year, and fourth-year students—and you could make sure that the number of men and women in each group is proportional to their enrollment at the school.

What to Ask and How to Ask It with Integrity Designing effective surveys can be challenging. Understanding the strengths and weaknesses of the kinds of questions that are frequently asked on surveys is a good way to get started. Figure 10.3 illustrates the main types of questions found on surveys. As you consider the types of questions you'll use, keep in mind the importance of asking questions that do not cue the people taking your survey to respond in a particular way. Consider, for example, how you might respond to the following questions.

Do you support increasing income tax rates to reduce the federal debt?

Do you support increasing income tax rates to ensure that future generations are not crushed under the burden of a spiraling federal debt?

Do you support increasing income tax rates to enable the federal government to continue its irresponsible and uncontrolled spending on entitlements?

Whether You Are Asking Your Questions Clearly Test your survey items before administering your survey by asking your classmates or family members to read your questions. A question that seems perfectly clear to you might confuse someone else. Rewrite the questions that confuse your "testers" and then test them again. Doing so will help you improve the clarity of your survey. Consider the evolution of the following question.

Original Question:

What can be done about voter turnout among younger voters?

Does "about voter turnout" mean increasing voter turnout, decreasing voter turnout, or encouraging younger voters to be better informed about candidates? Does the phrase "younger voters" mean 18-year-olds or 30-year-olds?

Revised Question:

In your opinion, what can be done to increase turnout among 18- to 24-year-old voters?

How to Distribute Your Survey Surveys are typically distributed via electronic mail, Web pages, or social networking sites, although a number of research writers still conduct paper-based surveys. The advantages of online surveys include the ease of distributing the survey to potential respondents, the growing number of tools that you can use to create surveys (such as SurveyGizmo, SurveyMonkey, Zoomerang, and Quibblo), and the ease of tabulating results with tools that break down responses and create charts from survey data. The disadvantages include the likelihood that the response rates to online surveys will be relatively low (compared to the total number of people who will learn about a survey) and that those who respond will do so because of a specific interest in the issue. In other words, you might find that most of your respondents have some sort of

III Collecting Information

Election Survey

Thank you for completing this survey.

A 1. Did you vote in the last presidential election?   ☐ yes   ☐ no

   2. I vote:

In every election	In most elections	In about half of the elections	Rarely	Never
☐	☐	☐	☐	☐

B 3. I have voted in the following types of elections (check all that apply):
   ☐ Regular local elections
   ☐ Special local elections
   ☐ Regular statewide elections
   ☐ National elections

C 4. Voting is a civic duty: ☐ true   ☐ false

D 5. All eligible voters should participate in local, state, and national elections:

Strongly Agree	Agree	Not Sure	Disagree	Strongly Disagree
☐	☐	☐	☐	☐

   6. Please rate the following reasons for voting on a 1-to-5 scale, in which 5 indicates very important and 1 indicates not at all important:

	1	2	3	4	5
To be a good citizen	☐	☐	☐	☐	☐
To have a say in how government affects my life	☐	☐	☐	☐	☐
To support a particular cause	☐	☐	☐	☐	☐
To vote against particular candidates	☐	☐	☐	☐	☐

E 7. Please rank the following types of elections from most important (4) to least important (1):
   _____ Presidential elections
   _____ Statewide elections
   _____ Local (city and county) elections
   _____ Student government elections

F 8. Please tell us what influenced your decision to vote or not vote in the last election.

FIGURE 10.3 Sample Survey

A Yes/no items divide respondents into two groups.

B Multiple-choice items indicate whether a respondent knows something or engages in specific behaviors. Because they seldom include every possible answer, be careful when including them.

C True/false items more often deal with attitudes or beliefs than with behaviors or events.

D Likert scales measure respondents' level of agreement with a statement, their assessment of something's importance, or how frequently they engage in a behavior.

E Ranking forces respondents to place items along a continuum.

F Short-answer items allow greater freedom of response, but can be difficult to tabulate.

TUTORIAL

How do I write a good survey question?

Developing a good survey question is challenging. The process is similar to writing an essay. The first drafts of survey questions serve to express your thoughts. Subsequent revisions help clarify questions for survey respondents. Keep your purpose in mind to be sure your question will elicit the information you need.

In this example, Chris Norris devised a survey question to find out how fellow students view heavy metal music.

1 Write a first draft of the question:

Do you listen to heavy metal music and why or why not?

2 Simplify the question:

Why do you listen—or not listen—to heavy metal music?

3 Consider alternative ways of asking a question — including whether it should be a question:

What are your reasons for listening—or not listening—to music by heavy metal bands like Slayer and Pantera?

4 Identify and then clarify key words and phrases:

List five words to describe music by heavy metal bands like Slayer and Pantera.

5 Ask for feedback from potential respondents. Review and clarify key words and phrases. Consider potential reactions to phrasing:

Please describe your reaction when you hear a song by heavy metal bands like Slayer or Pantera.

III Collecting Information

Review another example and work on refining survey questions at
bedfordresearcher.com. Click on Interactive Exercises.

interest or bias that leads them to want to respond and as a result might not form a representative sample of the group you hope to understand.

Paper-based surveys are most useful in situations where you can pass them out to a group, such as students in a class or people attending a meeting. If you are confident that the people in the class or at the meeting are likely to be representative of the group you are seeking to understand, then this can be a useful technique.

Asking people to respond to a survey over the phone tends to result in a low response rate and might be prohibited by local and state laws regarding telephone solicitations. In general, because of the low response rate to telephone surveys, it is seldom a productive tool for collecting survey responses.

Conduct Your Survey

The sheer number of surveys people are asked to complete these days has reduced the public's willingness to respond to them. In fact, a "good" response rate for a survey is 60 percent, and many professional pollsters find lower response rates acceptable.

Analyze Your Results

Once you've collected your surveys, you must tabulate your responses. It's usually best to tabulate survey responses using a spreadsheet program, which provides flexibility when you want to analyze your results. You can also organize the results in a table in a word processing program. Once you've tabulated the responses, spend time analyzing the results. You should look for trends in your data. For example, ask whether groups respond differently to particular questions, or whether age or experience seems to predict responses. Look as well for surprising results, such as unexpectedly high levels of agreement or disagreement with Likert-scale items or striking differences in the responses to short-answer questions.

As you conduct your analysis, keep in mind the need to ensure confidentiality for your respondents. Survey respondents usually do not expect their names to be revealed in reports about a survey or to find personally identifiable information in reports. As you review your responses, be on the lookout for information that might help someone identify a particular respondent. A respondent might reveal, for example, that she is the only Iraq War veteran in a particular writing class. If you find this kind of information, do not include it in your report.

CHECKLIST FOR CONDUCTING SURVEYS

☑ **Keep it short.** Surveys are most effective when they are brief. Don't exceed one page.

☑ **Format and distribute your survey appropriately.** If your survey is on paper, make sure the text is readable, there is plenty of room to write, and the page

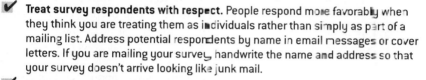

CHECKLIST FOR CONDUCTING INTERVIEWS (continued)

isn't crowded with questions. If you are distributing your survey through email, you can either insert the survey questions into the body of your email message or attach the survey as a word processing file. If you are distributing your survey on the Web, use the formatting tools in your Web survey tool to test out various layouts for your survey questions.

✔ **Explain the purpose of your survey.** Explaining who you are and how you will use the results of the survey in your research writing project can help increase a respondent's willingness to complete and return your survey.

✔ **Treat survey respondents with respect.** People respond more favorably when they think you are treating them as individuals rather than simply as part of a mailing list. Address potential respondents by name in email messages or cover letters. If you are mailing your survey, handwrite the name and address so that your survey doesn't arrive looking like junk mail.

✔ **Make it easy to return the survey.** If you are conducting your survey on the Web or via email, be sure to provide directions for submitting or returning completed surveys. If you are distributing the survey to students in classes, provide a large envelope with your name and contact information into which the surveys can be placed.

10e

How can I use correspondence to collect information?

Correspondence includes any textual communication, such as letters, faxes, and email. Correspondence can also take place through the communication tools available on social networking sites such as Facebook.

Although many research writers benefit from corresponding with experts, correspondence need not be sent only to experts. If you are writing an article about the effects of recent flooding in the Midwest, you could correspond with relatives, friends, or even strangers to ask them about their experiences with the floods. You can use their responses to illustrate the impact of the flood on average folks. You can also correspond with staff at government agencies, corporations, and organizations. Many of these institutions hire public relations personnel to respond to inquiries from the public.

Courtesy is essential when corresponding. Introduce yourself and explain the goals of your research writing project. Make sure that you are clear and ask specific questions. Thank your reader and indicate that you look forward to hearing from him or her. If you decide to send a letter via regular mail, include a self-addressed, stamped envelope to increase your chances of getting a response.

10f

How can I use public events and broadcast media to collect information?

Public events, such as lectures, conferences, and public meetings and hearings, often provide research writers with useful information. As with observations, you can record many public events by taking notes or bringing an audio or a video recorder. Be aware, however, that it is unethical to record events that specifically ask that you not do so. If you are asked not to record an event, find out whether a transcript, podcast, or video recording of the event will be available.

Radio and television are sources of information that research writers frequently overlook. News and information programs on television, such as *Nightline* and *60 Minutes*, might provide useful information about the conversation you plan to join. You may want to record the programs in order to examine them in detail. In addition, check the Web for radio programs and transcripts. National Public Radio's news information program *All Things Considered*, for instance, has audio archives going back to January 1996 that you can listen to on the Web (visit npr.org and search the program's archives). You can also record local public events that are broadcast on public access cable channels or streamed over the Web.

My Research Project

ASSESS THE RELEVANCE OF FIELD RESEARCH METHODS

Think about whether the field research methods discussed in this chapter might contribute to your research project. If you decide to use observations, interviews, surveys, correspondence, or other forms of field research, seek advice from researchers who have used these methods, or from your instructor or a librarian. Ask questions such as the following.

- How would field research methods help me accomplish my purpose for this project?
- How will my readers react to my use of evidence from field research methods?
- Is evidence from field research typically used in the type of document I plan to write?

In your research log, write down the responses you receive to these and related questions. Then decide whether using field research is a good choice for your project.

You can print or download this activity at **bedfordresearcher.com**.

> **QUICK REFERENCE**

Searching for Information with Field Research Methods

☑ Consider reasons for using field research. (p. 182)

☑ Plan and conduct interviews. (p. 184)

☑ Plan and conduct observations. (p. 191)

☑ Design, conduct, and analyze a survey. (p. 192)

☑ Use correspondence to collect information. (p. 197)

☑ Attend public events and view broadcast media to gather information about your issue. (p. 198)

III Collecting Information

The Bedford Researcher

I	Joining the Conversation
II	Working with Sources
III	Collecting Information
IV	**Writing Your Document**
V	Documenting Sources

PART IV

Writing Your Document

After you have collected information, you'll have a better understanding of the scope of your issue. In the chapters that follow, you'll learn how to use your new knowledge to create a well-written, well-designed document.

11

Developing Your Thesis Statement

Key Questions

As you shift your attention away from collecting and working with sources and toward crafting your own contribution to the conversation about your issue, you'll begin the process of planning your argument. That process begins with choosing your main point and drafting your thesis statement.

11a

How can I use my sources and position statement?

As you have collected, skimmed, critically read, and evaluated sources, you've almost certainly developed—and perhaps written, reviewed, and revised—a statement defining your position on your issue (p. 23). Your position statement served as your initial response to your research question (p. 40). As such, it helped you focus your search, critically read and evaluate your sources, and take effective notes. Now, it will serve as the foundation for your thesis statement, a formal statement of the main point you want to make about your issue in your document.

Your thesis statement provides a clear, focused expression of the main point you want to make. It is, in a nutshell, the most important idea or argument you want to convey to your readers. Your choice of a thesis statement will be influenced by what you've learned about your issue and by your writing situation. Before you try to draft your thesis statement, review your current position statement, review your notes, and consider your writing situation.

Review Your Position Statement

As you begin the process of deciding what you want to convey to your readers, reflect on your position on your issue. If you have already drafted a position statement, you can turn to it and ask whether it still represents the most important thing you want to say about your issue. If you haven't drafted a position statement, do so now. You can use brainstorming, looping, and other idea generation strategies to help formulate your position statement (p. 18).

Review Your Notes

With your position statement in mind, quickly review your notes. As you review your notes:

- identify important information, ideas, and arguments that you've come across in your reading
- consider whether the information, ideas, and arguments you've identified in your notes will allow you to pursue your personal, academic, and professional interests
- review and elaborate on ideas and arguments that you've come up with as a result of your own thinking about the subject
- consider how your own ideas and arguments might allow you to pursue your interests

As you carry out your review, reflect on your position statement. Ask how well it conveys the information, ideas, and arguments you would most like to address in your document. If you find that it does not fully capture your understanding of the issue—that is, if it doesn't seem to reflect the main point you want to make about your issue—revise your position statement.

Consider Your Purpose and Role

Reviewing your notes will help you deepen your understanding of your issue. That understanding, in turn, is likely to affect how you view your purpose and role as a writer and, by extension, the main point you want to make in your document. Use the following questions to guide how you think about your thesis statement.

- Have your purposes—the reasons you are working on this research writing project—changed since you started? If so, how do you view your purpose now?

- Has your role as a writer—for example, to inform or to solve a problem—changed since you started your research writing project? If so, how do you view your role now?

If your answers to any of these questions suggest that the main point you want to make has changed, revise your position statement.

Reflect on Your Readers

In the same way that you considered your purpose and role, ask whether focusing on a particular main point will help you address your readers' purposes, needs, interests, and backgrounds. If you find that your main point is not well aligned with your readers' concerns, revise your position statement.

11b

How can I draft my thesis statement?

To draft your thesis statement, consider what you learned through your reflections on your position statement, notes, and writing situation. Your work on your thesis statement will be affected by the type of document you plan to write and the information, ideas, and arguments you've encountered in your reading.

Identify Important Information, Ideas, and Arguments Associated with Your Position

Begin developing your thesis statement by identifying important information, ideas, and arguments related to your position on your issue. Examine your initial brainstorming or freewriting about your topic and issue. Review your research question and position statement for key words and phrases. Look through your notes to see how your sources consider questions related to your position. As you review your materials, identify important key words and phrases. You can use these words and phrases as you draft your thesis statement. Consider the following example, which shows how a writer identified key words and phrases in her research question and notes.

> **Research Question about Social Networking and Privacy:**
>
> *Is social networking more vulnerable to invasions of privacy than other forms of communication?*
>
> *Cardenas, Social Networking*
>
> *Teenagers often underestimate the dangers of revealing personal information online (p. 131).*
>
> *Preserving privacy is often at odds with joining social networking Web sites (p. 132).*

> *Individuals need to take responsibility for preserving sensitive, private information* (p. 132).
>
> *Even experienced Web users reveal personal, sensitive information by mistake* (p. 133)

Review the words and phrases you've identified as important and keep them in mind as you begin to draft alternative thesis statements.

Draft Alternatives

An effective thesis statement can invite your readers to learn something new, suggest that they change their attitudes or beliefs, or argue that they should take action of some kind. Consider how the following thesis statements reflect these three ways of explaining a position.

Position Statement:

Preserving privacy on social networking Web sites is an individual responsibility.

Thesis Statement: Asking Readers to Learn Something New

Social networking Web sites don't reveal personal information; people reveal personal information.

Thesis Statement: Asking Readers to Change Their Attitudes or Beliefs

We should view the use of social networking sites in educational settings with a great deal of caution.

Thesis Statement: Asking Readers to Take Action

People who use social networking Web sites should learn how to safeguard sensitive, personal information.

Experiment with different approaches to determine which one works best for your writing situation. The thesis statement you choose should convey your position in a way that addresses your purpose and your readers' needs, interests, values, beliefs, and knowledge of a subject.

Consider the Type of Document You Plan to Write

An effective thesis statement will reflect the type of document—or genre—you plan to write. Depending on the type of document, your readers will have different expectations about how you present your thesis statement. Readers of an academic essay are likely to expect a calm, clearly written statement of what you want them to learn, believe, or do. Readers of an informative newspaper article will expect you to identify, in a balanced and seemingly unbiased manner, what you want them to learn. Readers of an opinion column will expect you to be more assertive, and perhaps even more entertaining, about your position on an issue. Consider how the following thesis statements, all addressing problems with the recruitment of athletes at a college or university, reflect the type of document the writer plans to draft.

Argumentative Academic Essay:

The University should ensure that its recruiting practices are fully in compliance with NCAA regulations.

Informative Newspaper Article:

The University is taking steps to bring its recruiting practices in line with NCAA regulations.

Opinion Column:

The University's coaches need to get their act together before the NCAA slaps them with sanctions.

Focus Your Thesis Statement

A broad thesis statement does not encourage your readers to learn anything new, change their attitudes or beliefs, or take action. The following thesis statement is too broad.

Broad Thesis Statement:

Educating users of social networking sites about their dangers would be a good idea.

There's no conversation to be had about this topic because few people would argue with such a statement. A more focused thesis statement would define what should be done and who should do it.

Focused Thesis Statement:

The publishers of social networking Web sites should design their communication tools and Web page templates to highlight the dangers of publishing sensitive, personal information online.

To focus your thesis statement, ask what your readers would want to know about your subject, what attitudes should be changed, or what action should be taken. Consider their likely responses to your thesis statement and attempt to head off potential counterarguments or questions.

Table 11.1 presents the featured writers' movements from research question to position statement to thesis statement. Note how each thesis statement answers its research question and directs readers' attention to one aspect of the conversation, encourages them to change their attitudes or beliefs or urges them to take action of some kind.

> @ Read about the student writers discussed in this chapter at bedfordresearcher.com. Click on Featured Writers.

My Research Project

DEVELOP AND REFINE YOUR THESIS STATEMENT

In your research log, complete the following activity to draft your thesis statement.

1. My research question is:

2. My position statement is:

FEATURED WRITER	RESEARCH QUESTION	POSITION STATEMENT	THESIS STATEMENT
Alexis Alvarez	What are the effects of competitive soccer on adolescent girls?	Steroid use by adolescent girls involved in competitive sports should be addressed by educating athletes, parents, and coaches about health consequences and emphasizing fair play.	Although competitive sports can provide young female athletes with many benefits, they can also have negative effects, the worst of which is increasing drug use.
Nicholas Brothers	What dangers are associated with U.S. reliance on private military corporations in its war on terror?	The overreliance of the United States on private military corporations is a danger to national and international security.	By relying heavily on private military corporations to carry out military operations, the U.S. Department of Defense is undermining its own counterinsurgency efforts in Iraq and Afghanistan.
Pete Jacquez	What strategies, if any, should Coloradoans use to encourage local, state, and federal governments to increase U.S. use of wind-generated electrical power?	Coloradoans should encourage local, state, and federal governments to increase reliance on wind-generated electrical power through a mix of tax incentives and reduced regulation.	Coloradoans should lead a national movement toward increased use of wind power.
Elizabeth Leontiev	How can we reduce the economic impact of the war on drugs on South American coca farmers?	The U.S. and South American governments should adopt the "zero cocaine, not zero coca" policy.	The "zero cocaine, not zero coca" policy will boost the Bolivian economy, allow native Andeans to maintain their cultural practices, and reduce cocaine trafficking into the United States.
Chris Norris	What accounts for the resurgence in popularity of metal music?	Metal music has a political message, musical diversity, and a strong fan base.	With its political consciousness, diversity of musical subgenres, and thriving fan community, metal music today is undergoing a rebirth.
Cori Schmidtbauer	How does Portia's character in The Merchant of Venice fit in with Elizabethan ideas of women?	Portia appears to rebel against the expectations of Elizabethan culture.	By gaining the upper hand in traditionally male-dominated systems of exchange (notably marriage) and cross-dressing as a male lawyer to defend Antonio in court, Portia assaults the idea of the weak Renaissance woman from every angle. However, a fresh look at Portia — in a strange way — may have reflected Renaissance culture just as much as she contradicted it

3. My purpose for writing is:

4. My role is:

5. I want my thesis statement to reflect the following needs, interests, values, and beliefs of my readers:

6. I want my readers to do one or more of the following:
   - learn about . . .
   - change their attitudes or beliefs about . . .
   - take the following action:

7. I plan to write the following type of document:

8. The most important words and phrases in my research question are:

9. The most important words and phrases in my position statement are:

10. Building on my research question and position statement, my thesis statement is:

11. My readers are likely to respond to this thesis statement by asking the following questions or raising the following objections:

12. I can focus my thesis statement by rephrasing it:

You can print or download this activity at **bedfordresearcher.com.** Click on Activities.

> **QUICK REFERENCE**

Developing Your Thesis Statement

 Review and reflect on your research question, position statement, notes, and writing situation. (p. 203)

Draft your thesis statement. (p. 205)

IV Writing Your Document

12

Developing Your Argument

Key Questions

12a. How can I support my thesis statement?   210
Choose reasons
Select evidence to support your reasons
Decide how to appeal to your readers

12b. How can I assess the integrity of my argument?   215
Check for fallacies based on distraction
Look for fallacies based on questionable assumptions
Search for fallacies based on misrepresentation
Locate fallacies based on careless reasoning

Once you've determined your position on an issue and expressed it as a thesis statement, you've laid the foundation for developing your contribution to the conversation you've decided to join. Developing your argument involves identifying reasons to accept your thesis statement, selecting evidence to support your reasoning, and deciding how you'll appeal to your readers. To improve the overall effectiveness of your argument, you should also assess the integrity of your reasoning and evidence.

12a

How can I support my thesis statement?

Developing an effective argument involves far more than knowing what you want others to understand or believe or how you want them to act. It requires the development of a strategy to support your thesis statement. That strategy should reflect not only your purpose and role, but also your readers' needs, interests, values, beliefs, and knowledge of an issue. It should also take into account the conventions typically used in the type of document you plan to write.

Step 1: Choose Reasons

In longer documents, such as essays, reports, and Web sites, writers usually present several reasons to support their thesis statement. The kinds of reasons writers choose will vary according to the type of document they are writing. In informative articles in newspapers and magazines, for example, writers are likely to focus on the three or four most important aspects of the issue they want readers to understand. In blog posts that analyze an issue, in contrast, writers are likely to choose reasons that help readers understand the results of the analysis. In an argumentative essay, writers usually offer a series of claims that will lead readers to accept the argument they are advancing.

To choose the reasons you'll offer to support your thesis statement, generate ideas by brainstorming, freewriting, looping, or clustering. As you generate ideas, consider the following guidelines.

- Readers of reflective documents, such as some blog posts and academic essays, will expect you to focus on a particular subject. If you are writing a reflective document, ask which of your observations about a subject are most significant and what kind of impression you want to create for your readers.

- Readers of informative documents, such as reports, essays, and articles, expect you to help them understand something about an issue. As you plan an informative document, ask what you want to convey to your readers and what they are most likely to want to know about it.

- Readers of analytical documents, such as some articles in newspapers like the *New York Times* and the *Wall Street Journal*, expect a straightforward and logical presentation of the analysis. To meet readers' expectations about this kind of document, reflect on what your readers are likely to know about the issue, the kinds of questions they might have about it, and the overall conclusion you hope to share with them.

- Readers of evaluative documents, such as movie and media reviews and progress reports, expect you to provide a reasonable judgment based on a fairly selected set of criteria. As you choose reasons to accept your evaluation, ask what readers will want to gain from reading your document and what you want them to understand about the results of your evaluation.

- Readers of argumentative documents, such as argumentative essays, opinion columns, and blog posts, will expect you to provide a set of reasons for accepting your argument. As you choose your reasons, consider what your readers will know about the issue, how they are likely to respond to your overall argument, and the likely counterarguments they might propose.

Step 2: Select Evidence to Support Your Reasons

For every reason you offer to support your thesis statement, you'll need evidence—such as details, facts, personal observations, and expert opinions—to back up your assertions and help your readers understand your ideas.

You can draw evidence from your sources in the form of quotations, paraphrases, summaries, numerical data, and visual images. You can also gather evidence firsthand by conducting interviews, observations, and surveys, or by reflecting on your personal experience.

As you select supporting evidence, consider the type of document—or genre—you plan to write. The type of evidence used in various genres can differ in important ways. Articles in magazines, newspapers, and Web sites, for example, are more likely to rely on interviews, observations, and illustrations as primary sources of evidence than are academic essays, whose writers tend to draw information from published sources found in a library or database. Multimodal essays, in contrast, are likely to use not only textual information and images, but also audio, video, and animation.

My Research Project

SELECT EVIDENCE TO SUPPORT YOUR REASONS

Use the following prompts to help identify evidence to support your thesis statement.

1. List the reasons you are offering to support your thesis statement.

2. Identify relevant evidence, and then list the evidence below each reason. You might need to review your sources to locate additional evidence, or even obtain additional sources.

3. Determine whether you are relying too heavily on information from a single source.

4. Determine whether you are relying too heavily on one type of evidence.

5. Determine whether you've chosen evidence that is consistent with the type of document you plan to write.

You can download or print this activity at **bedfordresearcher.com**.

Step 3: Decide How to Appeal to Your Readers

For thousands of years, writers have appealed to readers to accept their ideas as reasonable and valid. Much of the work of ancient Greek and Roman thinkers such as Aristotle and Cicero revolved around strategies for presenting an argument to an audience. Their work continues to serve as a foundation for how we think about conveying information, ideas, and arguments to readers. In particular, the concept of an *appeal* to an audience plays a central role in thinking about how to develop an argument. Essentially, when you ask someone to accept your argument, you are appealing to them—you are asking them to consider what you have to say and, if they accept it as appropriate and valid, to believe or act in a certain way.

You can persuade your readers to accept your argument by appealing to authority, emotion, principles, values, beliefs, character, and logic.

Appeals to Authority   When you make an appeal to authority, you ask a reader to accept a reason because someone in a position of authority supports it. The evidence used to support this kind of appeal typically takes the form of quotations, paraphrases, or summaries of the ideas of experts on an issue, of political leaders, or of people who have been affected by an issue. As you consider potential reasons for accepting a reason, reflect on the notes you've taken on your sources. Ask whether you've identified experts, leaders, or people who have been affected by an issue, and then ask whether you can use them to convince your readers that your reason has merit.

Appeals to Emotion   Appeals to emotion attempt to elicit an emotional response to an issue. The famous "win one for the Gipper" speech delivered by Pat O'Brien, who was playing the part of Notre Dame coach Knute Rockne in the 1940 film *Knute Rockne: All American,* is an example of an appeal to emotion. At halftime during a game with Army, with Notre Dame trailing, he said:

> Well, boys . . . I haven't a thing to say. Played a great game . . . all of you. Great game. I guess we just can't expect to win 'em all.
>
> I'm going to tell you something I've kept to myself for years. None of you ever knew George Gipp. It was long before your time. But you know what a tradition he is at Notre Dame. . . . And the last thing he said to me—"Rock," he said, 'sometime, when the team is up against it—and the breaks are beating the boys—tell them to go out there with all they got and win just one for the Gipper . . . I don't know where I'll be then, Rock," he said, "but I'll know about it—and I'll be happy."

Using emotional appeals to frame an argument—that is, to help readers view an issue in a particular way—is a tried and true strategy. But use it carefully, if you use it at all. In some types of documents, such as scholarly articles and essays, emotional appeals are used infrequently, and readers of such documents are likely to ask why you would play on their emotions instead of making a logical appeal or appeals to authority.

Appeals to Principles, Values, and Beliefs   Appeals to principles, values, and beliefs rely on the assumption that your readers value a given set of principles. Religious and ethical arguments are often based on appeals to principles, such as the need to respect God, to love one another, to trust in the innate goodness of individuals, to believe that all of us are created equal, or to believe that security should never be purchased at the price of individual liberty. If you are considering making an appeal to principles, values, or beliefs, be sure your readers are likely to share the particular principle, value, or belief you will use.

Appeals to Character   Writers frequently use appeals to character. When politicians refer to their military experience, for example, they are saying, "Look at me. I'm a patriotic person who has served our country." When a celebrity endorses a product, he or she is saying, "You know and like me, so please believe me when I say that this product is worth purchasing." Appeals to character can also reflect a person's professional accomplishment. When scientists or philosophers present arguments, for example, they sometimes refer to their background and experience, or perhaps to their previous publications. In doing so, they are implicitly telling their readers that they have proven to be accurate and truthful in the past, and that readers can continue to trust them. Essentially, you can think of appeals to character as the "trust me" strategy. As you consider this kind of appeal, reflect on your character, accomplishments, and experiences, and ask how they might persuade your readers to trust you.

Appeals to Logic   When writers talk about logical appeals, they are referring to the concept of reasoning through a set of propositions to reach a considered conclusion. For example, you might argue that a suspect is guilty of murder because police found her fingerprints on a murder weapon, her DNA in blood under the murder victim's fingernails, scratches on the suspect's face, and video of the murder from a surveillance camera. Your argument would rely on the logical presentation of evidence to convince a jury that the suspect was the murderer and to persuade them to return a verdict of guilty. As you develop reasons to support your claim, consider using logical appeals such as deduction and induction.

Deduction is a form of logical reasoning that moves from general principles to a conclusion. It usually involves two propositions and a conclusion.

Proposition 1 (usually a general principle):	Stealing is wrong.
Proposition 2 (usually an observation):	John stole a candy bar from the store.
Conclusion (results of deductive analysis):	John's theft of the candy bar was wrong.

Deduction is often used in arguments about issues that have ethical and moral dimensions, such as birth control, welfare reform, and immigration policy.

Induction is a form of logical reasoning that moves from specific observations to general conclusions, often drawing on numerical data to reveal patterns. Medical researchers, for example, typically collect a large number of observations about the effectiveness and side effects of new medications and then analyze their observations to draw conclusions about the overall usefulness of the medications. Induction is based on probability. That is, it can tell you whether something seems likely to occur based on what has been observed. Three commonly used forms of induction are trend analysis (see p. 74), causal analysis, and data analysis (see p. 75).

You can use different types of appeals to support your argument. Emotional appeals can be mixed with appeals to character. A coach's address to a team before an important athletic competition might rely not only on appeals to emotion but also on appeals to character, calling attention to players' need to trust what the coach has to say and to trust in themselves and their own abilities. Similarly, appeals to principle can be combined with appeals to emotion and logic.

My Research Project

DECIDE HOW TO APPEAL TO YOUR READERS

To develop an argumentative strategy, reflect on your purpose, your readers, and your overall claim. In your research log record your responses to the following.

1. List each of your reasons.

2. Ask what sorts of appeals are best suited to each reason. Ask, for example, whether appeals to emotion, logic, or character are appropriate for a particular reason.

3. Sketch out promising appeals. Ask, for example, how you would appeal to authority, or how you would appeal to logic.

4. Ask how your readers are likely to respond to a given appeal.

5. Ask whether the kind of document you are writing lends itself to the use of particular appeals.

You can download or print this activity at **bedfordresearcher.com**.

12b

How can I assess the integrity of my argument?

If you're familiar with the "Buy this car, get a date with this girl (or guy)" school of advertising, you're aware of arguments that lack integrity. These kinds of arguments show a lack of respect toward readers. They also have a high likelihood of backfiring (the proven success of automobile ads filled with attractive young men and women notwithstanding), and readers who recognize errors in logic or the use of inappropriate emotional appeals are likely to reject an argument out of hand.

To ensure the integrity of your argument, acquaint yourself with common logical fallacies. Then check that your argument does not fall victim to them. Some of the most common logical fallacies are described below.

Check for Fallacies Based on Distraction

A red herring is an irrelevant and distracting point. The term originated with the practice of sweeping a red herring (a particularly fragrant type of fish) across the trail being followed by a pack of hunting dogs to throw them off the scent of their prey. A question such as *Why worry about the rising cost of tuition when the government is tapping our phones?*, for example, is a red herring (government surveillance has nothing to do with increases in college tuition).

Ad hominem attacks attempt to discredit an idea or argument by suggesting that a person or group associated with it should not be trusted. These kinds of attacks might be subtle or obvious. If you hear someone say that a proposed wind farm should be rejected because its main supporter cheated on her taxes, or that school vouchers are bad because a principal who swindled a school district supports them, you're listening to an ad hominem attack.

Irrelevant history is another form of distraction. Arguing that a proposal is bad because someone came up with the idea while he was using cocaine, for example, suggests that the state of mind of the person who originates an idea has something to do with its merits. It might well be the case that the idea is flawed, but your assessment should be based on an analysis of its strengths and weaknesses. Otherwise, you might as well say that an idea is undoubtedly sound because someone thought of it while they were sober.

Look for Fallacies Based on Questionable Assumptions

Sweeping generalizations, sometimes known as hasty generalizations, ignore the fact that there are exceptions to the rules. Arguing that the rich are conservative and always vote for Republicans, for example, assumes that anyone who is rich is just like everyone else who is rich. These kinds of arguments don't account for variation within a group, nor do they account for unusual situations that would mean the generalization doesn't apply.

Straw-man attacks oversimplify or distort other people's arguments in order to dismiss them. Just as a boxer can easily knock down a scarecrow, a writer who commits this fallacy might characterize an opposing position as more extreme than it actually is or refute obviously flawed counterarguments while ignoring valid objections.

Citing inappropriate authorities can take several forms: citing as an authority someone who is not an expert on a subject, citing a source with a strong bias on an issue, suggesting an individual voice represents consensus when that person's ideas are far from the mainstream, or treating paid celebrity endorsements as expert opinions.

Jumping on a bandwagon implies that if enough people believe something, it must be true. Also known as argument from consensus, it substitutes group thinking for careful analysis. The idea of jumping on a bandwagon refers to the practice, in early American politics, of parading a candidate through town on a bandwagon. To show support for the candidate, people would climb aboard the wagon.

Search for Fallacies Based on Misrepresentation

Stacking the deck refers to the practice of presenting evidence for only one side of an argument. Most readers will assume a writer has done this deliberately and wonder what he or she is trying to hide.

Base-rate fallacies are commonly found in arguments based on statistics. If you read that drinking coffee will triple your risk of developing cancer, you might be alarmed. If you knew that the risk rose from one in a billion to three in a billion, however, you might pour another cup.

Questionable analogies, also known as false analogies, make inappropriate comparisons. They are based on the assumption that, if two things are similar in one way, they must be similar in others. For example, a writer might argue that global warming is like a fever, and then argue that just as a fever usually runs its course on its own, so too will the climate recover without intervention.

Locate Fallacies Based on Careless Reasoning

Post hoc fallacies, formally known as *post hoc, ergo propter hoc* fallacies ("after this, so because of this"), argue that because something happened first, it caused something else. For example, a student might conclude that she received a low grade on an essay exam because she argued with an instructor during class. In fact, the real cause might have more to do with the quality of the exam responses.

Slippery slope arguments warn that a single step will inevitably lead to a bad situation. One of the most common arguments against decriminalizing marijuana, for example, is that it leads to the use of stronger narcotics. It might be that some heroin or cocaine addicts first tried marijuana, but there is no evidence that all marijuana users inevitably move on to harder drugs.

Either/or arguments present two choices, one of which is usually characterized as extremely undesirable. In fact, there might be a third choice, or a fourth, or a fifth.

Non sequiturs are statements that do not follow logically from what has been presented. Arguing, for example, that buying a particular type of car will lead to a successful love life is a non sequitur.

Circular reasoning, also known as begging the question, restates a point that has just been made as evidence for itself. Arguing that a decline in voter turnout is a result of fewer people voting is an example of circular reasoning.

> **QUICK REFERENCE**

Developing Your Argument

- ✔ Identify reasons to accept your thesis statement. (p. 211)
- ✔ Select evidence to support your reasoning. (p. 212)
- ✔ Decide how to appeal to your readers. (p. 212)
- ✔ Assess the integrity of your argument. (p. 215)

IV Writing Your Document

13

Organizing

> **Key Questions**

A well-organized document allows a reader to anticipate—or predict—what will come next. Choose an appropriate organizing pattern by reflecting on your writing situation, thesis statement, reasons, evidence, and appeals. Then use labeling, grouping, clustering, and mapping to arrange your argument and formal and informal outlining strategies to organize your document.

13a

What organizing pattern should I choose?

Organizing patterns provide an overall principle for arranging your argument and your research writing project document. Common organizing patterns include the following.

Chronology   The document's organization reflects the sequence in which events occur over time. For example, you might focus attention on a sequence of events in a recent election or during the course of a certain time span. If you are writing a research essay or developing a multimedia presentation about a historical issue, you might find this organizing pattern useful.

Description   The document provides a point-by-point description of the physical attributes of a subject. For example, you might focus on the typical architectural features of a suburb or use a spatial arrangement that mimics the movement of the human eye as it takes in an image (left to right, top to bottom, near to far, and so on). Description is best for documents that address physical spaces, objects, or people—things that we can see and observe—rather than theories or processes that are not visible.

Definition   The document lays out the distinguishing characteristics of a subject and then provides examples and reasoning to explain what differentiates it from similar subjects. For instance, an essay defining *pride* might begin by stating that it is an emotion and then move on to explain why that particular emotion is not as harmful as many people believe.

Cause/Effect   The document is organized according to factors that lead to (cause) an outcome (effect). For example, you might identify the reasons behind a recent strike by grocery store employees or the health risks that contribute to heart disease.

Process Explanation   The document outlines the steps involved in doing something or explains how something happens. You might, for example, help readers understand the stages of nuclear fission or teach them what steps to take in the event of a meltdown in a nearby power plant.

Pro/Con   Ideas and information are organized to favor one side of an argument. You might argue a series of points, for example, in favor of legislation calling for increased reliance on wind power (pro) or in opposition to a casino in your neighborhood (con).

Multiple Perspectives   The document arranges information, ideas and arguments according to a range of perspectives about a subject. Documents using this organizing pattern frequently provide an analysis supporting one perspective. For instance, a document addressing the use of tidal power as an alternative energy source might present the perspectives of utility company executives, environmentalists, oceanographers, legislators, and waterfront residents, ultimately favoring one group over the others.

Comparison/Contrast   The document identifies similarities and differences among the information, ideas, and arguments relevant to a subject. Documents that compare and contrast can be constructed in one of two ways. In the point-by-point approach, the writer presents each relevant point individually and then analyzes how that point operates in the two items being compared. In the whole-by-whole approach, the writer addresses the first item in its entirety, as a whole, and then moves on to the second item. For example, a document analyzing a policy initiative to decriminalize marijuana possession might compare current drug laws to alcohol prohibition or attempt to contrast medical and recreational uses of marijuana.

Strengths/Weaknesses   The document examines positive and negative aspects of a subject, such as increasing federal funding for health care by instituting a national lottery or the overall quality of life in a city. Documents using this organizing principle typically work toward a conclusion that one or two considerations outweigh the others.

Costs/Benefits   The tradeoffs associated with a subject, usually a choice or proposal of some sort, are considered in turn. For example, an evaluative essay might discuss why the expenses associated with implementing a particular educational initiative are justified (or not) by the potential for higher test scores.

Problem/Solution   Documents define a problem and discuss the appropriateness of one or more solutions. If multiple solutions are proposed, an argument is usually made for the superiority of one over the others. For instance, an informative article might explain the problem of "brain drain," in which highly educated and skilled workers move out of state and then argue in support of a proposal to retain and attract more skilled workers.

Your choice of organizing pattern will reflect your purpose and the role or roles you adopt as a writer. It should also reflect the argument you are making in your document and the reasons, evidence, and appeals you use to make your argument. Keep in mind as well that a writer may use more than one organizing pattern in a document. For instance, a process explanation often works in tandem with chronology, since both present steps in a sequence. Similarly, a document presenting multiple perspectives might also adopt a strengths/weaknesses pattern to evaluate the merits of each perspective.

? WHAT'S MY PURPOSE?

Your choice of organizing pattern will reflect your purpose and the role or roles you adopt as a writer. If you're adopting the role of *reporter*, for example, you might select chronology, cause/effect, or comparison/contrast. If you're adopting the role of *evaluator*, you're likely to choose from patterns such as strengths/weaknesses, pro/con, comparison/contrast, or multiple perspectives. If you're adopting the role of *problem solver*, you're likely to choose from patterns such as strengths/weaknesses, pro/con, comparison/contrast, or multiple perspectives. If you're adopting the role of *advocate*, you might opt for an organizing principle that is well suited to argumentation, such as pro/con or strengths/weaknesses.

13b

How can I arrange my argument?

Once you have selected an organizing pattern, you can use strategies such as labeling, grouping, clustering, and mapping to determine how to present your argument. These strategies will also help you later as you develop an outline for your document.

Label Evidence

Labeling can help you understand at a glance how and where you will use evidence from your sources. For example, you might label notes or sources containing the evidence you want to use in your introduction with "Introduction," those that you plan to use to define a concept with the name of that concept, and so on. If you have taken digital notes or saved digital sources, as Pete Jacquez did, you have a number of options (see Figure 13.1). Once you've labeled your notes and sources, you can organize them into groups or order them according to the outline you will create.

> @ Read about the student writers discussed in this chapter at becfordresearcher .com. Click on Featured Writers.

Economic Issues ———— Label at the top of a note in a word processing file.

Chasteen, Stephanie. (2004). Who Owns Wind? *Science and Spirit 15*(1), 12-15.

Focuses on the economic aspects, particularly motivations and market potential, of implementing wind power.

Key quotes:

"Technological advancements and federal tax credits have made wind energy potentially profitable, landing it on the radar screen of private developers and utilities" (p. 12).

"On a dollar-for-dollar basis, wind is cost-competitve with the soaring prices of natural gas. It's still more expensive than nuclear and coal power but studies suggest that when all costs (such as health care for coal miners stricken by black lung disease or federal subsidies of nuclear power) are taken into account, wind energy is actually cheaper" (p. 13).

FIGURE 13.1 Labeling Electronic Notes and Sources

IV Writing Your Document

Group Evidence

Grouping involves categorizing the evidence you've obtained from your sources. Paper-based notes and copies of sources can be placed in related piles or file folders; sources and notes in word processing files or a smartphone can be saved in larger files or placed in folders; items in Bookmarks or Favorites lists can be sorted by category (see Figure 13.2).

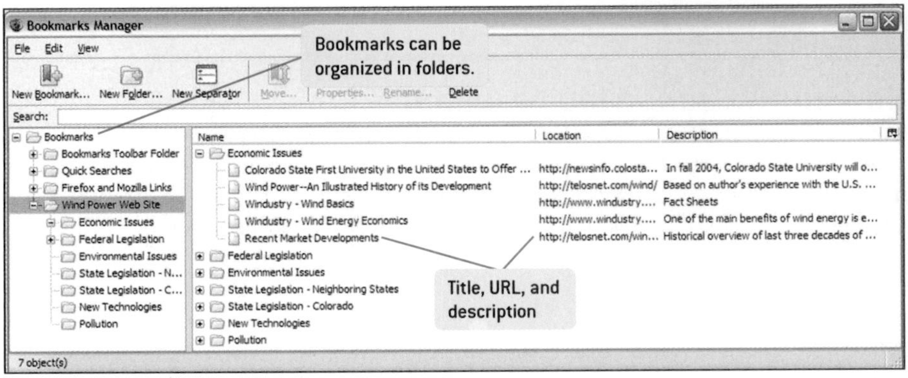

FIGURE 13.2 Grouping Electronic Notes and Sources

Use Clustering

Clustering can be used to explore the relationships among your thesis statement, reasons, and evidence. Clustering involves arranging these elements of your argument visually on a sheet of paper or on a computer screen. By putting your thesis statement at the center of the cluster and your reasons and evidence around it, you can explore how reasons and evidence relate to your main point, and how your reasons relate to each other.

Clustering can be used at several points in a research writing project: as you begin to explore your topic, as you brainstorm to come up with ideas, as you explore relationships among the material you've collected, and now as you begin to arrange your argument.

My Research Project

ARRANGE AN ARGUMENT BY CLUSTERING

Clustering can help you explore the relationships among your thesis statement, reasons, and evidence. To create a cluster:

1. In the middle of a sheet of paper, or in the center of a digital document (word processing file or graphics file), write your thesis statement.

2. Place your reasons around your thesis statement.

3. List the evidence you'll present to support your reasons next to each reason.

4. Think about the relationships among your main point, reasons, and evidence, and draw lines and circles to show those relationships.

5. Annotate your cluster to indicate the nature of the relationships you've identified.

You can print or download this activity at **bedfordresearcher.com**.

Use Mapping

You can use mapping to explore sequences of reasons and evidence. For example, you might use mapping to create a timeline or to show how an argument builds on one supporting point after another. This use of mapping is particularly effective as you begin to think about organizing your project document, and it often relies on the organizing patterns discussed on p. 218, such as chronology, cause/effect, comparison/contrast, cost/benefit, and problem/solution.

The following tutorial shows a map that Nicholas Brothers created to organize his thoughts about the argument in his research essay about U.S. reliance on private military corporations.

13c

How can I create an outline?

An outline represents the sequence in which your reasons and evidence will appear in your document. As you develop an outline, you'll make decisions about the order in which you will present your reasons and the evidence you'll use to back them up. Later, as you draft, your outline can serve as a plan for creating your document.

Create an Informal Outline

Informal outlines can take many forms: a brief list of words, a series of short phrases, or even a series of sentences. You can use informal outlines to remind yourself of key points to address in your document or of notes you should refer to when you begin drafting. Elizabeth Leontiev, who wrote a research essay about the impact of the U.S. war on drugs on South American coca farmers, created the informal outline shown in Figure 13.3. In her outline, each item represents a section she planned to include in her essay.

---

1. Introduction – what is coca? where is it grown?

2. Cultural and economic importance of coca crop

3. Evo Morales's plan: "zero cocaine, not zero coca"
   - Benefits of the Morales plan

4. Brief history of other plans and their failures
   - U.S. "war on drugs"
   - aerial fumigation / coca eradication
   - alternative cropping

5. Conclusion supporting the Morales plan

FIGURE 13.3 Elizabeth Leontiev's Informal Outline

TUTORIAL

How can I map my argument?

You can map your argument by arranging your reasons and evidence to support your thesis statement. In this example, Nicholas Brothers maps the reasons and evidence in his argumentative essay about U.S. reliance on private military corporations (PMCs) in its war on terror. Later, he will use this map as he develops his outline.

1 List your thesis statement.

2 Review your notes to identify reasons that help advance your thesis statement.

3 Based on the reasons you will use to help readers accept your thesis statement, choose an organizing pattern (see p. 218). Here, the writer chooses a cause/effect pattern to arrange his argument.

4 Use the organizing pattern to map your argument. Here, the writer maps the causes and effects of U.S. reliance on private military corporations.

5 List evidence near supporting points. Here, the writer includes references to sources in parentheses.

Review another example and work on mapping your own argument at **bedfordresearcher.com**. Click on Interactive Exercises.

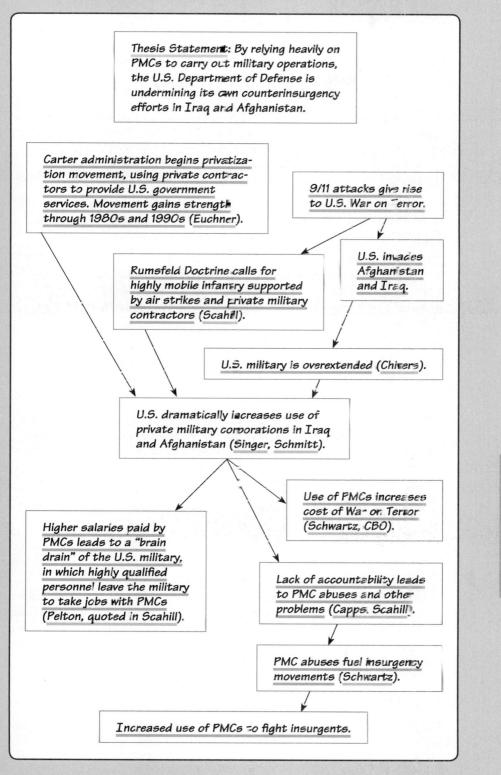

Thesis Statement: By relying heavily on PMCs to carry out military operations, the U.S. Department of Defense is undermining its own counterinsurgency efforts in Iraq and Afghanistan.

Carter administration begins privatization movement, using private contractors to provide U.S. government services. Movement gains strength through 1980s and 1990s (Euchner).

9/11 attacks give rise to U.S. War on Terror.

Rumsfeld Doctrine calls for highly mobile infantry supported by air strikes and private military contractors (Scahill).

U.S. invades Afghanistan and Iraq.

U.S. military is overextended (Chivers).

U.S. dramatically increases use of private military corporations in Iraq and Afghanistan (Singer, Schmitt).

Use of PMCs increases cost of War on Terror (Schwartz, CBO).

Higher salaries paid by PMCs leads to a "brain drain" of the U.S. military, in which highly qualified personnel leave the military to take jobs with PMCs (Pelton, quoted in Scahill).

Lack of accountability leads to PMC abuses and other problems (Capps, Scahill).

PMC abuses fuel insurgency movements (Schwartz).

Increased use of PMCs to fight insurgents.

IV Writing Your Document

Intro

Introduce private military corporations as integral to U.S. military operations. Present the many costs of PMCs to be examined.

Section 1

Explain the history of PMCs, from the Napoleonic era to today. Focus on the post-9/11 era and how privatization of the U.S. military has increased in the last ten years. Key sources: interview transcripts from Brothers and Euchner.

Section 2

Discuss the frequent use of PMCs in Iraq and Afghanistan, as well their diversified functions. Examine the distinction between PMCs and mercenaries. Key sources for background and argument: Scahill and Singer.

Section 3

Give examples of abuses and illegal acts by PMC contractors. Explain why contractors have not been convicted of crimes. Key sources for abuse evidence: Capps, Simpson, and Savage; key sources for lack of legal accountability: Singer, Yeoman, and Risen.

Section 4

Present the view that abuses by contractors undermine the image and goals of the U.S. military. Key sources: the Army Field Manual and the Congressional Research Service report.

Section 5

Discuss other "costs" of PMCs, in particular the amount of taxpayer money spent on them and the brain drain that occurs. Key sources: Stanger, Moshe, and Pelton.

Conclusion

Look at ways Americans can take civic action to end the overreliance on PMCs.

FIGURE 13.4 Nicholas Brothers's Thumbnail Outline

Nicholas Brothers wrote a "thumbnail outline," a type of informal outline, as he worked on his research essay about private military corporations. Nicholas identified the major sections he would include in his research essay and noted which sources he would use to provide background information and to support his argument (see Figure 13.4).

Create a Formal Outline

A formal outline provides a complete and accurate list of the points you want to address in your document. Formal outlines use Arabic numerals, letters, and

Roman numerals to indicate the hierarchy of information. An alternative approach, common in business and the sciences, uses numbering with decimal points:

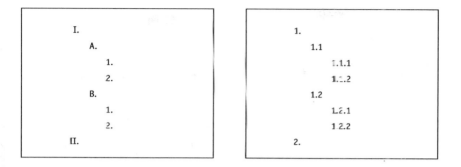

Writers use formal outlines to identify the hierarchy of information, ideas, and arguments. You can create a formal outline to identify

- your thesis statement
- your reasons
- the sequence in which those reasons should be presented
- evidence for your reasons
- the notes and sources you should refer to as you work on your document

The most common types of formal outlines are topical outlines and sentence outlines.

Topical Outlines   Topical outlines present the topics and subtopics you plan to include in your research document as a series of words and phrases. Items at the same level of importance should be phrased in parallel grammatical form.

In her topical outline for her research essay on steroid use among adolescent girls, Alexis Alvarez includes her thesis statement, suggests the key points she wants to make in her document, maps out the support for her points, and uses a conventional system of numbers and letters (see Figure 13.5).

Sentence Outlines   Sentence outlines use complete sentences to identify the points you want to cover (see Figure 13.6). Sentence outlines typically serve two purposes.

1. They begin the process of converting an outline into a draft of your document.

2. They help you assess the structure of a document that you have already written.

> @ Learn how to use bullets, numbering, and indentation to create outlines at bedfordresearcher.com. Click on How-To Guides.

When you've created your outline, ask whether it can serve as a blueprint for the first draft of your document. Taking the time to create an effective outline now will reduce the time needed to write your first draft later.

Thesis statement: Although competitive sports can provide young female athletes with many benefits, they can also have negative effects, the worst of which is increasing drug use.

I.   **Female Participation in Competitive Athletics**
   A.   Short history and current trends
   B.   Understanding the female athlete

II. **Positive Impact of Competitive Athletics**
   A.   Physiological (Kane & Larkin)
      1.   Reduced risk of obesity and heart disease
      2.   Increased immune functioning and prevention of certain cancers
      3.   Improved flexibility, strength, and aerobic power
   B.   Psychological (Kane & Larkin)
      1.   Improved self-esteem
      2.   Enhanced mental health
      3.   Effective in reducing symptoms of stress, anxiety, and depression
   C.   Sociological
      1.   Expansion of social boundaries
      2.   Teaches responsibility, discipline, and determination
      3.   Educational asset

III. **Negative Impact of Competitive Athletics**
   A.   Physiological (Graham)
      1.   Overtraining
      2.   Eating disorders
      3.   Exercise-induced amenorrhea and osteoporosis

FIGURE 13.5 Part of Alexis Alvarez's Topical Outline

Thesis statement: Although competitive sports can provide young female athletes with many benefits, they can also have negative effects, the worst of which is increasing drug use.

I.   Society has been concerned with the use of performance-enhancing drugs among younger male athletes, but many don't know that these drugs are also used by younger female athletes.
   A.   Women began participating in sports in the mid-19th century, although participation was not encouraged until recently. Millions of girls are involved in a wide range of physical activities and are participating in school-sponsored sports.
   B.   In response to pressures of competitive sports, girls' steroid use has increased and younger and younger girls are taking steroids.

II. Sports can benefit a girl's growth and development physiologically as well as psychologically and sociologically.
   A.   Participation in sports has a wide range of positive physiological effects on adolescent girls.
      1.   Studies have shown that participation in sports can reduce the risk of obesity and heart disease.
      2.   Studies have shown that participation in sports appear to increase immune functioning and prevent certain cancers.
      3.   Participation in sports has also been linked to improved flexibility, strength, and aerobic power.

FIGURE 13.6 Part of Alexis Alvarez's Sentence Outline

My Research Project

CREATE AND REVIEW YOUR OUTLINE

In your word processing program or in your research log, create an outline. If your word processing program has an outlining tool, use it to create a formal outline. In Microsoft Word, use Outline View (available in older versions of Word through the VIEW > OUTLINE menu command) to view your document in outline mode. Use the PROMOTE and DEMOTE buttons on the outlining toolbar to set the levels for entries in your outline. Use the COLLAPSE and EXPAND buttons to hide and show parts of your outline.

Review your outline by asking yourself the following questions.

1. Does my outline provide an effective organization for my document?

2. Have I covered all of my key points?

3. Have I addressed my key points in sufficient detail?

4. Do any sections seem out of order?

You can print or download this activity at **bedfordresearcher.com**.

> **QUICK REFERENCE**

Organizing

☑ Choose an organizing pattern for your document. (p. 218)

☑ Arrange your argument. (p. 221)

☑ Develop an informal outline. (p. 223)

☑ Create a formal outline. (p. 226)

IV Writing Your Document

14

Drafting

> ## Key Questions

If you're new to research writing, you might be surprised at how long it's taken to get to the chapter about writing your document. If you are an experienced research writer, you know that you've been writing it all along. Research writing isn't so much the act of putting words to paper or screen as it is the process of identifying and learning about an issue, reflecting on what you've learned, and contributing to the conversation about your issue.

14a

How can I use my outline to draft my document?

Your outline provides a framework you can use to draft your document. Your outline likely includes your plans for

- the points you will include in your document
- the order in which you will make your points
- the evidence you will use to support each point

? WHAT'S MY PURPOSE?

Review your purpose and your outline. Check whether you have organized your points in a way that will allow you to achieve your purpose and whether you are addressing the needs, interests, values, and beliefs of your readers.

If you have listed information about the sources you will use to support your points, you can check whether you are

- providing enough evidence to support your points
- relying too heavily on a limited number of sources
- relying too heavily on support from sources that favor one side of the conversation

As you prepare to draft your document, you might find it necessary to reorganize your ideas to achieve your purpose.

If you created an informal outline, it can be the skeleton of your document, and you can now begin fleshing out sections. Translate a bulleted list of items, for instance, into a series of brief sentences, or write paragraphs based on the key points in the outline. If you created a formal outline, such as a topical outline or a sentence outline, you can use each main point in the outline as a topic sentence for a paragraph. For example, you can form supporting sentences from the sub-points under each main point.

If your outline contains references to specific notes or sources, make sure that you use those notes in your draft. Take advantage of the time you spent thinking about which sources are most appropriate for a particular section of your document.

As you work on your document, you might find it necessary to reorganize your ideas. Think of your outline as a flexible guide rather than a rigid blueprint.

TUTORIAL

How do I use an outline to draft my document?

Use your outline as the "skeleton" of the first draft of your document. In this example, Alexis Alvarez expands her outline into a rough draft.

1 Save your outline with a new name, such as Draft1.doc.

2 Turn major headings in your outline into headings and subheadings in your draft.

3 Convert lower-level entries into topic sentences for paragraphs.

4 Use lists of items as sentences in each paragraph.

5 Locate evidence to support your points. Quote, paraphrase, and summarize sources identified in your outline.

---

1. Benefits of Sports for Girls
  a. Physical Health Benefits
    i. Reduces risks of adult-onset coronary disease and some cancers (Kane & Larkin, 1997)
    ii. Enhances immune system, posture, strength, flexibility, and heart-lung endurance (Kane & Larkin, 1997; "Sports in America," 1994)
  b. Mental Health Benefits (Kane & Larkin, 1997; Orozco interview)
    i. Positive body image
    ii. Confidence and self-esteem
    iii. Sense of control
  c. Social benefits (Orozco and Alvarez interviews)
2. Problems Caused by Sports for Girls
  a. Physical side effects

Girls and Sports: The Upside

According to Kane and Larkin (1997), adolescent girls who exercise regularly can lessen their risks for adult-onset coronary disease and certain cancers. Girls' involvement in sports and exercise also tends to improve immune functioning, posture, strength, flexibility, and heart-lung endurance (Kane & Larkin, 1997; "Sports in America," 1994).

In addition, competitive athletics can enhance mental health by offering adolescent girls positive feelings about body image; tangible experiences of competency, control, and success; improved self-esteem and self-confidence; and a way to reduce anxiety (Kane & Larkin, 1997). Juan Orozco, who has coached competitive soccer for nine years at the adolescent female level, confirmed that making a competitive sports team is a privilege that many girls work toward with determination and longing and that being picked to participate encourages these young athletes to believe in themselves and their abilities (personal interview, Sept. 22, 2004).

A final benefit is that sports expand social boundaries and teach many of the personal and social skills girls will need throughout their lives. According to Orozco, through competitive athletics girls learn a crucial lesson in how to

---

Review another example and work on using your outline to draft your document at **bedfordresearcher.com**. Click on Interactive Exercises.

14b

How can I draft effective paragraphs?

Writers use paragraphs to present and develop a central idea. Depending on the complexity of your argument and the type of document you are writing, a single paragraph might be all you need to present your reasoning and evidence, or it might play only a small role in conveying your thinking about an issue. You can create effective paragraphs by ensuring that they are focused, organized, and well developed. You can enhance the effectiveness of your document by creating transitions that clearly convey the relationships between paragraphs.

Focus on a Central Idea

Each of your paragraphs should focus on a single idea. Paragraphs often have a topic sentence in which the writer makes an assertion, offers an observation, or asks a question. The rest of the sentences in the paragraph elaborate on the topic. Consider the following paragraph, drawn from Nicholas Brothers's research essay.

> Given the potential costs in justice and national security, why hire contractors at all? Ironically, perhaps the most often-cited reason for using private contractors is that using these corporations saves the taxpayer money since the government can hire them on an as-needed basis and does not have to pay for contractors' training, health care, or pensions. Professor Allison Stanger of Middlebury College challenges this notion in her 2009 book *One Nation Under Contract: The Outsourcing of American Power and the Future of Foreign Policy* when she points out that nearly all private contractors previously served in the military, meaning that many of them are receiving pension payments anyway. Stanger writes that "the federal government is effectively paying for the training and retirement of the contractors it hires, all appearances to the contrary, as well as paying double or triple the daily rate for their services." Therefore the Department of Defense would actually save taxpayers money by reversing the trend of privatization.

The central idea of the paragraph follows an initial question.

The third and fourth sentences use evidence from a source to show the real cost of hiring contractors.

The final sentence draws a conclusion that supports the essay's thesis statement.

IV Writing Your Document

Follow an Organizing Pattern

Effective paragraphs follow an organizing pattern, often the same one that the document as a whole follows, such as:

- chronology: identifying the sequence in which events occur over time
- description: presenting the distinguishing features of an idea, a concept, or an event
- definition: explaining an idea, a concept, or an event

- cause/effect: identifying factors that lead to (cause) an outcome (effect)
- process explanation: tracing steps or explaining how something happened
- pro/con: presenting reasons and evidence in favor of and against an idea
- multiple perspectives: organizing according to a range of views
- comparison/contrast: exploring similarities and differences
- strengths/weaknesses: using a set of criteria to make judgments about an idea, a concept, an event, or an individual
- costs/benefits: presenting the tradeoffs involved in a choice
- problem/solution: defining a problem and presenting a solution

These common patterns help readers anticipate what you'll write. (See p. 218 to learn more about organizing patterns.) Readers who recognize a pattern, such as problem/solution, will find it easier to focus on your ideas and argument if they understand how you are organizing your paragraph. Note how the following paragraph, drawn from Alexis Alvarez, uses the problem/solution organizing pattern.

> What can we do to help adolescent female athletes avoid illicit drug use? How can we help them avoid the pitfalls of competitive athletics? Parents, coaches, and the athletes themselves all play a crucial role in averting bad choices. First, parents and coaches need to be aware that performance-enhancing drugs are a problem. Some adults believe that steroid use is either minimal or nonexistent among teenagers, but one study concluded that "over half the teens who use steroids start before age 16, sometimes with the encouragement of their parents.... Seven percent said they first took 'juice' by age ten" (Dudley, 1994, p. 235).

The paragraph begins by restating the problem.

The central idea of the paragraph is provided in the third sentence.

One part of the solution to the larger problem is provided.

The fifth sentence provides evidence from a source to illustrate the nature of the problem.

Use Details to Capture Your Readers' Attention

An effective paragraph does more than simply convey information—it provides details that bring an issue to life. Consider the differences between the following paragraphs:

Example 1: Minimal Details:

In fact, pollution from power plants may worsen as the demand for electric power continues to increase. Despite plans to build new power plants fueled by renewable energy and nuclear power, the U.S. Department of Energy projects that use of fossil fuels in power plants will actually increase. Moreover, Clayton (2004) notes that developing nations will also increase their reliance on fossil fuels. All of this is likely to lead to increased air pollution.

Example 2: Extensive, Concrete Details:

In fact, pollution from power plants may worsen as the demand for electric power continues to increase. The U.S. Department of Energy (2005b) predicts that, despite ongoing efforts to build power plants powered by renewable and nuclear energy,

U.S. demand for power generated by fossil fuels will keep growing. Moreover, demand in developing nations is expected to increase even more dramatically. China and India are poised to build a total of 775 new conventional power plants by 2012 (Clayton, 2004). The addition of so many new plants will almost certainly lead to more global air pollution in the near term.

Both examples, drawn from Pete Jacquez's Web site on wind energy, convey the same main point. The first example, however, does little more than state the facts. The second example provides details from a U.S. Department of Energy report about demand for power in the United States and offers statistics about the number of conventional power plants that are projected to be built in China and India in the next few years. These details allow readers to gain a more complete, and more concrete, understanding of the issue.

Integrate Information from Sources Effectively

Information from sources can be used to introduce an important concept, establish the strength of a writer's argument, and elaborate on the central idea of a paragraph. Writers frequently state a point, offer a reason to accept it, and support their reasoning with evidence from a source, typically in the form of quotations, paraphrases, and summaries. In the following example, drawn from Pete Jacquez's Web site, a quotation and a paraphrase are used to support a point introduced in the first sentence of the paragraph.

> In fact, pollution from power plants may worsen as the demand for electric power continues to increase. The U.S. Department of Energy (2005b) notes that "it is likely that the nation's reliance on fossil fuels to power an expanding economy will actually increase over at least the next two decades even with aggressive development and deployment of new renewable and nuclear technologies" (para. 1). Moreover, demand in developing nations is expected to increase even more dramatically. China and India are poised to build a total of 775 new conventional power plants by 2012 (Clayton, 2004). The addition of so many new plants will almost certainly lead to more global air pollution in the near term.

By quoting an authority on the issue, the U.S. Department of Energy, Pete strengthens his argument. The quotation, along with a subsequent paraphrase of a passage from another source, provides evidence to support his point. He follows the quotation and paraphrase with a sentence that restates the main point of the paragraph. (See Chapter 15 for more about integrating information.)

Create Transitions Within and Between Paragraphs

Transitions are words and phrases, such as *however* and *on the other hand*, that show the relationships between paragraphs and sentences. Transitions help readers understand how one sentence builds on another and how a new paragraph is related to the one that came before it. By signaling these relationships, they help readers anticipate how the information and ideas they are about to read are related to the information and ideas they've just read. Here are some common transitions and their functions.

IV Writing Your Document

To Help Readers Follow a Sequence:

Furthermore

In addition

Moreover

Next

First . . . Second . . . Third

To Elaborate or Provide Examples:

For example

For instance

Such as

In fact

Indeed

To illustrate

To Compare:

Similarly

In the same manner

Like

As in

To Contrast:

However

On the other hand

Nevertheless

Nonetheless

Despite

Although

To Signal a Concession:

I admit that

Of course

Granted

To Introduce a Conclusion:

As a result

As a consequence

Therefore

Thus

For this reason

As you create effective transitions, pay attention to the order in which you introduce new information and ideas in your paragraphs. In general, it is best to begin a sentence with a reference to information and ideas that have already been introduced and to introduce new information and ideas at the end of a sentence. For example, consider the following examples, which begin a new paragraph:

Introducing New Information First:
Admissions staff look at the kind of courses students are taking, in addition to looking at grades.

Building on Information that Has Already Been Introduced:
And it's not just grades that matter; admissions staff also look at the kind of courses students are taking.

The second example, by referring to information that has been introduced in the previous paragraph, provides an effective transition to a new paragraph, even as it introduces new information about additional college admissions criteria. In contrast, readers of the first example would not have the benefit of seeing how the new information fits into what they've already read.

14c

How can I draft my introduction?

All readers expect documents to include some sort of introduction. Whether they are reading a home page on a Web site or an opening paragraph in a research report, readers want to learn quickly what a document is about. Drafting an introduction involves framing your main point and choosing a strategy to begin your document.

Frame the Issue   [FRAMING MY ARGUMENT]

Your introduction provides a framework within which your readers can understand and interpret your contribution to the conversation about your issue. By calling attention to a specific situation, by asking a particular question, or by conveying a carefully chosen set of details, you can help your readers view your argument in a particular way. Consider for example, the differences between two introductions to an essay about buying habits among younger Americans.

> **Introduction 1:** In the face of an economic downturn, frugality is undergoing a revival in America. Young people are cutting up their credit cards, clipping coupons, and sticking to detailed budgets. In effect, they're adopting the very habits they mocked during the heady days of easy credit and weekend shopping sprees. Second-hand stores and thrift stores like Goodwill or the Salvation Army are drawing record numbers of customers, while once stable retail giants such as Circuit City and the Sharper Image have gone out of business (*Wall Street Journal*). In fact, retail sales during the Christmas season were down 2.8% last year, the lowest since 1995 (CNNMoney.com). The causes of this sea change in the spending habits of young Americans are complex and varied: high rates of unemployment, fewer jobs for recent college graduates, difficulty securing credit, and that elusive factor economists call "consumer confidence."

> **Introduction 2:** The new frugal spending habits of American consumers between the ages of 18 and 34 are endangering the very individuals who are trying to save money. Plagued with rising unemployment, widespread hiring freezes, and difficulty securing credit, young Americans are naturally turning to their spending habits as one area they can control. They are cutting down on how much money they spend in restaurants, bars, retail stores, and entertainment venues. As a result, usually robust Christmas sales were down an alarming 2.8% last year, the lowest since 1995 (CNNMoney.com). Even once stable retail giants such as Circuit City and the Sharper Image have gone out of business (*Wall Street Journal*). While the desire to hold onto their money is logical, all this coupon clipping, budgeting, and thrift-store shopping threatens the key to economic recovery, what economists call "consumer confidence." If we don't loosen our grip on our wallets and inject some much-needed cash into the system, we will face far more dire economic consequences in the years to come.

The first introduction frames the subject as an explanation of why younger Americans have changed their buying habits. The second introduction frames the subject as a warning that these changing habits might be causing more harm than good. While each introduction draws on the same basic information about current rates of spending, and while both will do a good job of introducing the essay, they ask readers to focus their attention on different aspects of the subject.

You can frame your discussion by calling attention to specific aspects of a topic, including:

- The agent: a person, an organization, or a thing that is acting in a particular way
- The action: what is being done by the actor
- The goal: why the actor carried out the action
- The result: the outcome of the action

Introduction 2: The new frugal spending habits of American consumers between the ages of 18 and 34 are endangering the very individuals who are trying to save money. Plagued with rising unemployment, widespread hiring freezes, and difficulty securing credit, young Americans are naturally turning to their spending habits as one area they can control. They are cutting down on how much money they spend in restaurants, bars, retail stores, and entertainment venues. As a result, usually robust Christmas sales were down an alarming 2.8% last year, the lowest since 1995 (CNNMoney.com). Even once stable retail giants such as Circuit City and the Sharper Image have gone out of business (*Wall Street Journal*). While the desire to hold onto their money is logical, all this coupon clipping, budgeting, and thrift-store shopping threatens the key to economic recovery, what economists call "consumer confidence." If we don't loosen our grip on our wallets and inject some much-needed cash into the system, we will face far more dire economic consequences in the years to come.

> Agent
> Action
> Goal
> Result

Select a Strategy for Your Introduction

You can introduce your document using one of several strategies.

State the Topic.   Tell your readers what your issue is, what conversation you are focusing on, and what your document will tell them about it, as in the following introduction.

> Artists and their artwork do not exist in a vacuum. The images artists create help shape and in turn are shaped by the society and culture in which they are created. The artists and artworks in the Dutch Baroque period are no exception.

Establish the Context.   In some cases, you'll want to give your readers background information about your subject or an overview of the conversation that has been taking place about it. Notice, for example, how Mark Hemingway sets up his article in *National Review Online* in response to media coverage of private military contractors.

> In the reams of media coverage surrounding the Blackwater incident last week one curious detail remains virtually unreported. The general theme of the coverage

remains that private military contractors are somehow "above the law," but almost no media sources have referred to the fact that, as of last fall, contractors are subject to the same Uniform Code of Military Justice that governs U.S. soldiers.

State Your Thesis.   If your research document presents an argument evaluation, solution, or interpretation, use your introduction to get right to your main point. In other words, lead with a thesis statement, as in the following introduction.

> While the private tragedies of its central characters have public implications, William Shakespeare's *Julius Caesar* is more about personal struggles than political ambition. It is easy to see the play as one whose focus is the political action of public events. The title character, after all, is at the height of political power. However, the interior lives of Julius Caesar, Marcus Brutus, and their wives offer a more engaging storyline. Shakespeare alternates between public and private scenes throughout the play to emphasize the conflict between duties of the Roman citizenry and the feelings and needs of the individual, but it is the "private mind and heart of the individual" (Edwards 105) that the reader is compelled to examine.

Define a Problem.   If your research has led you to propose a solution to a problem, you might begin your document by defining the problem. Alexis Alvarez used this strategy to introduce her essay.

> Almost daily, headlines and newscasters tell us about athletes' use of performance-enhancing drugs. Indeed, stories of such drug use seem to increase each year, with investigations of possible steroid use by college football players, by major league baseball players, and even by Olympic gold medalists. It is easy to gain the impression that many adult athletes, particularly males, may be using drugs in order to improve their performance and physical appearance. What may be surprising and even shocking to most of us, however, is that these drugs, especially anabolic steroids, are increasingly used by adolescent athletes and that girls are just as likely as boys to be users.

Read Alexis Alvarez's research essay on p. 382.

Make a Surprising Statement.   Grab your readers' attention by telling them something they don't already know. It's even better if the information is shocking, unusual, or strange.

> What is the most common cause of hunger in the world? Is it drought? Locusts? Crop diseases? Nope. Most hunger in the world has absolutely nothing to do with food shortages. Most people who go to bed hungry, both in rich and in poor countries, do so in places where markets are filled with food that they cannot have.

Ask a Question.   Asking a question invites your readers to become participants in the conversation. At the end of her introduction, Alexis Alvarez encouraged her readers to take an interest in the problem of steroid use by adolescent female athletes by asking a question.

> What role is competitive sports playing in this dangerous trend? Why are some girls feeling the need to ingest performance-enhancing drugs?

Tell a Story.   Everyone loves a story, assuming it's told well and has a point. This writer began her newspaper article about the benefit of writing by hand with a story of a young boy who struggles to master the skill.

> Ask preschooler Zane Pike to write his name or the alphabet, then watch this 4-year-old's stubborn side kick in. He spurns practice at school and tosses aside workbooks at home. But Angie Pike, Zane's mom, persists, believing that handwriting is a building block to learning. She's right. Using advanced tools such as magnetic resonance imaging, researchers are finding that writing by hand is more than just a way to communicate. The practice helps with learning letters and shapes, can improve idea composition and expression, and may aid fine motor-skill development.

Provide a Historical Account.   Historical accounts can help your readers understand the origins of a situation and how the situation has changed over time. A Web site focusing on relations between the People's Republic of China and Taiwan used this historical account:

> On February 21, 2000, the People's Republic of China (PRC) shocked the world with its release of the white paper "The One-China Principle and the Taiwan Issue." In this 18-page document, the Chinese government outlined its case that, in keeping with the "One China" principle to which the United States and Taiwan had allegedly agreed, Taiwan is the rightful property of the People's Republic of China, and revealed that it intended to use force if Taiwan did not move to reunite with the mainland.

Draw a Contrast.   Drawing a contrast asks your readers to begin making a comparison. Elizabeth Leontiev began her essay by contrasting what the word *cocaine* means to U.S. citizens and South American coca farmers.

> To most Americans, the word *cocaine* evokes images of the illegal white powder and those who abuse it, yet the word has a completely different meaning to the coca farmers of South America.

Read Elizabeth Leontiev's research essay on p. 357.

Lead with a Quotation.   A quotation allows your readers to learn about the issue from someone who knows it well or has been affected by it, as in the following introduction.

> "Without a few lucky breaks, we'd still be bagging groceries at Albertsons," says lead singer Rickie Jackson of the recent Grammy winning band, Soft Affections.

14d

How can I make sure my document is easy to follow?

A document that is well organized and well designed allows a reader to anticipate—or predict—what will come next, which helps readers understand your goals more easily. The test is whether your readers can move smoothly through your document without wondering, "Where did that come from?" As you draft, check whether your document is organized and designed consistently and predictably. You might find the following techniques useful.

Provide a Map. The most direct way of signaling the organization of your document is to provide a map in your introduction. You might write something like this: "This report will cover three approaches to treating cancer of the bladder: chemotherapy, a combination of chemotherapy and radiation, and surgical removal of the organ."

Use Headings and Subheadings. You can help your readers keep their place in your document by using headings and subheadings. Your formatting should distinguish between headings (major sections) and subheadings (subsections).

Provide Forecasts and Cross-References. Forecasts prepare your readers for a shift in your document, such as the boundary between one section and the next. A forecast at the end of a major section might say, "In the next section, you can read about...." Cross-references tell your readers that they can find related information in another section of the document or let them know that a particular issue will be addressed in greater detail elsewhere. On a Web site, forecasts and cross-references might take the form of small images, flags, or statements such as 'Continue to next section" or "Follow this link for more information."

Use a Menu. If you are writing a digital document such as a Web site, you can add a menu on the side, top, or bottom of your pages that readers can see as they work through your site. Pete Jacquez provided a menu on every page of his site (see Figure 14.1).

Pay Attention to Design Principles. As you write your document, pay attention to the principles of effective design. Using a readable body font that is clearly different from the font used for headings and subheadings for example, can improve readability significantly. Similarly, breaking out information using bulleted and numbered lists, providing descriptive page headers or footers, and integrating

FIGURE 14.1 Menu on Pete Jacquez's Web site The menu helps readers understand the organization of the site and move to pages within it.

illustrations effectively into your text can greatly enhance readability. If you are drafting a digital document, keep in mind the uses of digital illustrations. You can read more about design in Chapters 18 and 19.

14e

How can I draft my conclusion?

Your conclusion provides an opportunity to reinforce your message. It offers one last chance to achieve your purpose as a writer and to share your final thoughts about the issue with your readers.

Reinforce Your Points

At a minimum, your conclusion should summarize the reasons you've offered to support your thesis statement. You might also want to restate your thesis (in different words) to reinforce the main idea for readers. If you didn't include a thesis statement in your introduction, consider stating your main idea in your conclusion. Ending with a clear indication of what you want someone to think, believe, or do as a result of reading your document gives you one final opportunity to influence your readers.

Elizabeth Leontiev concluded her analysis of the impact of Evo Morales's vision for South American coca farmers like this:

> Through his bold program of "zero cocaine, not zero coca," Morales aims to improve the lives of Andean farmers and the economies of South American countries, while still remaining committed to controlling the illegal drug trade. Morales's example illustrates that it is time to work *with* coca farmers, rather than against them.

Select a Strategy for Your Conclusion

Conclusions that simply summarize a document, like Elizabeth's, are common — and sometimes effective, especially when the writer has presented complex concepts. But a conclusion can do much more than simply restate your argument. It can also give your readers an incentive to continue thinking about what they've read, to take action about the subject, or to read more about it.

As you draft, think about what you want to accomplish. You can choose from a range of strategies to write an effective conclusion.

Offer Additional Analysis. Extend your discussion of the issue by supplying additional insights. In his Web site about wind-generated electrical power, Pete Jacquez concluded his discussion of wind power and the environment by linking wind power to the production of hydrogen gas.

Another promising area—in terms of wind power's contribution to clean energy—is the role it can play in a "hydrogen economy." Because hydrogen gas, when burned, does not produce carbon dioxide (its only emission is water vapor), some legislators and environmentalists are looking to hydrogen as a replacement for fossil fuels. Generating hydrogen gas, however, requires power, and a number of plans to generate it rely on coal-powered plants. Wind-power advocates argue, instead, that wind turbines can supply the power needed to produce hydrogen gas. Recent government studies support this approach ("Wind Power Facts," 2004).

Speculate about the Future. Reflect on what might happen next. The author of an essay about the potential use of hydrogen as a fuel source, for example, might use this technique.

It is certain, though, that at some point the fossil fuels that have sustained our society's electricity and run our motor vehicles for over a century will run out—or become so expensive that they'll no longer provide an economically viable source of energy. Whether that day comes in five years or fifty, we need to shift to a new energy source—one that is practical, economical, and environmentally friendly. Hydrogen has demonstrated great promise as a new candidate for fuel. To realize that promise, however, we must work to remove the barriers that currently prevent hydrogen's emergence as a mainstay of our future economy.

Close with a Quotation. Select a quotation that does one of the following.

- offers deeper insight into the points you've made in your document
- sums up the points you've made in your document
- points to the future of the issue
- suggests a solution to a problem
- illustrates what you would like to see happen
- makes a further observation about the issue
- presents a personalized viewpoint from someone who has experienced the issue you are addressing

Alexis Alvarez used a quotation from a personal interview to underscore her main point about the use of steroids among adolescents girls involved in competitive sports.

In short, these athletes have not lost sight of the true objective of participating in sports—they know that their success is due to their efforts and not to the effects of a performance-enhancing drug. When asked what she would say to athletes considering steroid use, Melissa Alvarez said:

> If you are training and doing your best, you should not have to use steroids. At the end of the day, it is just a game. You should never put your health at risk for anything, or anyone. It should be your top priority. (personal communication, September 26, 2004)

Close with a Story. Tell a story about the issue you've discussed in your document. The story might suggest a potential solution to the problem, offer hope about a desired outcome, or illustrate what might happen if a desired outcome isn't realized. This writer concluded his newspaper article by continuing a story he used in his introduction:

> So [Scott] struggles to get a foothold in the civilian work force. His brother in Boston lost his roommate, and early last month Scott moved into the empty bedroom, with his parents paying Scott's share of the $2,000-a-month rent until the lease expires on Aug. 31. And if Scott does not have a job by then? "I'll do something temporary; I won't go back home," Scott said. "I'll be a bartender or get work through a temp agency. I hope I don't find myself in that position."

Close with a Question.   Questions provide an effective means of inviting readers to consider the implications of the ideas explored in an essay. After summarizing his position in his argumentative essay, Nicholas Brothers included a compelling question in his closing paragraph (see p. 417).

> In the end, we as voters and taxpayers must ask ourselves, who do we want to carry out U.S. defense missions abroad: those accountable to the U.S. military, or those beholden to private corporations?

Call Your Readers to Action.   Make a recommendation or urge your readers to do something specific. For example, you might ask them to participate in solving a problem by donating time, money, or effort to a project. Or you might ask them to write to someone, such as a politician or corporate executive, about an issue. Calls to action ask readers to do more than simply accept what you've written; they ask readers but to do something about it. Nicholas Brothers used this strategy in an earlier draft of his argumentative essay.

> On her Web site, Jan Schakowsky urges Americans to contact their representatives to co-sponsor the legislation and become citizen co-sponsors of the Stop Outsourcing Security Act themselves. Political action may be the most powerful remedy to our current state of apathy.

Link to Your Introduction.   This technique is sometimes called a "bookends" approach because it positions your introduction and conclusion as related ends of your document. The basic idea is to turn your conclusion into an extension of your introduction.

- If your introduction used a quotation, end with a related quotation or respond to the quotation.
- If your introduction used a story, extend that story or retell it with a different ending.
- If your introduction asked a question, answer the question, restate the question, or ask a new question.
- If your introduction defined a problem, then you can provide a solution to the problem, restate the problem, or suggest that readers need to move on to a new problem.

> **QUICK REFERENCE**

Drafting

☑ Use your outline to begin drafting your document. (p. 231)

☑ Develop effective paragraphs. (p. 233)

☑ Draft your introduction. (p. 237)

☑ Make your document easy to follow. (p. 240)

☑ Draft your conclusion. (p. 241)

15

Using Sources Effectively

As you draft your document, remember the range of strategies you can use to support your points, convey your ideas, and illustrate positions taken by other authors. This chapter discusses how you can use source information to meet the needs of your writing situation and addresses the primary techniques for integrating source information into your document: quotation, paraphrase, and summary. It also looks at techniques for working with numeric information, images, audio, video, and animations.

Much of the information in this chapter is based on MLA style, which is commonly used in the humanities. See Chapter 21 for more on MLA style and Chapters 22 to 24 for guidelines on APA, *Chicago*, and CSE styles.

15a

How can I use sources to accomplish my purposes as a writer?

Your sources can help you introduce ideas, contrast the ideas of other authors with your own, provide evidence for your points, define concepts, illustrate processes, clarify statements, set a mood, provide an example, and qualify or amplify a point. You can present information from sources in several ways:

- as a quotation, paraphrase, or summary
- as numerical information
- as illustrations such as images, audio, video, and animations

Depending on the point you want to make, some types of evidence might be more effective than others. The key is how your readers will react to the information you provide. In some cases, for example, numerical evidence might lend better support for a point than a quotation.

As you draft your document, consider how your use of sources can lead your readers to view your issue in terms that are most favorable to your purposes. By selecting source information carefully, you can make your point more directly than you might want to in your own words. Calling opponents of a proposal "inflexible" and "pig-headed," for example, might signal your biases too strongly. Quoting someone who uses those terms, however, allows you to get the point across without undermining an otherwise even and balanced tone.

The following are some of the most effective ways to use information, ideas, and arguments from sources to contribute to a written conversation about an issue.

Introduce an Idea or Argument

You can use a quotation, paraphrase, or summary to introduce an idea or argument to your readers. As you choose a quotation, paraphrase, or summary, keep in mind that it will call your readers' attention to particular aspects of your argument.

Consider how the following quotation, for instance, leads readers to view a public debate about education reform as a battle between reformers and an entrenched teachers union.

> "The teachers union has balked at even the most reasonable proposals for school reform," said Mary Sweeney, press secretary for Save Our Schools, which has

sponsored a referendum on the November ballot calling for funding for their voucher plan. "We believe
the November election will send a wake-up call about
the need to rethink their obstructionist behaviors."

> Phrases such as "balked at even the most reasonable proposals" and "their obstructionist behavior" place the blame for the problem on the teachers union.

If Sweeney and supporters of Referendum D are
successful, the educational landscape in . . .

In contrast, note how the following quotation frames the debate as a question
of how best to spend scarce education funds.

"In the past decade, state and local funding of public education in real dollars has
declined by 7.2 percent," said Jeffrey Allister, state chair of the governor's Special
Commission on Education Reform. "Referendum D, if passed, would further
erode that funding by shifting state dollars to private
schools."

> Phrases such as "funding of public education in real dollars has declined" and "further erode that funding" call attention to the financial challenges faced by schools.

As the state considers the merits of Referendum D,
which would institute the first statewide voucher program in the United States, opponents of the measure
have . . .

Contrast Ideas or Arguments

When you want to indicate that disagreement exists on an issue, you can use
source information to illustrate the nature and intensity of the disagreements.
The following example uses partial quotations (see p. 253) to highlight differences in proposed solutions to a problem.

> Solutions to the state's higher education funding shortfall range from traditional
> approaches, such as raising taxes, to more radical solutions, among them privatiz-
> ing state colleges and universities. Advocates of increased taxes, such as Vincent
> Richards of the Higher Education Coalition, argue that declines in state funding
> of higher education "must be reversed immediately or we will find ourselves in a
> situation where we are closing rural community colleges and only the wealthiest
> among us will have access to the best education" (A4). Those in favor of privatiz-
> ing higher education suggest, however, that free market approaches will ultimately
> bring about "a fairer situation in which the poor, many of whom have no interest
> in higher education, are no longer asked to subsidize higher and higher faculty
> salaries and larger football stadiums" (Pieters 23).

Base your choices about how to contrast ideas and arguments on the clarity and
conciseness of your sources and on the effects you hope to achieve. If you want
to express complex ideas as concisely as possible, you might use paraphrase and
summary. If you want to convey the emotional qualities of an author's position
on an issue, use quotations.

Provide Evidence for Your Argument

Arguments that consist of a series of unsupported assertions amount to little
more than a request for a reader's trust. Even when the writer is eminently trust-
worthy, most readers find such arguments easy to dismiss. In contrast, providing

evidence to support your assertions increases the likelihood that your readers will accept your argument. Note the differences between the following passages.

Unsupported Assertion:

Given a choice between two products of comparable quality, reputation, and cost, American consumers are far more likely to purchase goods that use environmentally friendly packaging. Encouraging the use of such packaging is a good idea for America.

> No evidence is provided to support the writer's assertion.

Supported Assertion:

Given a choice between two products of comparable quality, reputation, and cost, American consumers are far more likely to purchase goods that use environmentally friendly packaging. A recent study by the High Plains Research Institute found that the shelf life of several biodegradable plastics not only exceeded the shelf life of the products they were used to package, but also cost less to produce (Chen and Lohann 33). In addition, a study by the Consumer Products Institute found that, when made aware that products were packaged in environmentally friendly materials, consumers were more likely to buy those products.

> Summaries of the results of two studies provide evidence for the assertion made in the first sentence.

Similarly, visual sources can lend support to an assertion. For example, an assertion about the unintended consequences of military action might be accompanied by a photograph of a war-torn street or a wounded child.

Align Your Argument with an Authority

Aligning an argument with an authority—such as a subject matter expert, a scientist, a politician, or a religious figure—allows you to borrow someone else's credibility and status. Start by making an assertion and follow it with supporting information from a source, such as a quotation, paraphrase, or source summary.

> Although voice recognition appears to be a promising technology, challenges associated with vocabulary, homonyms, and accents have slowed its widespread implementation. "The computer right now can do a very good job of voice recognition," said Bill Gates, co-founder and former chairman of Microsoft Corporation. "It certainly will re-define the way we think of the machines when we have that voice input" (Gates, par. 42).

Define a Concept, Illustrate a Process, or Clarify a Statement

Writers commonly turn to information from sources to define concepts, illustrate processes, or clarify statements when the information is clearer and more concise than what they might write themselves. You might define a concept by quoting or paraphrasing a dictionary or encyclopedia, or use an illustration to help readers understand a complex process, such as the steps involved in cellular respiration.

Writers also use information from sources to clarify their statements. A writer might amplify a statement by providing examples from sources or qualify a statement by noting that it applies only to specific situations and then use a quotation or paraphrase from a source to back that up.

> Studies have found connections between weight loss and coffee intake. This doesn't mean that drinking a couple of cups of coffee each day leads to weight loss. However, three recent studies reported that individuals who increased their coffee intake from fewer than three cups to more than eight cups of coffee per day experienced weight losses of up to 7 percent over a two month period (Chang, Johnson and Salazar, Neiman). "It may be that increased caffeine intake led to a higher metabolic level, which in turn led to weight loss," noted John Chang, a senior researcher at the Centers for Disease Control. "Or it might be that drinking so much coffee depressed participants' appetites" (232).

Set a Mood

You can also choose quotations and illustrations with an eye toward establishing an overall mood for your readers. The emotional impact of images of a celebration at a sporting event, an expression of grief at a funeral, or a calming mountain vista can lead your readers to react in specific ways to your document. Similarly, a striking quote, such as "The screams of pain coming out of that room will stay with me as long as I live," can evoke a specific mood among your readers.

Provide an Example

It's often better to *show* with an example than to *tell* with a general description. Examples provide concrete evidence in your document. Note how the writer of the following passage used an example from a well-known film to illustrate a point about her family's relationship with food.

> And the obsession with eating! My grandmother feeds us constantly. My dad and I always laugh at that scene in *Goodfellas* where the mobsters show up at two in the morning after killing someone, and one mobster's mother whips up a full pasta meal for them. We know that my grandmother would do the same thing: "Are you hungry? Here, sit, eat!" Grandma holds interventions over pasta. If she is unhappy with something someone in the family is doing, she invites everyone over for pasta and we hash it out together.

Amplify or Qualify a Point

You can use amplification to expand the scope of a point. Consider how information from a source is used in the following example to broaden a discussion of the dangers football players face when they add bulk.

> NFL offensive linemen who weigh less than 300 pounds are often described as "undersized," so it's no surprise that young football players are getting the message that bigger is better—and bulking up. A recent study of high school linemen in Iowa showed that 45% were overweight and 9% were severely obese, while only 18% of other young males were overweight; even more troubling, a study in Michigan revealed that among football players from ages 9 to 14, 45% could be considered overweight or obese (as cited in Longman, 2007).

Qualifications, in contrast, allow you to narrow the scope of a statement, reducing the possibility that your readers might misunderstand your meaning. Note how the writer made it clear that deaths related to weight gain are a rare occurrence in football.

> Although such fatalities are unusual, a growing number of doctors believe that use of dietary supplements increases the risk of heat stroke among football players.

15b

How can I integrate sources into my draft?

You can integrate information, ideas, and arguments from sources into your draft by quoting, paraphrasing, summarizing, presenting numerical information, and using illustrations. As you do so, make a point of distinguishing your ideas and information from those found in your sources.

Identify Your Sources

You should identify the sources of information in your document for several reasons. First, doing so fulfills your obligation to document your sources. Second, it allows you (and your readers) to recognize the boundaries between your ideas and those borrowed from sources. Third, it can help you strengthen your document by calling attention to the qualifications or experiences of the person whose ideas you are incorporating.

Use Attributions and In-Text Citations   Whenever you quote, paraphrase, or summarize, distinguish between your ideas and information obtained through your sources by using attributions — brief comments such as "according to" or "as the author points out" — to alert your readers that the point is not your own.

Writers who use MLA or APA documentation format also provide citations — or acknowledgments of source information — within the text of their document to indicate where borrowed material ends. These citations, in turn, refer readers to a list of works cited or a list of references at the end of the document.

Note the following examples, which use attributions and in-text citations:

MLA Style:

Pamela Coke argues, "Education reform is the best solution for fixing our public schools" (22).

> Attributions identify the author of the quotations.

"Education reform is the best solution for fixing our public schools" (Coke 22).

> MLA-style in-text citations include the author's name and exact page reference.

APA Style:

Pamela Coke (2008) has argued, "Education reform is the best solution for fixing our public schools" (p. 22).

"Education reform is the best solution for fixing our public schools" (Coke, 2008, p. 22).

> APA-style in-text citations include the author's name, publication date, and exact page reference.

As you acknowledge material you've borrowed from sources, you'll want to vary the wording of your attributions. As you do, be aware of the way that the verbs in attributions can convey important shades of meaning—for example, the difference between writing that someone "alleged" something and someone "confirmed" something.

Some Common Attributions:

according to	claimed	expressed	reported
acknowledged	commented	inquired	said
affirmed	confirmed	interpreted	stated
alleged	declared	mused	suggested
asked	denied	noted	thought
asserted	described	observed	wondered
assumed	disputed	pointed out	wrote
believed	emphasized	remarked	

You can learn more about in-text citations and the MLA, APA, *Chicago*, and CSE documentation systems in Part 5.

Provide a Context   Skilled writers know the importance of providing a context for the source information they include in their documents. It's not enough to simply put text within two quotation marks and move on. Such "orphan quotations"—quotations dropped into a paragraph without any introduction—are confusing. Worse, paraphrases and summaries inserted without context can easily be mistaken for the writer's own work.

To provide a clear context for your source information, establish why the quotation, paraphrase, or summary is reliable by identifying the source's credentials. In addition, indicate how it relates to your main idea and what it contributes to the point you are making. If you don't, readers will wonder why it's there.

However, Wechsler et al. (2003) of the Harvard School of Public Health analyzed trends at schools using social norms marketing and revealed that the campaigns did not necessarily decrease student drinking; in some cases, schools even reported higher alcohol consumption, according to seven criteria that measured whether students drank, how much, and how often. As the researchers explained, "individual students' drinking behaviors align more closely to the drinking behaviors of their immediate social group rather than to the overall student population at a given school" (paras. 30–33).

> Attribution identifies the source as experts.

> Writer follows APA style; parenthetical citation identifies the paragraph numbers where the quotation was found.

Quote Strategically

A well-chosen quotation can have a powerful impact on your readers' perception of your argument and on the overall quality of your document. Quotations can also add a sense of immediacy by bringing in the voice of someone who has been affected by an issue or lend a sense of authority to your argument by conveying the words of an expert. Quotations can range in form from brief, partial quotations to extended, block quotations. As you integrate quotations into your document, remember that you might need to modify them to suit your purpose and fit the flow of your sentences. When you do, be careful to punctuate them properly.

Use Partial, Complete, and Block Quotations   Quotations can be parts of sentences (partial), whole sentences (complete), or long passages (block). When you choose one type of quotation over another, consider the length and complexity of the passage as well as the obligation to convey ideas and information fairly.

Partial Quotations   Partial quotations can be a single word, phrase, or most of a sentence. They are often used to convey a well-turned phrase or to complete a sentence using important words from a source, as in the following example.

> Nadine K. Maxwell, a guidance services coordinator in Fairfax, Virginia, says that students' chances of being admitted can be greater if they apply early, although this varies from school to school and year to year and "may depend upon the applicant pool at the school where they are applying" (32).

Quotation marks indicate the borrowed phrase.

Source information, including the number of the page containing the quotation, is clearly identified

Complete Quotations   Complete quotations are typically one or more complete sentences and are most often used when the meaning of the passage cannot be conveyed adequately by a few well-chosen words, as in the following example.

> I smiled when I read Elizabeth Gilbert's memoir *Eat, Pray, Love*. She writes, "The Neapolitan women in particular are such a gang of tough-voiced, loud-mouthed, generous, nosy dames, all bossy and annoyed and right up in your face just trying to friggin' *help* you for chrissake, you dope — *why they gotta do every-thing around here?*" (78).

Since the source of the quotation is identified in an attribution ("Elizabeth Gilbert's memoir . . ."), only the page number appears in the citation at the end of the sentence.

Block Quotations   Block quotations are extended quotations (usually more than four typed lines) that are set off in a block from the rest of the text. In general, use a colon to introduce the quotation, indent the entire quotation one inch (or ten spaces) from the left margin, and include source information according to the documentation system you are using (such as MLA, APA, *Chicago*, or CSE). Since the blocked text indicates to your readers that you are quoting directly, you do not need to include quotation marks.

In the article "In the Best Interest of America, Affirmative Action in Higher Education Is a Must," William H. Gray III states:

Quotation marks are not used to surround block quotations.

> High school achievement and test scores are considered to be very important criteria in the admissions process by most of the four-year public degree-granting colleges and universities. Nonetheless, high school grades and test scores are not the only factors considered by colleges and universities in the admissions process. Other factors that

influence college admissions decisions include high school rank, being an athlete, alumni connections, extracurricular activities, special talents, and other personal characteristics of applicants. (par. 5)

> In block quotations, the citation information is placed after the period.

> A paragraph number is provided for an online source.

Modify Quotations as Appropriate   [FRAMING MY ARGUMENT]   You can modify quotations to fit your draft. It is acceptable, for example, to delete unnecessary words or to change the tense of a word in a partial quotation so that it fits your sentence. For example, if you wanted to change the tense of a verb in a partial quotation so that it fits the sentence, you would use brackets to indicate the change.

Original Quotation:

"They treated us like family and refused to accept a tip."

Quotation Modified Using Brackets:

> Brackets indicate a word that has been changed.

It's a place where the staff treats you "like family and [refuses] to accept a tip," said travel writer Melissa Ancomi.

Keep in mind, however, that research writers have an obligation to quote sources accurately and fairly. You should indicate when you have added or deleted words, and you should not modify quotations in a way that distorts their meaning.

The most useful strategies you can use to modify quotations include using ellipses (...) to indicate deleted words, using brackets [ ] to clarify meaning, and using "sic" to note errors in a source. You can learn more about modifying quotations using these strategies on pages 104–105.

Punctuate Quotations Correctly   The rules for punctuating quotations are as follows.

- Use double quotation marks (" ") around partial or complete quotations. Do not use quotation marks for block quotations.

- Use single quotation marks (' ') to indicate quoted material within a quotation:

  "The hotel manager told us to 'make ourselves at home.'"

- In most cases, place punctuation marks such as commas, periods, question marks, and exclamation points inside quotation marks:

  Dawn Smith asked an important question: "Do college students understand the importance of avoiding running up credit card debt?"

- Place colons and semicolons outside quotation marks:

  Many young consumers consider themselves "free at last"; all too often, however, they find that freedom has its costs.

- Do not put a punctuation mark that ends your own sentence inside quotation marks if doing so will alter the meaning of the original text. In the following example, the original quotation is not a question, so the question mark should be placed after the quotation mark:

> But what can be gained from following the committee's recommendation that the state should "avoid, without exceptions, any proposed tax hike"?

- When citation information is provided after a quotation, place the punctuation mark (comma, period, semicolon, colon, or question mark) after the parenthetical citation. In a block quotation, place the end punctuation before the parenthetical citation.

> "Preliminary reports have been consistent," Yates notes. "Without immediate changes to current practices, we will deplete known supplies by mid-century" (335).

- Use three spaced periods (ellipsis) to indicate an omission within a sentence:

> According to critic Joe Robinson, Americans are overworked: "Ask Americans how things are really going and you'll hear stories of . . . fifty- and sixty-hour weeks with no letup in sight" (467).

- Place a period before the ellipsis to indicate an omission at the end of a sentence:

> The most recent information indicates, says Chen, that "we can expect a significant increase in costs by the end of the decade. . . . Those costs, however, should ramp up slowly" (35).

Paraphrase Information, Ideas, and Arguments

A paraphrase is a restatement, in your own words, of a passage from a source. Unlike summaries, which are shorter than the text being summarized, paraphrases are about as long as the text on which they are based. Paraphrases can be used to illustrate or support a point you make in your document or to illustrate another author's argument about an issue.

Your notes are likely to include a number of paraphrases of information, ideas, and arguments from your sources. (See Chapter 6 to learn how to write a paraphrase.) To integrate these paraphrases into your document, begin by making sure your paraphrase is an accurate and fair representation of the source. Reread the source to double-check the accuracy and fairness of your paraphrase, then revise the paraphrase so that it fits the context and tone of your document. Use attributions to ensure a smooth transition from your ideas to the ideas found in the source.

In the following example, note how Alexis Alvarez lets her readers know where her statement ends and where the support for her statement, in the form of a paraphrase, begins.

> Competitive sports also teach athletes how to cope with failure — Alexis's idea
> as well as success. In the best of situations, as Sieghart (2004)
> noted, athletes are able to assess their achievements realistically,
> letting neither winning nor losing consume their reality.

The source of paraphrase is cited per APA style.

An attribution marks transition from Alexis's idea to source ideas.

TUTORIAL

How do I integrate a quotation into my draft?

After you select a passage to quote, you'll need to acknowledge the source, punctuate the quotation properly, and provide a context for the information. This example uses MLA style; be sure to follow the guidelines for the documentation style you are using.

Original Passage

1 Locate the passage you want to quote and identify the text you want to include in the quotation.

But there is still a black cloud hovering over this seemingly sunny scenario. Wind turbines remain expensive to build — often prohibitively so. On average, it costs about $1 million per megawatt to construct a wind turbine farm, compared to about $600,000 per megawatt for a conventional gas-fired power plant; in the economic calculations of power companies, the fact that wind is free doesn't close this gap. In short, the price of building wind power must come down if it's ever to be more than a niche technology.

Source: Fairley, Peter. "Wind Power for Pennies." *Technology Review* 105.6 (2002): 40–46. Print.

2 Add quotation marks or, if the quotation is long, set the text in a block (see p. 253). If you modify the passage, use ellipses and brackets appropriately (see p. 254).

"Wind turbines remain expensive to build. . . . On average, it costs about $1 million per megawatt to construct a wind turbine farm, compared to about $600,000 per megawatt for a conventional gas-fired power plant"

3 Identify the source of the quotation and the location, such as the page number. Give the author's qualifications in an author tag if you haven't already done so for this source in your document.

In his article "Wind Power for Pennies," Peter Fairley notes, "Wind turbines remain expensive to build. On average, it costs about $1 million per megawatt to construct a wind turbine farm, compared to about $600,000 per megawatt for a conventional gas-fired power plant" (40).

4 Avoid "orphan quotations" by providing a context for your quotation. Introduce the quotation and indicate how it relates to your argument.

At this point, some still argue that the price of wind power is too steep. In his article "Wind Power for Pennies," Peter Fairley notes, "Wind turbines remain expensive to build. . . . On average, it costs about $1 million per megawatt to construct a wind turbine farm, compared to about $600,000 per megawatt for a conventional gas-fired power plant" (40). These differences in cost are then passed on to the consumer in the form of higher energy costs for wind-generated electricity.

Review another example and work on quoting your own sources at **bedfordresearcher.com**. Click on Interactive Exercises.

Summarize

A summary is a concise statement, written in your own words, of information found in a source (see p. 108 to learn about summarizing entire sources and lengthy passages within a source). When you integrate a summary into your draft, review the source to make sure your summary is an accurate and fair representation of the ideas in the original source. Be careful, as well, to identify the source and include a citation. You can summarize an entire source, parts of a particular source, or a group of sources to support your argument.

Summarize an Entire Source

Research writers frequently summarize an entire work. In some cases, the summary might occupy one or more paragraphs or be integrated into a discussion contained in one or more paragraphs. In other cases, the summary might be as brief as a single sentence.

Alexis Alvarez summarized a report issued by the Centers for Disease Control and Prevention in her research essay about steroid use by adolescent girls involved in competitive sports.

> In May 2004, the Centers for Disease Control and Prevention (CDC) published its latest figures on self-reported drug use among young people in grades 9 through 12. The CDC study, "Youth Risk Behavior Surveillance — December 2003," found that 6.1% of its survey participants reported using steroids at least once, up from 2.2% in 1993. The report also showed that use of steroids appears to be increasing among younger girls: While only 3.3% of 12th-grade girls reported using steroids, 7.3% of 9th-grade girls reported using them. Moreover, girls might be starting to use steroids at a higher rate than boys. The CDC study indicated that 9th-grade girls had reported slightly higher rates of steroid use than boys (7.3% and 6.9% respectively), while 10th-, 11th-, and 12th-grade girls all reported lower use than boys.

The author, title, and publication date are identified in the text, so parenthetical citation is not required for either MLA or APA style.

The main point of the report.

Additional information from the report.

In contrast, Alexis offered a much briefer, "nutshell" summary of a related source.

> A 2003 article in *Drug Week* stated that girls who participate in sports more than eight hours a week are at considerable risk for taking many illicit drugs: The higher the level at which athletes compete, the higher their risk for substance abuse ("Sporting Activities").

Summarize Specific Ideas and Information from a Source

You can also use summaries to convey key information or ideas from a source. In his research essay, Nicholas Brothers summarized a section of a book about private military corporations.

> A look at definitions in Singer's *Corporate Warriors* reveals that PMCs and traditional mercenaries differ in several key ways. Perhaps the most important difference is that a private military corporation is just that:

The summary is introduced with the author and specific source of the ideas.

IV Writing Your Document

a legal corporate entity[10] (as opposed to the illegal adventurer or rag-tag squad evoked by the word "mercenary"). Another significant distinction is that PMCs offer a wide range of services . . . while mercenaries can rarely do more than engage in combat.

> Per Chicago style, a citation appears as a numbered footnote.

Summarize a Group of Sources   In addition to summarizing a single source, research writers often summarize groups of sources. It's not unusual, for instance, to encounter in research documents phrases such as "Numerous authors have argued . . ." or "The research in this area seems to indicate that . . . ." Such collective summaries allow you to establish a point briefly and with authority. They are effective particularly at the beginning of a document, when you are establishing a foundation for your argument, and can serve as a transitional device when you move from one major section of the document to another.

When you are summarizing a group of sources, separate the citations with a semicolon. MLA guidelines require including author and page information, as in the following example.

> Several critics have argued that the Hemingway code hero is not always male (Graulich 217; Sherman 78; Watters 33).

APA guidelines require including author and date information, as in the following example:

> The benefits of early detection of breast cancer have been well documented (Page, 2007; Richards, 2007; Vincent, 2008).

Present Numerical Information

If it suits the issue you are addressing, you might use numerical information, such as statistics, in your document. You can present this information within sentences, or you might use tables, charts, or graphs, as Pete Jacquez did on his Web site about wind power (see Figure 15.1). Keep in mind that you still need to accurately and fairly present the numerical information in your document and clearly identify the source of the information, just as you would for textual information. For more information about using tables, charts, and graphs, see pp. 291–95.

Use Images, Audio, Video, and Animations

Including images in your print document and images, audio, video or animation files in your electronic document can enhance its effectiveness. Use caution, however, when taking images and audio, video, or animations from other sources. Simply copying a photograph into your document might be a form of plagiarism. The same is true of audio, video, and animations files.

Chris Norris carefully documented the sources of the images, audio clips, and video clips he used in his multimodal research essay. Since he was writing an academic essay—rather than a document intended for publication and wide distribution—he did not seek permission to use the images, audio, and video that

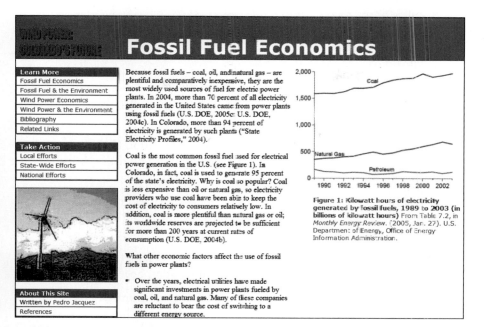

FIGURE 15.1 Chart on Pete Jacquez's Web Site

he had found in other sources. (In contrast, the publisher of this book sought and received permission to publish those materials.)

15c

How should I document my sources?

You should cite your sources within the text of your document as well as provide complete publication information for each source you've used. Fully documenting your sources in this way can help you achieve your purpose as a writer, such as establishing your authority and persuading your readers. It also helps you avoid

Information Literacy

If you are creating a digital document, such as a Web page or a multimedia presentation, use the following approach to integrating digital illustrations.

- Make a link between your document and a document that contains an image, sound clip, or video clip — rather than simply copying the image and placing it in your document.
- If it isn't possible or appropriate to create a link to another document, you should contact the owner of the image, sound clip, or video clip for permission to use it.
- If you cannot contact the owner, review the fair use guidelines discussed on page 125 for guidance about using the material.

As you've done for the other sources you cite in your document, make sure you fairly present images, audio, or video and identify their author or creator.

plagiarism, gives credit to others who have written about an issue, and creates a record of their work that your readers can follow and build upon.

Choose a Documentation System

The documentation systems most commonly used in academic disciplines are the following.

- **MLA** This style, from the Modern Language Association (MLA), is used primarily in the humanities — English, philosophy, linguistics, world languages, and so on. See Chapter 21.

- **APA** This style, from the American Psychological Association, is used mainly in the social sciences — psychology, sociology, anthropology, political science, economics, education, and so on. See Chapter 22.

- *Chicago* Developed by the University of Chicago Press, this style is used primarily in history, journalism, and the humanities. See Chapter 23.

- **CSE** This style, from the Council of Science Editors (formerly the Council of Biology Editors), is used mainly in the physical and life sciences — chemistry, geology, biology, botany, and so on — and in mathematics. See Chapter 24.

Your choice of documentation system will be guided by the discipline or field within which you are writing and by any requirements associated with your research writing project. If your project has been assigned to you, ask the person who assigned it or someone who has written a similar document which documentation system you should use. If you are working on a project for a writing class, your instructor will most likely tell you which documentation system to follow.

Your choice will also be guided by the genre you have chosen for your document. For example, while academic essays and articles appearing in scholarly journals typically use a documentation system such as MLA or APA, newspaper and magazine articles often do not and rely instead on identification of sources in the main text of the document rather than in a works cited or references list. If you write a digital document that cites other online sources, you might simply link to those sources.

Provide In-Text References and Publication Information

The specific format of your in-text citations will depend on the documentation system you use. If you use MLA or APA style, you'll cite — or formally acknowledge — information in the text using parentheses and add a list of sources to the end of your document. Key publication information is usually provided in a works cited list (MLA) and CSE, reference list (APA), or bibliography (*Chicago*). This list appears at the end of the document and includes the following information about each source.

- author(s) and/or editor(s)
- title
- publication date
- publisher and city of publication (for books)
- periodical name, volume, issue, and page numbers (for articles)
- URL and access date (for online publications)

Each documentation system creates an association between citations in the text of a document and the works cited or reference page. See Part V for documentation models.

Check for Unattributed Sources in Your Document

Writers sometimes neglect to identify the sources from which they have drawn their information. You should include a complete citation for each source you refer to in your document. The citation should appear in the text of the document (as an in-text citation, footnote, or endnote) or in a works cited list, reference list, or bibliography.

In the following MLA-style examples, the writer includes parenthetical citations that refer readers to a list of works cited at the end of the document. Note that MLA style allows for a combination of attributions and parenthetical information to refer to sources.

Reid Vincent argues, "We must explore emerging energy technologies before we reach a peak oil crisis" (322).

"We must explore emerging energy technologies before we reach a peak oil crisis" (Vincent 322).

MLA-style in-text citations include the author's name and exact page reference.

Distinguish Between Your Ideas and Ideas in Your Sources

Failing to distinguish between your ideas and ideas drawn from your sources can lead readers to think other writers' ideas are yours. Examine how the writer of the following passage might have failed to distinguish his ideas from those of Joel Levine and Lawrence May, authors of a source used in the essay.

Failing to Credit Ideas to a Source:

According to Joel Levine and Lawrence May, authors of *Getting In*, entrance exams are an extremely important part of a student's college application and carry a great deal of weight. In fact, a college entrance examination is one of the two most significant factors in getting into college. The other, unsurprisingly, is high school grades.

Because the second and third sentences fail to identify Levine and May as the source of the information about the second important factor affecting admissions decisions—high school grades—the passage implies that the writer of the research essay is the source of that information.

In contrast, the writer actually included the following passage in the essay.

Giving Credit to the Source:

According to Joel Levine and Lawrence May, authors of *Getting In*, entrance exams are an extremely important part of a student's college application and carry a great deal of weight. In fact, they claim that a college entrance examination is "one of the two most significant factors" in getting into college (the other, unsurprisingly, being high school grades).

> The attribution, "they claim," credits Levine and May as the source of the information.

> Quotation marks are used to indicate a partial quotation.

To distinguish between your ideas and those obtained through your sources, use attributions—words or phrases that alert your readers to the source of the ideas or information you are using. As you take notes and draft your document, use the name of an author or the title of the source you're drawing from each time you introduce ideas from a source.

Examples of Attributions:

According to Scott McPherson . . .

Jill Bedard writes . . .

Tom Huckin reports . . .

Kate Kiefer observes . . .

Bob Phelps suggests . . .

In the words of Pamela Coke . . .

As Ellen Page tells it . . .

Reid Vincent indicates . . .

Jessica Richards calls our attention to . . .

> **QUICK REFERENCE**

Using Sources Effectively

- ✔ Use source information to accomplish your purpose. (p. 247)
- ✔ Integrate quotations appropriately. (p. 252)
- ✔ Integrate paraphrases appropriately. (p. 255)
- ✔ Integrate summaries appropriately. (p. 257)
- ✔ Integrate numerical information appropriately. (p. 258)
- ✔ Integrate images, audio, video, and animations appropriately. (p. 258)
- ✔ Choose a documentation system. (p. 260)
- ✔ Provide in-text references and a works cited or reference list. (p. 260)
- ✔ Check for unattributed sources in your document. (p. 261)
- ✔ Distinguish between your work and information, ideas, and arguments from your sources. (p. 261)

16

Writing with Style

Key Questions

In many cases, participants in a written conversation never meet. Your document might well be the only point of contact between you and your readers. If you want your readers to form a positive opinion of you and your ideas, you'll need to attend not only to what you say but also to how you say it. Although each writer and every teacher of writing defines *style* differently, and the definition of *appropriate style*—like appropriate behavior—can vary widely by writing situation, you'll find that paying attention to a few aspects of style can vastly improve the quality of any document you write.

16a

How can I begin to write with style?

Good style begins with an understanding of your writing situation. By reading the work of other writers addressing your issue, you can gain insights into the appropriate style for the conversation you've decided to join. For example, if you are involved in an issue that is being addressed by scholars working in the social sciences, you might find that documents written about your issue use long and fairly complex sentences, do not use *I* or other first-person pronouns, and cite sources using the American Psychological Association's documentation system. You might also find that the authors of the documents you have read are cautious about making strong claims—that they hedge their claims through the use of phrases such as "these results appear to suggest" or "it appears that." In contrast, if you are involved in an issue that is being written about in the popular media, such the *Wall Street Journal, Time* magazine, or CNN.com, you might find that the sentences are comparatively brief, occasionally refer to the author in first person, cite sources in a general way in the body of the document, and are more likely to make strong claims.

In addition to understanding your writing situation, you can draw on a number of general principles to develop an appropriate style. Regardless of the issue you are addressing, your readers will appreciate it if you write concisely, use active voice and passive voice effectively, adopt a consistent point of view, vary the structure of your sentences, and choose your words carefully.

Write Concisely

Readers don't want to work any harder than necessary to understand and engage with the information, ideas, and arguments in a document. They get unhappy if they find it hard to read a document—so unhappy, in fact, that they'll often give up on a document that's hard to read.

One of the keys to writing clearly is keeping your words to a minimum. Consider the following examples.

> Please join me, Dr. Watson. I have concluded that I am in a situation in which I require your assistance.
>
> Come here, Dr. Watson. I need you.
>
> Help!

The second example, reputed to be the first words ever spoken on a telephone, was spoken by Alexander Graham Bell after he'd spilled acid on his pants. Had he spoken the first sentence instead, he might have wasted crucial time while he waited a few extra seconds for his assistant to figure out what he was being asked to do. It's possible that the simple exclamation of "Help!" might have been even more effective and would certainly have taken less time to utter. Then again, it might have been too vague for his assistant to figure out just how he needed to act and what sort of help was required.

In general, if two sentences provide the same information, you'll find that the briefer sentence is easier to understand. In some cases, however, writing too little will leave your readers wondering what you are trying to get across.

Three techniques can help you write more concisely.

- **Remove unnecessary modifiers.** Unnecessary modifiers are words that provide little or no additional information to a reader, such as *fine, many, somewhat, great, quite, sort of, lots, really,* and *very.*

Example Sentence with Unnecessary Modifiers:

The Volvo S80 serves as a really excellent example of a very fine performance sedan.

Revised Example:

The Volvo S80 serves as an excellent example of a performance sedan.

- **Remove unnecessary introductory phrases.** Avoid phrases such as *there are, there is, these have, these are, here are, here is, it has been reported that, it has been said that, it is evident that, it is obvious that,* and so on. Sentences beginning with *it goes without saying,* for example, allow you to emphasize a point, but you can often recast such sentences more concisely by simply stating the point.

Example Sentence with Unnecessary Introductory Phrase:

It goes without saying that drinking water should be clean.

Revised Example:

Drinking water should be clean.

- **Eliminate stock phrases.** Search your document for phrases that you can replace with one or two words, such as the following.

Stock Phrase:	Alternative:
as a matter of fact	in fact
at all times	always
at that point in time	then
at this point in time	now, currently
at the present time	now, currently
because of the fact that	because
by means of	by
due to the fact that	because
in order to	to
in spite of the fact that	although, though
in the event that	if

Example Sentence with Stock Phrase:

Call the security desk in the event that the alarm sounds.

Revised Example:

Call the security desk if the alarm sounds.

TUTORIAL

How can I write concisely?

Write concisely by removing unnecessary modifiers, unnecessary introductory phrases, and stock phrases. In this example, Elizabeth Leontiev revises a wordy, vague sentence into a more concise, specific one.

Original Sentence:
There are many problems that the peasants of South America face due to the fact that America has declared war on drugs.

1 Remove unnecessary introductory phrases such as *there are* and *it is*. Often, these phrases are clues that you are using the passive voice. Rephrase the sentence using the active voice.

The peasants of South America face many problems due to the fact that America has declared war on drugs.

2 Remove unnecessary modifiers — words that provide little or no additional information to a reader — such as *fine, many, somewhat, great, quite, sort of, lots, really,* and *very*. Instead, supply specific information.

The peasants of South America face serious hardship, including poverty and cultural degradation, due to the fact that America has declared war on drugs.

3 Eliminate stock phrases such as *in order to* and *at this point in time*. Often, you can substitute a single strong word for an entire stock phrase. Similarly, use apostrophes to show possession, rather than *of* phrases.

Concise Sentence:
South American peasants face serious hardship, including poverty and cultural degradation, because of America's war on drugs.

Review another example and work on writing concisely at **bedfordresearcher.com**. Click on Interactive Exercises.

IV Writing Your Document

Use Active and Passive Voice Effectively

Active and passive voice refer to two distinct types of sentences. A sentence written in active voice specifies an actor—a person or thing—who carries out an action:

Active Voice:

Juan took an exam.
The tornado leveled the town.

In contrast, a sentence written in passive voice indicates that something was done, but does not specify who or what did it:

Passive Voice:

The exam was taken.
The town was leveled.

In general, you'll want to emphasize the actor because sentences written in active voice are easier to understand and provide more information.

Passive voice, however, can be effective when active voice would require the inclusion of unnecessary information. Many scientific experiments, for example, are conducted by large teams of researchers. Few readers would want to know which members of the team carried out every task discussed in an article about the experiment. Rather than using active voice, as in "Janelle Knott, assisted by Jen Lee and Victor Garza, anesthetized the mice, and then Jen Lee and Richard Simpson examined their eyes for lesions," you can use passive voice, as in "The mice were anesthetized and their eyes were examined for lesions." In this case, the sentence written in passive voice is clearer, easier to understand, and does not include unnecessary information.

Passive voice is also useful if you wish to emphasize the recipient of the action, rather than the person or thing carrying out the action. Police reports, for example, often use passive voice, as in "The suspect was apprehended at the corner of Oak and Main Streets."

Adopt a Consistent Point of View

Writers adopt a particular point of view as they write:

- first person: *I, we*
- second person: *you*
- third person: *she, he, it, one, they*, or nouns that describe a particular group or individual, such as *doctors, teachers, engineer, lawyer, Mr. Smith*, or *Lee Chen.*

When writers shift their point of view within a sentence, readers notice—and sometimes have to stop and ask themselves what just happened. Consider the following example.

Shift in Point of View:

After the climbers reached the summit in record time, we burst into song.

IV Writing Your Document

The sentence begins with a third-person point of view (*the climbers*) and then shifts to first-person (*we*). The sentence would be easier to understand if it were written in either first- or third-person.

Consistent Point of View:

After the climbers reached the summit in record time, they burst into song.
After we reached the summit in record time, we burst into song.

Choose Your Words Carefully   [FRAMING MY ARGUMENT]

Pay attention to level of formality and the extent to which specialized terms are used in the conversation about your issue. Pay attention as well to the variety and specificity of your words.

Formality   Your reading of other documents that contribute to the conversation about your issue will give you insights into the level of formality you should strive for when you draft, revise, and edit your document. Some written conversations, such as those conducted on blogs and Web discussion forums, are relatively informal and can even show evidence of lack of respect for the opinions of other participants in the discussion. Others, such as those conducted through scholarly journals or magazines such as the *Nation* or *Atlantic Monthly*, adopt a formal, restrained tone. Still others, such as those conducted through many popular media outlets, are casual but respectful. As you read about your issue, note the level of formality and the manner in which writers refer to ideas and arguments in other sources.

Informal Writing:

It was awesome to see how well the U.S. soccer team did in the last World Cup.

Formal Writing:

The performance of the U.S. soccer team in the most recent World Cup was gratifying.

Specialized Language   Specialized language, sometimes called jargon, can allow writers and readers to communicate effectively and efficiently—but only if both parties are familiar with the terms. If you are contributing to a conversation in which specialized language is used heavily, familiarize yourself with the terms your readers will expect you to use. For example, if you plan to write an article for a Web site that focuses on motorcycle touring, you can write more concisely and with greater accuracy if you use the proper terminology.

Ineffective Use of General Language:

Braking that involves a mechanism that coordinates proportionally the amount of pressure applied to your front and rear brakes during turns that get progressively tighter can be hazardous if you fail to initiate the turn properly.

Effective Use of Specialized Language:

Linked braking during decreasing-radius turns can be hazardous if you fail to initiate the turn properly.

In contrast, readers who are unfamiliar with specialized language will find it more difficult to understand your point. Most people in the United States, for example, have at least a passing familiarity with basketball, but many would find it difficult to understand the following statement.

Ineffective Use of Specialized Language for a General Audience:

Box-and-one defenses are largely ineffective against well-executed pick-and-roll plays that result not in shots, but in skip passes, particularly if the pick-and-rolls are initiated on the baseline.

Variety   Variety is not only the spice of life—it's also the key ingredient in an effective document. Even a well-conceptualized and thoroughly supported argument can fail to impress if it's presented in dull, monotonous language. Consider the differences between the following examples.

Lack of Varied Word Choice:

The U.S. space program has benefited the United States in more ways than most U.S. government programs, largely because of the important technologies that have found their way into the U.S. economy

Varied Word Choice:

NASA has benefited the nation in more ways than most federal programs, largely because of the important technologies that have found their way into the U.S. economy.

16b

How can I polish my style?

You can improve the overall quality of your document by varying your sentence patterns to produce an appealing rhythm, creating effective transitions, varying your source attributions, avoiding sexist language, consulting a handbook, and reading widely.

Vary Your Sentence Structure

On a basic level, there are four types of sentences.

Statements:	Dick runs quickly.
Questions:	How quickly did Dick run?
Commands:	Run, Dick, run.
Exclamations:	Way to go, Dick!

There are also four basic sentence structures, distinguished by the types and numbers of *clauses* they contain. A clause—a sequence of words containing a subject and a verb—can be either *independent* or *dependent*. (Sometimes these types of clauses are referred to as *main* and *subordinate*, respectively.) The primary difference between these types of clauses is that independent clauses can function on their own as a complete sentence, while dependent clauses cannot.

Simple (a single independent clause):

Jane runs quickly.

Compound (two or more independent clauses):

Jane runs quickly, but she doesn't run as quickly as Dick.

Complex (an independent clause and a dependent clause):

Although Jane runs quickly, Dick is quicker.

Dependent clause   Independent clause

Compound-Complex (two or more independent clauses and at least one dependent clause):

All things considered, the Dick and Jane readers were wildly successful, but they have faded into the comfortable oblivion of history.

Dependent clause

Independent clause

Independent clause

Mixing sentence types and structures helps to produce an appealing rhythm in your writing. If you neglect to vary your sentences, on the other hand, your readers are likely to find your document monotonous and boring. To keep your readers' interest, vary your sentence type, structure, and length. Consider the following examples.

Similar Sentence Structure and Length:

We decided to spend the morning at El Rastro. El Rastro is a Sunday morning flea market extraordinaire. We decided to take the subway to get there. A man stood quite close as we got on. I found this strange in an uncrowded subway station. Then I felt his hand in my left pocket. I also felt his hand on my back. It's a good thing that I'm ticklish. I instinctively shrugged away from his hands. Then I swore loudly and imaginatively at him. (It's inappropriate to swear on a Sunday in Spain. I wouldn't have done it under normal circumstances.) He had almost gotten away with my sunglasses. This would almost certainly have disappointed him. I know it would have inconvenienced me.

> Each sentence uses the same sentence type (statements) and the same simple sentence structure. Sentence length ranges from seven to nine words.

Varied Sentence Structure and Length:

We decided to spend the morning at El Rastro, a Sunday morning flea market extraordinaire. As we got on the subway to get to El Rastro, I noticed that a man was standing quite close to me — strange, since the subway wasn't crowded. Then I felt his hand in my left pocket and his hand on my back. (Fortunately, I'm ticklish.) "What the heck?" I thought, instinctively shrugging away and swearing at him (an inappropriate thing to do on a Sunday morning in Spain, but I was caught off guard). He had almost gotten away with my sunglasses, which would have disappointed him and inconvenienced me.

> Sentence types include statements and questions. Sentence structures include simple, compound, and complex. Sentence length ranges from three to twenty-eight words.

Create Effective Transitions

Transitions help readers understand the relationships between sentences, paragraphs, and even sections of a document. Essentially, they smooth the way for readers, helping them understand how information, ideas, and arguments are related to each other. Transitions are most effective when they don't call attention to themselves, but instead move the reader's eye along to the next sentence, paragraph, or section. Consider the following examples of the steps involved in preparing fish.

No Transitions:

Catch the fish. Clean the fish. Filet the fish. Cook the fish. Eat the fish. Catch another fish.

Inconsistent Transitions:

First, catch the fish. Secondly, clean the fish. When you've done that, filet the fish. Next, cook the fish. Fifth, eat the fish. After all is said and done, catch another fish.

Consistent Transitions:

First, catch the fish. Second, clean the fish. Third, filet the fish. Fourth, cook the fish. Fifth, eat the fish. Finally, catch another fish.

Transitions frequently appear as words and phrases, such as those used in the previous example. They can also take the form of sentences and paragraphs. Transitional sentences often appear at the ends or beginnings of paragraphs and serve to link two paragraphs. Transitional paragraphs call attention to a major shift in focus within a document. Several examples of transitions are found below.

Transitional Words:

First, second, third, . . . finally
However
Nonetheless

Transitional Phrases:

On the one hand, . . . on the other hand
As a result
In turn

Transitional Sentences:

The results of the tests revealed a surprising trend.
Incredibly, the outcome was far better than we could have hoped.

Transitional Paragraphs:

In the next section, we explore the reasons behind this surprising development. We focus first on the event itself. Then we consider the reasons underlying the event. Our goal is to call attention to the unique set of relationships that made this development possible.

IV Writing Your Document

Transitions can also be created in the form of headings and subheadings. Section headings serve as transitions by signaling to the reader, through formatting that differs from body text, that a new section is beginning. You can read more about headings and subheadings on p. 241.

Introduce Other Authors Effectively   [FRAMING MY ARGUMENT]

Readers appreciate clear indications of the source of a quotation, paraphrase, or summary. (For more information about these methods of integrating the work of other authors, see Chapter 15.) Far too many writers show little imagination in their decisions about how to introduce that work.

Common Attributions:

The author wrote . . .
The author said . . .
The author stated . . .

Somewhat More Imaginative Attributions:

The author expressed the opinion that . . .
The author denied this, noting . . .
In response, the author observed that . . .

To make your writing stand out, vary the words and phrases you use to identify the sources of the information, ideas, and arguments used in your document. As you work on your document, be aware of the way that attributions can convey important shades of meaning—for example, the difference between saying that someone "alleged" something and someone "confirmed" something.

Avoid Sexist Language

It is still technically correct to use male pronouns, such as *he, him,* and *his,* when the gender of a noun, such as *doctor* or *nurse,* is unspecified. Most readers, however, object to this assumption—or they are at least sensitive to it. Readers are even more likely to object if you make the mistake of referring to representatives of particular professions using gender-specific pronouns.

> When describing your symptoms to a doctor, be sure to tell him everything that's relevant. Similarly, when a nurse is taking your blood pressure, feel free to let her know how you feel.

By implying that all doctors are male and all nurses are female, the writer of this passage plays into common stereotypes. The result is that many readers will form a negative opinion of the writer.

To avoid sexist language, recast your sentences so that generic references, such as *a doctor,* are plural, such as *doctors,* as in the following example.

Sexist Language:

A doctor who pursues an advanced specialization might need to spend as many as 15 years of study before he can go into practice on his own.

IV Writing Your Document

Nonsexist Language:

Doctors who pursue advanced specializations might need to spend as many as 15 years of study before they can go into practice on their own.

Consult a Good Handbook

The strategies discussed in this chapter provide a good starting point for improving your style. Your decisions about style, however, are likely to touch on a far wider range of concerns than are addressed here. As you work to improve your writing, consult a good handbook. You'll find detailed discussions and numerous examples of strategies you can use to polish your style.

Read Widely

The most effective means of improving your style might be the most enjoyable: Read as widely and as frequently as you can. Reading widely will expose you to the styles used by published authors—and you'll find that effective style comes in almost as many varieties as there are authors. Reading frequently will keep you engaged with words, and you'll find that you can draw on them more easily as you work on your own writing.

 QUICK REFERENCE

Writing with Style
- ✔ Write concisely. (p. 264)
- ✔ Use active and passive voice to accomplish your purpose. (p. 267)
- ✔ Adopt a consistent point of view. (p. 267)
- ✔ Pay attention to word choice. (p. 268)
- ✔ Use transitions effectively. (p. 271)
- ✔ Introduce the work of other authors effectively. (p. 272)
- ✔ Avoid sexist language. (p. 272)
- ✔ Consult a handbook. (p. 273)
- ✔ Read widely. (p. 273)

IV Writing Your Document

17

Revising and Editing

> **Key Questions**

When writers revise and edit, they evaluate the effectiveness of their drafts and, if necessary, work to improve them. Although the two processes are related, they focus on different aspects of a document. To revise is to assess how well a document responds to a specific writing situation, makes an argument, presents reasons, and uses evidence. To edit is to evaluate and improve the expression—at the sentence and word levels—of the information, ideas, and arguments in the document.

17a

What should I focus on as I revise my document?

Revising involves rethinking and re-envisioning your document. It focuses on such big-picture issues as whether the document you've drafted is appropriate for your writing situation; whether your argument is sound and well supported; whether you've organized and presented your information, ideas, and arguments clearly and effectively; and whether you've made appropriate decisions about genre and design.

Consider Your Writing Situation

As you revise, ask whether your document helps you achieve your purpose.

> **?** **WHAT'S MY PURPOSE?**
>
> Review your purpose in your research log. If your assignment directed you to inform readers about a particular subject, see whether you've provided appropriate information, whether you've given enough information, and whether that information is presented clearly. If your purpose is to convince or persuade your readers in some way, ask whether you have chosen appropriate reasons and evidence and presented your argument as effectively as you can.

Review as well your readers' needs, interests, values, beliefs, and knowledge of the issue. It's useful during revision to imagine how your readers will react to your document by asking questions such as these.

- Will my readers trust what I have to say? How can I establish my credibility?
- Will my readers have other ideas about how to address this issue? How can I convince them that they should believe what I say?
- Will my readers find my evidence appropriate and accurate? Is my selection of evidence consistent with their values and beliefs?

Finally, identify your requirements, limitations, and opportunities. Ask yourself whether you've met the specific requirements of the assignment, such as length and number of sources. Evaluate your efforts to work around limitations, such as lack of access to information. Think about whether you've taken full advantage of your opportunities and any new ones that have come your way.

Consider Your Argument and Ideas   [FRAMING MY ARGUMENT]

As you revise, ask how well you are conveying your argument and ideas to your readers. First, check the clarity of your thesis statement. Is it phrased in a way that is compatible with the needs, interests, values, and beliefs of your readers?

Second, ask whether the argument and ideas in your document help your readers understand and accept your thesis statement. As you make this assessment, keep in mind the role or roles you've decided to adopt — such as informing your readers, interpreting or analyzing, or advocating for a particular position.

Consider Your Use and Integration of Sources

Think about how you've used source information in your document. First, review the amount of support you've provided for your points and the appropriateness of that support for your purpose and readers. Then, if you are arguing about an issue, determine whether you've identified and addressed reasonable opposing viewpoints.

It's also important that you integrate your sources effectively into your document and acknowledge them according to the documentation system you are following. Ensure that you have cited all your sources and that you've clearly distinguished between your ideas and those of other writers. Review your works cited or reference list for completeness and accuracy. Remember that improper documentation can reduce your document's effectiveness and your credibility.

Consider the Structure and Organization of Your Document

Your readers should be able to locate information and ideas easily. As you read your introduction, ask whether it clearly and concisely conveys your main point and whether it helps your readers anticipate the structure and organization of your document. Reflect on the appropriateness of your organizing pattern (see p. 218) for your purpose and readers. If you've used headings and subheadings, evaluate their effectiveness.

Make sure your document is easy to read. Check for effective paragraphing and paragraph structure. If you have a number of small paragraphs, you might combine paragraphs with similar ideas. If you have a number of long paragraphs, break them up and add transitions. Finally, ask whether your conclusion leaves your readers with something to think about. The most effective conclusions typically provide more than a document summary.

Consider Genre and Design

Consider both the genre — or type — of document that you are writing (see p. 6) and your use of design principles and elements (see Chapter 18). Since you are writing in a particular genre, such as a source-based argumentative essay or an article for a popular magazine, ask whether the choices you've made about the content and style of your document are consistent with your readers' expectations about that type of document. Be sure to consider, for example, issues such as level of formality, accepted sources of evidence, and organization.

Take a careful look, as well, at how you've designed your document. Does it resemble what your readers will expect? For example, if you're writing an academic essay, have you double-spaced your lines, used a readable font, and set wide margins? If you are creating a Web site, have you made it easy for your readers to find their way around? Have you used design principles and elements to achieve your purpose and address the needs and interests of your readers?

17b

What strategies should I use to revise?

As you revise, you can draw on strategies for reviewing and improving your document. These strategies range from saving multiple drafts of your document to assessing its argument and organization to obtaining feedback from others.

Save Multiple Drafts

You might not be happy with every revision you make. To avoid wishing that you hadn't made extensive revisions to a draft of your document, save a new copy of your draft before every major revising session. Name your drafts by number — as in Draft1.doc, Draft2.doc, and so on — or by date, as in Draft-April6.doc and Draft-April10.doc. Or come up with a naming system that works for you. What's important is that you save multiple versions of your drafts in case you don't like the changes you've made.

Highlight Your Main Point, Reasons, and Evidence

As you revise, ensure that your main point (usually expressed as a thesis statement), reasons, and evidence are fully developed. An effective way to do this is to identify and examine each element in your draft, both individually and as a group of related points. If you are working with a printed document, use a highlighter, colored pens or pencils, or sticky notes. If you are working in a word processing program, use the highlighting tools to mark the text. You might use different colors to highlight your main point, supporting points, and evidence. If you are focusing solely on the evidence in your document, use different colors to highlight evidence from different sources (to help you check whether you are relying too heavily on a single source) or to differentiate the type of evidence you are using (such as quotations, paraphrases, summaries, and numerical data).

Challenge Your Assumptions

It's easy to agree with an argument that you've developed. Challenge your main idea, reasons, and evidence by using one of the following strategies. Keep track of your challenges by using the Comment tool in your word processor.

- **Put yourself in the place of your readers.** As you read, pretend that you are one of your readers. Try to imagine a single reader — or, if you're ambitious, a group of readers. Ask questions they might ask. Imagine concerns they might bring to their reading of your document. A reader interested in solving a problem might ask, for example, whether a proposed solution is cost effective, is more appropriate than alternative solutions, or has unacceptable side effects. As you revise, take these questions and concerns into account.

- **Play devil's advocate.** A devil's advocate raises reasonable objections to ideas and arguments. As you review your document, identify your key claims and pose reasonable objections to them. Make note of these potential objections and take them into account as you revise.

- **Play the "so what?" game.** As you read your document, ask why readers would care about what you are saying. By asking "so what?" questions, you can gain a better understanding of what your readers are likely to care about and how they might respond to your arguments and ideas. Make note of your responses to these questions and consider them as you revise.

Scan, Outline, and Map Your Document

Use the following strategies to review the structure and organization of your document.

- **Scan headings and subheadings.** If you have used headings and subheadings, they can help you track the overall flow of your argument and ideas. Ask whether the organization they reveal is appropriate for your writing situation and your role as a writer.

- **Scan the first sentence of each paragraph.** A quick reading of the first sentence in each paragraph can reveal points at which your argument shifts. As you note these shifts, think about whether they are appropriate and effective.

As you review the organization and structure of your document, reflect on whether it is appropriate given your purpose, readers, argument, and available information.

> @ Learn how to use the Styles tools in your word processor at **bedfordresearcher.com**. Click on How-To Guides.

IV Writing Your Document

Information Literacy

- **Outline Your Document.** Create a topical or sentence outline of your document (see p. 227) to assess its structure and organization. This strategy, sometimes called a reverse outline, helps you identify the sequence of your points and amount of space you've devoted to each aspect of your document. If you are viewing your document in a word processor, use the Styles tool to assign levels to headings in your document and then view it in outline view.

- **Map Your Document.** On paper in a word processor or in a graphics program, draw a map of your document. Like an outline, a map can help you identify the organization of your points and the amount of evidence you've used to support them.

TUTORIAL

How do I strengthen my argument during revision?

By this point in your research writing process, you are probably quite comfortable with your argument. But what would a reader with fresh eyes think? Imagine that you are a reader encountering this essay for the first time, then respond as author.

	Reader's Comments	**Author's Responses**
① Look for confusing or unclear points. As you read the essay, do any questions form in your mind? Write down your questions, then—wearing your author's hat again—consider how your essay can address them more fully.	— You mention various genres of metal music, but how are they different from each other?	— Must distinguish the genres more clearly; define "nu-metal" and "metalcore." Maybe include examples to clarify?
	— You say that the rise of grunge in the '90s caused the decline of metal's popularity, but then you say there was a thriving underground. Seems contradictory.	— Need to sort out the chronology. Metal *did* decline in popularity during the heyday of grunge, but there were still devoted fans in the "underground" movement.
② Play devil's advocate. Identify your key claims and pose reasonable objections to them. Consider how you could address them in your essay.	— You claim that metal has diversity, but all the song lyrics you include are about the war. Seems like that's the only topic addressed in these songs.	— Need to include different song lyrics about other issues, too — animal rights, the environment, racism, nuclear weapons, etc. Use Cattle Decapitation as an example.
③ Play the "so what?" game. As a reader, consider why you should care about this topic. Then respond to help readers identify the significance of your issue.	— What if I'm not interested in heavy metal or just don't like the sound? Why should I pay attention?	— Mention recent protests and demonstrations against heavy metal groups to show that it is *still* a controversial issue.
		— Show bands' MySpace pages to illustrate its popularity and relevance among young fans today.

Review another example and learn more about revising your document at **bedfordresearcher.com.** Click on Interactive Exercises.

Ask for Feedback

After spending long hours on a project, you may find it difficult to identify problems your readers might have with your draft. You might read the same paragraph eight times, failing to notice that the evidence you are using to support a point actually contradicts it. Or you might not notice that your document's organization could confuse your readers. You can ask for feedback on your draft from a friend, relative, colleague, or writing center tutor. It's generally a good idea to ask for help from someone who will be frank as well as supportive and to be specific about the kinds of comments you're looking for. Hearing "it's just fine" from a reviewer will not help you to revise.

> ### QUICK REFERENCE

Revising

☑ **Review your research writing situation.** Ask whether your document helps you achieve your purposes; addresses your readers' needs, interests, values, and beliefs; meets your requirements; effectively works around limitations; and takes advantage of opportunities. (p. 275)

☑ **Evaluate your argument and ideas.** Ask whether your document provides a clear and appropriate thesis statement and whether your argument and ideas support your thesis statement and are consistent with your roles. (p. 275)

☑ **Assess your use and integration of sources.** Ask whether you have offered adequate support for your points, considered reasonable opposing viewpoints, integrated and acknowledged your sources, and distinguished between your work and that of other writers. (p. 276)

☑ **Examine the structure and organization of your document.** Ask whether the introduction is clear and concise, clearly conveys your main point, and helps your readers anticipate the structure of your document. Also think about whether the organizational structure is easy to follow, paragraphs are easy to read, and transitions are effective. Ask whether the conclusion provides more than a summary of the document. (p. 276)

☑ **Evaluate genre and design.** Ask whether the genre you've created helps you accomplish your purpose. Check that you've followed the style and design conventions associated with the type of document you've created. (p. 276)

☑ **Use effective revision strategies.** Create multiple drafts to preserve earlier work; review your document to assess its argument and organization; get feedback from other writers. (p. 277)

17c

What should I focus on as I edit my document?

Editing involves assessing the effectiveness, accuracy, and appropriateness of the words and sentences in a document. Before you begin to edit, remember that editing focuses on the words and sentences in your document, not on its overall

IV Writing Your Document

structure or ideas. If you're uncertain about whether you've organized your document as effectively as possible or whether you've provided enough support for your argument, deal with those issues first. In the same way that you wouldn't start painting a house until you've finished building the walls, hold off on editing until you're confident that you're finished revising.

Focus on Accuracy

You'll risk damaging your credibility if you provide inaccurate information in your document. To reduce this risk, do the following.

- **Check your facts and figures.** Your readers might think you're deliberately misleading them if you fail to provide accurate information. As you edit, return to your original sources or your notes to check any facts and figures.

- **Check every quotation.** Return to your original sources or consult your notes to ensure that you have quoted each source exactly. Make sure that you have noted any changes to a quotation with an ellipsis or brackets (p. 104), and make sure that those changes haven't altered the original meaning of the passage. Make sure you have cited the source in the text and in a works cited or reference list.

- **Check the spelling of every name.** Don't rely on spelling checkers, which provide the correct spelling for only the most common or prominent names.

Focus on Economy

Editing for economy involves reducing the number of words needed to express an idea or convey information to your readers. Removing unnecessary modifiers and wordy introductory or stock phrases can make your writing more concise and to-the-point (see p. 264). Editing for economy generally makes it easier for your readers to understand your meaning. However, you should use care when you edit for economy; your readers still need to understand the point you are trying to make.

Focus on Consistency

Editing your project document for consistency helps you present information in a uniform way. Use the following techniques to edit for consistency.

- **Treat concepts consistently.** Review your document for consistent treatment of concepts, information, ideas, definitions, and anecdotes.

- **Use numbers consistently.** Check the documentation system you are using for its guidelines on the treatment of numbers. You might find that you should spell out the numbers zero through ten and use Arabic numerals for numbers larger than ten.

- **Treat your sources consistently.** Avoid referring to some sources using first names and to others using honorifics, such as *Dr., Mr.,* or *Ms.* Also check that you have cited your sources appropriately for the documentation style you are using, such as MLA or APA. Review each reference for consistent presentation of names, page numbers, and publication dates.

- **Format your document consistently.** Avoid any inconsistencies in your use of fonts, headings and subheadings, and tables and figures.

Focus on Style

Your readers will judge you—and what you have to say—not only on what you say but on how you say it. Edit for matters of style by choosing the right words, using active and passive voice appropriately, adopting a consistent point of view, rewriting complex sentences, varying your sentence length and structure, providing transitions, and avoiding sexist language (see Chapter 16).

Focus on Spelling, Grammar, and Punctuation

Poor spelling doesn't necessarily affect your ability to get your point across—in most cases readers will understand even the most atrociously spelled document—but it does affect what your readers think of you. Ignore enough spelling errors in your document and you'll erode their confidence in your ability to present information or make an argument. The same goes for grammar and punctuation. If you haven't made sure that subjects and verbs agree and that sentences end with the appropriate punctuation, a reader might not trust that you have presented your facts correctly.

17d

What strategies should I use to edit?

Thorough editing involves making several passes through your document to ensure that you've addressed accuracy, economy, and consistency; style; and spelling, grammar, and punctuation. The following tips can make that process both easier and more productive.

Read Carefully

As you've worked on your document, you've become quite familiar with it. As a result, it can be easy to read what you meant to write instead of what you actually wrote. The following strategies can help you read with fresh eyes:

- **Set your document aside before you edit.** If time permits, allow a day or two to pass before you begin editing your document. Taking time off between revising and editing can help you see your writing with new eyes.

- **Pause between sentences for a quick check.** Avoid getting caught up in the flow of your document—where the meaning takes precedence over the structure and expression of your sentences—by stopping after each sentence. Slowing down can help you identify problems with your text.

- **Read aloud.** Reading your document aloud can help you find problems that might not be apparent when it's read silently.

- **Read in reverse order.** To check for problems with individual sentences, start at the end of your document and read the last sentence first, then work backward through the document. To check for problems at the word level, read each word starting with the last one in the document. Disrupting the normal flow of your document can alert you to problems that might not stand out when it's read normally.

Mark and Search Your Document

Use the following marking and searching strategies to edit for accuracy, consistency, and use of sexist language.

Mark Your Document. As you read, use a highlighting pen or the Highlighter tool in your word processor to mark errors or information that should be double-checked. Consider using different colors to highlight specific types of problems, such as sexist language or inconsistent use of formal titles.

> @ Learn how to use the Highlighting, Search and Replace, and Split Window tools in your word processor at bedfordresearcher.com. Click on How-To Guides.

Use Spelling, Grammar, and Style Tools with Caution

Most word processors provide tools to check spelling, grammar, punctuation, and style. Used with an awareness of their limitations, these tools can significantly reduce the effort required to edit a document. Spelling checkers have two primary limitations. First, they can't identify words that are spelled correctly but misused—such as *to/two/too*, *their/they're/there*, and *advice/advise*. Second, spelling checkers are ineffective when they run into a word they don't recognize, such as proper

IV Writing Your Document

Information Literacy

Use the Find and Replace Tools. Use your word processor to edit concepts, names, numbers, and titles for consistency and accuracy. Once you've identified a word or phrase that you'd like to check or change, you can search for it throughout your document. If you are referring to sources using a parenthetical style, such as MLA or APA, use the Find tool to search for an opening parenthesis. If you discover that you've consistently misspelled a word or name, use the Replace tool to correct it throughout your document.

Use the Split Window Tool. Some word processors allow you to split your window so that you can view different parts of your document at the same time. Use this tool to ensure that you are referring to a concept in the same way throughout your document or to check for consistent use of fonts, headings, subheadings, illustrations, and tables.

names, technical and scientific terms, and unusual words. To compound this problem, spelling checkers often suggest replacement words. If you take the advice, you'll end up with a paper full of incorrect words and misspelled names.

@ Learn how to use the Spelling, Grammar, and Style tools in your word processor at bedfordresearcher.com. Click on How-To Guides.

Ask for Feedback

One of the biggest challenges writers face is reading a draft of their own work as a reader rather than as the writer. Because you know what you're trying to say, you'll find it easy to understand your draft. And because you've read and reread your document so many times, you're likely to overlook errors in spelling, punctuation, and grammar. After you've edited your document, ask a friend, relative, or classmate to proofread it and to make note of any problems.

> ## QUICK REFERENCE

Editing

- ✔ **Ensure your document is accurate.** Check facts and figures, quotations, and spelling of names. (p. 281)

- ✔ **Strive for economy.** Remove unnecessary modifiers, eliminate unnecessary introductory phrases, and avoid use of stock phrases. (p. 281)

- ✔ **Ensure that your document is consistent.** Use concepts, numbers, and source information consistently. Check your document for consistent use of formatting and design. (p. 281)

- ✔ **Use appropriate tone and style.** Use appropriate words, rewrite overly complex sentences, and vary sentence length and structure. (p. 282)

- ✔ **Check for correct spelling, grammar, and punctuation.** Use your word processor's spelling, grammar, punctuation, and style tools; consult a handbook and dictionary; and ask someone to proofread your draft. (p. 282)

IV Writing Your Document

Information Literacy

The main limitation of spelling checkers and grammar, punctuation, and style checkers is inaccurate advice. Although much of the advice they offer is sound, a significant proportion is not. If you are confident about your knowledge of grammar, punctuation, and style, you can use the grammar and style-checking tools in your word processor to identify potential problem areas in your document. You'll find that these tools can point out problems you might have overlooked, such as a subject-verb disagreement that occurred when you revised a sentence. However, if you don't have a strong knowledge of grammar, punctuation, and style, you can easily be misled by inaccurate advice.

If you have any doubts about advice from your spelling checker, consult an up-to-date dictionary. If you have concerns about the suggestions you receive from your grammar, punctuation, and style checker, consult a good handbook.

18

Understanding Design Principles

Key Questions

18a. How can I use design effectively? 286
Understand design principles
Design for a purpose
Design for your readers
Design to address genre conventions

18b. What design elements can I use? 290
Use fonts, line spacing, and alignment
Use page layout elements
Use color, shading, borders, and rules
Use illustrations

The design decisions you make will play a critical role in how your readers understand, react to, and work with your document. Understanding design principles and elements, as well as the design conventions of documents typically assigned in college courses, can help you craft a unique and substantial contribution to a conversation.

The growing sophistication of word processing, Web editing, and presentation programs along with access to high-quality color printers have given writers a great deal of control over the design of their documents. Design opportunities, from choosing appropriate fonts to presenting information in charts and tables to selecting compelling illustrations, can have powerful effects on how you shape and present your ideas and how your readers understand and react to your document.

18a

How can I use design effectively?

Although the most important factor in the success of your research writing project is the ability to express your ideas and arguments clearly, you should also think about how the design of your document can help you achieve your purpose, affect your readers, and meet their expectations.

Understand Design Principles

Before you begin formatting text and inserting illustrations, consider how the document design principles of *balance, emphasis, placement, repetition,* and *consistency* can help you accomplish your goals as a writer.

Balance is the vertical and horizontal alignment of elements on your pages (see Figure 18.1). Symmetrical designs create a sense of rest and stability and tend to lead the reader's eye to focus on a particular part of a document. In contrast, asymmetrical—or unbalanced—designs suggest movement and guide readers' eyes across the page.

Emphasis is the placement and formatting of elements, such as headings and subheadings, so they catch your readers' attention. You can emphasize an element in a document by using a color or font that distinguishes it from other elements,

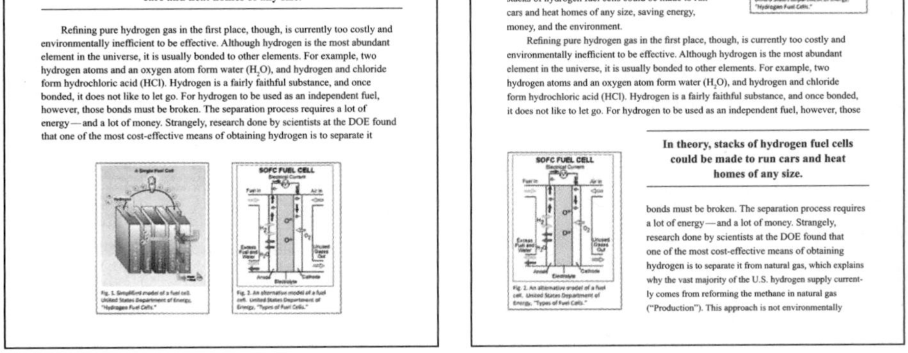

Hydrogen Economy: The Role of Fuel Cells

The key to a hydrogen economy is the fuel cell, which uses hydrogen gas and oxygen to produce electricity. In a way, a fuel cell is like a battery, but it never requires charging and it produces only electricity, heat, and water vapor (see Fig. 1). The U.S. Department of Energy (DOE) explains that hydrogen fuel cells use electrode plates to separate hydrogen's protons and electrons, diverting the stream of electrons to create electricity. A "stack" of fuel cells is scalable, so the same basic structure has many different uses ("Hydrogen Fuel"). In theory, stacks of hydrogen fuel cells could be made to run cars and heat homes of any size, saving energy, money, and the environment.

In theory, stacks of hydrogen fuel cells could be made to run cars and heat homes of any size.

Refining pure hydrogen gas in the first place, though, is currently too costly and environmentally inefficient to be effective. Although hydrogen is the most abundant element in the universe, it is usually bonded to other elements. For example, two hydrogen atoms and an oxygen atom form water (H_2O), and hydrogen and chloride form hydrochloric acid (HCl). Hydrogen is a fairly faithful substance, and once bonded, it does not like to let go. For hydrogen to be used as an independent fuel, however, those bonds must be broken. The separation process requires a lot of energy—and a lot of money. Strangely, research done by scientists at the DOE found that one of the most cost-effective means of obtaining hydrogen is to separate it

Fig. 1. Simplified model of a fuel cell. United States Department of Energy. "Hydrogen Fuel Cells."

Fig. 2. An alternative model of a fuel cell. United States Department of Energy. "Types of Fuel Cells."

Hydrogen Economy: The Role of Fuel Cells

The key to a hydrogen economy is the fuel cell, which uses hydrogen gas and oxygen to produce electricity. In a way, a fuel cell is like a battery, but it never requires charging and it produces only electricity, heat, and water vapor (see Fig. 1). The U.S. Department of Energy (DOE) explains that hydrogen fuel cells use electrode plates to separate hydrogen's protons and electrons, diverting the stream of electrons to create electricity. A "stack" of fuel cells is scalable, so the same basic structure has many different uses ("Hydrogen Fuel"). In theory, stacks of hydrogen fuel cells could be made to run cars and heat homes of any size, saving energy, money, and the environment.

Fig. 1. Simplified model of a fuel cell. United States Department of Energy. "Hydrogen Fuel Cells."

Refining pure hydrogen gas in the first place, though, is currently too costly and environmentally inefficient to be effective. Although hydrogen is the most abundant element in the universe, it is usually bonded to other elements. For example, two hydrogen atoms and an oxygen atom form water (H_2O), and hydrogen and chloride form hydrochloric acid (HCl). Hydrogen is a fairly faithful substance, and once bonded, it does not like to let go. For hydrogen to be used as an independent fuel, however, those

In theory, stacks of hydrogen fuel cells could be made to run cars and heat homes of any size.

bonds must be broken. The separation process requires a lot of energy—and a lot of money. Strangely, research done by scientists at the DOE found that one of the most cost-effective means of obtaining hydrogen is to separate it from natural gas, which explains why the vast majority of the U.S. hydrogen supply currently comes from reforming the methane in natural gas ("Production"). This approach is not environmentally

Fig. 2. An alternative model of a fuel cell. United States Department of Energy. "Types of Fuel Cells."

FIGURE 18.1 Symmetrical (left) and Asymmetrical (right) Layouts

by placing a border around it and adding a shaded background, or by using an illustration, such as a photograph, drawing, or graph.

Placement is the location of elements on your pages. Placing elements next to or near each other suggests that they are related. Illustrations, for example, are usually placed near the passages in which they are mentioned.

Repetition is the use of elements, such as headers and footers, navigation menus, and page numbers, across the pages in your document. As readers move from page to page, they tend to expect navigation elements, such as page numbers, to appear in the same place. In addition, repeated elements, such as a logo or Web navigation menu, help establish a sense of identity across the pages in your document.

Consistency is the extent to which you format and place text and illustrations in the same way throughout your document. Treating each design element—such as illustrations, headings, and footnotes—consistently will help your readers recognize the different roles played by the elements in your document and, by extension, help them locate the information they seek. A consistent design can also convey a sense of competence and professionalism to your readers, increasing their confidence in the quality and credibility of your document.

You should also keep two other principles in mind: moderation and simplicity. An overly complex design can work against the effectiveness of a document by obscuring important ideas and information. The best approach is to use design elements moderately to create a simple yet effective design.

Design for a Purpose

A well-designed document presents your information, ideas, and arguments in a manner that helps you accomplish your purpose. Your purpose, as a result, should inform your design decisions.

IV Writing Your Document

? WHAT'S MY PURPOSE?

In your research log, review your purpose to determine if you might use design to achieve the following goals.

- **Setting a Tone.** One of the most powerful tools writers have for accomplishing their purpose is establishing an emotional context for their readers. Drawing on the design principles of balance and placement, you can set a tone by using a particular color scheme, such as bright, cheerful hues, or by selecting photographs or drawings with a strong emotional impact (see Figure 18.2).
- **Helping Readers Understand a Point.** You might use the design principles of emphasis and placement to introduce and help readers understand your points. Headings or pull quotes can call your readers' attention to important ideas and information. To introduce a main point, you might use a contrasting font or color

↓

to signal the importance of the information. To highlight a definition or example, you might use borders or place the passage in a pull quote. You can also help readers understand a point by using illustrations.

- **Convincing Readers to Accept a Point.** The key to convincing readers is providing them with appropriate, relevant evidence. Drawing on the principles of emphasis and placement, you can use illustrations, marginal glosses, pull quotes, and bulleted lists to call attention to that evidence.

- **Clarifying Complex Concepts.** Sometimes a picture really is worth a thousand words. Rather than attempting to explain a complex concept using text alone, use an illustration. A well-chosen, well-placed photograph, flow chart, diagram, or table can define a complex concept such as photosynthesis in far less space, and in many cases far more effectively, than a long passage of text. You can also clarify the key elements of a complex concept with bulleted and numbered lists.

FIGURE 18.2 Using Images to Create an Emotional Impact

How is the photograph likely to influence the reader's response to the headline?

From *Newsweek*, January 25, 2010. © 2010 The Newsweek/Daily Beast Company LLC. All rights reserved. Used by permission and protected by the Copyright Laws of the United States. The printing, copying, redistribution, or retransmission of the material without express written permission is prohibited.

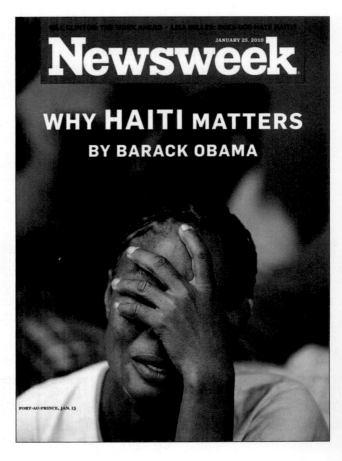

Design for Your Readers

A well-designed document helps readers understand the organization of the document, locate information and ideas, and recognize the function of parts of the document. It is also easy on your readers' eyes: Readers working with a well-designed document will not have to strain to read the text or discern illustrations. Use document design to do the following.

Help Readers Understand the Organization of a Document. You can use headings and subheadings to signal the content of each part of the document. If you do, keep in mind the design principles of emphasis and consistency: Format your headings in a consistent manner that helps them stand out from other parts of the document (see Figure 18.3).

Help Readers Locate Information and Ideas. Many longer print documents use tables of contents and indexes to help readers locate information and ideas. Web sites typically provide a mix of menus and navigation headers and footers to help readers move around the site. When these navigation aids are integrated into pages, they are often distinguished from the surrounding text by the use of bordered or shaded boxes or through the use of contrasting fonts.

Help Readers Recognize the Function of Parts of a Document. If you include passages that differ from the main text of your document, such as sidebars and "For More Information" sections, help readers understand their function by

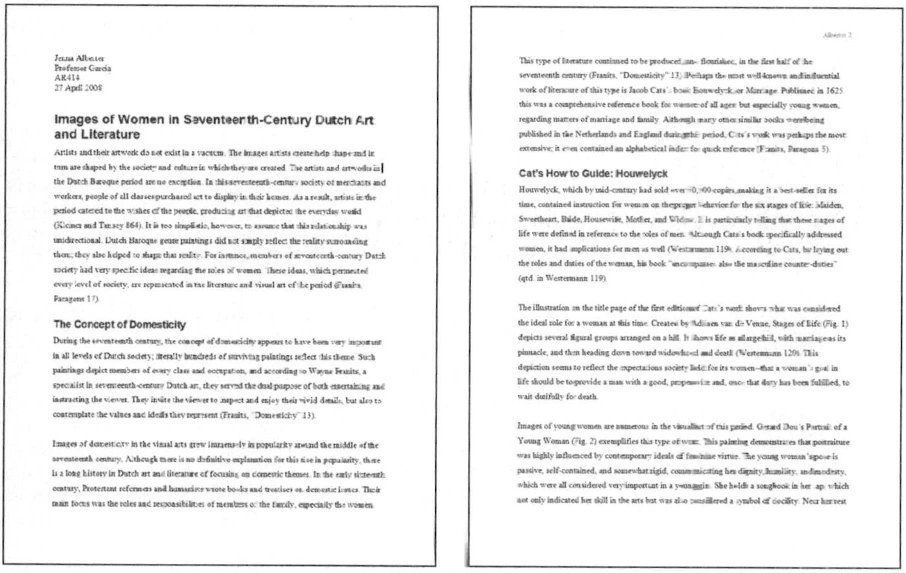

Jenna Alberter
Professor Garcia
AR414
27 April 2008

Images of Women in Seventeenth-Century Dutch Art and Literature

Artists and their artwork do not exist in a vacuum. The images artists create help shape and in turn are shaped by the society and culture in which they are created. The artists and artworks in the Dutch Baroque period are no exception. In this seventeenth-century society of merchants and workers, people of all classes purchased art to display in their homes. As a result, artists in the period catered to the wishes of the people, producing art that depicted the everyday world (Kleiner and Tansey 864). It is too simplistic, however, to assume that this relationship was unidirectional. Dutch Baroque genre paintings did not simply reflect the reality surrounding them; they also helped to shape that reality. For instance, members of seventeenth-century Dutch society had very specific ideas regarding the roles of women. These ideas, which permeated every level of society, are represented in the literature and visual art of the period (Franits, Paragons 17).

The Concept of Domesticity

During the seventeenth century, the concept of domesticity appears to have been very important in all levels of Dutch society; literally hundreds of surviving paintings reflect this theme. Such paintings depict members of every class and occupation, and according to Wayne Franits, a specialist in seventeenth-century Dutch art, they served the dual purpose of both entertaining and instructing the viewer. They invite the viewer to inspect and enjoy their vivid details, but also to contemplate the values and ideals they represent (Franits, "Domesticity" 13).

Images of domesticity in the visual arts grew immensely in popularity around the middle of the seventeenth century. Although there is no definitive explanation for this rise in popularity, there is a long history in Dutch art and literature of focusing on domestic themes. In the early sixteenth century, Protestant reformers and humanists wrote books and treatises on domestic issues. Their main focus was the roles and responsibilities of members of the family, especially the women

This type of literature continued to be produced and flourished in the first half of the seventeenth century (Franits, "Domesticity" 13). Perhaps the most well-known and influential work of literature of this type is Jacob Cats's book Houwelyck, or Marriage. Published in 1625 this was a comprehensive reference book for women of all ages but especially young women, regarding matters of marriage and family. Although many other similar books were being published in the Netherlands and England during this period, Cats's work was perhaps the most extensive; it even contained an alphabetical index for quick reference (Franits, Paragons 5).

Cat's How to Guide: Houwelyck

Houwelyck, which by mid-century had sold over 50,000 copies, making it a best-seller for its time, contained instruction for women on the proper behavior for the six stages of life: Maiden, Sweetheart, Bride, Housewife, Mother, and Widow. It is particularly telling that these stages of life were defined in reference to the roles of men. Although Cats's book specifically addressed women, it had implications for men as well (Westermann 119). According to Cats, by laying out the roles and duties of the woman, his book "encompasses also the masculine counter-duties" (qtd. in Westermann 119).

The illustration on the title page of the first edition of Cats's work shows what was considered the ideal role for a woman at this time. Created by Adriaen van de Venne, Stages of Life (Fig. 1) depicts several figural groups arranged on a hill. It shows life as a large hill, with marriage as its pinnacle, and then heading down toward widowhood and death (Westermann 120). This depiction seems to reflect the expectations society held for its women—that a woman's goal in life should be to provide a man with a good, proper wife and, once that duty has been fulfilled, to wait dutifully for death.

Images of young women are numerous in the visual art of this period. Gerard Dou's Portrait of a Young Woman (Fig. 2) exemplifies this type of work. This painting demonstrates that portraiture was highly influenced by contemporary ideals of feminine virtue. The young woman's pose is passive, self-contained, and somewhat rigid, communicating her dignity, humility, and modesty, which were all considered very important in a young virgin. She holds a songbook in her lap, which not only indicated her skill in the arts but was also considered a symbol of docility. Near her rest

FIGURE 18.3 Headings and Subheadings in a Research Essay
Use of a contrasting font and color helps readers understand the document's organization.

designing them to stand out visually. Using emphasis, for example, you might format a sidebar in an article with a shaded or colored box. Similarly, you might format a list of related readings or Web links in a contrasting font or color.

Design to Address Genre Conventions

Understanding the design conventions of the type of document you plan to write will help you create a document that meets the expectations of your readers. Genres are characterized not only by distinctive writing styles, types of evidence, and organizing patterns, but also by distinctive types of design. An article in a magazine such as *Time* or *Newsweek,* for example, is characterized by the use of columns, headings and subheadings, pull quotes, and illustrations, while an academic essay is characterized by wide margins, double-spaced lines, and comparatively restrained use of color and illustrations. Your readers will expect your document to be similar in design to other examples of that genre. This doesn't mean that you can't depart from those conventions should the need arise, but it does mean that you should take your readers' expectations into account as you design your document.

18b

What design elements can I use?

Understanding the range of design elements at your disposal will enable you to decide which of these options to use as you design your document. These elements include fonts, line spacing, and alignment; page layout strategies; color, shading, borders, and rules; and illustrations.

Use Fonts, Line Spacing, and Alignment

Fonts, line spacing, and alignment choices are the most common design decisions made by writers. They are also among the most important, since poor choices can make a document difficult to read. Figures 18.4 and 18.5 provide an overview of the key features of fonts and the uses of fonts, line spacing, and alignment.

> @ Learn more about formatting fonts, line spacing, and alignment at bedfordresearcher .com. Click on How-To Guides.

Use Page Layout Elements

Page layout is the placement of text, illustrations, and other objects on a page or screen. Successful page layout draws on a number of design elements, including white space, margins, columns, headers and footers, page numbers, headings, lists, captions, marginal glosses and pull quotes, and sidebars. Figure 18.6 illustrates these design elements.

> @ Learn more about creating effective page layouts at bedfordresearcher.com. Click on How-To Guides.

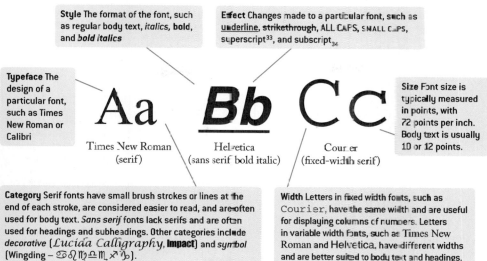

Style The format of the font, such as regular body text, *italics*, **bold**, and ***bold italics***

Effect Changes made to a particular font, such as underline, strikethrough, ALL CAPS, SMALL CAPS, superscript[33], and subscript[34]

Typeface The design of a particular font, such as Times New Roman or Calibri

Size Font size is typically measured in points, with 72 points per inch. Body text is usually 10 or 12 points.

Times New Roman (serif)

Helvetica (sans serif bold italic)

Courier (fixed-width serif)

Category Serif fonts have small brush strokes or lines at the end of each stroke, are considered easier to read, and are often used for body text. *Sans serif* fonts lack serifs and are often used for headings and subheadings. Other categories include decorative (*Lucida Calligraphy*, **Impact**) and *symbol* (Wingding – ✆♋🜙♏♏♍ ⚹ ✌).

Width Letters in fixed width fonts, such as Courier, have the same width and are useful for displaying columns of numbers. Letters in variable width fonts, such as Times New Roman and Helvetica, have different widths and are better suited to body text and headings.

FIGURE 18.4 Font Basics

Use Color, Shading, Borders, and Rules

Color, shading, borders, and rules (lines running horizontally or vertically on a page) can increase the overall attractiveness of your document, call attention to important information, help readers understand the organization of your document, help readers recognize the function of specific passages of text, and signal transitions between sections (see Figure 18.7). As you use these design elements, exercise restraint. Avoid using more than three colors on a page unless you are using a photograph or work of art. Be cautious, as well, about using multiple styles of rules or borders in a document.

> Learn more about formatting color, borders, shading, and rules at bedfordresearcher.com. Click on How-To Guides.

Use Illustrations [FRAMING MY ARGUMENT]

Illustrations—charts, graphs, tables, photographs and other images, animations, audio clips, and video clips—can expand on or demonstrate points made in the text of your document. They can also reduce the text needed to make a point, help readers better understand your points, and increase the visual appeal of your document.

Photographs and Other Images Photographs and other images, such as drawings, paintings, and sketches, are frequently used to set a mood, emphasize a point, or demonstrate a point more fully than is possible with text alone.

Charts and Graphs Charts and graphs represent information visually. They are used to make a point more succinctly than is possible with text alone or to

Line spacing refers to the amount of space between lines of text. Larger line spacing appears easier to read, so you'll often find increased line spacing used in introductory paragraphs, executive summaries (which provide an overview of a longer document), and sidebars (see p. 293). When text is crammed together vertically, it is difficult to read and add comments. Keep this in mind if you are creating a document such as an essay on which someone else might write comments.

(see p. 293)

CLIMATE COUNTDOWN

Best-case scenario for a Copenhagen deal? Twice the warming the planet can take.
BY BILL McKIBBEN

TOO HOT TO HANDLE

wo decades ago, when I was writing what would be one of the first books on global warming, I interviewed a professor at Harvard's Kennedy School of Government, one of the few academics already thinking about the emerging problem. He hemmed and hawed for a little while, and then he said, "This is the public policy problem from hell. There are just too many conflicting interests. It won't be solved."

This December may be the last real chance to prove him wrong as the nations of the world meet in Copenhagen for a climate conference billed as make or break, do or die, perhaps quite literally sink or swim. In fact, you could make a fair argument that this will be the most important diplomatic gathering in the world's history. Versailles, sure. Yalta, yes–but their failures were measured in decades of pain and millions of lives. Failure to rein in climate change will reverberate for tens of thousands of years, across generations not even yet imagined.

Which is not to say the 12 days of final negotiations will be august or easy to follow or even coherent. I remember the last big talks of this sort, in Kyoto in 1997. The sessions took place, as they will in Copenhagen, in a conference center miles from town. It became its own insulated world, with reporters and delegates and oil company lobbyists and NGO representatives endlessly querying each other about what was going on. (There was even a daily paper, and sometimes a parody version.) The answer to the queries was always the same: We're waiting for the US and the Europeans to strike a deal. The official palaver was taking place in a big hall, with delegates making amendments and offering motions, but all the real action was behind closed doors.

ILLUSTRATION BY ANITA KUNZ

12 MOTHER JONES | NOVEMBER/DECEMBER 2009

Alignment refers to the horizontal arrangement of text and illustrations (such as photos and drawings). You can select four types of alignment.
- **Left alignment** has a straight left margin and a "ragged right" margin; it is typically the easiest to read.
- **Right alignment** has a straight right margin and a ragged left margin.
- **Centered alignment** is seldom used for body text but can make headings stand out.
- **Justified alignment** has straight alignment on both the left and right margins. It adds a polished look and can be effective in documents that use columns — but it also produces irregular word spacing and hyphenation, which can slow the reading process.

Fonts are a complete set of type of a particular size and typeface. As you choose fonts, consider the following.
- **Select fonts that are easy to read.** For body text, avoid decorative fonts and italics.
- **Select fonts that complement each other.** A serif body font, such as Times New Roman or Garamond, works well with a sans serif heading font, such as Arial, Helvetica, or Calibri.
- **Exercise restraint.** Generally, use no more than four different fonts in a document.

FIGURE 18.5 Using Fonts, Line Spacing, and Alignment

Pull quotes highlight a passage of text — frequently a quotation — through the use of borders, white space, distinctive fonts, size, and contrasting colors.

Numbered and bulleted lists (not shown) display brief passages of related information using numbers or symbols (usually round "bullets"). The surrounding white space draws the eye to the list, highlighting the information for your readers, while the brief content in each entry can make concepts or processes easier to understand.

Sidebars (not shown) are brief discussions of information related to but not a central part of your document. Sidebars simplify the task of integrating supporting information into the body of the article by setting that information off in a clearly defined area.

White space — literally, empty space — frames and separates elements on a page.

Columns generally appear in newspaper and magazine articles — and, to a growing extent, articles published on the Web. Essays, on the other hand, are typically formatted in a single column. Columns can improve the readability of a document by limiting the eyes' physical movement across the page and by framing other elements.

Childhood immunization is the most cost-effective technology in public health, doctors say. That message is getting out around the world. BY KAREN SPRINGEN AND SAM SEIBERT

On the March To Eradicate Child Illness

DR. BRUCE AYLWARD IS YIELDING NO GROUND. AS COordinator of the World Health Organization's $4 billion Global Polio Eradication Initiative, Aylward runs a worldwide immunization program that is supposed to eliminate the virus forever by the end of this year. He's still not ready to push back the schedule, even though cases of the devastating childhood illness have been popping up in countries like Indonesia and Yemen, where it was wiped out long ago. "The virus has never been in this much trouble," he insists. When the global campaign began in 1988, the disease was paralyzing 350,000 or more victims a year on five continents—mostly children. So far this year, the number of confirmed cases hasn't passed the low hundreds. Now, says Aylward, the essential thing is to finish wiping out the disease. "If we blink," he says, "it will be not hundreds, but hundreds of thousands."

People forget too quickly the horrors of sicknesses like polio. In 1954, the year before Jonas Salk introduced his vaccine, the virus killed more than 3,000 Americans and crippled roughly 20,000 others. Today the United States has been effectively polio-free for more than a quarter century. That success story is hardly unique. A century ago, before childhood immunization became routine in America, the upper-respiratory infection known as diphtheria was a worse killer than cancer. Now the United States gets an average of three cases a year. Whooping cough, measles, mumps and rubella have become rarities in America. Wider vaccine coverage could further reduce the burden of other important illnesses already in decline, like hepatitis A, hepatitis B, chickenpox and invasive disease from *Haemophilus influenzae* type b (Hib for short), a bacterial meningitis that can cause deafness or mental retardation in children when it doesn't kill them outright.

But the economics of vaccines can be as cruel as any disease. A third of the world gets none of the childhood immunizations that are routine in the West. More than 2 million children a year die as a result, according to Dr. Julian Lob-Levyt, executive secretary of the Global Alliance for Vaccines and Immunization. For drugmakers, the profitability of developing and distributing vaccines tends to be marginal at best, and medical aid to the Third World is chronically underfunded. And yet for humanity as a whole, immunization programs pay huge dividends, not only in lives saved but in reduced medical and social burdens. "The cost benefit of vaccines is overwhelmingly the best investment yield in biomedicine and health," says Dr. Anthony Fauci, director of the National Institute of Allergy and Infectious Diseases. "It is much more economical to prevent a disease than to treat a disease." "[Immunization] is the most cost-effective technology in public health, bar any," says Lob-Levyt.

That fact is a powerful motivation for scientists, relief groups, philanthropists and others in the fight against communicable diseases. Earlier this year the Bill & Melinda Gates Foundation teamed up with the Norwegian government to make a joint pledge of $1 billion for standard childhood immunizations in the Third World. Meanwhile, immunologists are working to expand their arsenal. A few of the most promising targets:

Dengue Health workers have spent decades in a losing fight to stop the mosquito that transmits dengue. Every year the hot-climate viral illness infects as many as 100 million people, many of them children. Roughly 500,000 end up hospitalized for intravenous feedings, oxygen and sometimes transfusions. Up to 5 percent die anyway. "Parents go through hell," says Scott Halstead, research director for the Pediatric Dengue Vaccine Initiative. One form of the disease, dengue hemorrhagic fever, mimics the Ebola virus: victims bleed from their bodily orifices as they die. Now scientists at Aventis and GlaxoSmithKline are closing in on vaccines to ward off the disease. Studies are underway in Vietnam, Thailand and Nicaragua, and Halstead says the result could be available by 2010—for under $2 a dose, he hopes. The best thing about dengue is that it needs human hosts to survive. If a population is immunized, the disease will be gone, no matter how bad the mosquitoes get.

Pneumococcus *Streptococcus pneumoniae*, also known as pneumococcus, kills more than 1 million children a year around

DEATH IN THE AIR

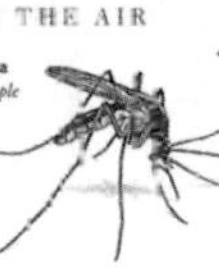

The mosquitoborne illness **malaria** *infects more than 300 million people a year, mostly in the developing world. (About 1,300 cases are diagnosed in the United States.) Of more than 1 million deaths annually, most occur among children under 5.*

Margins are the white space between the edge of the page or screen (top, bottom, right, and left) and text or graphics in your document.

Headings and subheadings identify sections and subsections, serve as transitions, and allow readers to locate information more easily.

Marginal glosses are brief notes in a margin that explain or expand on text in the body of the document.

Headers, footers, and page numbers (not shown) appear at the top or bottom of the page, set apart from the main text. They help readers find their way through a document; they provide information, such as the title of the document, its publication date, and its author; and they frame a page visually.

Captions describe or explain an illustration, such as a photograph or chart.

FIGURE 18.6 Using Page Layout Elements

Signal the organization of a document. In a longer print document, headers, footers, headings, and subheadings might be formatted with a particular color to help readers recognize which section they are reading. On a Web site, pages in each section could share the same background or heading color.

Call attention to important information. Color, borders, shading, and rules can subtly yet clearly emphasize an illustration, such as a table or chart, or an important passage of text, by distinguishing it from the surrounding body text.

Signal the function of text. A colored or shaded background, as well as colored type, can be used to differentiate captions and pull quotes from body text. Rules can also separate columns of text on a page or screen.

Be consistent. Use the same colors for top-level headings throughout your document, another color for lower-level headings, and so on. Use the same borders and shading for sidebars. Use rules consistently in pull quotes, headers, and footers. Don't mix and match.

Understand the effects of color. Some effects are physical. Bright yellow, for example, can tire your readers' eyes. Other effects are emotional — and are often linked to readers' cultural backgrounds. In many cultures, green is regarded as soothing because it is associated with nature and growth. Red, in contrast, is often associated with danger. As a result, it tends to attract attention.

FIGURE 18.7 Using Color, Borders, Shading, and Rules

TUTORIAL

How can I use illustrations in my document?

Illustrations can enhance the effectiveness of your document by reducing word length, clarifying your argument, increasing visual appeal, and helping readers follow your argument. In this example, pages from an essay written by Elizabeth Leontiev show how illustrations can enhance the effectiveness of a document.

Review your draft to determine where you could use illustrations to accomplish the following.

1 **Reduce the text needed to make a point.** Elizabeth found this graph from a reliable source — the United Nations Office on Drugs and Crime. It presents significant data in a concise fashion and illustrates that coca cultivation in Bolivia did not increase after Evo Morales became president.

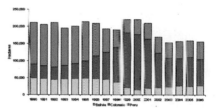

2 **Expand on or demonstrate your argument.** Illustrations can clarify and offer context for the information you provide. The graph Elizabeth uses not only supports her point about Evo Morales's plan, but it also illustrates that Bolivia's coca production is minimal compared with that of other coca-producing countries.

3 **Increase the visual appeal of your document.** Striking and colorful, this photograph of manual coca plant eradication attracts the reader's eye on the page.

4 **Help readers better understand your reasons.** The photograph shows the audience a scene that coca farmers who live in poverty must dread. It creates an emotional appeal by showing exactly how the war on drugs is fought — by soldiers with machetes.

Review another example and learn more about working with images at **bedfordresearcher.com**. Click on Interactive Exercises.

IV Writing Your Document

present complex information in a compact and more accessible form. They frequently rely on numerical information.

Tables Like charts and graphs, tables can present complex information, both textual and numerical, in a compact form.

Other Digital Illustrations Digital publications allow you to include a wider range of illustrations, including audio, video, and animations that bring sound and movement to your document.

> @ Learn more about working with illustrations at bedfordresearcher.com. Click on How-To Guides.

As you work with illustrations, keep the following guidelines in mind.

- **Use an illustration for a purpose.** Illustrations are best used when they serve a clear function in your document. Avoid including illustrations simply because you think they might make your document "look better."

- **Place illustrations near the text they illustrate.** In general, place illustrations as close as possible to the point where they are mentioned in the text. If they are not explicitly mentioned (as is often the case with photographs), place them at a point where they will seem most relevant to the information and ideas being discussed.

- **Include a title or caption that identifies or explains the illustration.** The documentation style you are using, such as MLA or APA, will usually offer advice on the placement and format of titles and captions. In general, documentation systems suggest that you distinguish between tables and figures (which include other illustrations), number tables and figures in the order in which they appear in the document, and use compound numbering of tables and figures in longer documents (for example, the second table in Chapter 5 would be labeled "Table 5.2"). Consult the documentation system you are using for specific guidelines on illustrations.

The following tutorial can help you determine whether to use illustrations in your document.

> **> QUICK REFERENCE**
>
> ### Understanding Design Principles
>
> ✔ Understand the design principles of balance, emphasis, placement, repetition, and consistency. (p. 286)
>
> ✔ Design to achieve your purposes. (p. 287)
>
> ✔ Design to address your readers' needs, interests, values, and beliefs. (p. 289)
>
> ✔ Design to address genre conventions. (p. 290)
>
> ✔ Use design elements — such as fonts, line spacing, alignment, page layout, color, shading, borders, rules, and illustrations — effectively and appropriately to increase the readability and effectiveness of your document. (p. 290)

19

Designing Documents and Presentations

Key Questions

Readers familiar with particular genres — or types — of documents, such as academic essays, newspaper columns, informative Web sites, and feature articles, expect documents in a genre to share a particular look and feel. Newspaper articles, for example, are typically laid out in narrow columns of text and are often accompanied by captioned photographs. As you design your document, consider the typical design characteristics associated with the type of document you've chosen. Attending to these conventions will allow you to meet the expectations of your readers. It will also help convey an impression of competence and professionalism.

19a

How can I design academic essays?

The design of academic essays is neither flashy nor complex. Their most obvious design features — wide margins, readable fonts, and double-spaced lines — are intended to help their intended audience, typically instructors and classmates, read and review them.

Consider Your Purpose

Because the writing assignments given by most college instructors have focused on the written expression of ideas and arguments, academic essays have tended to use images sparingly, if at all, and to make limited use of design elements such as color, shading, borders, and rules. With changes in word-processing technology, however, writers of academic essays have begun to take advantage of these design elements. Some writers use color to differentiate headings and subheadings, for example, while others include sidebars, images, tables, and charts. Other writers, who expect their essays to be read on a computer or tablet, also use embedded video clips, sound files, and animations as illustrations.

Consider Reader Expectations about Design

In general, instructors will expect you to design your essay with wide margins (typically one inch or more), double-spaced lines, and a readable font such as 12-point Times New Roman or 11-point Calibri. If you are uncertain about your instructor's preferences, ask for guidance.

IV Writing Your Document

View an Essay

The pages in Figures 19.1 through 19.4 are from an essay written by a student for his composition class. They reflect his awareness of the instructor's expectations about line spacing, margins, documentation system, page numbers, and a heading.

CHECKLIST FOR DESIGNING ACADEMIC ESSAYS

✔ Cover page with title, name, and course information [depending on your instructor's preferences]

✔ Readable body font (example: 12-point Times New Roman)

✔ Double-spaced lines

✔ Wide margins, one inch or larger

✔ Consistent use of assigned documentation system

✔ Headers and footers in a readable font distinct from body font

✔ If used, headings and subheadings formatted in fonts and colors that distinguish them from the body text and show relative importance of heading levels

✔ If used, illustrations labeled and placed either within the text near relevant passages or in an appendix, according to instructor's preferences

FIGURE 19.1 Cover Page for an Academic Essay

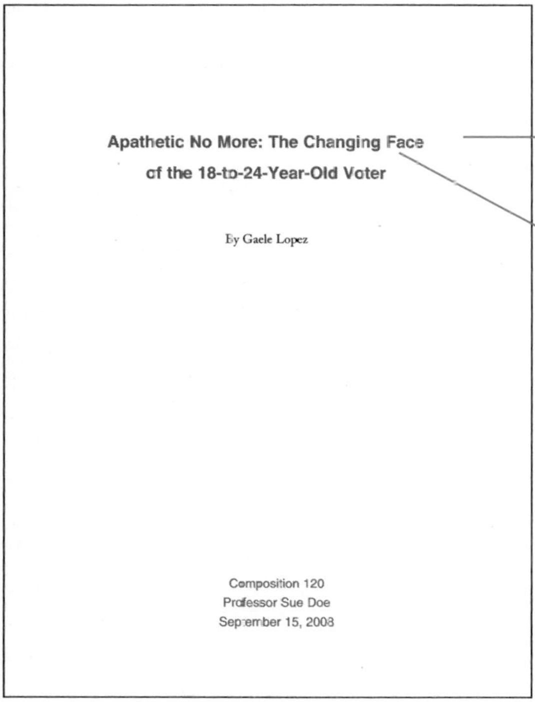

Apathetic No More: The Changing Face
of the 18-to-24-Year-Old Voter

By Gaele Lopez

Cover page provides title, author, information about the course, and date the essay was turned in.

A larger, boldface font distinguishes title from other information on the page.

Composition 120
Professor Sue Doe
September 15, 2008

FIGURE 19.2 First Page of an Academic Essay

A header with writer's last name and page number is repeated at the top of each page.

Title is repeated on first page of essay in a larger, colored, sans serif font that distinguishes it from the body text.

Body text is set in a serif font, which is more readable than most sans serif fonts.

All body text is formatted consistently.

One-inch margins and double-spaced lines provide space for the teacher to write comments.

A graph appears near its mention in the text, supporting claims made there.

Lopez 2

**Apathetic No More: The Changing Face of the
18-to-24-Year-Old Voter**

Ever since 1972, when 18-year-olds gained the right to vote, voter turnout among America's youth has been significantly lower than that of older Americans. Following an initial turnout of 52 percent of younger registered voters in 1972, the percentage declined to an all-time low of only 32 percent in the 1996 presidential election, nearly 30 points below the turnout of voters over the age of 30 (see Figure 1). By the late 1990s, calls for voter reform – even to the point of suggesting that the vote be limited to those over 30, a suggestion once made by Winston Churchill – became all too common. When the 2000 presidential elections showed virtually no change in voting rates, commentators weighed in with criticisms that, at best, portrayed the youngest members of our society as apathetic when it came to politics and, at worst, as a bunch of freeloading slackers.

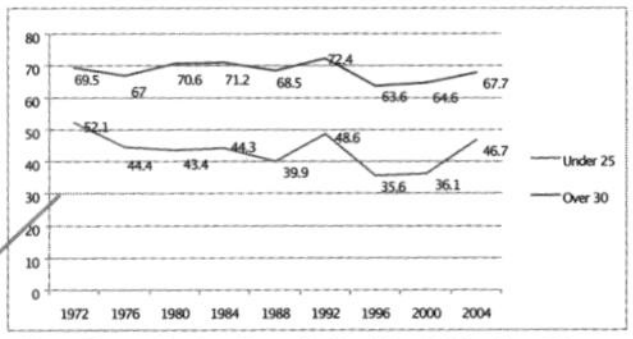

Figure 1. Voter Turnout by Age Group in Presidential Elections (Source: Lopez, Kirby, and Sagoff, 12)

Fortunately, times change. In 2004, turnout among younger voters increased to nearly 47 percent, and by the 2008 elections it seemed likely that turnout might be higher than that recorded in 1972, when anger and frustration over the Vietnam war resulted in the largest turnout to date among younger voters.

FIGURE 19.3 Interior Page of an Academic Essay

Lopez 3

In the 2008 primaries, turnouts among younger voters doubled, tripled, and in some case quadrupled the turnouts recorded in any previous primary (Pew Charitable Trust, par. 2). Analysts – even some of those who had suggested raising the voting age – quickly began to investigate why younger voters were turning out in such unprecedented numbers, what impact their votes would have on the upcoming presidential election, and what this change in behavior would have on future elections.

Factors Contributing to the Change in Voting Behaviors

Why the sudden change? Or is it as sudden as it seems? Analysts Mark Hugo Lopez, Emily Kirby, and Jared Sagoff, writing after the 2004 presidential elections, pointed to "the confluence of extensive voter outreach efforts, a close election, and high levels of interest in the 2004 campaign" as factors that drove turnout among younger voters to "levels not seen since 1992" (1). They cautioned, however, that it was unclear whether the 2004 results were indicators of a significant change or simply an aberration.

It would appear, based on patterns seen in the 2006 mid-term elections and in the 2008 presidential primaries, that there really is evidence of a change. In its report on record turnout in the 2008 primaries and caucuses, the Pew Charitable Trust notes,

> The research showed that college students are deeply concerned about issues, involved personally as volunteers and ready to consider voting. But they want political leaders to be positive, to address real problems and to call on all Americans to be constructively involved (par. 5).

As we look toward the fall 2008 elections, it seems clear that young voters will not only play an important role in the election, but might in fact play the deciding role. Voters such as Reid Vincent,

A heading, formatted in blue and using a sans serif font that differs from the serif body font, calls attention to a shift in Gaele's argument.

Block quotation is set off by indenting the margins on both sides. Quotation marks are not needed for block quotations.

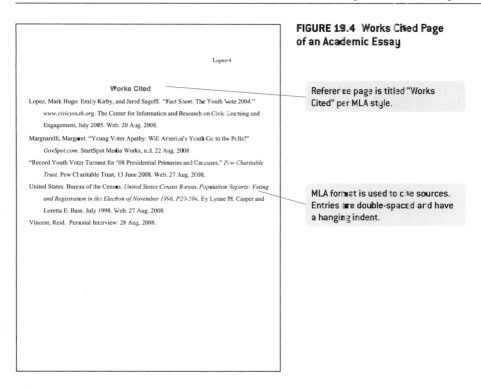

FIGURE 19.4 Works Cited Page of an Academic Essay

Reference page is titled "Works Cited" per MLA style.

MLA format is used to cite sources. Entries are double-spaced and have a hanging indent.

For another sample essay formatted in MLA style, see p. 357. For a sample essay formatted in APA style, see p. 382. For a sample essay formatted in *Chicago* style, see p. 412.

19b

How can I design multimodal essays?

Multimodal essays are characterized by their essayistic form and their use of multiple types of illustrations. As essays, they present information in a linear sequence, one idea after another. As multimodal documents, they combine text with images, animation, sound, and/or video to establish a line of argument and support the writer's points.

Consider Your Purpose

Multimodal essays require careful selection and organization of sources not only for their content, but also for the manner in which they appeal to readers. Depending on your argument, you might find that an embedded video clip is likely to be more effective than an audio clip or image. In each case, your purpose and understanding of your readers' needs, interests, values, beliefs, background, and knowledge of the issue will affect your decisions about content and design.

IV Writing Your Document

Consider Reader Expectations about Design

Multimodal essays have emerged quite recently as a distinct genre. Your readers are likely to expect only that you'll provide a linear document that contains one or more types of embedded media; uses fonts, colors, borders, and lines consistently and effectively; and is designed to be viewed on a computer screen or tablet. If you develop an extended essay, such as the multimodal essay created by Chris Norris, your readers are also likely to expect you to provide navigation aids, such as tables of contents and page links, that will allow them to move easily to different parts of the essay.

Choose Your Design Tools

Multimodal essays vary widely not only in form, but also in the software used to create them. You can create multimedia essays using a word processing program such as Microsoft Word or Apple Pages, a multimedia presentation program such as PowerPoint or KeyNote, or Web site development programs such as Dreamweaver. As you choose your design tools, consider how their distinctive features will help you accomplish your goals as a writer. A word processing program might be a better choice than a multimedia presentation program, for example, if you plan to rely more heavily on text than on images and video. In contrast, a program such as PowerPoint offers more options for including multimedia elements than most word processing or Web development programs.

View a Multimodal Essay

Figures 19.5 through 19.8 show a selection of slides from the multimodal essay written by Chris Norris. Chris developed his essay with PowerPoint. Note his use of text, illustrations, color, headings and subheadings, sidebars, and lists to clearly convey his argument about the resurgence in the popularity of metal music.

IV Writing Your Document

CHECKLIST FOR MULTIMODAL ESSAYS

✔ Overall design consistent across pages (placement of titles and text; use of fonts, colors, rules, illustrations)

✔ Readable heading and subheading fonts (example: 16-point Times New Roman or Verdana)

✔ Readable body font designed for on-screen reading (example: 11-point Calibri or Georgia)

✔ Appropriate and consistent color scheme

✔ Text presented in brief, readable chunks, using bulleted and numbered lists when appropriate

✔ Illustrations labeled and placed near relevant text passages

✔ If used, transitions between pages (dissolves, page flips) quick and not distracting

✔ If used, background sound clear but not distracting

A table of contents, set in a manner similar to a Web page, allows quick access to pages in the essay.

The title and subtitle are presented in large, readable fonts in colors that contrast with the background.

Second Coming
The Resurgence of Heavy Metal in Popular Music

INTRODUCTION

SOCIAL AND
POLITICAL
DIALOGUE

DIVERSITY

SOCIAL
COMMUNITY

CONCLUSION

REFERENCES

HOME

A photograph draws the reader's eye and sets the tone for the essay.

FIGURE 19.5

Body text is presented in a readable sans-serif font that contrasts with the background.

Photographs illustrate key ideas in the text.

Introduction

INTRODUCTION

SOCIAL AND
POLITICAL
DIALOGUE

DIVERSITY

SOCIAL
COMMUNITY

CONCLUSION

REFERENCES

HOME

Heavy metal music has a turbulent history, partly due to its loud, harsh style but especially because of its lyrics. At the height of its popularity in the 1980s, heavy metal's antisocial and violent themes spurred many critics to try to eliminate this genre of music. Ultimately, though, it was the rising popularity of grunge bands such as Nirvana and Pearl Jam in the late 1980s and early 1990s that led to metal's decline. The sold-out stadium tours were all but a memory to the majority of bands that once thrived in the genre. In the past ten years, however, numerous bands and their fans have begun to rekindle the heavy metal flame. By addressing complex social and political issues, by incorporating diverse musical styles, and by cultivating a strong fan community, heavy metal is undergoing a rebirth.

HEAVY METAL: (NOUN) 2- A TYPE OF HIGHLY AMPLIFIED HARSH-SOUNDING ROCK MUSIC WITH A STRONG BEAT.
-OXFORD ENGLISH DICTIONARY

Source information and credits are provided for photographs.

FIGURE 19.6

IV Writing Your Document

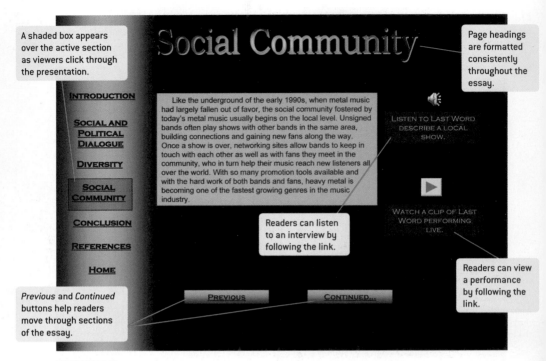

A shaded box appears over the active section as viewers click through the presentation.

Page headings are formatted consistently throughout the essay.

Readers can listen to an interview by following the link.

Readers can view a performance by following the link.

Previous and *Continued* buttons help readers move through sections of the essay.

FIGURE 19.7

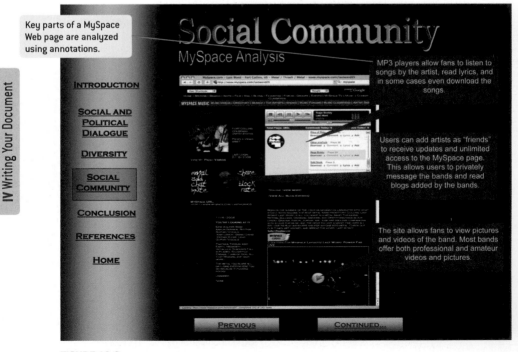

Key parts of a MySpace Web page are analyzed using annotations.

FIGURE 19.8

19c

How can I design articles?

Articles appear in a wide range of publications, including newspapers, magazines, scholarly and professional journals, and Web sites, among others. Articles rely heavily on information obtained from sources such as books, Web sites, government reports, interviews, surveys, and observation. Article writers should consider several factors that affect design: the overall design of the publication in which they hope to place their article, the audience the publication addresses, the subjects typically written about in the publication, and the style and tone used in other articles in the publication.

Consider Your Purpose

Articles are written for a wide range of purposes, from informing to evaluating to entertaining to persuading or convincing. As you consider potential design choices, keep your purpose in mind. If you are informing your readers about a complex concept, for example, you might use a diagram or chart to convey information in a way that would be difficult to do through words alone. If you are trying to persuade your readers to take action, you might select a color scheme that sets a particular mood or insert an image that invokes a strong emotional response.

Consider Reader Expectations about Design

Because most articles are written for a specific publication, writers typically have a clear picture of their readers (age, income, education, hobbies, and so forth) and can develop a line of argument that directly addresses their needs and interests. An article about an election, for example, might report on turnout among younger voters, offer a profile of a recently elected senator from the Midwest, or describe the activities of an organization such as the League of Women Voters.

Depending on the publication you are targeting, your article might use headings and subheadings, columns, sidebars, pull quotes, and a wide array of illustrations. To gain an understanding of your readers' expectations about the design of your article, scan other articles in the publication. Take note of the range of design choices in the articles. Then read a few of the articles more closely to gain insights into the choices the writers made as they wrote and designed their articles.

View an Article

The four related articles in Figure 19.9 were published in the *Daily Californian*, the student newspaper at the University of California, Berkeley. Paired with a photo montage later in the issue, the articles use font formatting and visual elements to set a mood, call attention to key points, and convey information.

IV Writing Your Document

A large headline contrasts with the text and the headlines for individual articles.

Bylines are set in bold and sans serif to differentiate them from main body text.

Newspaper articles are formatted in columns.

A large photograph, framed by the articles, adds visual interest and information. A caption and photographer credit appear below.

FIGURE 19.9A Articles in *The Daily Californian*

CHECKLIST FOR DESIGNING ARTICLES

✔ Column layout appropriate for target publication and target audience

✔ Line spacing typically single-space

✔ Readable body font (example: 10- or 11-point Century Schoolbook)

✔ Color, borders, shading, and rules used appropriately

✔ Heading and subheadings formatted in font and colors that distinguish them from body text and show the relative importance of heading levels

✔ Illustrations labeled and placed near relevant passages

The articles are continued later in the newspaper.

A montage of photographs provides additional information about the protests.

FIGURE 19.9B Articles in *The Daily Californian.*

19d

How can I design Web sites?

Web sites consist of linked pages, typically organized through a home page and navigational devices such as menus, tables of contents, indexes, and site maps. The main pages of Web sites usually provide broad overviews of the topic, and related pages add detailed information.

Consider Your Purpose

Web sites are able to engage readers in ways that print documents cannot: They can link directly to related sites, allow visitors to access video and audio files, and support communication among the site's readers and writers. This wealth of design and navigation options, however, carries significant design challenges for writers. As you consider your purpose in developing a Web site, you must reflect not only on what you hope to accomplish—informing or persuading readers, for example—but also on design elements that can help you achieve your purpose. Key considerations include helping readers move easily through your site, formatting text to highlight important information and ideas, and selecting effective digital illustrations.

Consider Reader Expectations about Design

Given the wide range of individuals with access to the Web, writers must anticipate the needs of a much more diverse group of readers than is the case with documents distributed in print. Designers of Web sites, as a result, typically attempt to provide their readers with a significant amount of guidance about the purpose, content, and organization of their sites on the pages writers usually visit first. This guidance can include site menus, tables of contents, links to pages that provide information about the site, and links to pages that provide contact information.

Over the past decade, the appearance of many Web sites has grown similar to that of magazines, with a heavy use of images and other illustrations. Writers typically design a Web site with many of the same considerations they apply to the pages in a magazine article, choosing a unified color scheme, formatting headings and subheadings consistently across pages, and using borders, shading, and rules in a manner similar to that of many print publications. They must also address, however, the placement and appearance of navigation menus and digital illustrations, such as audio and video clips, animations, and embedded programs and downloadable files.

View Pages from a Web Site

Figures 19.10 through 19.12 show pages from Pete Jacquez's Web site about wind-generated electrical power.

> @ Learn more about creating and designing Web sites at bedfordresearcher.com. Click on How-To Guides.

CHECKLIST FOR DESIGNING WEB SITES

✔ Organizational structure consistent with the purpose of the site and the needs and expectations of readers

✔ Home page provides links to main pages on the site

✔ Home page and main pages offer navigation tools appropriate for readers of the site

✔ Overall design consistent across the site (placement of titles, text, and navigation tools; use of fonts, colors, rules, and illustrations)

✔ Information presented in brief, readable chunks, using bulleted and numbered lists whenever possible

---

CHECKLIST FOR DESIGNING WEB SITES (continued)

✔ Readable body font in font family designed for on-screen reading (examples: 11-point Verdana or Georgia)

✔ Headings and subheadings formatted in fonts and colors that distinguish them from body text and show relative importance of heading levels

✔ Labels, captions, and pop-up flags used to help readers understand links and images

✔ Color used to set a mood, highlight information, and help readers understand the function of text and illustrations on the site

✔ Illustrations placed near the passages to which they refer

✔ Images kept as small (in kilobytes) as possible, while being clear and easy to see

✔ Contact information and other relevant information included and easy to locate

---

A side menu provides links to pages on the site.

A large heading identifies the issue addressed by the site.

WIND POWER: COLORADO'S FUTURE

Learn More
Fossil Fuel Economics
Fossil Fuel & the Environment
Wind Power Economics
Wind Power & the Environment
Bibliography
Related Links

Take Action
Local Efforts
State-Wide Efforts
National Efforts

About This Site
Written by Pedro Jacquez
References

With the flip of a switch, electricity is there. It powers our lights, televisions, stereos, computers, clothes washers, and refrigerators. Once a luxury, electric power has become a staple of modern life. Yet it is a necessity that Americans consume with little regard for its sources – or its costs.

In Colorado, as in other states, the majority of electricity is produced by power plants that burn fossil fuels, usually coal, oil, or natural gas (U.S. Department of Energy [DOE], 2004c). Unfortunately, the mass production of electricity has significantly reduced supplies of these non-renewable natural resources. It has also increased air pollution and spurred global warming.

What can we do to reduce these negative effects of power plants ? One promising approach is to increase our reliance on wind-generated electrical power. Wind power, as it has come to be known, is a cost-effective alternative to power from fossil-fuel-based power plants – and is likely to become even more attractive as the costs of fossil fuels continue to rise. Perhaps more important, wind power generates no air pollution or greenhouse gases.

A new state constitutional amendment (which mandates that clean power be used to generate some electricity) has put Colorado at the forefront of efforts to increase the use of wind power (Gonzalez-Estay, 2004). But more must be done. Coloradoans should lead a national movement to increase the use of wind power. Through this site, you will learn how you can help in that effort. You'll find background information about the environmental and economic issues associated with generating electrical power through fossil fuel and wind. You'll also find an annotated bibliography and a list of links to other sites addressing wind power.

The average visitor to Vail and other upscale ski resorts has come to expect elaborate lighting schemes. Most visitors, however, don't even think about the economic costs and environmental impacts of generating electricity through conventional fossil fuels.

Caption is set off from body text with a different font (Verdana) and contrasting color.

Site information is provided. A list of references cited in the site is available.

A photograph illustrates a key point raised in the body text.

Body text is formatted in a 12-point serif font that is easy to read.

FIGURE 19.10 Web Site Home Page

IV Writing Your Document

A link to the home page is provided on all other pages.

Headings are formatted in a large sans-serif font that contrasts with the body text.

A chart provides information about wind power economics.

Wind Power Economics

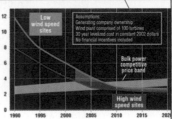

Learn More
Fossil Fuel Economics
Fossil Fuel & the Environment
Wind Power Economics
Wind Power & the Environment
Bibliography
Related Links

Take Action
Local Efforts
State-Wide Efforts
National Efforts

About This Site
Written by Pedro Jacquez
References

Today, wind power accounts for less than one-tenth of one percent of all electrical power generated in the United States (U. S. General Accounting Office [GAO], 2004). This represents a four-fold increase since 1990, however, and growth is expected to continue for the foreseeable future (U. S. GAO, 2004). The majority of wind power installations are in ten Midwestern and Western states: California, Colorado, Iowa, Minnesota, New Mexico, Oklahoma, Oregon, Texas, Washington, and Wyoming. These states have the natural conditions required for wind power: large open spaces with annual wind speeds of at least 16 miles per hour.

Since the late 1990s, the cost of wind power has become competitive with that of power generated by fossil-fuel power plants. As you can see in Figure 2, the cost of wind power now falls within the same "competitive price bard" as fossil fuels. In large part, this decline in cost can be attributed to improvements in technology, which are likely to continue. Flowers (2005) estimates that the average output of large wind turbines will increase from their current capacity of 1.5 megawatts to 5 megawatts by 2010. In addition, as the number of wind farms increases nationwide, the cost of producing wind turbines has declined (Colorado Green Power, 2005).

Government support of wind power has also helped the industry. The federal government offers a

Figure 2: Cost of electricity produced by wind power, 1990 to 2020 (in Year-2002 constant dollars). From U.S. Department of Energy, National Renewable Energy Laboratory. (2004, March). *Wind Power: Today and Tomorrow.*

The side menu appears in the same place on each page of the site.

Extra space after each paragraph helps differentiate one from another.

The figure title is followed by source information.

FIGURE 19.11 Web Site Content Page

IV Writing Your Document

An annotated bibliography provides information for visitors to the site.

Links to other documents are signaled by a contrasting blue color.

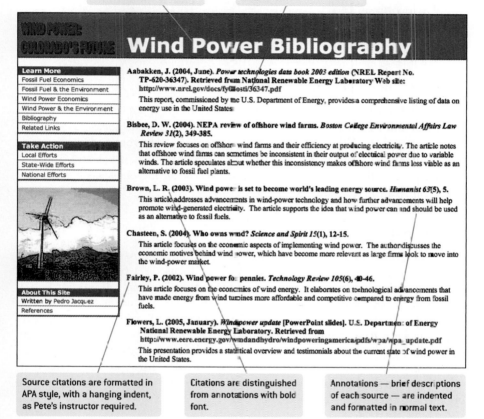

Source citations are formatted in APA style, with a hanging indent, as Pete's instructor required.

Citations are distinguished from annotations with bold font.

Annotations — brief descriptions of each source — are indented and formatted in normal text.

FIGURE 19.12 Annotated Bibliography Web Page

19e

How can I design oral presentations?

Writers are often asked to make a presentation, lead a discussion, or share their thoughts through speaking rather than writing. The ability to present your ideas through an oral presentation is an important skill that you'll use not only in your courses, but also throughout your professional and personal life.

Designing an effective oral presentation involves much more than simply taking what you've written and reading it aloud. When you're physically present to share your ideas, your ability to connect personally with your audience is affected by your choice of words, your physical appearance, your use of gestures and other forms of nonverbal communication, your ability to maintain eye contact, and variation in your tone of voice. In addition, your connection with your audience is affected by their ability to follow your line of argument. As you design your presentation, remember that most people find it more difficult to understand complex information, ideas, and arguments when they hear it than when they read (or reread) it. Focus, as a result, on how you can help your listeners follow your line of argument and see you as a credible presenter.

Consider Your Purpose and Audience

The most important thing to remember about designing an oral presentation is engaging your audience and keeping them interested in your ideas. As you plan your presentation, ask what you want to accomplish, what your audience expects to hear, and how you can balance your purpose with their needs and interests. The answers to these questions will shape everything in your speech from language choices to visual aids.

Narrow Your Scope

It is important to consider how much your audience knows about your topic. With their knowledge and expertise in mind, focus on a few key points and decide how much detail you'll need to provide to help them follow your line of argument. If you have already drafted a written document, use it as the basis for your presentation, but don't try to cover every point and every piece of supporting evidence you've included in your document. Draw on your thesis statement, supporting points, and conclusions to create a brief overview of your presentation that you can use in your introductory remarks. This "preview statement" will help your audience gain an understanding of your line of argument and the organization right from the start.

Create a Barebones Outline

Once you've developed a focus for your presentation and determined its main point and general organization, you can create an outline. It's a good idea to begin with a basic outline that includes the following.

- An opening line that captures the attention of your audience
- A statement of your main point, typically in the form of a thesis statement
- A sentence establishing your credibility and purpose; your audience should understand that you care about and understand the issue, either through personal experience or through research, and that they can trust what you have to say
- Two to four key points
- Evidence to support your key points
- Transition statements to guide your audience through your talk
- A conclusion that reinforces your audience's understanding of the main ideas they should take away from your talk

- A closing line or an invitation to ask questions that makes it clear to your audience that you have finished your presentation

Think about Language

In an oral presentation, you'll use spoken language to connect personally with your audience. Through your choice of words, phrases, metaphors, imagery, and turns of speech, you'll engage your listeners in your argument and ideas. Your choices about how to address your audience should be made with the goal of engaging them in your issue. For example, you might talk about how your issue affects "us" and ask them to consider what "we" should do to address it.

As you consider your language choices, keep in mind that spoken language is usually more casual than written language. If you adopt the formal tone of an academic research essay, you might sound stiff and unnatural. Keep in mind, as well, the power of repetition in oral presentations. You'll help your audience follow your line of argument by stating important points more than once and in different ways. Finally, consider the role of emotional appeals in your presentation. To connect personally with your audience and to engage your audience with your issue, you should explore the use of vivid descriptions, surprising statistics, and humor. Don't rely heavily on emotional appeals, however. To maintain your credibility, you'll want to balance emotional appeals with logic by presenting sound reasoning and support for your argument.

Design Speaker's Notes

Although many speakers write their presentations word for word, this strategy usually does not produce outstanding results. It's better to develop a set of speaker's notes to prompt yourself as you present your points. Using notes, instead of a word-for-word speech, will force you to speak directly to your listeners. Many seasoned speakers use note cards for their speaker's notes, as they are easy to hold in one hand and are not as distracting as fluttering paper. As you prepare your notes, make sure that they are easy to read, so that you can view your next point with a quick glance. You should include the following information in your speaker's notes.

- Your opening line, written out in full, in case your mind goes blank due to nervousness
- Your preview statement
- Any statements that you need to give word for word, such as carefully worded observations about a controversial point or clear descriptions of a complex concept
- Your supporting points and reminders of important evidence, including direct quotes, statistics, and names of important people
- Transition sentences from one part of the presentation to the next
- Memory prompts for parts of your presentation that you've found yourself forgetting as you practice
- Reminders to use a visual aid, such as a chart

Engage with Your Audience

When you give an oral presentation, *how* you say something is almost as important in getting your message across as *what* you say. Important parts of your delivery include the following.

- **Maintain eye contact with your audience.** Eye contact communicates that you know your topic and that you care about making sure the audience understands your argument.

- **Vary the pitch of your voice.** Speaking in a monotone is the fastest way to put your audience to sleep. When you mention a startling statistic, raise your pitch. To demonstrate weight and importance, go to a lower register in your voice. Practice using vocal variety to make sure that it sounds natural.

- **Speak loudly.** You might feel like you're yelling, but the audience will let you know (by looking surprised) if you are too loud. Speakers rarely are.

- **Articulate every word clearly.** Consonants are often dropped in casual conversation, so you should pay attention to making them clearer than you would in normal speaking.

- **Slow down.** Most presenters speak much too quickly. Slow down your normal rate of speaking to make sure that the audience has time to process your words.

View Speaker's Notes

Figures 19.13 through 19.15 show speaker's notes from Alexis Alvarez's oral presentation on the use of steroids by adolescent girls involved in sports.

CHECKLIST FOR DESIGNING ORAL PRESENTATIONS

✔ Determine the presentation's purpose.

✔ Narrow your presentation's scope to between two and four key points.

✔ Write a preview statement.

✔ Choose supporting evidence for your key points.

✔ Create a basic outline of your presentation.

✔ Prepare speaker's notes that you can read easily and quickly.

✔ Consider how the size and physical arrangement of the room will affect your ability to interact with your audience.

✔ Practice your presentation and ask for feedback from your practice audience.

✔ Arrive early to ensure adequate time for setup.

✔ During the presentation, observe and respond to your audience.

✔ Vary the pitch of your voice, speak loudly, and clearly articulate your words.

1: Intro

Barry Bonds, A-Rod, Marion Jones, Lance Armstrong—what do all of these big names have in common? **(pause, wait for audience response)**

1. **All accused of using performance-enhancing drugs**

2. **Used to seeing athletes break records, find out later about steroid use**

3. **Happening for younger athletes—including young women**

> Include nonverbal cues in your note cards. This will remind you to interact with your audience.

> Use short phrases to cue your thoughts.

FIGURE 19.13 Note Card with a Nonverbal Cue

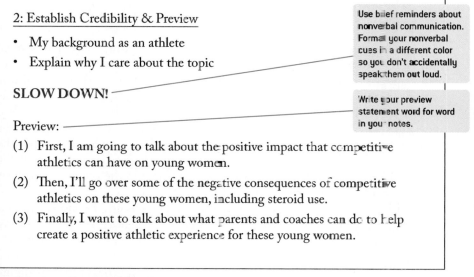

2: Establish Credibility & Preview

- My background as an athlete
- Explain why I care about the topic

SLOW DOWN!

Preview:

(1) First, I am going to talk about the positive impact that competitive athletics can have on young women.

(2) Then, I'll go over some of the negative consequences of competitive athletics on these young women, including steroid use.

(3) Finally, I want to talk about what parents and coaches can do to help create a positive athletic experience for these young women.

> Use brief reminders about nonverbal communication. Format your nonverbal cues in a different color so you don't accidentally speak them out loud.

> Write your preview statement word for word in your notes.

FIGURE 19.14 Note Card with a Preview Statement

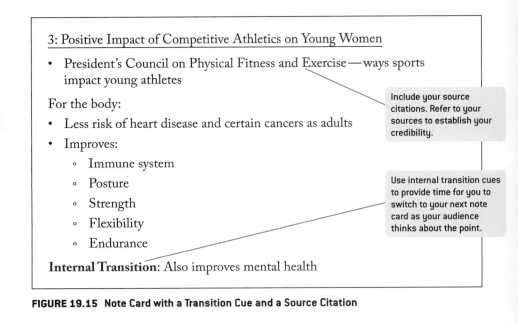

3: Positive Impact of Competitive Athletics on Young Women

- President's Council on Physical Fitness and Exercise — ways sports impact young athletes

For the body:

- Less risk of heart disease and certain cancers as adults
- Improves:
  ○ Immune system
  ○ Posture
  ○ Strength
  ○ Flexibility
  ○ Endurance

Internal Transition: Also improves mental health

Include your source citations. Refer to your sources to establish your credibility.

Use internal transition cues to provide time for you to switch to your next note card as your audience thinks about the point.

FIGURE 19.15 Note Card with a Transition Cue and a Source Citation

19f

How can I design multimedia presentations?

Multimedia presentations allow you to illustrate points using more than spoken words alone, allowing your audience to follow your argument more easily and to better understand complex ideas. During these presentations, slides containing text or graphics are projected on a screen and, in some cases, audio, video, or animations are played. Multimedia presentations can also include links to the Web and embedded applications, such as spreadsheets. Some multimedia presentations are created for delivery via the Web, allowing a larger audience to access the presentation. Web-based multimedia presentations can be designed so that the speaker either appears in a smaller video window next to the presentation slides or provides a voiceover for each slide.

Multimedia presentation programs, such as PowerPoint, Keynote, Impress, and Google Presentations, allow writers to create well-designed presentations. More specialized programs are also available for particular types of presentations. Prezi (prezi.com) and Ahead (ahead.com), for example, allow you to create "zooming" presentations that can be useful for creative purposes such as digital storytelling. VuVox (vuvox.com), in contrast, arranges slides along a timeline.

Consider Your Purpose

A strong multimedia presentation highlights your points without stealing the show. When used with moderation and created according to good design principles, multimedia elements can add credibility to a presentation, aid your ability to make your argument, and help your audience better understand complex ideas. A presentation on recent changes in education policy, for example, might include video clips in which students, teachers, parents, and community members discuss the effects of those policies or the reasons leading to their development. A presentation on social networking might include links to social networking sites, a chart illustrating the growth in use of such sites over the past decade, or screenshots showing a range of purposes for which such sites are used.

Consider Audience Expectations about Design

Poorly designed multimedia presentations sometimes seem as numerous as grains of sand on a Caribbean beach. Audiences in settings ranging from business meetings to conferences to lecture halls have been subjected to them, and perhaps you have been too. If so, you'll be aware of the benefits of keeping in mind the following design guidelines.

- Keep text to a minimum. A general rule is six words per bullet point, six bullet points per slide, and no more than six slides in a row of all text.
- Use readable fonts, such as 44-point Corbel for headings and 28-point Calibri for body text.
- To enhance the readability of slides, use either a light background with dark text or a dark background with light text.
- Choose a color scheme that reflects the purpose and tone of your line of argument. Use bright colors, for example, for a light-hearted topic. Use neutral colors for a serious presentation.
- Use audio, video, and animation with moderation. Generally, clips should run no longer than one minute each.
- Be consistent in your choice of fonts, colors, and page layout.
- Avoid the use of slow or overly complex transitions between slides.
- Avoid the use of distracting sound effects on slides or during slide transitions.

View a Presentation

Figures 19.16 through 19.19 show slides from a multimedia presentation designed by Elizabeth Leontiev.

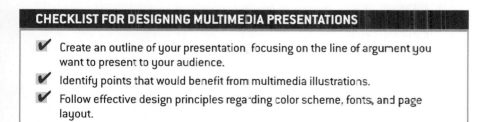

CHECKLIST FOR DESIGNING MULTIMEDIA PRESENTATIONS

- ✔ Create an outline of your presentation focusing on the line of argument you want to present to your audience.
- ✔ Identify points that would benefit from multimedia illustrations.
- ✔ Follow effective design principles regarding color scheme, fonts, and page layout.

CHECKLIST FOR DESIGNING MULTIMEDIA PRESENTATIONS (continued)

✔ Use multimedia elements in moderation.

✔ To ensure that your slides are readable and well designed, preview your presentation on a screen similar in size to what you will be using during your talk.

✔ Face your audience as you make your presentation.

✔ Use multimedia elements to advance your line of argument, pointing out important information and illustrations on slides.

✔ Create a backup plan in case technology fails. Consider using handouts as a backup.

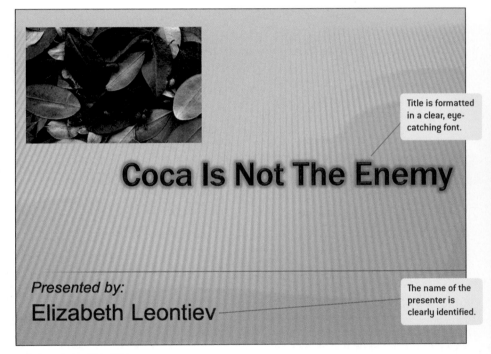

FIGURE 19.16 Title Slide

IV Writing Your Document

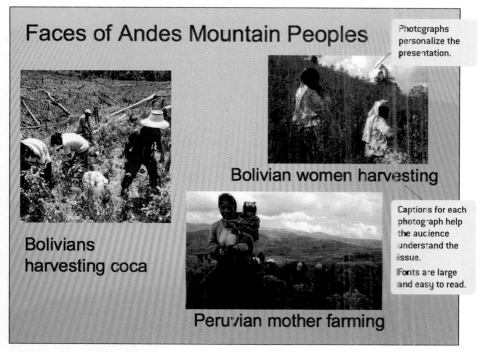

FIGURE 19.17 Slide with Photographs and Captions

FIGURE 19.18 Slide Supporting the Writer's Presentation

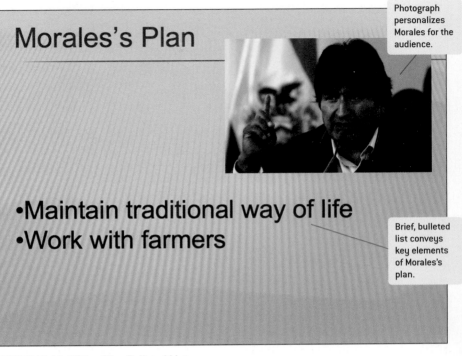

Photograph personalizes Morales for the audience.

Brief, bulleted list conveys key elements of Morales's plan.

FIGURE 19.19 Slide with a Bulleted List

19g

How can I design poster presentations?

Poster presentations are often given at conferences, workshops, or symposiums for particular disciplines and professions. Most poster exhibitions involve numerous presenters, typically in a large room or hallway, and audience members who look for posters that interest them.

Consider Your Purpose and Audience

Your audience will usually have some background knowledge in the discipline or area that your presentation addresses. For example, if you are giving a poster presentation at a microbiology conference, it is safe to assume that the individuals who stop to talk with you will have at least a basic understanding of the central terminology and research methods used in the discipline. You should expect that most members of your audience will spend about five minutes talking with you about a poster. Be prepared, as a result, to provide a brief overview of your project, its key findings, and their significance. You might find it useful to create speaker's notes that you can view between discussions to remind yourself of the key points you want to make.

Be prepared, as well, for likely questions and challenges. The individuals who stop to talk with you will usually have a strong interest in your issue and will want to know what you've learned about it.

Consider Audience Expectations about Design

Posters typically include a large, explanatory title; an abstract that describes your study and its findings; a list of key research questions or a description of the problem or issue that you've addressed; a brief description of your methods; a summary of results; and a list of conclusions and implications. It's best to organize your poster left to right and top to bottom, as most of the people who view your poster will begin reading in the upper left corner. Your poster should be clearly organized and able to stand on its own—that is, your poster should have just enough information to allow someone to gain an understanding of your project and findings.

As you plan your presentation, consider the following design guidelines.

- Limit your use of text by using bulleted and numbered lists, tables, charts, graphs, images, photographs, and diagrams to present information.
- Format your poster so that all text and illustrations can be read from four feet away.
- Use a limited number of complementary fonts.
- Use empty space (sometimes called "white space") to reduce clutter and help your audience identify important information.
- Choose a color scheme that is consistent with your purpose.
- Use color to create interest and capture audience attention.

View a Poster

Figure 19.20 shows a poster about private military corporations developed by Nicholas Brothers.

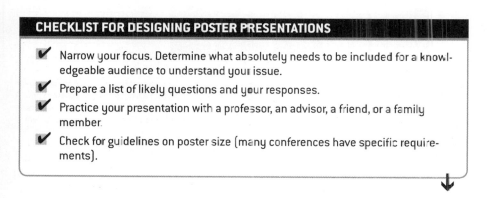

CHECKLIST FOR DESIGNING POSTER PRESENTATIONS

- ✔ Narrow your focus. Determine what absolutely needs to be included for a knowledgeable audience to understand your issue.
- ✔ Prepare a list of likely questions and your responses.
- ✔ Practice your presentation with a professor, an advisor, a friend, or a family member.
- ✔ Check for guidelines on poster size (many conferences have specific requirements).

IV Writing Your Document

CHECKLIST FOR DESIGNING POSTER PRESENTATIONS (continued)

✔ Plan for the physical setup of your poster. Will you need some sort of stand, or are you mounting your material on a board that stands on its own?

✔ Consider how to transport your poster to the site.

✔ During your presentation, remember that most questions are posed out of curiosity, not to catch you off guard. Be polite and professional, and avoid becoming defensive.

✔ Be prepared to share a handout about your project or even a complete written document.

Bulleted lists are used to present information clearly and concisely.

Charts present complex information in a compact form.

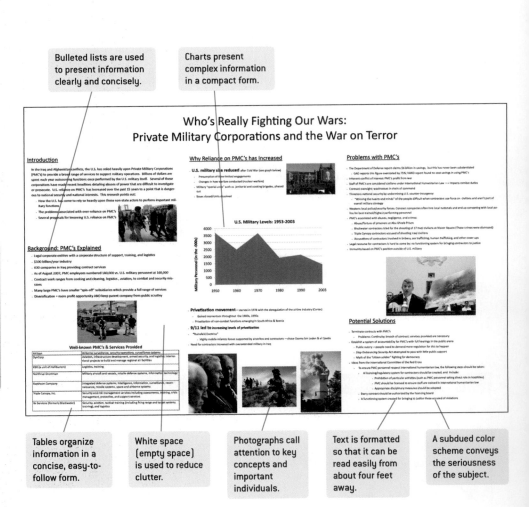

Tables organize information in a concise, easy-to-follow form.

White space (empty space) is used to reduce clutter.

Photographs call attention to key concepts and important individuals.

Text is formatted so that it can be read easily from about four feet away.

A subdued color scheme conveys the seriousness of the subject.

FIGURE 19.20 Poster for a Presentation

IV Writing Your Document

> **QUICK REFERENCE**

Designing Documents and Presentations

☑ Consider purpose, audience, and design expectations as you create an academic essay. (p. 298)

☑ Consider purpose, audience, and design expectations as you create a multimodal essay. (p. 301)

☑ Consider purpose, audience, and cesign expectations as ycu create an article. (p. 305)

☑ Consider purpose, audience, and design expectations as you create a Web site. (p. 307)

☑ Consider purpose, scope, language, and your audience's expectations as you create speaker's notes and prepare to make an oral presentation. (p. 311)

☑ Consider purpose, audience, technology tools, and design expectations as you create a multimedia presentation. (p. 316)

☑ Consider purpose, design expectations, and interaction with your audience as you create a poster presentation. (p. 320)

The Bedford Researcher

I	Joining the Conversation
II	Working with Sources
III	Collecting Information
IV	Writing Your Document
V	**Documenting Sources**

PART V

Documenting Sources

As you complete your work on your research writing project, you can turn your attention fully to the task of citing and documenting your sources. This section discusses reasons to document your sources and describes four major documentation systems: MLA, APA, *Chicago,* and CSE.

20

Understanding Documentation Systems

> **Key Questions**
>
> **20a. What is a documentation system and which one should I use?** 327
>
> **20b. How should I document my sources?** 329

Research writers document their sources to avoid plagiarism, give credit to others who have written about an issue, and create a record of their work that others can follow and build upon. These reasons illustrate the concept of writing as participation in a community of writers and readers. By documenting your sources, you show that you are aware that other writers have contributed to the conversation about your issue and that you respect them enough to acknowledge their contributions. In turn, you expect that writers who read your document will cite your work.

> **? WHAT'S MY PURPOSE?**
>
> Documenting your sources can help you achieve your purpose as a writer, such as establishing your authority and persuading your readers. If your readers find that you haven't documented your sources, they'll either suspect that you're careless or decide that you're dishonest. In either case, they won't trust what you have to say.

20a

What is a documentation system and which one should I use?

Many professional organizations and publications have developed their own rules for formatting documents and citing sources. As a result, writers in many disciplines know how to cite their sources clearly and consistently, and their readers know what to expect. For example, imagine that a psychologist is writing an article for the *Journal of Counseling Psychology*. The writer is likely to know that submissions to the journal go through a rigorous review for substance and style before being accepted for publication. Among its expectations, the journal requires that writers use the documentation system created by the American Psychological Association (APA). Given the high level of competition for space in the journal, the writer knows that even if the article is substantive and compelling, it will not be accepted for publication if it does not use APA style appropriately. After ensuring the article is clearly written and well argued, the writer double-checks the article to ensure it follows the formatting and source citation guidelines specified by the APA documentation system.

Several of the documentation systems most commonly used in the various academic disciplines are covered in this book.

- **MLA** This style, from the Modern Language Association, is used primarily in the humanities—English, philosophy, linguistics, world languages, and so on. See Chapter 21.

- **APA** This style, from the American Psychological Association, is used mainly in the social sciences—psychology, sociology, anthropology, political science, economics, education, and so on. See Chapter 22.

- *Chicago* Developed by the University of Chicago Press, this style is used primarily in history, journalism, and the humanities. See Chapter 23.

- **CSE** This style, from the Council of Science Editors (formerly the Council of Biology Editors), is used mainly in the physical and life sciences—chemistry, geology, biology, botany, and so on—and in mathematics. See Chapter 24.

Your choice of documentation system will be guided by the discipline or field within which you are writing and by any requirements associated with your research writing project. If your project has been assigned to you, ask the person who assigned it or someone who has written a similar document which documentation system you should use. If you are working on a project for a writing class, your instructor will most likely tell you which documentation system to follow.

If you don't have access to advice about which documentation system is best for your project, consider the discipline in which you are writing. In engineering and business, for example, a wide range of documentation styles are used, with most of them specific to scholarly journals or specializations within the discipline. Consider as well the genre you have chosen for your project document. The manner in which sources are cited can vary widely from one type of document to another. For example, while academic essays and articles appearing in scholarly journals typically use a documentation system such as MLA, APA, *Chicago*, or CSE, newspaper and magazine articles often do not and rely instead on identification of sources in the main text of the document rather than in a works cited or reference list.

20b

How should I document my sources?

How you document sources will depend on your writing situation. Most often, you will

1. provide a reference to your source within the text
2. provide a complete set of citations, or formal acknowledgments, for your sources in a works cited or reference list

The specific format of your in-text citations will depend on the documentation system you use. If you use MLA or APA style, you'll cite—or formally acknowledge—information in the text using parentheses and add a list of sources to the end of your document. If you use the *Chicago* notes style, you'll acknowledge your sources in footnotes or endnotes and supply a bibliography at the end of your document. If you use the CSE citation-sequence style, you will number the citations in your text and list your sources in the order in which they are referenced. If you write an electronic document that cites other online sources, you might simply link to your sources.

Table 20.1 presents examples of in-text citations and works cited or reference list entries for each of these major documentation styles. As Table 20.1 shows, although each style differs from the others, especially in the handling of in-text citations, they share a number of similarities.

With the exception of Web style, key publication information is usually provided in a works cited list, reference list, or bibliography. These lists appear at the end of the document and include the following information about each source.

- author(s) and/or editor(s)
- title
- publication date
- publisher and city of publication (for books)
- periodical name, volume, issue, and page numbers (for articles)
- URL and access date (for online publications)

Each documentation system creates an association between citations in the text of a document and the works cited page.

My Research Project

REVIEW YOUR WORKING BIBLIOGRAPHY

Start by reviewing the source citations in your working bibliography. Make sure that you've used the appropriate documentation system and entered sufficient source information to fully document your sources. If you have used the bibliography tools at **bedfordresearcher.com**, you can select from several documentation systems.

TABLE 20.1 EXAMPLES OF IN-TEXT CITATIONS AND BIBLIOGRAPHIC ENTRIES FOR MAJOR DOCUMENTATION STYLES

STYLE	IN-TEXT CITATION	WORKS CITED OR REFERENCE LIST ENTRY
MLA Style	Over the past few years, the Bolivian government has not seen much economic growth (Gordon 16).	Gordon, Gretchen. "The United States, Bolivia, and the Political Economy of Coca." *Multinational Monitor* 27.1 (2006): 15-20. Print.
APA Style	Over the past few years, the Bolivian government has not seen much economic growth (Gordon, 2006, p.16).	Gordon, G. (2006). The United States, Bolivia, and the political economy of coca. *Multinational Monitor, 27*(1), 15-20.
Chicago Style: Notes System	Over the past few years, the Bolivian government has not seen much economic growth.[3]	Gordon, Gretchen. "The United States, Bolivia, and the Political Economy of Coca." *Multinational Monitor* 27, no. 1 (2006): 15-20.
	3. Gretchen Gordon, "The United States, Bolivia, and the Political Economy of Coca," *Multinational Monitor 27,* no. 1 (2006): 16.	*Note: The citation is placed in a footnote or endnote, and again in the bibliography.*
CSE Style: Citation-Sequence System	Over the past few years, the Bolivian government has not seen much economic growth.[3]	3. Gordon G. The United States, Bolivia, and the political economy of coca. Multinational Monitor. 2006;27(1):15-20.
		Note: Numbered citations are placed in the reference list in the order in which they appear in the text.
Web Style	Gordon notes that, over the past few years, the Bolivian government has not seen much economic growth.	Many Web documents will link directly to a cited work, as shown here. Or they may use a style such as MLA, APA, *Chicago*, or CSE.

> **QUICK REFERENCE**

Understanding Documentation Systems

✔ Choose an appropriate documentation system. (p. 327)

✔ Document your sources in your text and, depending on the documentation system, create a works cited list, reference list, or bibliography. Review your sources for accuracy and completeness. (p. 329)

V Documenting Sources

21

Using MLA Style

> **Key Questions**
>
> **21a. How do I cite sources within the text of my document? 334**
>
> **21b. How do I prepare the list of works cited? 337**

Modern Language Association (MLA) style, used primarily in the humanities, emphasizes the authors of a source and the pages on which information is located in the source. Writers who use the MLA documentation system cite, or formally acknowledge, source information within their text using parentheses, and they provide a list of sources in a works cited list at the end of their document.

For more information about MLA style, consult the *MLA Handbook for Writers of Research Papers,* Seventh Edition. Information about the MLA Handbook can also be found at mla.org.

To see featured writer Elizabeth Leontiev's research essay, formatted in MLA style, turn to p. 357.

> @ Use the Bedford Bibliographer at bedfordresearcher.com to create an MLA-style bibliography.

CITATIONS WITHIN YOUR TEXT

1. Basic format for direct quotation   334
2. Basic format for a summary or paraphrase   334
3. Entire source   335
4. Corporate or group author   335
5. Unknown author   335
6. Two or more works by the same author   335
7. Two or more authors with the same last name   335
8. Two or three authors   335
9. Four or more authors   336
10. Literary work   336
11. Work in an anthology   336
12. Sacred text   336
13. Two or more works   336
14. Source quoted in another source   336
15. Print source without page numbers   336
16. Electronic or nonprint source   337

ENTRIES IN YOUR WORKS CITED LIST

MLA

V Documenting Sources

21a

How do I cite sources within the text of my document?

MLA style uses parentheses for in-text citations to acknowledge the use of another author's words, facts, and ideas. When you refer to a source within your text, place the author's last name and specific page number(s)—if the source is paginated—within parentheses. Your reader then can go to the works cited list at the end of your document and find a full citation there.

1. Basic Format for Direct Quotation   Often you will want to name the author of a source within your sentence rather than in a parenthetical citation. By doing so, you create a context for the material (words, facts, or ideas) that you are including and indicate where the information from the author begins. When you are using a direct quotation from a source and have named the author in your sentence, place only the page number in parentheses after the quotation. The period follows the parentheses.

> Vargas reports that "each year, unintentional drownings kill more than 830 children younger than 14 and cause, on average, 3,600 injuries" (B01).

When you have not mentioned the author in your sentence, you must place the author's name and the page number in parentheses after the quotation. Again, the period follows the parentheses.

> After car accidents, "drowning is the second-leading cause of unintentional deaths" among toddlers (Vargas B01).

When you are using a block (or extended) quotation, the parenthetical citation comes after the final punctuation and a single space.

If you continue to refer to a single source for several sentences in a row within one paragraph—and without intervening references to another source—you may reserve your reference to the end of the paragraph. However, be sure to include all of the relevant page numbers.

2. Basic Format for a Summary or Paraphrase   When you are summarizing or paraphrasing information gained from a source, you are still required to cite the source. If you name the author in your sentence, place only the page number in parentheses after the paraphrase or summary. Punctuation marks follow the parentheses. When you have not mentioned the author in your sentence, you must place the author's name and the page number in parentheses after the quotation.

> Vargas points out that drowning doesn't happen in the manner you might expect; children slip under water quietly, making very little noise to alert unsuspecting parents or guardians (B01).

3. Entire Source   If you are referring to an entire source rather than to a specific page or pages, you will not need a parenthetical citation.

> The explorations of race in ZZ Packer's *Drinking Coffee Elsewhere* can be linked thematically to the treatment of immigrants in Lahiri's work.

4. Corporate or Group Author   Cite the corporation or group as you would an individual author. You may use abbreviations for the source in subsequent references if you add the abbreviation in parentheses at the first mention of the name.

> The Brown University Office of Financial Aid (BUOFA) has adopted a policy that first-year students will not be expected to work as part of their financial aid package (12). BUOFA will award these students a one-time grant to help compensate for the income lost by not working (14).

5. Unknown Author   If you are citing a source that has no known author, such as the book *Through Palestine with the 20th Machine Gun Squadron*, use a brief version of the title in the parenthetical citation.

> The members of the squadron rode horses while the cooks were issued bicycles, requiring the cooks to exert quite a lot of effort pedaling through the desert sand (*Through Palestine* 17).

6. Two or More Works by the Same Author   For references to authors with more than one work in your works cited list, insert a short version of the title between author and page number, separating the author and the title with a comma.

> (Ishiguro, *Unconsoled* 146)

> (Ishiguro, *Remains* 77)

7. Two or More Authors with the Same Last Name   Include the first initial and last name in the parenthetical citations.

> (G. Martin 354)

> (F. Martin 169)

8. Two or Three Authors   Include the last name of each author in your citation.

> Casting physically attractive actors wins points with film audiences: "Primitive as the association between outward strength and moral force may be, it has its undeniable appeal" (Clarke, Johnson, and Evans 228).

9. Four or More Authors Use only the last name of the first author and the abbreviation "et al." (Latin for "and others"). Note that there is no comma between the author's name and "et al."

> (Barnes et al. 44)

10. Literary Work Along with the page number(s), give other identifying information, such as a chapter, scene, or line number, that will help readers find the passage.

> The sense of social claustrophobia is never as palpable in *The Age of Innocence* as when Newland realizes that all of New York society has conspired to cover up what it believes to be an affair between him and Madame Olenska (Wharton 339; ch. 33).

11. Work in an Anthology Cite the author of the work, not the editor of the anthology. (See also #34 on p. 341.)

> In "Beneath the Deep, Slow Motion," Leo says, "The Chinese call anger a weary bird with no place to roost" (Barkley 163).

12. Sacred Text Give the name of the edition you are using along with the chapter and verse (or their equivalent).

> He should consider that "Where no counsel is, the people fall: but in the multitude of counselors there is safety" (*King James Bible*, Prov. 11.14).

> In the Qu'ran, sinners are said to be blind to their sins ("The Cow" 2.7).

13. Two or More Works Use a semicolon to separate entries.

> Forethought is key in survival, whether it involves remembering extra water on a safari trail or gathering food for a long winter in ancient times (Wither and Hosking 4; Estes and Otte 2).

14. Source Quoted in Another Source Ideally, you will be able to find the primary, or original, source for material used in your research project document. If you quote or paraphrase a secondary source—a source that contains information about a primary source—use the abbreviation "qtd. in" (for "quoted in") when you cite the source.

> President Leonid Kuchma insisted that "we cannot in any instance allow the disintegration or division of Ukraine" (qtd. in Lisova A1).

15. Print Source without Page Numbers If no page numbers are provided, list only the author's name in parentheses.

Although his work has been influenced by many graphic artists, it remains essentially text based (Fitzgerald).

16. Electronic or Nonprint Source   Give a page, section, paragraph, or screen number, if used, in the parenthetical citation.

Teters believes the mascots dehumanize Native Americans, allowing spectators to dismiss the Native Americans' true culture as well as their hardships (Saraceno, par. 20).

21b

How do I prepare the list of works cited?

MLA-style research documents include a reference list titled "Works Cited," which begins on a new page at the end of the document. If you wish to acknowledge sources that you read but did not cite in your text, you may title the list "Works Consulted" and include them. The list is alphabetized by author. If the author's name is unknown, alphabetize the entry using the title of the source. To cite more than one work by the same author, use the author's name in the first entry. Thereafter, use three hyphens followed by a period in place of the author's name; list the entries alphabetically by title. All entries in the list are double-spaced, with no extra space between entries. Entries are formatted with a hanging indent: The first line of an entry is flush with the left margin and subsequent lines are indented one-half inch or five spaces.

In longer documents, a list of works cited may be given at the end of each chapter or section. In electronic documents that use links, such as a Web site, the list of works cited is often a separate page to which other pages are linked. To see a works cited list in MLA style, see p. 361.

> @ Use the Bedford Bibliographer at bedfordresearcher.com to create an MLA-style bibliography.

Books, Conference Proceedings, and Dissertations

17. One Author

Boyd, Gerald M. *My Times in Black and White: Race and Power at the New York Times*. Chicago: Hill, 2010. Print

18. Two or Three Authors   List all the authors in the same order as on the title page, last name first for only the first author listed. Use commas to separate authors' names.

Datta, Sona, Pratapaditya Pal, and Rivka Israel. *Urban Patua: The Art of Jamini Roy*. Mumbai: Marg, 2010. Print.

Siegel, Ben, and Jay L. Halio. *Playful and Serious: Philip Roth as a Comic Writer*. Newark: U of Delaware P, 2010. Print.

TUTORIAL

How do I cite books using MLA style?

When citing a book, use the information from the title page and the copyright page (on the reverse side of the title page), not from the book's cover or a library catalog.

   Consult pp. 337–42 for additional models for citing books.

Book cover from *Confessions of a Young Novelist* by Umberto Eco. Copyright © 2011 by the President and Fellows of Harvard College, appears courtesy of Harvard University Press.

Eco, Umberto. *Confessions of a Young Novelist*. Cambridge: Harvard UP.

2011. Print.

A **The author.** Give the last name first, followed by a comma, the first name, and the middle initial (if given). Omit titles such as *MD*, *PhD*, or *Sir*; include suffixes after the name and a comma (O'Driscoll, Gerald P., Jr.). End with a period.

B **The title.** Give the full title; include the subtitle (if any), preceded by a colon. Italicize the title and subtitle; capitalize all major words. End with a period.

C **The city of publication.** If more than one city is given, use the first one listed. Insert a colon.

D **The publisher.** Give a shortened version of the publisher's name (*Harper* for HarperCollins Publishers; *Palgrave* for Palgrave Macmillan; *Oxford UP* for Oxford University Press). Do not include the words *Publisher* or *Inc.* Follow with a comma.

E **The year of publication.** If more than one copyright date is given, use the most recent one. Use "n.d." if no date is given. End with a period.

F **The medium of publication.** Use *Print*. End with a period.

Use the bibliography tools at **bedfordresearcher.com** to create a bibliography formatted in MLA style.

19. Four or More Authors   Provide the first author's name (last name first) followed by a comma, and then the abbreviation "et al." (Latin for "and others").

Levin, Miriam, et al. *Urban Modernity: Cultural Innovation in the Second
   Industrial Revolution.* Cambridge: MIT P, 2010. Print.

20. Corporate or Group Author   Write out the full name of the corporation or group, and cite the name as you would an author. This name is often also the name of the publisher.

National Geographic. *In Focus: National Geographic Greatest Portraits.*
   Washington: Natl. Geographic, 2010. Print.

21. Unknown Author   When no author is listed on the title or copyright page, begin the entry with the title of the work. Alphabetize the entry by the first word of the title other than *A, An,* or *The.*

The Book of Nature. Munich: Kunth, 2010. Print.

22. Two or More Books by the Same Author   List the entries alphabetically by title.

Chopra, Deepak. *Muhammad: A Story of the Last Prophet.* New York: Harper,
   2010. Print.

- - -. *Why Is God Laughing? The Path to Joy and Spiritual Optimism.* New
   York: Harmony, 2008. Print.

23. Editor(s)   Use the abbreviation "ed." or "eds."

Olson, Gregory Allen, ed. *Landmark Speeches on the Vietnam War.* College
   Station: Texas A&M UP, 2010. Print.

24. Translated Book   List the author first and then the title, followed by the name of the translator and publication information. Use the abbreviation "Trans."

Eco, Umberto. *History of Beauty.* Trans. Alastair McEwen. New York: Rizzoli,
   2010. Print.

25. Book in a Language Other Than English   You may give a translation of the book's title in brackets.

Márquez, Gabriel García. *Del amor y otros demonios [Of Love and Other
   Demons].* New York: Vintage, 2010. Print.

26. Edition Other Than the First   Include the number of the edition and the abbreviation "ed." after the title.

Gmelch, George, Robert V. Kemper, and Walter P. Zenner. *Urban Life: Readings in the Anthropology of the City.* 5th ed. Long Grove: Waveland, 2010. Print.

27. Multivolume Work   Include the total number of volumes and the abbreviation "vols." after the title.

Taylor, Quintard. *From Timbuktu to Katrina: Sources in African-American History.* 2 vols. Boston: Wadsworth, 2007. Print.

If you have used only one of the volumes in your document, include the volume number after the title. Then list the total number of volumes after the medium of publication.

Campbell, Gordon. *The Grove Encyclopedia of Classical Art and Architecture.* Vol. 1. New York: Oxford UP, 2007. Print. 2 vols.

28. Book in a Series   If a series name and/or number appears on the title page, include it at the end of the citation, after the medium. If the word "Series" is part of the series name, use the abbreviation "Ser."

Hernández, Felipe, Peter Kellett, and Lea K. Allen, eds. *Rethinking the Informal City: Critical Perspectives from Latin America.* New York: Berghahn, 2010. Print. Remapping Cultural History 11.

29. Republished Book   Indicate the original date of publication after the title.

Melville, Herman. *Bartleby, the Scrivener: A Story of Wall-Street.* 1853. Champaign: Book Jungle, 2010. Print.

30. Book with a Title within the Title

Stuckey, Sterling. *African Culture and Melville's Art: The Creative Process in* Benito Cereno *and* Moby-Dick. New York: Oxford UP, 2009. Print.

31. Author with an Editor   Include the name of the editor (first name first) after the title.

Twain, Mark. *Autobiography of Mark Twain.* Ed. Harriet Elinor Smith. Vol. 1. Berkeley: U of California P, 2010. Print.

32. Anthology   To cite an anthology of essays, stories, or poems or a collection of articles, list the editor or editors first (as on the title page), followed by the abbreviation "ed." or "eds."

Schmidt, Elizabeth, ed. *The Poets Laureate Anthology.* New York: Norton, 2010. Print.

33. Foreword, Introduction, Preface, or Afterword   Begin with the author of the part you are citing and the name of that part. Continue with the title of the work and its author (first name first), following "By." At the end of the entry, list the inclusive page numbers on which the part of the book appears.

Wakeling, Edward. Foreword. *The Mystery of Lewis Carroll: Discovering the Whimsical, Thoughtful and Sometimes Lonely Man Who Created* Alice in Wonderland. By Jenny Woolf. New York: St. Martin's, 2010. ix-x. Print.

If the author of the foreword or other part is also the author of the work, use only the last name after "By."

Olson, Gregory Allen. Introduction. *Landmark Speeches on the Vietnam War.* By Olson. College Station: Texas A&M UP, 2010. 1-12. Print.

If the foreword or other part has a title, include the title in quotation marks between the author and the name of the part.

Walker, Alice. "Learning to Dance." Preface. *Hard Times Require Furious Dancing.* By Walker. Novato: New World, 2010. xv-xvi. Print.

34. Chapter in an Edited Book or Selection in an Anthology   Begin your citation with the author and the title of the chapter or selection. Follow this with the title of the anthology or collection, the abbreviation "Ed." (meaning "Edited by"), and names of the editors (first name first) as well as publication information. At the end of your entry, give the inclusive page numbers for the selection or chapter.

Simmons, James. "The Not Yet Ancient Mariner." *An Anthology of Modern Irish Poetry.* Ed. Wes Davis. Cambridge: Belknap-Harvard UP. 2010. 277. Print.

35. Two or More Works from One Anthology   To avoid repeating the same information about the anthology several times, include the anthology itself in your list of works cited.

Fishkin, Shelley Fisher, ed. *The Mark Twain Anthology: Great Writers on His Life and Works.* New York: Lib. Classics, 2010. Print.

In the entries for individual selections or chapters, list the author and title of the selection (in quotation marks) and cross-reference the anthology by giving the editor's name and the page numbers on which the selection appears. with no comma between them. Do not include the medium of publication.

Eliot, T. S. "Huck and Oliver." Fishkin 246-51.

Kipling, Rudyard. "On the Art of Mark Twain." Fishkin 66-77.

MLA

V Documenting Sources

36. Screenplay

Cholodenko, Lisa, and Stuart Blumberg. *The Kids Are All Right: The Shooting Script*. New York: Newmarket, 2011. Print.

37. Published Proceedings of a Conference   Provide information as you would for a book, adding information about the conference after the title: the date, sponsors, and location of the conference. Then add the publication data as for a book. End with the medium.

Becker, Michael, and Andrew McKenzie, eds. *Proceedings of the 3rd Conference on the Semantics of Underrepresented Languages in the Americas*. 11-13 May 2007, Graduate Linguistics Student Assn., UMass Amherst. Amherst: GLSA, 2007. Print.

38. Paper Published in Proceedings of a Conference   Treat a selection from conference proceedings as you would a selection in an edited collection.

Chang, Charles B. "Learning to Produce a Multidimensional Laryngeal Contrast." *New Sounds 2010: Proceedings of the 6th International Symposium on the Acquisition of Second Language Speech*. Ed. K. Dziubalska-Kołaczyk, M. Wrembel, and M. Kul. 1-3 May 2010, School of English, Adam Mickiewicz University. Poznan: Adam Mickiewicz University. 89-94. Print.

39. Sacred Text   Include the title of the version as it appears on the title page. If the title does not identify the version, place that information directly after the title.

Holy Bible: New Revised Standard Version. Nashville: Abingdon, 2010. Print.

40. Published Dissertation or Thesis   Cite as you would a book, with the title in italics, but include information specific to the dissertation, such as the school and the year the dissertation was accepted.

Crites, Danya Alexandra. *From Mosque to Cathedral: The Social and Political Significations of Mudejar in Late Medieval Seville*. Diss. U of Iowa, 2010. Iowa City: U of Iowa, 2010. Print.

41. Unpublished Dissertation or Thesis   Place the title of the thesis or dissertation in quotation marks and add information about the type of dissertation, the school, and the date.

Higgins, Wayne C. "Urban Regeneration: Enabled by Mobility Centric Architecture." MA thesis. MIT, 2010. Print.

42. Abstract of a Dissertation or Thesis   Treat an abstract as you would an article in a journal. First give the information for the dissertation. Then add the source, abbreviated either *DA* or *DAI* (for *Dissertation Abstracts* or *Dissertation Abstracts International*), volume number, year (in parentheses), and item number page numbers.

Kennedy-O'Neill, Joy D. "The Sacred and the Sublime: Caves in American
    Literature." Diss. Indiana U of Pennsylvania, 2007. *DAI* 68.3 (2007):
    3258663. Print.

Sources in Journals, Magazines, and Newspapers

43. Article in a Journal Paginated by Volume   Most journals continue pagination for an entire year, beginning again at page 1 only in the first volume of the next year. After the journal title (omit introductory articles such as *The*), list the volume number and issue number (if any) with a period between them, the year of publication in parentheses, a colon, and inclusive page numbers. End with the medium.

Kinzser, Charles K. "Considering Literacy and Policy in the Context of Digital
    Environments." *Language Arts* 88.1 (2010): 51-61. Print.

44. Article in a Journal Paginated by Issue   Some journals begin at page 1 for every issue. After the volume number, add a period and the issue number, with no space.

Love, Jessica. "They Get to Me: A Young Psycholinguist Confesses Her Strong
    Attraction to Pronouns." *American Scholar* 79.2 (2010): 64-71. Print.

45. Article That Skips Pages   Give only the first page number and a plus sign (+), with no space between.

Mahler, Jonathan. "The Second Coming." *New York Times Magazine* 15 Aug.
    2010: 30+. Print.

46. Article with a Quotation in the Title   Enclose the quotation in single quotation marks within the article title, which is enclosed in double quotation marks.

Jones, Vanessa E. "'They're Sitting Right Next to Us': On College Campuses,
    Students Continue to Struggle with Ethnic Tensions and Racist
    Attitudes." *Boston Globe* 5 Dec. 2007: F1+. Print.

47. Article in a Monthly or Bimonthly Magazine   After the author's name and title of the article, list the title of the magazine, the date (use abbreviations for all months except May, June, and July), and the inclusive pages.

TUTORIAL

How do I cite articles from periodicals using MLA style?

Periodicals include journals, magazines, and newspapers. This page gives an example of a citation for a print journal article. Models for citing articles from magazines and newspapers are on pp. 342–44.

If you need to cite a periodical article you accessed electronically, follow the guidelines below and see also p. 350.

A **B**

Fisher, Mark. "Visionary Television: *World on a Wire* and *Artemis 81*." *Film*

C **D** **E** **F** **G**

Quarterly 64.2 (Winter 2010): 58-63. Print.

A **The author.** Give the last name first, followed by a comma, the first name, and the middle initial (if given). Omit titles such as *MD*, *PhD*, or *Sir*; include suffixes after the name and a comma (O'Driscoll, Gerald P., Jr.). End with a period.

B **The article title.** Give the full title; include the subtitle (if any), preceded by a colon. Enclose the title and subtitle in quotation marks, and capitalize all major words. Place a period inside the closing quotation mark.

C **The periodical title.** Italicize the periodical title; exclude any initial *A*, *An*, or *The*; capitalize all major words.

D **The volume number and issue number.** For journals, include the volume number; if the journal uses issue numbers, include a period (no space) and then the issue number as well.

E **The date of publication.** For journals, give the year in parentheses followed by a colon. For monthly magazines, don't use parentheses; give the month and year. For weekly magazines and newspapers, don't use parentheses; give the day, month, and year (in that order). Abbreviate the names of all months except May, June, and July.

F **Inclusive page number(s).** For numbers 100 and above, give only the last two digits and any other preceding digits if different from the first number (22-28, 402-10, 1437-45, 592-603). If an article continues on nonconsecutive pages, include the first page number followed by a plus sign. Include section letters for newspapers, if relevant. End with a period.

G **The medium of publication.** For print publications, use *Print*. End with a period.

Use the bibliography tools at **bedfordresearcher.com** to create a bibliography formatted in MLA style.

McArdle, Megan. "The Freeloaders: How a Generation of File-Sharers Is
Ruining the Future of Entertainment." *Atlantic* May 2010: 34-35. Print.

48. Article in a Weekly or Biweekly Magazine Give the exact date of publication, inverted.

Kaplan, David A. "Climate Science under Attack." *Fortune* 18 Oct. 2010: 34.
Print.

49. Article in a Daily Newspaper If the title of the newspaper begins with
The, omit the word. If the newspaper is not a national newspaper (such as the
Wall Street Journal, Christian Science Monitor, or *Chronicle of Higher Education*) or
the city of publication is not part of its title, give the name of the city in square
brackets [Cincinnati] after the title. List the date in inverted order and, if the
masthead indicates that the paper has more than one edition, give this information after the date ("natl. ed.," "late ed."). Follow with a colon and a space, and
end with the page numbers (use the section letter before the page number if the
newspaper uses letters to designate sections). If the article does not appear on
consecutive pages, write only the first page number and a plus sign (+), with no
space between.

Saltzman, Jonathan. "Judge OK's Class-Action Smoker Suit." *Boston Globe*
25 June 2010: B1. Print.

50. Unsigned Article in a Newspaper or Magazine Begin with the title of the
article. Alphabetize by the first word other than *A, An,* or *The*.

"FDA Sends e-Cigarette Companies a Warning." *Detroit News* 10 Sept. 2010:
A22. Print.

51. Editorial in a Newspaper Include the word "Editorial" after the title.

"The Spill and Energy Bill." Editorial. *New York Times* 5 June 2010: A20.
Print.

52. Letter to the Editor Include the word "Letter" after the title.

Hasl, Rudy. "Jefferson's Mammoth." Letter. *Smithsonian* June 2010: 6. Print.

53. Review After the author and title of the review, include the words "Rev.
of," followed by the title of the work under review; a comma; the word "by" (for
a book) or "dir." (for a play or film); and the name of the author or director.
Continue with publication information for the review.

Hornaday, Ann. "A Tough Tale Told with Tenderness." Rev. of *The Fighter*,
dir. David O. Russell. *Washington Post* 17 Dec. 2010: T23. Print.

MLA

V Documenting Sources

54. Published Interview   Begin with the person interviewed. If the published interview has a title, give it in quotation marks. If not, write the word "Interview" (no quotation marks or italics). If an interviewer is identified and relevant to your project, give that name next. Then supply the publication data.

Kelley, Kitty. "The Secret Sharer." Interview by Deborah Solomon. *New York Times Magazine* 11 Apr. 2010: MM18. Print.

55. Article in a Special Issue   After the author and the title of the article (in quotation marks) include the title of the special issue (in italics), then write the words "Spec. issue of" before the regular title of the periodical.

Feldman, Elliot. "Old Hippy in Hollywood." *View of the Arts 2007*. Spec. issue of *Scene 4 Magazine* Jan. 2007: 72-79. Print.

Print Reference Works

56. Encyclopedia, Dictionary, Thesaurus, Handbook, or Almanac   Cite as you would a book (see p. 337).

57. Entry in an Encyclopedia, Dictionary, Thesaurus, Handbook, or Almanac
In many cases, the entries and articles in reference works are unsigned. Therefore, begin your citation with the title of the entry in quotation marks, followed by a period. Give the title of the reference work, italicized, and the edition and year of publication. Include the editor's name if the reference work is not well known. If the entries in the work are arranged alphabetically, you may omit the volume and page numbers.

"Go Figure." *Oxford Dictionary of English Idioms*. 3rd ed. 2010. Print.

If you cite a specific definition, include that information after the title of the entry, adding the abbreviation "Def." and the number of the definition.

"Heterodox." Def. 1. *Oxford English Dictionary*. 3rd ed. 2010. Print.

If a reference work is not well known (perhaps because it includes highly specialized information), provide all of the bibliographic information.

"Loyalty Oaths." *Encyclopedia of American Immigration*. Pasadena: Salem, 2010. Print.

58. Map or Chart   Generally, treat a map or chart as you would a book without authors. Give its title (italicized), the word "Map" or "Chart," and publication information. For a map in an atlas, give the map title (in quotation marks) followed by publication information for the atlas and page numbers for the map. If the creator of the map or chart is listed, use his or her name as you would an author's name.

Benchmark Recreation Map: Oregon. Map. Chicago: Rand, 2010. Print.

"Africa: Political." Map. *Oxford Atlas of the World.* 17th ed. New York: Oxford
UP, 2010. 255. Print.

59. Government Publications In most cases, cite the government agency as
the author. If there is a named author, editor, or compiler, provide that name after
the title. Use the abbreviations "Dept." for department, "Cong." for Congress,
"S." for Senate, "H." or "HR" for House of Representatives, "Res." for resolution,
"Rept." for report, "Doc." for document, and "GPO" for Government Printing
Office.

United States. Cong. House. Committee on Science and Technology.
*America Competes: Big Picture Perspectives on the Need for Innovation,
Investments in R&D, and a Commitment to STEM Education.* 111th Cong.,
2nd sess. Serial no. 111-70. Washington: GPO, 2010. Print.

For congressional bills (not reports or resolutions), do not include a period after
the abbreviations "S" or "HR".

If you are citing from the *Congressional Record,* the entry is simply *Cong. Rec.*
followed by the date, a colon, and the page numbers.

60. Pamphlet Format the entry as you would for a book (see p. 337).

American Diabetes Association. *Everyday Choices for a Healthier Life.*
Alexandria: Amer. Diabetes Assn., 2007. Print.

Field Sources

61. Personal Interview Place the name of the person interviewed first, words
to indicate how the interview was conducted ("Personal interview," "Telephone
interview," or "E-mail interview"), and the date.

Templeton, Santo. Personal interview. 4 Oct. 2010.

62. Unpublished Letter If written to you, give the writer's name, the words
"Letter to the author" (no quotation marks or italics), and the date the letter was
written. End with the form of the material use "MS" (for manuscript) for a letter
written by hand and "TS" (for typescript) for typed letters.

Wilden, Raquel. Letter to the author. 11 Aug. 2010. TS.

If the letter was written to someone else, give that name rather than "the author."

63. Lecture or Public Address Give the speaker's name and the title of the lecture (if there is one). If the lecture was part of a meeting or convention, identify
that event. Conclude with the event data, including venue, city, and date. End
with the appropriate label ("Lecture," "Panel discussion," "Reading").

Joseph, Branden. "1962." Dept. of Art History, U of Chicago, Cochrane Art
Center, Chicago. 11 Mar. 2010. Lecture.

Media Sources

64. Film or Video Recording   Generally begin with the title of the film or recording (italicized). Always supply the name of the director (following the abbreviation "Dir."), the distributor, and the year of original release. You may also
insert other relevant information, such as the names of performers or screenplay
writers, before the distributor.

True Grit. Dir. Ethan Coen and Joel Coen. Perf. Jeff Bridges and Matt Damon.
Paramount, 2010. Film.

If you wish to emphasize an individual's role in the film or movie, such as the
director or screenplay writer, you may list that name first.

Olivier, Laurence, dir. and perf. *Hamlet*. Paramount, 1948. Film.

For media other than film (such as videotape and DVD), cite it as for a film but
identify the medium at the end.

Guess Who's Coming to Dinner. Dir. Stanley Kramer. 1967. Sony Pictures
Home Entertainment, 2008. DVD.

65. Television Program   If the program has named episodes or segments, list
those in quotation marks. Then include the title of the program or series (italicized), the network, the station's call letters and city (if any), and the date on
which you watched the program. If there are relevant persons to name (such as
an author, director, host, narrator, or actor), include that information after the
title. Add the medium at the end.

"Strange Bedfellows." *Big Love*. HBO. 24 Jan. 2010. Television.

66. Radio Program   Cite as you would a television program.

Fresh Air. Host Terry Gross. Natl. Public Radio. WHYY, Philadelphia. 20 Oct.
2010. Radio.

67. Radio or Television Interview   Provide the name of the person interviewed
and the title of the interview. If there is no title, write "Interview" and, if relevant,
the name of the interviewer. Then provide the name of the program, the network,
the call letters of the station, the city, and the date.

Assange, Julian. Interview by Katie Couric. *CBS Evening News*. CBS. KCTV,
Kansas City. 20 Dec. 2010. Television.

68. Sound Recording   Begin with the name of the person whose work you want to highlight: the composer, the conductor, or the performer. Next list the title, followed by names of other artists (composer, conductor, performers), with abbreviations indicating their roles. The recording information includes the manufacturer and the date. Add the medium of the recording at the end (CD, LP, Audiocassette, Audiotape, or MP3 file).

Gershwin, George. *Rhapsody in Blue*. Royal Philharmonic Orch. Cond. Leonard
    Slatkin. EMI Gold, 2007. CD.

If you wish to cite a particular track on the recording, give its performer and title (in quotation marks) and then proceed with the information about the recording. For live recordings, include the date of the performance between the title and the recording data.

Cash, Johnny. "Folsom Prison Blues." *The Great Lost Performance*. Rec.
    27 July 1990. Island, 2007. MP3 file.

69. Musical Composition   Give the composer and title. Italicize the title unless it identifies the composition by form ("symphony," "suite"), number ("op. 39," "K. 231"), or key ("E flat").

Berlioz, Hector. Symphonie Fantastique. op. 14.

If you are referring to a published score, provide publication data as you would for a book. Insert the date of composition between the title and the publication information and capitalize the abbreviations *no.* and *op.*

McKinley, Roger. *Jackson Pollock the Musical*. 2007. Manchester: Michael
    Butterworth, 2007. Print.

70. Live Performance   Generally, begin with the title of the performance (italicized). Then give the author and director; the major performers; and theater, city, and date.

1776. By Peter Stone. Dir. Jon Huffman. Perf. Peter Riopelle, Mark Sawyer-
    Daily, and Mason Stewart. Bomhard Theatre, Louisville. 27 June 2010.
    Performance.

71. Work of Art   Give the name of the artist, the title of the work (italicized), the date of composition, the medium of composition, and the name of the collection, museum or owner, and the city. If you are citing artwork published in a book, add the publication information for the book and the medium of publication ("Print") at the end.

Attia, Kader. *Sleeping from Memory*. 2007. Foam and plywood. Inst. of
    Contemporary Art, Boston.

72. Advertisement   Provide the name of the product, service, or organization being advertised, followed by the word "Advertisement." Then provide the usual publication information.

Bose. Advertisement. *Sports Illustrated* 4 Oct. 2010: 69. Print.

73. Cartoon   Treat a cartoon like an article in a newspaper or magazine. Give the cartoonist's name, the title of the cartoon if there is one (in quotation marks), the word "Cartoon," and the publication data for the source.

Chast, Roz. "Dadonomics." Cartoon. *New Yorker* 1 Nov. 2010: 75. Print.

Electronic Sources

74. Article from an Online Database or Subscription Service   Cite it as you would a print article, then give the name of the database in italics, the medium consulted ("Web"), and the date you accessed the article. (See also p. 355.)

Barrett, Lynn. "Effective School Libraries: Evidence of Impact on Student
    Achievement." *School Librarian* 58.3 (2010): 136. *Academic OneFile.*
    Web. 17 Dec. 2010.

75. Abstract from an Online Database   Provide the publication information for the source, followed by the word "Abstract," the name of the database, the medium ("Web"), and the date you accessed it.

Thompson, June. "Mothers Who Do Not Breastfeed More Likely to Develop
    Type-2 Diabetes." *Community Practitioner* 83.10 (2010): 41. Abstract.
    Health Reference Center Academic. Web. 29 Nov. 2010.

76. Entire Web Site   Provide the name of the Web site in italics, the sponsor or publisher, the date of publication or last update, the medium, and the date of access.

Solar System Exploration. NASA, 10 June 2011. Web. 15 June 2011.

77. Work from a Professional or Commercial Web Site   Include the author (if available), the title of the document in quotation marks, and the title of the Web site in italics. Then give the sponsor or publisher, the date of publication or last update, the medium, and the access date. (See also p. 356.)

"Transitioning to Kindergarten: A Toolkit for Early Childhood Educators."
    Get Ready to Read! Natl. Center for Learning Disabilities, 2010. Web.
    8 Nov. 2010.

TUTORIAL

How do I cite articles from databases using MLA style?

Libraries subscribe to services such as LexisNexis, ProQuest, InfoTrac, and EBSCOhost that provide access to databases of electronic texts. The databases provide publication information, abstracts, and the complete text of documents in a specific subject area, discipline, or profession. (See also Chapter 8.)

A **B**

Kostelac, Sofia. "'The Body Is His, Pulse and Motion': Violence and Desire in

C **D**

Yvonne Vera's *The Stone Virgins.*" *Research in African Literatures* 41.3

E **F** **G** **H** **I**

(2010): 75-88. *Expanded Academic ASAP.* Web. 27 Jan. 2011.

A   **The author.** Give the last name first, followed by a comma and the first name. Omit titles such as *MD*, *PhD*, or *Sir*; include suffixes after the name and a comma (O'Driscoll, Gerald P., Jr.). End with a period.

B   **The article title.** Give the title and subtitle (if any), preceded by a colon. Enclose the full title in quotation marks, and capitalize all major words. Place a period inside the closing quotation mark.

C   **The periodical title.** Italicize the periodical title; exclude any initial *A*, *An*, or *The*; capitalize all major words.

D   **The volume number and issue number if appropriate.** For journals, give the volume number; if the journal uses issue numbers, include a period (no space) and then the issue number as well.

E   **The date of publication.** For journals, give the year in parentheses, followed by a colon. For monthly magazines, don't use parentheses; give the month and year. For weekly magazines and newspapers, give the day, month, and year.

F   **Inclusive page number(s).** For numbers 100 and above, give only the last two digits and any other preceding digits if different from the first number (22-28, 402-10, 1437-45, 592-603). Include section letters for newspapers, if relevant.

G   **The name of the database.** Italicize the name of the database, followed by a period.

H   **The medium consulted.** Use *Web* followed by a period.

I   **The date of access.** Use the day-month-year format; abbreviate all months except May, June, and July. End with a period.

Use the bibliography tools at **bedfordresearcher.com** to create a bibliography formatted in MLA style.

78. Academic Course or Department Web Site   For a course page, give the name of the instructor, the course title in italics, a description such as "Course home page," the course dates, the department, the institution, the medium, and the access date. For a department page, give the department name, a description such as "Home page," the institution, the date of the last update, the medium, and your access date.

Global Studies Dept. *Crossing Borders: Islam and the West.* Course home
     page. Spring 2011. International Programs, Alfred U. Web. 20 Jan. 2011.

Dept. of English and Technical Communication. Home page. Missouri U of
     Science and Technology, 2010. Web. 22 Mar. 2010.

79. Work from a Personal Web Site   Include the name of the person who created the site. If the site has no title, give a description such as "Home page." Then follow with the sponsor of the Web site, the date of the last update, the medium ("Web"), and your date of access.

Gibson, Shimon. Home page. HarperCollins, 2010. Web. 22 Aug. 2010.

80. Message Posted to a Newsgroup, Electronic Mailing List, or Online Discussion Forum   Cite the name of the person who posted the message; the title (from the subject line, in quotation marks); if the posting has no title, add the phrase "Online posting"; then add the name of the Web site (italicized), the sponsor or publisher, the date of the message, the medium ("Web"), and the date you accessed the posting.

Hillestad, Sharon. "Re: Vocabulary Reading Comprehension." *Learning
     Disabilities Discussion List.* Natl. Inst. for Literacy, 23 Dec. 2010. Web.
     30 Dec. 2010.

81. Article Posted on a Wiki

"Pointillism." *Wikipedia.* Wikimedia Foundation, 21 Dec. 2010. Web. 31 Dec.
     2010.

82. Entire Blog   To cite an entire Weblog, give the author (if available), the title of the Weblog (italicized), the sponsor or publisher (if none, use "N.p."), the date of publication or last update, the medium ("Web"), and the date of access.

Paper Cuts: A Blog about Books. New York Times, 2010. Web. 1 Oct. 2010.

83. Entry or Comment Posted on a Blog   To cite an entry or a comment on a Weblog, give the author of the entry or comment (if available), the title of the entry or comment in quotation marks, the title of the blog (italicized), the sponsor or publisher, the date the material was posted, the medium, and the access date.

TUTORIAL

How do I cite works from Web sites using MLA style?

You will likely need to search the site to find some of the citation information you need. For some sites, all of the details may not be available; find as many as you can. Remember that the publication you provide should allow readers to retrace your steps electronically to locate the sources. Consult pages 348–52 for additional models for citing Web sources.

A **B**

Cogan, Laura. "Naomie Kremer: The Vocabulary of Obsession and Obsessiveness."

C **D** **E** **F**

ZYZZYVA. The Last Word: West Coast Writers and Artists, 28 Mar. 2011. Web.

G

13 May 2011.

A **The author of the work.** Give the last name first, followed by a comma, the first name, and the middle initial (if given). Omit titles such as *MD, PhD,* or *Sir*; include suffixes after the name and a comma (O'Driscoll, Gerald P., Jr.). Insert a period. If no author is given, begin with the title of the work.

B **The title of the work.** Give the full title; include the subtitle (if any), preceded by a colon. Enclose the title and subtitle in quotation marks, and capitalize all major words. Place a period inside the closing quotation mark. If you are citing an entire Web site, begin with the title of the Web site.

C **The title of the Web site.** Give the title of the entire site italicized. If there is no clear title and it is a personal home page, use "Home page" without italicizing it. End with a period.

D **The name of the sponsoring organization.** Look for the sponsor's name at the bottom of the site's home page. Follow with a comma.

E **The date of publication or most recent update.** Use the day-month-year format; abbreviate all months except May, June, and July. End with a period.

F **The medium consulted.** For works found online, use *Web* followed by a period.

G **The date you accessed it.** Give the most recent date you accessed the site. End with a period.

Use the bibliography tools at **bedfordresearcher.com** to create a bibliography formatted in MLA style.

MLA

V Documenting Sources

Lalami, Laila. "Quotable: Cormac McCarthy." *Laila Lalami*. Laila Lalami,
     28 Apr. 2010. Web. 17 Aug. 2010.

84. Email message   Cite the sender of the message; the title (from the subject line, in quotation marks); "Message to" the recipient of the message; the date of the message; and the medium ("E-mail"). (Note that MLA style is to hyphenate "e-mail.")

Willford, Latrisha. "Critique of 'Anna's Ordinary Blues.'" Message to the
     author. 19 Aug. 2010. E-mail.

Pabon, Xavier. "Brainstorming for Essay." Message to Brayden Perry. 24 Apr.
     2011. E-mail.

85. Online Book   Cite an online book as you would a print book; then give title of the database or Web site (italicized), the medium ("Web"), and the access date (see also #17 on p. 337).

James, Marlon. *The Book of Night Women*. New York: Riverhead, 2009. *Google
     Books*. Web. 20 Aug. 2010.

86. Article in an Online Periodical   Provide the author, the title of the article (in quotation marks), and the name of the Web site (in italics). Then add the publisher or sponsor, the date of publication, the medium, and your date of access (see also #43 on p. 342).

Jackson, Nicholas. "Taking Care of Your Personal Archives." *Atlantic*.
     Atlantic Monthly Group, 11 Nov. 2010. Web. 21 Dec. 2010.

87. Online Poem   Cite an online poem as you would a print poem, followed by the name of the site, the sponsoring organization (if any), the date of publication or latest update, the medium, and the date of access.

Rich, Susan. "Letter to the End of the Year." *The Alchemist's Kitchen*.
     Buffalo: White Pine P, 2010. *Verse Daily*. Verse Daily, 11 Sept. 2010.
     Web. 16 Nov. 2010.

88. Online Editorial or Letter to the Editor   Include "Letter" or "Editorial" after the title (if any). Follow with the title of the Web site, the sponsor or publisher, the date of publication, medium, and date of access (see also #51 and #52 on p. 343).

Spiro, Ira. "Latino Voters? In GOP's Dreams." Letter. *Los Angeles Times*. Los
     Angeles Times, 19 Dec. 2010. Web. 21 Dec. 2010.

89. Online Review   (See also #53 on p. 345.)

Dargis, Manohla. "Millions of Friends but Not Very Popular." Rev. of *The Social Network*, dir. David Fincher. *New York Times*. New York Times, 23 Sept. 2010. Web. 27 Oct. 2010.

90. Entry in an Online Reference Work   (See also #57 on p. 346.)

"Existentialism. " *Encyclopaedia Britannica Online*. Encyclopaedia Britannica, 2010. Web. 23 Apr. 2010.

91. Online Film or Video Clip   (See also #64 on p. 348.)

Eastwood, Clint, dir. *Hereafter*. 2010. *Momesh.com*. Web. 22 Dec. 2010.

DeGeneres, Ellen. "It Gets Better." *YouTube*. YouTube, 30 Sept. 2010. Web. 22 Feb. 2011.

92. Online Work of Art or Image   Cite like a work of art but omit the medium of composition, and after the location, add the title of the Web site or database (italicized), the medium consulted ("Web"), and your date of access. (See also #71 on p. 349.)

Johns, Jasper. *Perilous Night*. 1982. Natl. Gallery of Art, Washington. *National Gallery of Art*. Web. 10 Mar. 2010.

Haglundc. *Coyote Watching*. 4 Feb. 2008. *Flickr.com*. Web. 25 Mar. 2010.

93. Online Map or Chart   (See also #58 on p. 346.)

"Fisherman's Wharf, San Francisco." Map. *Google Maps*. Google, 2010. Web. 19 Sept. 2010.

94. Online Advertisement   Give the item or organization being advertised followed by the word "Advertisement." Then add the information about the Web site. (See also #72 on p. 350.)

Jobs on Demand. Advertisement. *Ohio.com*. Ohio.com, 2011. Web. 2 Feb. 2011.

95. Other Online Sources   For other online sources, adapt the guidelines to the medium. Include as much information as necessary for your readers to easily find your source. The examples below are for a radio program available in an online archive, and an online archive of oral-history interviews.

"True Urban Legends." Host Ira Glass. *This American Life*. Chicago Public Radio. WBEZ, Chicago. 23 Apr. 2010 MP3 file. 18 Aug. 2010.

Bruno, Angelo, and Eddie Nieves. "I Think I Could Have Done Another 31
      Years." *StoryCorps*. StoryCorps, n.d. Web. 2 Dec. 2010.

96. CD-ROM   Treat a CD-ROM as you would a book, noting "CD-ROM" as
the medium.

Orman, Suze. *Stop Identity Theft Now Kit*. Salt Lake City: TrustID, 2008.
      CD-ROM.

97. Multidisc CD-ROM   Either give the total number of discs or, if you used only
one of the discs, give the number of that disc.

Lindley, Philip, and Alex Moseley. *English Parish Churches*. Turnhout:
      Brepols, 2007. CD-ROM. Disc 2.

98. Computer Software or Video Game   Cite computer software as you would
a book. Provide additional information about the medium on which it is distributed (CD-ROM, Xbox 360, etc.) and the version.

Uncharted: Drake's Fortune. Foster City: Sony Computer Entertainment, 2007.
      CD-ROM.

MLA-Style Research Essay

Leontiev   1

Elizabeth Leontiev

Professor Lynda Haas

WR 39C

10 June 2010

Coca Is Not the Enemy

To most Americans, the word *cocaine* evokes images of the illegal white powder and those who abuse it, yet the word has a different meaning to the coca farmers of South America. *Erythroxylum coca*, or the tropical coca plant, has been grown in the mountainous regions of Colombia, Bolivia, and Peru since 3000 BC. The coca plant has been valued for centuries by indigenous South American cultures for its ability to alleviate pain and combat fatigue and hunger (Forero, "Bolivia's Knot"). Just as many Americans drink coffee every day, natives of the Andes Mountains chew coca leaves and drink coca tea for a mild stimulant effect. Easy to grow, not addictive, and offering many medicinal benefits, coca is part of the everyday lives of the people in this region.

Aside from its medicinal and cultural value, coca is also important to Andean farmers economically, as a result of a long history of illegal drug trafficking. Dried coca leaves mixed with lime paste or alkaline ashes produce cocaine—a highly addictive substance that delivers euphoric sensations accompanied by hallucinations (Gibson). Supplying the coca for the illegal drug trade accounts for a tremendous portion of the Bolivian, Peruvian, and Colombian economies. In Bolivia, for example, it has been estimated that coca makes up anywhere from one-third to three-quarters of the country's total exports (Kurtz-Phelan 108). In 1990 the Bolivian president even asserted that 70% of the Bolivian gross domestic product was due to the coca trade (Kurtz-Phelan 108).

Despite such statistics, for most farmers in the region growing coca is about making a living and supporting their families, not becoming wealthy or furthering the use of cocaine. More than half of Bolivians live in poverty, with a large portion earning less than $2 a day (U.S. Foreign Affairs, Defense, and Trade Div. 2). In the words of one coca farmer, "'The U.S. says 'Coca is cocaine, coca is cocaine,' but it isn't,' says Argote. 'Coca is the tree of the poor'" (Schultz and Gordon). Can we reduce cocaine trafficking without eliminating coca? Evo Morales, the current president of Bolivia, believes the answer is "yes" and has advocated a "zero cocaine, not zero coca" policy in his country. This policy would allow native Andeans to maintain their cultural practices, boost South American economies, and channel coca into a new market, away from cocaine traffickers. For all of these reasons, the Morales plan should become a model for other coca-growing countries.

Morales gained recognition for his "zero cocaine, not zero coca" program during his 2005 presidential campaign. His policy aims to legalize the coca crop but not the cocaine that is produced from that crop. He also expressed a desire to get the United Nations to rescind its 1961 convention declaring coca an illegal narcotic. In December 2005, Morales won the election with more than 50% of the vote, and he made history as the first indigenous Bolivian president (Forero, "Coca").

Morales's plan promotes the best interests of the Andean farmers and offers multiple economic and social benefits. First, South American countries would be able to export non-narcotic coca-based products, such as soaps, toothpaste, tea, alcohol, and candies (Logan). Products like these are already being produced for local use in Bolivia, and manufacturers would like to seek an international market for them. These new coca products would stimulate the Bolivian economy and put money in the pockets of coca growers to support their families, rather than in the pockets of the drug lords. Second, if the market for legal coca were to increase, farmers would be able to make a legal living from a crop that has long been a mainstay of their culture. With legal coca products, the indigenous people of the Andes would not have to sacrifice their way of life. Finally, an increase in the demand for legal coca products might also result in less cocaine being trafficked illegally around the world, since more of the raw material for cocaine will be used for new legal coca products.

In order to understand the benefits of Morales's plan, we must first investigate the failures of the alternatives. The United States has been waging various "wars on drugs" for decades, spending up to $1 billion trying to control cocaine trafficking from South America (Forero, "Bolivia's Knot"). In the 1990s the United States shifted its efforts from fighting the trafficking of cocaine to eliminating the source of the drug—the coca plants growing in Bolivia, Colombia, and Peru. Coca eradication has taken two main forms. In Bolivia, bands of soldiers move through the countryside using machetes to hack away coca plants (see Fig. 1). This process is slow and dangerous, and there have been reports of human rights abuses and extreme violence against the peasant farmers who grow coca (Gordon 16). In nearby

A brief title distinguishes two sources by the same author.

Elizabeth addresses counter-arguments and provides support for her assertion.

Reference to a photograph included in the essay.

Leontiev   3

Colombia, the United States funded aerial fumigation programs to poison the coca fields: native farmers complain that the herbicide used in the fumigation is causing health problems and environmental pollution ("US Weighs Cost"). By destroying coca plants in Colombia, the United States has "left 500 million people poorer" (Padgett 8). It is unclear whether fumigation results in any benefit, since farmers respond by moving farther and farther into the jungle and replanting their crops there (Otis). Such dense areas are harder to see and therefore harder to fumigate effectively.

FIG. 1. Manual eradication of a coca field in Chapare, Bolivia. United Nations Office on Drugs and Crime.

> Caption includes figure number and source information.

Another U.S. effort encouraged farmers to replace coca with other crops, like coffee, bananas, and pineapples. Alternative crop programs seem like a good idea because they will get rid of the coca farms, but they have their own drawbacks. First, as coca grower Leonida Zurita-Vargas noted in her 2003 *New York Times* opinion column, transporting heavy fruits like pineapples from the mountainous coca-growing regions is expensive and difficult. Second, growers are seldom willing to give up coca farming because they can make more money by selling coca than any other crop. Even with government incentives for alternative cropping, coca remains more profitable, a big inducement for poor farmers who can barely support their families and send their children to school. The *Houston Chronicle* reports that even in areas where farmers have planted alternative crops, the farmers are being lured back to the coca plant by larger profits (Otis). One coca farmer asserted that by growing coca,

> The in-text citation provides just the author's name, since the online source did not include page numbers.

Leontiev   4

he could "make ten times what he would make by growing pineapples
or yucca" (Harman). Ultimately, alternative cropping means less coca
production overall, which will drive up coca prices and encourage
more farmers to abandon their alternative crops and return to coca.

After decades of legislation and various eradication programs,
cocaine trafficking remains a major problem. The most recent data
show that coca cultivation throughout the region remains steady (see
Fig. 2). Contrary to dire predictions, there has been no major spike
in Bolivian coca production since Morales was elected at the end of
2005. Furthermore, critics argue that cocaine is no less available in
the United States than before eradication began, and street prices
remain low (Forero, "Colombia's Coca"). Instead of curbing cocaine
trafficking, America's war on drugs has turned out to be a war against
the peasants of Colombia, Bolivia, and Peru.

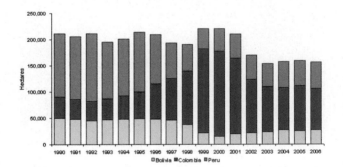

FIG. 2. Coca cultivation in the Andean region, 1990–2006. United Nations Office on
Drugs and Crime.

Throughout the years, the various wars on drugs have failed to
produce effective results for the United States. The programs of alternative cropping and eradication did not succeed due to the legislators'
inability to see life through the eyes of the coca farmers—something
Evo Morales is able to do. In 2006, Morales addressed the UN General
Assembly and waved a coca leaf in the air: "[This] is a green coca
leaf, it is not the white of cocaine. [T]his coca leaf represents Andean
culture; it is a coca leaf that represents the environment and the hope
of our peoples." Through his bold program of "zero cocaine, not zero
coca," Morales aims to improve the lives of Andean farmers and the
economies of South American countries, while still remaining committed
to controlling the illegal drug trade. Morales's example illustrates that
it is time to work *with* coca farmers, rather than against them.

The conclusion
reinforces
Elizabeth's
thesis
statement.

MLA

V Documenting Sources

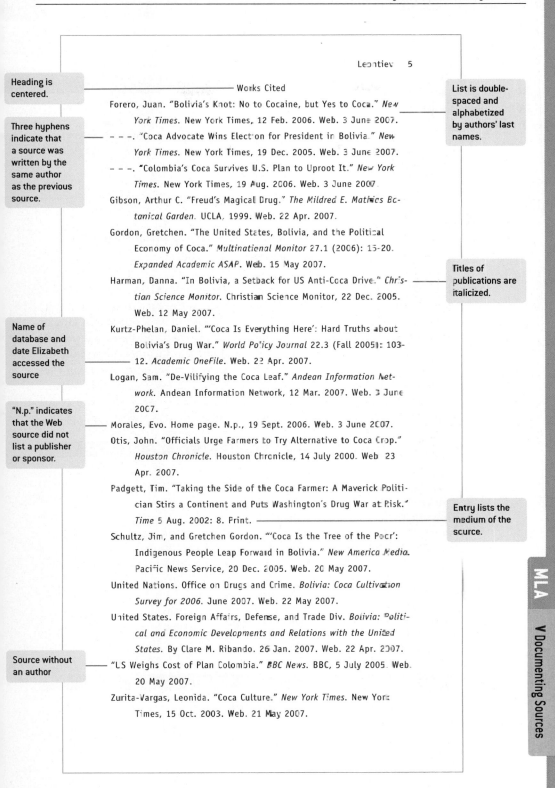

Leontiev   5

Works Cited

Forero, Juan. "Bolivia's Knot: No to Cocaine, but Yes to Coca." *New York Times*. New York Times, 12 Feb. 2006. Web. 3 June 2007.

- - -. "Coca Advocate Wins Election for President in Bolivia." *New York Times*. New York Times, 19 Dec. 2005. Web. 3 June 2007.

- - -. "Colombia's Coca Survives U.S. Plan to Uproot It." *New York Times*. New York Times, 19 Aug. 2006. Web. 3 June 2007.

Gibson, Arthur C. "Freud's Magical Drug." *The Mildred E. Mathias Botanical Garden*. UCLA, 1999. Web. 22 Apr. 2007.

Gordon, Gretchen. "The United States, Bolivia, and the Political Economy of Coca." *Multinational Monitor* 27.1 (2006): 15-20. *Expanded Academic ASAP*. Web. 15 May 2007.

Harman, Danna. "In Bolivia, a Setback for US Anti-Coca Drive." *Christian Science Monitor*. Christian Science Monitor, 22 Dec. 2005. Web. 12 May 2007.

Kurtz-Phelan, Daniel. "'Coca Is Everything Here': Hard Truths about Bolivia's Drug War." *World Policy Journal* 22.3 (Fall 2005): 103-12. *Academic OneFile*. Web. 22 Apr. 2007.

Logan, Sam. "De-Vilifying the Coca Leaf." *Andean Information Network*. Andean Information Network, 12 Mar. 2007. Web. 3 June 2007.

Morales, Evo. Home page. N.p., 19 Sept. 2006. Web. 3 June 2007.

Otis, John. "Officials Urge Farmers to Try Alternative to Coca Crop." *Houston Chronicle*. Houston Chronicle, 14 July 2000. Web. 23 Apr. 2007.

Padgett, Tim. "Taking the Side of the Coca Farmer: A Maverick Politician Stirs a Continent and Puts Washington's Drug War at Risk." *Time* 5 Aug. 2002: 8. Print.

Schultz, Jim, and Gretchen Gordon. "'Coca Is the Tree of the Poor': Indigenous People Leap Forward in Bolivia." *New America Media*. Pacific News Service, 20 Dec. 2005. Web. 20 May 2007.

United Nations. Office on Drugs and Crime. *Bolivia: Coca Cultivation Survey for 2006*. June 2007. Web. 22 May 2007.

United States. Foreign Affairs, Defense, and Trade Div. *Bolivia: Political and Economic Developments and Relations with the United States*. By Clare M. Ribando. 26 Jan. 2007. Web. 22 Apr. 2007.

"US Weighs Cost of Plan Colombia." *BBC News*. BBC, 5 July 2005. Web. 20 May 2007.

Zurita-Vargas, Leonida. "Coca Culture." *New York Times*. New York Times, 15 Oct. 2003. Web. 21 May 2007.

22

Using APA Style

> **Key Questions**
>
> **22a. How do I cite sources within the text of my document?** 364
>
> **22b. How do I prepare the reference list?** 367

American Psychological Association (APA) style, used primarily in the social sciences and in some of the natural sciences, emphasizes the author(s) and publication date of a source. Writers who use the APA documentation system cite, or formally acknowledge, information within their text using parentheses and provide a list of sources, called a reference list, at the end of their document. For more information about APA style, consult the *Publication Manual of the American Psychological Association,* Sixth Edition, and the *APA Style Guide to Electronic References.* Information about these publications can be found on the APA Web site at apa .org. To see Alexis Alvarez's research essay, formatted in APA style, turn to p. 382.

CITATIONS WITHIN YOUR TEXT

ENTRIES IN YOUR REFERENCE LIST

Books, Conference Proceedings, and Dissertations

Sources in Journals, Magazines, and Newspapers

Print Reference Works

Field Sources

Media Sources

Electronic Sources

22a

How do I cite sources within the text of my document?

APA uses an author-date form of in-text citation to acknowledge the use of another writer's words, facts, or ideas. When you refer to a source, insert a parenthetical note that gives the author's last name and the year of the publication, separated by a comma. Even when your reference list includes the day or month of publication, the in-text citation should include only the year. For a quotation, the citation in parentheses also includes the page(s) on which the quotation can be found, if the source has page numbers. Note that APA style requires using the past tense or present perfect tense to introduce the material you are citing: *Renfrew argued* or *Renfrew has argued.*

1. Basic Format for Direct Quotation   When you are using a direct quotation from a source and have named the author in your sentence, place the publication date in parentheses directly after the author's last name. Include the page number (with "p." for page) in parentheses after the quotation.

> Horowitz (2009) noted that "the fact of dogs' relatively weak visual capacity turns out to be a boon to them" (p. 135).

If you are using a direct quotation from a source and have not mentioned the author's name in your sentence, place the author's last name, the publication date, and the page number in parentheses.

> (Horowitz, 2009, p. 265).

2. Basic Format for Summary or Paraphrase When you are summarizing or paraphrasing, place the author's last name and date either in the sentence or in parentheses at the end of the sentence. Include a page or chapter reference if it would help readers find the original material in a longer work.

> Baker (2011) questions how advances in artificial intelligence might undermine the value of human intelligence and knowledge in some realms (p. 15).

> As the Watson experiment demonstrates, even the physical appearance of artificial intelligence devices is shaped by human preconceptions—and fears—of technology (Baker, 2011, p. 112).

3. Two Authors List the last names of both authors in every mention in the text. If you mention the authors' names in a sentence, use the word "and" to separate the last names, as shown in the first example. If you place the authors' names in the parenthetical citation, use an ampersand (&) to separate the last names, as shown in the second example.

> Drlica and Perlin (2011) wrote that "although many infections tend to occur in persons having weakened immune systems, MRSA can infect anyone" (p. 3).

> Everyone is susceptible to MRSA, not just those who are already weak or ill (Drlica & Perlin, 2011, p. 3).

4. Three, Four, or Five Authors In parentheses, name all the authors the first time you cite the source, using an ampersand (&) before the last author's name. In subsequent references to the source, use the last name of the first author followed by the abbreviation "et al." (Latin for "and others").

> Visual illusions serve an important scientific purpose in illustrating the brain's processes (Macknik, Martinez-Conde, & Blakeselee, 2010). Neuroscientists have found much value in studying magic and how it subverts the brain's expectations of visual input (Macknik et al., 2010).

5. More Than Five Authors In all references to the source, give the first author's last name followed by "et al."

> Coles et al. (2011) demonstrated the correlation between prenatal alcohol exposure, smaller brain size, and diminished memory function.

6. Corporate or Group Author In general, cite the full name of the corporation or group the first time it is mentioned in your text. If you add an abbreviation for the group in square brackets the first time you cite the source, you can use the abbreviation in subsequent citations.

Reactions to the idea of global climate change vary widely and are subject to many influences, including personal beliefs and cultural values (American Psychological Association [APA], 2010, p. 6). Similarly, the psychosocial effects of the signs of climate change, such as fear and anxiety over dwindling natural resources or unusual weather patterns, are functions of individual and cultural contexts (APA, 2010, p. 7).

7. Unknown Author   Sources with unknown authors are listed by title in the list of references. In your in-text citation, shorten the title as much as possible without introducing confusion. Add quotation marks to article titles, and italicize book titles.

The debate over evolution and creationism continues in the wake of recent scientific discoveries ("Fossil," 2011).

If a source identifies its author as "Anonymous," use that word to cite the author of the source.

The rise in coastal water levels has been referred to as a national crisis (Anonymous, 2011).

8. Two or More Works   List the sources in alphabetical order and separate them with semicolons. If you are referring to two or more sources by the same author, order those sources chronologically.

While the rush of adrenaline experienced during combat can be life saving at the time, adrenaline levels in combat veterans can remain high even after their return home, resulting in an array of stress-related health problems (Friedman & Sloane, 2008; Hoge, 2010).

9. Source Quoted in Another Source   Ideally, you will be able to find the primary, or original, source for material used in your research writing project document. If you quote or paraphrase a secondary source—a source that contains information about a primary source—mention the primary source and indicate that it was cited in the secondary source. Include the secondary source in your reference list.

Hall et al. (2008) have shown that self-regulation can create positive habits that can restore a person's ability to adapt to changing circumstances (as cited in Segerstrom et al., 2011, p. 25).

10. Source with No Page Numbers   Many Web sources lack stable page numbers. If the source has numbered paragraphs, include the paragraph number using the abbreviation "para." If the paragraphs are not numbered, include the section heading and indicate which paragraph in that section you are referring to.

Tomasulo (2011) suggested that "there is a pattern to who and how we love" based on an attraction to traits that are familiar to us (para. 10).

11. Two or More Authors with the Same Last Name Use the authors' initials in each citation.

While C. Smith (2009) has noted an increase in early childhood psychiatric disorders, L. W. Smith (2010) suggested that many of these diagnoses in very young children might be inaccurate.

12. Email and Other Personal Communication Give the first initial(s) and last name of the person with whom you corresponded, the words "personal communication," and the date. Don't include personal communication in your reference list.

(A. L. Chan, personal communication, October 9, 2010)

13. Document from a Web Site To cite a quotation from a Web site, give the page number or paragraph number, if indicated, and include the source in your reference list.

Lehrer (2011) noted that the era of the "lone genius" may be ending, replaced instead by collaborative thinking and research (para. 13).

22b

How do I prepare the reference list?

The reference list contains publication information for all sources that you have cited within your document, with one main exception. Personal communications—such as correspondence, email messages, and interviews—are cited only in the text of the document.

Begin the list on a new page at the end of the document and center the title "References" at the top. Organize the list alphabetically by author; if the source is an organization, alphabetize the source by the name of the organization. All of the entries should be double-spaced with no extra space between entries. Entries are formatted with a hanging indent: The first line of an entry is flush with the left margin and subsequent lines are indented one-half inch or five spaces. In longer documents, a reference list could be given at the end of each chapter or section. In electronic documents that use links, such as Web sites, the reference list is often a separate page to which other pages are linked. For an example of a reference list in APA style, see p. 390.

Books, Conference Proceedings, and Dissertations

14. One Author

Skloot, R. (2010). *The immortal life of Henrietta Lacks*. New York, NY: Crown.

15. Two or More Authors   List the authors in the same order as the title page does, each with last name first. Use commas to separate authors and use an ampersand (&) before the final author's name. List every author up to seven; for a work with more than seven authors, give the first six names followed by a comma, three ellipsis dots, and the final author's name. (Do not use an ampersand.)

Kraybill, D. B., Nolt, S. M., & Weaver-Zercher, D. (2010). *The Amish way: Patient faith in a perilous world*. San Francisco, CA: Jossey-Bass.

16. Corporate or Group Author   Write out the full name of a corporate or group author. If the corporation is also the publisher, use "Author" for the publisher's name.

National Geographic. (2010). *Water: Our thirsty world*. Washington, DC: Author.

17. Unknown Author   When there is no author listed on the title or copyright page, begin the entry with the title of the work. Alphabetize the entry by the first significant word of the title (not including *A*, *An*, or *The*).

On the road of life. (2007). Naperville, IL: Sourcebooks.

18. Two or More Works by the Same Author(s)   Give the author's name in each entry and list the works in chronological order.

Kozol, J. (2006). *The shame of the nation: The restoration of apartheid schooling in America*. New York, NY: Crown.

Kozol, J. (2007). *Letters to a young teacher*. New York, NY: Crown.

19. Translated Book   List the author first followed by the year of publication, the title, and the translator (in parentheses, identified by the abbreviation "Trans."). Place the original date of the work's publication at the end of the entry.

Philipponnat, O., & Lienhardt, P. (2010). *The life of Irene Nemirovsky, 1903–1942* (E. Cameron, Trans.). New York, NY: Knopf.

20. Book in a Series

Frasier, J. D. (2010). *Forensic science*. Very short introductions 211 [Series]. Oxford, England: Oxford University Press.

TUTORIAL

How do I cite books using APA style?

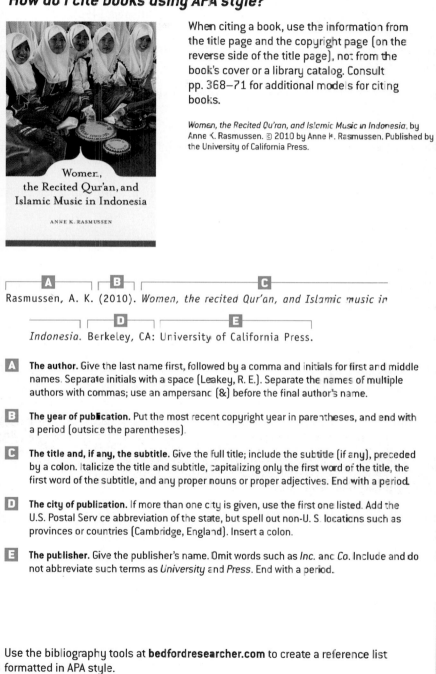

When citing a book, use the information from the title page and the copyright page (on the reverse side of the title page), not from the book's cover or a library catalog. Consult pp. 368–71 for additional models for citing books.

Women, the Recited Qu'ran, and Islamic Music in Indonesia, by Anne K. Rasmussen. © 2010 by Anne K. Rasmussen. Published by the University of California Press.

Women, the Recited Qur'an, and Islamic Music in Indonesia

ANNE K. RASMUSSEN

A   **B**   **C**

Rasmussen, A. K. (2010). *Women, the recited Qur'an, and Islamic music in*

D   **E**

Indonesia. Berkeley, CA: University of California Press.

A **The author.** Give the last name first, followed by a comma and initials for first and middle names. Separate initials with a space (Leakey, R. E.). Separate the names of multiple authors with commas; use an ampersand (&) before the final author's name.

B **The year of publication.** Put the most recent copyright year in parentheses, and end with a period (outside the parentheses).

C **The title and, if any, the subtitle.** Give the full title; include the subtitle (if any), preceded by a colon. Italicize the title and subtitle, capitalizing only the first word of the title, the first word of the subtitle, and any proper nouns or proper adjectives. End with a period.

D **The city of publication.** If more than one city is given, use the first one listed. Add the U.S. Postal Service abbreviation of the state, but spell out non-U.S. locations such as provinces or countries (Cambridge, England). Insert a colon.

E **The publisher.** Give the publisher's name. Omit words such as *Inc.* and *Co.* Include and do not abbreviate such terms as *University* and *Press.* End with a period.

Use the bibliography tools at **bedfordresearcher.com** to create a reference list formatted in APA style.

APA

V Documenting Sources

21. Republication

Freud, S. (2010). *The interpretation of dreams* (J. Strachey, Ed. & Trans.).
    New York, NY: Basic Books. (Original work published 1955)

22. Book in an Edition Other Than the First   Note the edition ("2nd ed.," "Rev.
ed.") after the title.

Sowell, T. (2010). *Basic economics: A common sense guide to the economy*
    (4th ed.). New York, NY: Basic Books.

23. Multivolume Work   Include the number of volumes in parentheses after
the title.

Delbanco, N., & Cheuse, A. (Eds.). (2010). *Literature: Craft and voice* (Vols.
    1-3). Boston: McGraw-Hill.

If you have used only one volume in a multivolume work, identify that volume
by number and by title.

Delbanco, N., & Cheuse, A. (Eds.). (2010). *Literature: Craft and voice: Vol. 1.*
    Fiction. Boston: McGraw-Hill.

24. Editor   Include "Ed." or "Eds." in parentheses.

Bryson, B. (Ed.). (2010). *Seeing further: The story of science, discovery, and*
    the genius of the Royal Society. New York, NY: Morrow.

25. Author with an Editor   Include the editor's name and the abbreviation
"Ed." in parentheses after the title.

Mencken, H. L. (2010). *Mencken: Prejudices, first, second, and third* (M. E.
    Rodgers, Ed.). New York, NY: Library of America.

26. Anthology   To cite an entire anthology of essays or collection of articles,
list the editor or editors first, followed by the abbreviation "Ed." or "Eds." in
parentheses.

Van Wormer, K. S., & Thyer, B. A. (Eds.). (2010). *Evidence-based practice*
    in the field of substance abuse: A book of readings. Thousand Oaks, CA:
    Sage.

27. Chapter in an Edited Book or Selection in an Anthology   Begin the entry
with the author, the publication date, and the title of the chapter or selection
(not italicized). Follow this with the names of the editors (initials first) and the

abbreviation "Ed." or "Eds." in parentheses, the title of the anthology or collection (italicized), inclusive page numbers for the chapter or selection (in parentheses, with abbreviation "pp."), and place and publisher.

Wahab, S. (2010). Motivational interviewing and social work practice. In K. S. Van Wormer & B. A. Thyer (Eds.), *Evidence-based practice in the field of substance abuse: A book of readings* (pp. 197-210). Thousand Oaks, CA: Sage.

28. Foreword, Introduction, Preface, or Afterword   Treat as you would a chapter in a book.

Wong, H. K. (2010). Introduction. In C. Asquith, *The emergency teacher: The inspirational story of a new teacher in an inner-city school* (pp vi-vii). New York, NY: Skyhorse.

29. Published Proceedings of a Conference   Cite information as you would for a book.

Doherty, G. W. (Ed.). (2007). *Proceedings of the 5th Rocky Mountain region disaster mental health conference.* Ann Arbor, MI: Loving Healing Press.

30. Paper Published in the Proceedings of a Conference   Treat a conference paper as you would a selection from an edited collection.

Justice, P. (2007). Care for the caretaker. In G. W. Doherty (Ed.), *Proceedings of the 5th Rocky Mountain region disaster mental health conference* (pp. 89-92). Ann Arbor, MI: Loving Healing Press.

31. Sacred Text   Treat as you would a book (see p. 368).

The Holy Bible: King James version. (2010). Quartercentenary Ed. Oxford, England: Oxford University Press.

32. Published Dissertation or Thesis   If a published dissertation or thesis is available through a database, give the author, date, title, and a description in parentheses ("Doctoral dissertation" or "Master's thesis"). Then give information about the database and any accession or order number in parentheses.

Burke, C. R. (2010). *Black parents at predominantly white schools: An exploratory study of race and parent involvement* (Doctoral dissertation, Rutgers University). Retrieved from http://hdl.rutgers.edu/1782.2/ rucore10001800001.ETD.000052864

33. Unpublished Dissertation or Thesis   Format as you would a book, replacing the publisher information with the phrase "Unpublished doctoral dissertation" or "Unpublished master's thesis," followed by information about the college or university.

Connolly, P. (2007). *A comparison of two forms of spatial ability development treatment* (Unpublished doctoral dissertation). Purdue University, West Lafayette, IN.

34. Abstract of a Dissertation or Thesis   Treat an abstract as you would an article in a journal. Follow with the *Dissertation Abstracts International* information obtained from UMI.

San Martin, D. (2007). Treatment goals of adult mental health patients: A literature review. *Dissertation Abstracts International, 68*(04). (UMI No. 3264598)

Sources in Journals, Magazines, and Newspapers

35. Article in a Journal Paginated by Volume   Most journals continue page numbers throughout an entire annual volume, beginning again at page 1 only in the first volume of the next year. After the author and publication year, provide the article title, the journal title, the volume number (italicized), and the inclusive page numbers.

Pope, N. D., & Kang, B. (2010). Residential relocation in later life: A comparison of proactive and reactive moves. *Journal of Housing for the Elderly, 24,* 193-207. doi:10.1080/02763891003757122

36. Article in a Journal Paginated by Issue   Some journals begin at page 1 for every issue. Include the issue number (in parentheses, not italicized) after the volume number.

Carlozzi, N. E., Horner, M. D., Kose, S., Yamanaka, K., Mishory, A., Mu, Q., . . . George, M. S. (2010). Personality and reaction time after sleep deprivation. *Current Psychology, 29*(1), 24-33. doi:10.1007/s12144-009-9068-8

37. Article in a Magazine   The author's name and the publication date are followed by the title of the article, the magazine title (italicized), and the volume number, if any (also italicized). Include all page numbers.

Senior, J. (2010, June 28-July). Divorce liberation. *New York,* 20.

TUTORIAL

How do I cite articles from periodicals using APA style?

Green travel: Food lovers down on the farm

The Organic Top:
20 products that are good for
body, soul and planet

Profit with a
purpose:
A new way
to think
about
investing

Ode
FOR INTELLIGENT OPTIMISTS

Your
brain is a
rain forest

ADHD, dyslexia
and other mental
disorders are
serious and disabling,
but they also have
hidden strengths.
Why brain diversity is as
enriching—and essential—
as biodiversity

Periodicals include journals, magazines, and newspapers. This page gives an example of a citation for a print journal article. Models for citing articles from magazines and newspapers are on pp. 372–74. If you need to cite a periodical article you accessed electronically, follow the guidelines below and see pp. 376–81.

A **B** **C** **D** **E** **F**

Armstrong. T. (2010, April/May). Your brain is a rain forest. *Ode, 8*(3), 36-43.

A **The author.** Give the last name first, followed by a comma and initials for first and middle names. Separate the names of multiple authors with commas; use an ampersand (&) before the final author's name.

B **The year of publication.** Put the year in parentheses and end with a period (outside the parentheses). For magazines and newspapers, include the month and, if relevant, the day (2010, April 13).

C **The article title.** Give the full title; include the subtitle (if any), preceded by a colon. Do not underline, italicize, or put the title in quotation marks. Capitalize only the first word of the title, the first word of the subtitle, and any proper nouns or proper adjectives. End with a period.

D **The periodical title.** Italicize the periodical title, and capitalize all major words. Insert a comma.

E **The volume and issue number, if relevant.** For journals, include the volume number, italicized. If each issue starts with page 1, include the issue number in parentheses, not italicized. Insert a comma.

F **Inclusive page number(s).** Give all of the numbers in full (248-254, not 248-54). For newspapers, include the abbreviation *p.* for page and section letters, if relevant (p. B12). End with a period.

Use the bibliography tools at **bedfordresearcher.com** to create a reference list formatted in APA style.

APA

V Documenting Sources

38. Article in a Newspaper   List the author's name and the complete date (year first). Next give the article title followed by the name of the newspaper (italicized). Include all page numbers, preceded by "p." or "pp."

Filipov, D. (2010, October 1). Diehards say texting tough to kick. *The Boston Globe*, p. B8.

39. Unsigned Article in a Newspaper   Begin with the article title, and alphabetize in the reference list by the first word in the title other than *A*, *An*, or *The*. Use "p." or "pp." before page numbers.

UN: 2010 tied for warmest year on record. (2011, January 20). *The Chicago Sun-Times*, p. C2.

40. Letter to the Editor   Include the words "Letter to the editor" in square brackets after the title of the letter, if any.

Kropf, B. (2010, November 16). Good policy isn't the provenance of any ethnic group [Letter to the editor]. *The Wall Street Journal*, p. A15.

41. Review   After the title of the review, include the words "Review of the book . . ." or "Review of the film . . ." and so on in brackets, followed by the title of the work reviewed.

Hertzberg, H. (2010, October 25). Politics and prose [Review of the book *Daniel Patrick Moynihan: A Portrait in Letters of an American Visionary*, by D. P. Moynihan & S. R. Weisman]. *The New Yorker*, 78-82.

When the review is untitled, follow the date with the bracketed information.

Turan, K. (2010, November 26). [Review of the film *The King's Speech*, 2010]. *The Los Angeles Times*, p. D1.

42. Published Interview   Cite a published interview like a journal article (see p. 372).

Massondo, A. (2010, July). Yellow-card journalism [Interview by C. Barron]. *Harper's, 321*(1921), 17-18.

43. Two or More Works by the Same Author in the Same Year   List the works alphabetically and include lowercase letters (*a*, *b*, etc.) after the dates.

Iglehart, J. K. (2010a). The ACA's new weapons against health care fraud. *The New England Journal of Medicine, 363*, 1589-1591.

Iglehart, J. K. (2010b). Health reform, primary care, and graduate medical education. *The New England Journal of Medicine, 363*, 584-590.

Print Reference Works

44. Encyclopedia, Dictionary, Thesaurus, Handbook, or Almanac Cite a reference work, such as an encyclopedia or a dictionary, as you would a book (see p. 368).

Priest, S. H. (Ed.). (2010). *Encyclopedia of science and technology*
  communication (Vols. 1-2). Thousand Oaks, CA: Sage.

45. Entry in an Encyclopedia, Dictionary, Thesaurus, Handbook, or Almanac Begin your citation with the name of the author or, if the entry is unsigned, the title of the entry. Proceed with the date, the entry title (if not already given), the title of the reference work, the edition number, and the pages.

Human genome project. (2010). In S. H. Priest (Ed.), *Encyclopedia of*
  science and technology communication (Vol. 1, pp. 374-379). Thousand
  Oaks, CA: Sage.

46. Government Publication Give the name of the department (or office, agency, or committee) that issued the report as the author. If the document has a report or special file number, place that in parentheses after the title.

U.S. Department of Health and Human Services. (2010). *Ending the tobacco*
  epidemic: A tobacco control strategic action plan for the U.S. Department
  of Health and Human Services. Washington, DC: Government Printing
  Office.

47. Pamphlet Format the entry as you would a book (see p. 368).

Rosie's Place. (2007). *Rosie's Place . . . creating community: A directory of*
  programs and happenings. Boston, MA: Author.

Field Sources

48. Personal Interview Treat unpublished interviews as personal communications and include them in your text only (see p. 367). Do not cite personal interviews in your reference list.

49. Letter Cite a personal letter only in the text (see p. 367), not in the reference list.

50. Lecture or Public Address Cite a lecture or public address the same way you would cite an unpublished paper presented at a conference.

Lander, E. (2010, April 19). Secrets of the human genome. Lecture presented
  at Princeton University, Princeton, NJ.

Media Sources

51. Film or Video Recording   List the director and producer (if available), the date of release, the title followed by "Motion picture" in square brackets, the country where the film was made, and the studio or distributor.

Aronofsky, D. (Director). (2010). *Black swan* [Motion picture]. United States: Fox Searchlight.

52. Television Program   Cite as you would a chapter in a book. List the director (if available), the broadcast date, the title followed by "Television broadcast" or "Television series episode" in square brackets. Then add information on the series, location, and station.

Jennings, T. (Writer, Producer, & Director), & Bomse, S. (Writer). (2010, August 25). Law and disorder [Television series episode]. In D. Fanning (Executive Producer), *Frontline*. Boston, MA: WGBH.

53. Radio Program   List the host, the broadcast date, the title followed by "Radio broadcast," or "Radio series episode," in square brackets.

Young, R. (Host). (2011, January 21). Center focuses on treating Alzheimer's by comforting residents, not medicating them [Radio series episode]. In K. McKenna (Senior Producer), *Here and now*. Boston, MA: WBUR.

54. Sound Recording   Name the author of the song; the date; the song title followed by "On" and the recording title in italics; the medium (in square brackets); and the production data.

Ruffins, K. (2010). More today than yesterday. On *Happy talk* [MP3]. New Orleans, LA: Basin Street Records.

Electronic Sources

55. Article with a DOI   A DOI (Digital Object Identifier) is a unique number assigned to specific content, such as a journal article. If a DOI is available, include it; you do not need to provide a database name or URL.

Schwander, T., Vuilleumier, S., Dubman, J., & Crespi, B. J. (2010). Positive feedback in the transition from sexual reproduction to parthenogenesis. *Proceedings of the Royal Society Biology, 277*, 1435-1442. doi:10.1098/rspb.2009.2113

56. Article without a DOI   If no DOI (Digital Object Identifier) is provided, give the exact URL for the article or for the home page of the journal, if access requires a subscription.

TUTORIAL

How do I cite articles from databases using APA style?

Libraries subscribe to services such as LexisNexis, ProQuest, InfoTrac, and EBSCOhost that provide access to databases of electronic texts. The databases provide publication information, abstracts, and the complete text of documents in a specific subject area, discipline, or profession. (See also Chapter 8.)

| A | B | C |

Resnick, D. B. (2010). Urban sprawl, smart growth, and deliberative democracy.

| D | E | F | G |

American Journal of Public Health, *100,* 1852-1856. doi:10.2105/

AJPH.2009.182501

A   **The author.** Give the last name first, followed by a comma and initials. Separate the names of multiple authors with commas; use an ampersand (&) before the final author's name.

B   **The date of publication.** Put the year in parentheses and end with a period (outside the parentheses). For magazines and newspapers, include the month and, if relevant, the day (2010, April 13).

C   **The article title.** Give the full title; include the subtitle (if any), preceded by a colon. Do not underline, italicize, or put the title or subtitle in quotation marks. Capitalize only the first word of the title, the first word of the subtitle, and any proper nouns or proper adjectives. End with a period.

D   **The periodical title.** Italicize the periodical title, and capitalize all major words. Insert a comma.

E   **The volume number and issue number.** For journals, include the volume number, italicized. If each issue starts with page 1, include the issue number in parentheses, not italicized. Insert a comma.

F   **Inclusive page numbers(s).** Give all of the numbers in full (317-327, not 317-27). For newspapers, include the abbreviation p. for page and section letters, if relevant (p. B12). End with a period.

G   **The DOI.** Give the unique Digital Object Identifier (DOI); you do not need to provide a retrieval date, database name, or URL. If there is no DOI, include the words "Retrieved from" and the URL of the publication's home page.

Use the bibliography tools at **bedfordresearcher.com** to create a reference list formatted in APA style.

APA

V Documenting Sources

Stieb, J. A. (2011). Understanding engineering professionalism: A reflection on the rights of engineers. *Science and Engineering Ethics, 17*(1), 149-169. Retrieved from http://springerlink.com/content/ r58q044521917785/

If the article comes from a database, give the URL of the home page of the journal.

Robertson, L. A. (2010). The spiritual competency scale. *Counseling and Values, 55*(1), 6-24. Retrieved from http://www.counseling.org

57. Article in an Online Periodical   Publication information is followed by the URL. Since the article was published online, it is unlikely to have page numbers. Note that the first example is for an online journal, while the second is for online magazine content not found in the print version.

Rusanen, M., Kivipelto, M., Quesenberry, C. P., Zhou, J., & Whitmer, R. A. (2010). Heavy smoking in midlife and long-term risk of Alzheimer disease and vascular dementia. *Archives of Internal Medicine.* doi:10.1001/archinternmed.2010.393

Okrent, D., & Gray, S. (2010, November 11). "How to shrink a city." *Time.* Retrieved from http://www.time.com

58. Online Book   Cite the electronic version only if a print version is not available or is hard to find.

Ducot, C. (n.d.). *An end to anxiety* (E. Pichel-Juan, Trans.). Retrieved from http://www.onlineoriginals.com

59. Entry in an Online Reference Work   Give the URL for the home or index page.

Cultural anthropology. (2010). In *Encyclopædia Britannica.* Retrieved from http://www.britannica.com/eb/

60. Nonperiodical Web Document   For a stand-alone Web source, such as a report, an online brochure, or a blog, cite as much of the following information as possible: author, publication date, document title, and the URL. Include a retrieval date before the URL if the material is likely to be changed or updated, or if it lacks a set publication date, edition, or version number. A retrieval date is generally not necessary when citing electronic books and journal articles.

Mayo Clinic. (n.d.). *Quit smoking.* Retrieved from http://www.mayoclinic .com/health/quit-smoking/MY00433

For a chapter or section within a Web document, identify the section as well as the main document.

Davis, J. L. (n.d.). Coping with anxiety. In *Anxiety and panic disorders guide*. Retrieved from http://www.webmd.com/anxiety-panic/guide/coping-with-anxiety

For a document within a government agency, university, or other complex Web site, include the name of the agency or organization before the URL.

American Psychological Association. (n.d.). *Careers in psychology*. Retrieved from the American Psychological Association website: http://www.apa.org/topics/psychologycareer.html

61. Email Message or Real-Time Communication   Because email messages are difficult or impossible for your readers to retrieve, APA does not recommend including them in your reference list. You should treat them as personal communications and cite them parenthetically in your text (see #12 on p. 367).

62. Article Posted on a Wiki   Since the material on a Wiki is likely to change, include a retrieval date.

Sensory deprivation. (n.d.). In *Wikipedia*. Retrieved December 15, 2010, from http://en.wikipedia.org/wiki/Sensory_deprivation

63. Message Posted to a Newsgroup, Electronic Mailing List, or Online Discussion Forum   List the author, posting date, message title, and a description of the message in brackets. Then add the retrieval information, including the name of the list or forum.

Wolf, J. (2010, October 12). Girlhood Studies receives a Highly Commended Certificate for the ALPSP 201 Best New Journal award [Electronic mailing list message]. Retrieved from Childhood discussion list: http://h-net.msu.edu/cgi-bin/logbrowse.pl?trx=lm&list=h-childhood

64. Entry or Comment on a Blog   To cite an entry on a Web log, give the author (or screen name, if available), the date the material was posted, the title of the entry, a description of the entry in brackets, and the URL. To cite a comment on a blog post, use the description "Web log comment" in brackets.

Lunde, A. (2010, October 30). For caregivers, it's OK to feel good and bad [Web log post]. Retrieved from http://www.mayoclinic.com/health/alzheimers-caregivers/MY01563

Jane. (2010, November 10). Re: For caregivers, it's OK to feel good and bad [Web log comment]. Retrieved from http://www.mayoclinic.com/health/alzheimers-caregivers/MY01563_comments#post

TUTORIAL

How do I cite works from Web sites using APA style?

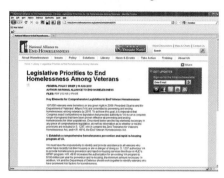

You will likely need to search the Web site to find some of the citation information you need. For some sites, all of the details may not be available; find as many as you can. Remember that the citation you provide should allow readers to retrace your steps electronically to locate the sources. Consult pp. 376–81 for additional models for citing Web sources.

A   **B**   **C**

National Alliance to End Homelessness. (2010, August). *Legislative priorities*

D

to end homelessness among veterans. Retrieved from http://

www.endhomelessness.org/content/article/detail/2570

A   **The author of the work.** Give the last name first, followed by a comma and initials. Separate the names of multiple authors with commas; use an ampersand (&) before the final author's name.

B   **The date of publication.** Put the year in parentheses and include the month, if available. If there is no date, use *n.d.* in parentheses. End with a period (outside the parentheses).

C   **The title of the work.** Give the full title, italicized; include the subtitle (if any), preceded by a colon. Capitalize only the first word of the title, the first word of the subtitle, and any proper nouns or proper adjectives.

D   **Retrieval information.** Include a retrieval date if the material is likely to be changed or updated, or if it lacks a set publication date. (Since this report has a set publication date, the retrieval date is not necessary.) End with the URL.

Use the bibliography tools at **bedfordresearcher.com** to create a reference list formatted in APA style.

65. Video Posted Online   After the title of the video, include the words "Video file" in brackets. If there is no author's name, list the screen name provided.

AskSanAnything. (2010, November 1). Month 1 done: How many inches and
    pounds down? [Video file]. Retrieved from http://losethefatkeepthefab
    .blogspot.com/

GeckoGeekFr. (2010, January 6). How to make a traditional origami
    crane [Video file]. Retrieved from http://www.youtube.com/
    watch?v=jUZaOWibCcs

66. Image Posted Online

Wolff, M. K. (2010, November 15). Mussels in a creamy garlic sauce
    [Photograph]. Retrieved from http://www.whatsforlunchhoney.net

67. Presentation Slides

Jessedee. (n.d.). 5 Presentation lessons from *The King's Speech* [PowerPoint
    slides]. Retrieved from http://www.slideshare.net/jessedee/
    presentation-lessons-from-the-kings-speech-6551851

68. Podcast

Jones, C. (2010, May 21). *Learning and becoming: The construction of
    identity in urban classrooms* [Audio podcast]. Retrieved from Swarthmore
    College Web site: http://media.swarthmore.edu/faculty_lectures/?p=182

69. Computer Software   Sometimes a person is named as having rights to the program, software, or language: In that case, list that person as the author. Otherwise, begin the entry with the name of the program and identify the source in square brackets after the name as "Computer software." Treat the organization that produces the software as the publisher. If you're referring to a specific version that isn't included in the name, put this information immediately after the title in parentheses.

Microsoft Office 2010 [Computer software]. Redmond, WA: Microsoft.

Other Sources

70. General Advice about Other Sources   For citing other types of sources, APA suggests that you use as a guide a source type listed in their manual that most closely resembles the type of source you want to cite

APA-Style Research Essay

Girls, Sports, and Steroids   1

> **APA notes that requirements for title pages on student papers vary. Check with your instructor before following this example.**

> **Title of essay**

> **Writer's name**

Girls, Sports, and Steroids

Alexis Alvarez

English 110, Section 4

Professor Desai

November 22, 2010

> **Title of course, instructor's name, and date**

Girls, Sports, and Steroids 2

Girls, Sports, and Steroids

Almost daily, headlines and newscasters tell us about athletes' use of performance-enhancing drugs. Indeed, stories of such drug use seem to increase each year, with investigations of possible steroid use by college football players, by major league baseball players, and even by Olympic gold medalists. It is easy to gain the impression that many adult athletes, particularly males, may be using drugs in order to improve their performance and physical appearance. What may be surprising and even shocking to most of us, however, is that these drugs, especially anabolic steroids, are increasingly used by adolescent athletes and that girls are just as likely as boys to be users.

In May 2004, the Centers for Disease Control and Prevention (CDC) published its latest figures on self-reported drug use among young people in grades 9 through 12. The CDC study, "Youth Risk Behavior Surveillance — December 2003," found that 6.1% of its survey participants reported using steroids at least once, up from 2.2% in 1993. The report also showed that use of steroids appears to be increasing among younger girls: While only 3.3% of 12th-grade girls reported using steroids, 7.3% of 9th-grade girls reported using them. Moreover, girls might be starting to use steroids at a higher rate than boys. The CDC study indicated that 9th-grade girls had reported slightly higher rates of steroid use than boys (7.3% and 6.9% respectively), while 10th-, 11th-, and 12th-grade girls all reported lower use than boys. Other studies support the conclusion that steroid use is both widespread and rising quickly among adolescent girls. According to Mundell (2004), experts estimate that as many as a million high school students have used steroids — and that a significant percentage of that group are girls. Moreover, since the late 1990s, studies have shown that steroid use is increasing among adolescent girls. In 1998, *Teacher Magazine* reported that steroid use among high school girls had increased 300% since 1991, from 0.4% of all high school girls to 1.4% ("Girls and Steroids," 1998). And Manning (2002) wrote, "A 1999 Youth Risk Behavior Surveillance study by the Centers for Disease Control and the 2001 Monitoring the Future survey both show steady growth in steroid use by 8th- to 12th-graders" ("As Kids Use Steroids," para. 2).

What role are competitive sports playing in this dangerous trend? Why are some girls feeling the need to ingest performance-enhancing drugs? Although competitive sports can provide young female athletes with many benefits, they can also have negative effects, the worst of which is increasing drug use. Let's look first at the positives.

Title of essay repeated

Alexis's statement is likely to surprise readers, drawing them into the essay.

Effective use of statistical evidence shows growth of the problem over time.

Source of paraphrased information is acknowledged using APA's parenthetical reference system.

A source that does not have an author is identified by shortened title and publication year.

Section heading and paragraph number are given for location of material quoted from an online source.

Thesis states Alexis's main point.

Headings, boldface and centered throughout, help readers follow the essay's organization.

Shortened name of the council; it was introduced by its full name the first time it was cited.

An author tag alerts readers that information is taken from a source.

Girls, Sports, and Steroids 3

Title of essay, shortened if necessary, followed by page number

Girls and Sports: The Upside

Millions of girls are now involved in a variety of sports activi-ties, and girls' participation in school athletics and community-based programs continues to increase. As the President's Council on Physi-cal Fitness and Sport (1997) has pointed out, when girls participate in competitive sports, their lives can be affected in a number of positive and interrelated ways. Physical and psychological health, a positive sense of identity, good relationships with friends and family, and improved performance in school all work together to influence a girl's complete growth and development.

According to the President's Council (1997), adolescent girls who exercise regularly can lessen their risks for adult-onset coronary disease and certain cancers. Girls' involvement in sports and exercise also tends to improve immune functioning, posture, strength, flex-ibility, and heart-lung endurance (President's Council, 1997; Dudley, 1994).

Two sources are cited in one parenthetical citation.

In addition, competitive athletics can enhance mental health by offering adolescent girls positive feelings about body image; tangible experiences of competency, control, and success; improved self-esteem and self-confidence; and a way to reduce anxiety (President's Council, 1997). Juan Orozco, who has coached adolescent females in competitive soccer for nine years, confirmed that making a competitive sports team is a privilege that many girls work toward with determination and longing and that being picked to participate encourages these young athletes to believe in themselves and their abilities (personal communication, September 22, 2010).

Personal com-munication — an interview — is cited in the text of the document, but not in the reference list.

A final benefit is that sports expand social boundaries and teach many of the personal and social skills girls will need through-out their lives. According to Orozco, through competitive athletics girls learn a crucial lesson in how to interact with, get along with, and depend on athletes from different social and economic groups. In short, they learn to adapt to and enjoy each other's differences. Melissa Alvarez, a 17-year-old athlete who has participated in high school basketball and club soccer, draws a similar conclusion. In an interview, she stated that sports "give you something to work for as an individual and as a team. You learn self-discipline and dedication, which are essential skills to have in life" (personal communication, September 26, 2007). Competitive sports also teach athletes how to cope with failure as well as success. In the best of situations, as Sieghart (2004) noted, athletes are able to assess their achievements realistically, letting neither winning nor losing consume their reality.

Girls, Sports, and Steroids 4

Girls and Sports: The Downside

In spite of the many positive effects of competitive athletics, sports can have a negative impact on girls' bodies and minds, and some girls falter under the pressure to succeed. Overtraining, eating disorders, and exercise-induced amenorrhea (which may result in osteoporosis) are some of the most common negative physical side effects that young female athletes experience; negative psychological and social side effects include increased stress and anxiety and a loss of self-confidence. Let's look at each of these effects.

Negative Physical Side Effects

Overtraining occurs when your body can no longer adapt to increasing workloads — instead of building up, it breaks down. When a young girl overtrains, her body's balance between training and recovery is lost. Because the athlete's body can't recover, her performance stays flat and she cannot improve. Overtraining also makes a young female athlete prone to a variety of physical and psychological ills, such as unusual fatigue, irritability, feelings of apathy, and menstrual irregularities (Graham, 1999).

Another negative effect is amenorrhea, which refers to an atypical inability to menstruate. Graham (1999) pointed out, "in some sports as many as 50% of the athletes who are competitive may suffer from what's known as exercise-induced or athletic amenorrhea" (p. 26). Furthermore, research has shown that when a woman does not menstruate regularly, she loses bone density and becomes more prone to stress fractures (cracks in bones, especially hands and feet) and osteoporosis later in life. Amenorrhea can be caused by inadequate nutrition as well as by overtraining, both of which cause the athlete to burn more calories than she eats. As a result, her body shuts down its reproductive function to conserve energy (Graham, 1999).

The tendency to develop an eating disorder, such as anorexia or bulimia, is a third possible effect. Although young women may develop eating disorders for a variety of reasons, Graham (1999) noted, "Disordered eating is high among female athletes competing in sports where leanness and/or a specific weight are considered important for either performance or appearance" (p. 74). Being slim and trim may be the goal of many adolescent female athletes, but when they seek that goal by means of an eating disorder, they hinder their athletic performance. A calorie deficit actually decreases immune function, reduces aerobic capacity, decreases muscle mass and strength, and causes low energy and fatigue (Graham, 1999).

Page number identifies the location of material quoted from a print source.

APA

V Documenting Sources

Girls, Sports, and Steroids 5

Negative Psychological and Social Effects

Just as a girl's body and mind often benefit from sports, so too are body and mind linked when it comes to those aspects of sports that are not positive. Often, negative physical effects occur because female athletes feel the need to win at any cost and the pressure to attain an unrealistic ideal. They may resort to extremes such as overtraining in order to have the "ideal" body or be the "best of the best." When they can't meet these expectations, some girl athletes lose self-confidence and become overly stressed and anxious. In fact, they may see their failures as a serious threat to their self-esteem (Davies & Armstrong, 1989).

Pressures at home, at school, among friends, and from coaches can be daunting as well because young athletes tend to worry about the actions and reactions of the people who make up their social circles (Brown & Branta, 1988). In addition, learning to balance the demands of sports, school, family, and fun can be incredibly fatiguing. Juan Orozco recalled that some of the girls he coached were involved in three sports at a time and still had to keep their grades up in order to participate (personal communication, September 22, 2007). Add to these demands the pressure from parents, and real problems can occur. Gary Anderson, a girls' basketball coach for more than two decades, has seen it all: parents who are overly dramatic, teams that serve primarily as stages for a few superstar athletes, and girls who seem "factory-installed with a sense of entitlement simply because they know their way around a ball and a pair of high-tops" (Dexheimer, 2004, para. 15). All of these situations and pressures affect young female athletes and can result in their making some regrettable, if not devastating, choices.

Girls' Reactions: Burnout and Steroids

What happens when these young women decide the pressure is too much? What measures will they take to lighten their load? Some of these athletes simply burn out. They stop participating in competitive athletics because the pressure and anxiety make them physically ill. They no longer enjoy competitive sports, but consider them a torment to be endured. In fact, according to Davies and Armstrong (1989), it is not unusual for promising 12-year-olds to abandon the game entirely by the age of 16 and move on to less distressing pastimes. Melissa Alvarez had one such experience while playing high school basketball. The coach put so much pressure on her that her stomach began to ache during games and during practice. The more the coach yelled, the worse she played, but when the coach was absent, her performance improved dramatically and her stomach problems disappeared. Eventually, Melissa quit the basketball team

Subheadings are set in boldface and aligned flush left to differentiate them from higher-level headings.

A partial quotation is integrated into the sentence.

Girls, Sports, and Steroids 6

because the game had become a burden instead of something she enjoyed (M. Alvarez, personal communication, September 26, 2007).

An alternative much more dangerous than burnout, however, is the use of performance-enhancing drugs such as anabolic steroids. A 2003 article in *Drug Week* stated that girls who participate in sports more than eight hours a week are at considerable risk for taking many illicit drugs: The higher the level at which athletes compete, the higher their risk for substance abuse ("Sporting Activities").

Teenage girls take steroids for some of the same reasons that professional athletes do — to increase stamina and strength and to acquire a lean, muscular body. However, girls also take steroids to compete for athletic scholarships ("Girls and Steroids," 1998). According to Charles Yesalis, a professor of sports science and senior author of a Penn State report, a lot of young women see steroid use as an investment in their future; athletes can take the hormones for a few months in high school, qualify for a college scholarship, and then stop taking the drugs before sophisticated lab tests can spot them (Faigenbaum, Zaichkowsky, Gardner, & Micheli, 1993). What teenagers don't realize, though, is that even a few months of steroid use can permanently damage the heart, trigger liver failure, stunt physical growth, and put a woman's childbearing ability at risk. Steroids cause muscles to outgrow and injure the tendons and ligaments that attach them to the bone (Faigenbaum et al., 1998). As Farnaz Khadem, spokeswoman for the World Anti-Doping Agency has emphasized, "A lot of these young people have no idea of what this is doing to their bodies. This is a real health danger" (DeNoon, 2004).

Although health is the most important concern in the issue of steroid use, it is not the only one. Possessing or selling steroids without a prescription is a crime, so those who are involved in such activities may also endure criminal penalties (Gorman, 1998). Young women who use steroids are resorting to illegal actions and may eventually be labeled as "criminals," a label that will follow them for the rest of their lives. Doors to coaching jobs, teaching careers, and many other occupations may be shut permanently if one has a criminal past.

How Girl Athletes Can Avoid Steroid Use

What can we do to help adolescent female athletes avoid illicit drug use? How can we help them avoid the pitfalls of competitive athletics? Parents, coaches, and the athletes themselves all play a crucial role in averting bad choices. First, parents and coaches need to be aware that performance-enhancing drugs are a problem. Some adults believe that steroid use is either minimal or nonexistent among teenagers, but one study concluded that "over half the teens

---

Since the publication year is given in the sentence, it is not included in the citation.

In APA style, the first parenthetical reference to a source with three to five authors lists all authors . . .

. . . subsequent references to the source use "et al." in place of all but the first author.

Girls, Sports, and Steroids 7

who use steroids start before age 16, sometimes with the encourage-
ment of their parents. . . . Seven percent said they first took 'juice'
by age ten" (Dudley, 1994, p. 235).

> An ellipsis indicates that words from the source were not included in the quotation.

Parents need to take the time to know their children and know
what their children are doing. Coaches must know their players well
enough to be able to identify a child in trouble. When asked what
parents and coaches could do to help girl athletes remain healthy
and not use drugs or overwork themselves, Juan Orozco offered the
following advice:

> An athlete should be happy in her activity of choice, and
> her parents should encourage her desires to do well. Parents
> should be involved in her life and let her know that her efforts
> are valued highly, but they also need to be on the lookout
> for danger signs — such as unusual weight loss or moodiness.
> As a coach, I need to know the personalities of my players
> and get them to trust me, not only as their coach but as their
> friend — someone they can talk to if they have a problem.
> (personal communication, September 22, 2010)

> Extended quotation is set off in block style without quotation marks.

It is also important for parents and coaches to teach the
athletes how to develop a healthy lifestyle and not focus only
on winning. If an athlete seems to take her sport too seriously,
parents might negotiate with her, encouraging her to balance
sports with other endeavors. Some parents and coaches push kids
too hard, teaching them to win at any cost. In fact, a number of
researchers believe that some parents and coaches are actually
purchasing expensive black-market steroids for their young athletes
(Kendrick). As University of Massachusetts researcher Avery Faigenbaum has put it, "I don't know a lot of ten-year-olds who have a
couple of hundred dollars — to spend on drugs or anything else"
(Kendrick, "Parents as Pushers," para. 1).

Athletes, too, must take responsibility for their own lives. Adolescent girls should try to resist undue pressures imposed by parents,
coaches, and society. They must learn about the damage steroids can
cause and understand that pursuing an "ideal" body type is not only
unrealistic but also unhealthy (Yiannakis & Melnick, 2001). Most of
all, young female athletes need to know that they are more important
than the competition. No scholarship or medal is worth liver failure
or losing the ability to bear children.

The vast majority of excellent athletes do not overtrain, become
bulimic, or wind up using steroids. Clearly, they have learned to
avoid the pitfalls of competitive athletics. They believe in themselves
and their abilities and know how to balance sports and other activities. They have learned how to sacrifice and work hard, but not at

Girls, Sports, and Steroics 8

the expense of their integrity or health. In short, these athletes have not lost sight of the true objective of participating in sports — they know that their success is due to their efforts and not to the effects of a performance-enhancing drug. When asked what she would say to athletes considering steroid use, Melissa Alvarez said:

> If you are training and doing your best, you should not have to use steroids. At the end of the day, it is just a game. You should never put your health at risk for anything, or anyone. It should be your top priority. (personal communication, September 26, 2010)

In the essay's conclusion, Alexis uses a quotation to reinforce her main point.

Girls, Sports, and Steroids 9

References

Brown, E. W., & Branta, C. F. (Eds.). (1988). *Competitive sports for children and youth: An overview of issues and research.* Champaign, IL: Human Kinetics.

Centers for Disease Control and Prevention. (2004, May 21). Youth risk behavior surveillance — December 2003. *Morbidity and Mortality Weekly Report 53* (Report no. SS-2). Retrieved from http://www.cdc.gov/mmwr/PDF/SS/SS5302.pdf

Costello, B. (2004, July 4). Too late? Survey suggests millions of kids could be juicing. *New York Post.* Retrieved from http://www.nypost.com

Davies, D., & Armstrong, M. (1989). *Psychological factors in competitive sport.* New York, NY: Falmer Press.

DeNoon, D. (2004, August 4). *Steroid use: Hitting closer to home.* Retrieved from http://webmd.com/fitness-exercise/features/steroid-use-hitting-closer-to-home

Dexheimer, E. (2004, May 13). Nothing to lose: The Colorado Impact teaches girls about life — then hoops. *Denver Westword.* Retrieved from http://www.westword.com

Dudley, W. (Ed.). (1994). *Sports in America: Opposing viewpoints.* San Diego, CA: Greenhaven Press.

Faigenbaum, A. D., Zaichowsky, L. D., Gardner, D. E., & Micheli, L. J. (1998). Anabolic steroid use by male and female middle school students. *Pediatrics, 101*(5), e6. doi:10.1542/peds.101.5.e6

Girls and steroids. (1998). *Teacher Magazine 9*(5), 11. Retrieved from http://www.teachermagazine.org

Gorman, C. (1998, August 10). Girls on steroids. *Time 152*(6), 93. Retrieved from http://www.time.com

Graham, J. (1999). *The athletic woman's sourcebook.* New York, NY: Avon Books.

Kendrick, C. (n.d.). *Seduced by steroids.* Retrieved from http://life.familyeducation.com/drugs-and-alcohol/sports/36182.html

Manning, A. (2002, July 9). Kids, steroids don't mix. *USA Today.* Retrieved from http://www.usatoday.com

Mundell, E. J. (2004, May 12). Schools struggle to control steroid use. *HealthDay.* Retrieved from http://www.healthday.com

President's Council on Physical Fitness and Sports. (1997, May). *Physical activity and sport in the lives of girls: Physical and mental health dimensions from an interdisciplinary approach.* Retrieved from University of Minnesota, Tucker Center for

---

Annotations (left margin):

Sources alphabetized by author's name or, if no author, by title

First line of each entry starts at left margin, additional lines indented one-half inch, or five spaces

Online newspaper article

Book with two authors

Source URL given

Edited book

Online article with a DOI

Online articles without DOIs

Book with one author

Nonperiodical web document

Online newspaper article

Annotations (right margin):

List of references on a separate page, heading centered

Edited book

Online government report

In source titles, only capitalize first words, words following a colon or question mark, and proper nouns

Titles of books and journals italicized

Nonperiodical Web site

URL of publication's home page

Side tab:
APA

V Documenting Sources

Girls, Sports, and Steroids 10

Research on Girls and Women in Sport Web site: http://cehd.umn.

edu/tuckercenter/projects/PresidentsCouncil/

pcpfs_report.pdf

Online newspaper article

Sieghart, M. A. (2004, August 27). Competitive sport is harsh and

unforgiving: That's why it's good for children. *The Times* of

London. Retrieved from http://www.the-times.co.uk

Sporting activities impact illegal drug use among male and female

teenagers. (2003, September 26). *Drug Week,* pp. 16-17.

Magazine article without a named author

Book editors identified with (Ed.) or (Eds.)

Yiannakis, A., & Melnick, M. J. (Eds.). (2001). *Contemporary issues in*

sociology of sport. Champaign, IL: Human Kinetics.

23

Using *Chicago* Style

> **Key Questions**
>
> **23a. How do I cite sources within the text of my document?** 394
>
> **23b. How do I format notes and prepare the bibliography?** 396

The documentation style described in *The Chicago Manual of Style: The Essential Guide for Writers, Editors, and Publishers*, Sixteenth Edition, is used in the humanities and in some of the social sciences. The *Manual* recommends two systems, an author-date system similar to the APA system (see Chapter 22) and a notes system. This chapter describes and provides models for the notes system.

In the notes system, researchers acknowledge their sources in footnotes or endnotes. Footnotes appear at the bottom of a printed page, whereas endnotes appear at the end of the document. Although a bibliography can be omitted when using the note system (since all relevant publication information is provided in the notes), the manual encourages authors to provide a bibliography or list of works cited in documents when more than a few sources are cited. For more information about this system, consult *The Chicago Manual of Style*. Information about the manual can also be found at chicagomanualofstyle.org.

To see Nicholas Brothers's research essay, formatted in *Chicago* style, turn to p. 412.

CITATIONS WITHIN YOUR TEXT

1. Numbering   394
2. Placement of the note numbers in the text   394
3. Placement of notes   395
4. Including page numbers in a note   395
5. Cross-referencing notes   395
6. Citing the same source in multiple notes   395
7. Citing a source quoted in another source   395

23a

How do I cite sources within the text of my document?

Chicago uses footnotes or endnotes. Notes can also be used to expand on points made in the text—that is, notes can contain both citation information and commentary on the text. For electronic documents such as Web sites that consist of multiple "pages" of text, footnotes can take the form of links to notes at the end of a "page" or to pop-up windows that display the notes.

The first time you refer to a source in a note, provide complete publication information for the source. In subsequent references, you need to cite only the author's last name, a shortened version of the title, and the page numbers (if the source has page numbers) to which you refer. Separate the elements with commas and end with a period. *Chicago* style italicizes titles of books and periodicals.

The following examples illustrate the most common ways of citing sources within the text of your document using *Chicago*'s note system.

1. Numbering   Notes should be numbered consecutively throughout your work, beginning with 1.

2. Placement of the Note Numbers in the Text   Place the number for a note at the end of the sentence containing the reference after punctuation and outside any parentheses. If you are citing the source of material that comes before an em dash (or two hyphens) used to separate parts of a sentence, the note number should precede the dash. Note numbers are set as superscripts.

> Lee and Calandra suggest that the poor organization of online historical documents may impair students' ability to conduct research without guidance.[1]

Tomlinson points out that the erosion of Fiji's culture was accelerated by both British and Indian immigration[2] — though the two immigrant groups inhabited very different roles and social classes.

3. Placement of Notes   You may choose between footnotes, which appear at the bottom of the page containing corresponding note numbers, and endnotes, which appear at the end of the document in a section titled "Notes." Longer works, such as books, typically use endnotes. The choice depends on the expectations of your readers and your preferences. Regardless of placement, notes are numbered consecutively throughout the document. If you use a bibliography, it follows the last page of text or the last page of endnotes. Model notes for various types of sources appear in section 23b, which begins on p. 396.

4. Including Page Numbers in a Note   Use page numbers whenever you refer to a specific page of a source rather than to the source as a whole. The use of page numbers is required for quotations.

4. Amy Hanson, *Baby Boomers and Beyond: Tapping the Ministry, Talents, and Passions of Adults over Fifty* (San Francisco: Jossey-Bass, 2010), 156.

5. Cross-Referencing Notes   If you are referring to a source identified in a previous note, you can refer to that note instead of repeating the information.

5. See note 3 above.

6. Citing the Same Source in Multiple Notes   If you refer to the same source in two or more notes, provide a full citation in the first note. In subsequent notes, provide the author's last name, a brief version of the title, and the page number. If you are referring to the same source cited in the previous note, you can use the Latin abbreviation "ibid." (for *ibidem,* or *in the same place*).

1. John Mosier, *Deathride: Hitler vs. Stalin; The Eastern Front, 1941–1945* (New York: Simon & Schuster, 2010), 26.

2. Ibid., 54.

6. Mosier, *Deathride*, 131.

7. Citing a Source Quoted in Another Source

7. José María Arguedas, *Obras Completa* (Lima: Editorial Horizonte, 1983), 1:129, quoted in Alberto Flores Galindo et al., *In Search of an Inca: Identity and Utopia in the Andes* (New York: Cambridge University Press, 2010), 199.

23b

How do I format notes and prepare the bibliography?

The Chicago Manual of Style provides guidelines for formatting notes and entries in a bibliography of works that are relevant to but not necessarily cited within your document. In print documents and linear documents that are distributed electronically (such as a word processing file or a newsgroup post), the bibliography appears at the end of the document. In longer documents, a bibliography could be given at the end of each chapter or section. In electronic documents that use links, such as a Web site, the bibliography is often a separate page to which other pages are linked. To see a bibliography in *Chicago* style, see p. 421.

For notes, include the number of the note, indented and not superscripted, followed by these elements:

- author's name (first name first)
- title (followed by the title of the complete work if the source is an article, chapter, or other short work contained in a larger work)
- publisher (for a book) or publication title (for a journal, magazine, or newspaper)
- date
- page(s) being cited

For entries in the bibliography, include these elements:

- author's name (last name first)
- title (followed by the title of the complete work if the source is an article, chapter, or other short work contained in a larger work)
- publisher (for a book) or publication title (for a journal, magazine, or newspaper)
- date
- page(s) (if the source is a shorter work included in a complete work)

Keep in mind that well-known reference works, such as encyclopedias, and all types of personal communication—personal interviews, letters, surveys, email messages, online discussion groups—are cited in a note only. They are not usually included in the bibliography.

Note: For each type of source, a pair of examples is presented in this section: a model note followed by a model bibliographic entry.

Books, Conference Proceedings, and Dissertations

8. One Author   Use the basic format described on p. 397.

When citing a book, use the information from the title page and the copyright page (on the reverse side of the title page), not from the book's cover or a library catalog.

TUTORIAL

How do I cite books using Chicago style?

When citing a book, use the information from the title page and the copyright page (on the reverse side of the title page), not from the book's cover or a library catalog. This tutorial gives an example of a *Chicago*-style footnote or endnote. An example of the bibliography entry for this source is at the bottom of the page.

Consult pp. 396–402 for additional models for citing books.

Note

A ┌─────────┐ **B** ┌──────────────────────────────────┐
1. David Tracey, *Urban Agriculture: Ideas and Designs for the New Food*

C ┌──────────────────────────────┐ **D** ┌─────┐
Revolution (Gabriola Island, BC: New Society Publishers, 2011), 80-83.

A **The author.** In the note, give the first name first. Follow the last name with a comma. Separate the names of multiple authors with commas; use the word *and* before the final author's name.

B **The title.** Give the full title; include the subtitle (if any), preceded by a colon. Italicize the title and subtitle, capitalizing all major words.

C **Publication information.** Enclose the city, publisher, and date in parentheses. If more than one city is given, use the first one listed. For a city that may be unfamiliar to your readers or confused with another city, add an abbreviation of the state, country, or province (Cambridge, MA or Waterloo, ON). Insert a colon.

Give the publisher's name. Omit words such as *Inc.* and *Co.* Include and do not abbreviate such terms as *Books* and *Press*. Insert a comma.

Give the year of publication, using the most recent copyright year. Close the parentheses and insert a comma.

D **Inclusive page number(s).** Give the specific page or pages on which you found the information. For numbers 100 and above, give only the last two digits and any other preceding digits if different from the first number (22-28, 402-10, 1437-45, 599-603).

Bibliography Entry
In the bibliography, give the author's last name first, and separate the elements with periods. Do not enclose the publication information in parentheses.

Tracey, David. *Urban Agriculture: Ideas and Designs for the New Food Revolution.* Gabriola Island, BC: New Society Publishers, 2011.

Chicago

V Documenting Sources

8. Jeff Shesol, *Supreme Power: Franklin Roosevelt vs. the Supreme Court* (New York: Norton, 2010), 132.

Shesol, Jeff. *Supreme Power: Franklin Roosevelt vs. the Supreme Court.* New York: Norton, 2010.

9. Two or Three Authors List the authors in the order in which they appear on the title page. In a note, list the first name for each author first. In the bibliography, list the first author's last name first and list the first names for each other author first.

9. Robert A. Jerin and Laura J. Moriarty, *The Victims of Crime* (Upper Saddle River, NJ: Pearson Prentice Hall, 2010), 259.

Jerin, Robert A., and Laura J. Moriarty. *The Victims of Crime.* Upper Saddle River, NJ: Pearson Prentice Hall, 2010.

10. Four or More Authors In a note, give only the first author's name followed by "et al." (Latin for "and others"). In the bibliography, list all the authors that appear on the title page.

10. Harry Markopolos et al., *No One Would Listen: A True Financial Thriller* (Hoboken, NJ: Wiley, 2010), 179.

Markopolos, Harry, Frank Casey, Neil Chelo, Gaytri Kachroo, and Michael Ocrant. *No One Would Listen: A True Financial Thriller.* Hoboken, NJ: Wiley, 2010.

11. Corporate or Group Author Use the corporation or group as the author; it may also be the publisher.

11. International Monetary Fund, *Regional Economic Outlook: Middle East and Central Asia* (Washington, DC: International Monetary Fund, 2010), 26.

International Monetary Fund. *Regional Economic Outlook: Middle East and Central Asia.* Washington, DC: International Monetary Fund, 2010.

12. Unknown Author When no author is listed on the title or copyright page, begin the entry with the title of the work. In the bibliography, alphabetize the entry by the first word other than *A, An,* or *The.*

12. *Through Palestine with the 20th Machine Gun Squadron* (Arlington, VA: IndyPublish, 2007), 63.

Through Palestine with the 20th Machine Gun Squadron. Arlington, VA: IndyPublish, 2007.

13. Translated Book   List the author first and the translator after the title. Use the abbreviation "trans." in a note, but spell out "Translated by" in the bibliography.

13. Nujood Ali and Delphine Minoui, *I Am Nujood, Age 10 and Divorced,* trans. Linda Coverdale (New York: Three Rivers Press, 2010), 34.

Ali, Nujood, and Delphine Minoui. *I Am Nujood, Age 10 and Divorced.* Translated by Linda Coverdale. New York: Three Rivers Press, 2010.

14. Edition Other Than the First   Give edition information after the title.

14. Alan Brinkley, *The Unfinished Nation: A Concise History of the American People,* 6th ed. (New York: McGraw-Hill, 2010), 527.

Brinkley, Alan. *The Unfinished Nation: A Concise History of the American People.* 6th ed. New York: McGraw-Hill, 2010.

15. Untitled Volume in a Multivolume Work   In the notes, give the volume number and page number, separated by a colon, for the specific location of the information referred to in your text. In the bibliography, if you have used all the volumes, give the total number of volumes after the title, using the abbreviation "vols." ("2 vols." or "4 vols."). If you have used one volume, give the abbreviation "Vol." and the volume number after the title.

15. Christopher Edgar and Ron Padgett, eds., *Educating the Imagination: Essays and Ideas for Teachers and Writers* (New York: Teachers & Writers Collaborative, 2007), 1:84-87.

Edgar, Christopher, and Ron Padgett, eds. *Educating the Imagination: Essays and Ideas for Teachers and Writers.* Vol. 1. New York: Teachers & Writers Collaborative, 2007.

16. Titled Volume in a Multivolume Work   Give the title of the volume to which you refer, followed by the volume number and the general title for the entire work.

16. Dietrich Bonhoeffer, *Letters and Papers from Prison,* ed. John W. de Grunchy, trans. Isabel Best et al., vol. 8 of *Dietrich Bonhoeffer Works* (Minneapolis: Fortress Press, 2010), 564.

Chicago

V Documenting Sources

Bonhoeffer, Dietrich. *Letters and Papers from Prison*. Edited by John W. De Grunchy. Translated by Isabel Best, Lisa E. Dahill, Richard Krauss, and Nancy Lukens. Vol. 8 of *Dietrich Bonhoeffer Works*. Minneapolis: Fortress Press, 2010.

17. Book in a Series The series name follows the title and is capitalized as a title but is not italicized. If the series numbers its volumes, include that information as well.

17. Michael F. Holt, *Franklin Pierce*, American Presidents Series 14 (New York: Times Books/Henry Holt, 2010), 7.

Holt, Michael F. *Franklin Pierce*. American Presidents Series 14. New York: Times Books/Henry Holt, 2010.

18. Republished Book Place the original publication date before the publication information for the reprint.

18. James, King of England, *The Political Works of James I*, ed. Charles Howard McIlwain (1918; repr., Whitefish, MT: Kessinger, 2010), 74.

James, King of England. *The Political Works of James I*. Edited by Charles Howard McIlwain. 1918. Reprint, Whitefish, MT: Kessinger, 2010.

19. Author with an Editor List the author at the beginning of the citation and add the editor's name after the title. In notes, use the abbreviation "ed." before the editor's name. In the bibliography, include the phrase "Edited by" before the editor's name.

19. H. L. Mencken, *Thirty-five Years of Newspaper Work: A Memoir,* ed. Fred Hobson, Vincent Fitzpatrick, and Bradford Jacobs (Baltimore: Johns Hopkins University Press, 2006), 330-32.

Mencken, H. L. *Thirty-five Years of Newspaper Work: A Memoir*. Edited by Fred Hobson, Vincent Fitzpatrick, and Bradford Jacobs. Baltimore: Johns Hopkins University Press, 2006.

20. Anthology or Collection with an Editor To cite an entire anthology or collection of articles, give the editor(s) before the title of the collection, adding a comma and the abbreviation "ed." or "eds."

20. Michael Krausz, ed., *Relativism: A Contemporary Anthology* (New York: Columbia University Press, 2010).

Krausz, Michael, ed. *Relativism: A Contemporary Anthology*. New York: Columbia University Press, 2010.

21. Foreword, Introduction, Preface, or Afterword Give the name of the writer of the foreword, introduction, preface, or afterword followed by the appropriate phrase ("introduction to," "preface to," and so on) before the title of the book. If the writer of the introduction or other part differs from the writer of the book, after the title insert the word "by" and the author's name.

21. Martin Stannard, preface to *Muriel Spark: The Biography* (New York: Norton, 2010).

Stannard, Martin. Preface to *Muriel Spark: The Biography*, xv–xxvi. New York: Norton, 2010.

22. Chapter in a Book or Selection in an Anthology Give the author and title (in quotation marks) for the chapter or selection. Then give the title, editor (if any), and publication data for the book or anthology. In the bibliography, give the inclusive page numbers before the publication data.

22. William Dalrymple, "The Monk's Tale," in *Nine Lives: In Search of the Sacred in Modern India* (New York: Knopf, 2010), 151.

Dalrymple, William. "The Monk's Tale." In *Nine Lives: In Search of the Sacred in Modern India*, 142–71. New York: Knopf, 2010.

23. Published Proceedings of a Conference Cite as for an anthology or collection with an editor (see also #20 on p. 400).

23. Derek McAuley and Simon Peyton-Jones, *Proceedings of the 2010 ACM-BCS Visions of Computer Science Conference* (Swindon, UK: British Informatics Society, 2010).

McAuley, Derek, and Simon Peyton-Jones. *Proceedings of the 2010 ACM-BCS Visions of Computer Science Conference.* Swindon, UK: British Informatics Society, 2010.

24. Paper Published in the Proceedings of a Conference Cite as a chapter in an edited book (see also #22 above).

24. Dale Miller, "Finding Unity in Computational Logic," in *Proceedings of the 2010 ACM-BCS Visions of Computer Science Conference* (Swindon, UK: British Informatics Society, 2010), 2.

Miller, Dale. "Finding Unity in Computational Logic." In *Proceedings of the 2010 ACM-BCS Visions of Computer Science Conference*, 1–13. Swindon, UK: British Informatics Society, 2010.

Chicago

V Documenting Sources

25. Sacred Text   Cite sacred texts only within the text of your document. A note should include the book, chapter, and verse, but not a page number.

> 25. Deut. 5:1-21 (New Revised Standard Version).

26. Published Dissertation or Thesis   Give the author and title, the phrase "PhD diss." or "master's thesis," followed by information about the institution that granted the degree and the year. Include publication number from ProQuest if appropriate.

> 26. Anthony Colello, *Affirmative Action Bans and Minority Employment: Washington State's Initiative 200* (PhD diss., Georgetown University, 2011), 41-2, ProQuest (AAT 1491319).

> Colello, Anthony. *Affirmative Action Bans and Minority Employment: Washington State's Initiative 200.* PhD diss., Georgetown University, 2011. ProQuest (ATT 1491319).

27. Unpublished Dissertation or Thesis   Give the author and title, in quotation marks. Then include the phrase "PhD diss." or "master's thesis," information about the institution that granted the degree, and the date.

> 27. Jamil Edwin, "Evaluation of a Military Family Support Program: The Case of Operation: Military Kids in Indiana" (PhD diss., Purdue University, 2007), 77-79.

> Edwin, Jamil. "Evaluation of a Military Family Support Program: The Case of Operation: Military Kids in Indiana." PhD diss., Purdue University, 2007.

28. Abstract of a Dissertation or Thesis   Provide information as you would for an article in a journal (see also #29 below). Add information about *Dissertation Abstracts International.*

> 28. Machiko Inagawa, "Japanese American Experiences in Internment Camps during World War II as Represented by Children's and Adolescent Literature" (PhD diss., University of Arizona, 2007), abstract, *Dissertation Abstracts International* 67 (2007): 122.

> Inagawa, Machiko. "Japanese American Experiences in Internment Camps during World War II as Represented by Children's and Adolescent Literature." PhD diss., University of Arizona, 2007. Abstract. *Dissertation Abstracts International* 67 (2007): 122.

TUTORIAL

How do I cite articles from periodicals using Chicago style?

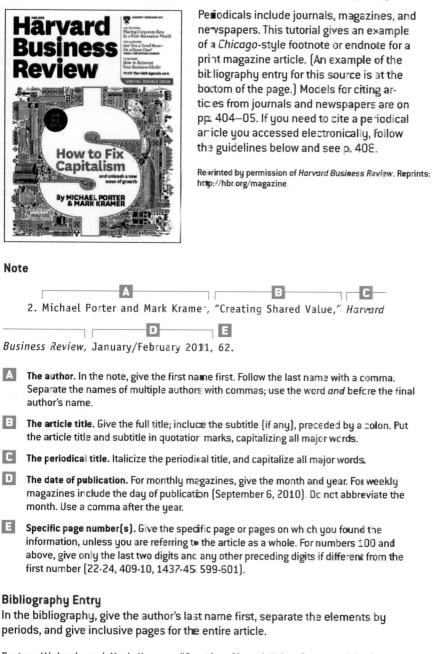

Periodicals include journals, magazines, and newspapers. This tutorial gives an example of a *Chicago*-style footnote or endnote for a print magazine article. (An example of the bibliography entry for this source is at the bottom of the page.) Models for citing articles from journals and newspapers are on pp. 404–05. If you need to cite a periodical article you accessed electronically, follow the guidelines below and see p. 408.

Reprinted by permission of *Harvard Business Review*. Reprints: http://hbr.org/magazine.

Note

2. Michael Porter and Mark Kramer, "Creating Shared Value," *Harvard*
Ⓐ — title Ⓑ — title Ⓒ

Business Review, January/February 2011, 62.
Ⓓ Ⓔ

Ⓐ **The author.** In the note, give the first name first. Follow the last name with a comma. Separate the names of multiple authors with commas; use the word *and* before the final author's name.

Ⓑ **The article title.** Give the full title; include the subtitle (if any), preceded by a colon. Put the article title and subtitle in quotation marks, capitalizing all major words.

Ⓒ **The periodical title.** Italicize the periodical title, and capitalize all major words.

Ⓓ **The date of publication.** For monthly magazines, give the month and year. For weekly magazines include the day of publication (September 6, 2010). Do not abbreviate the month. Use a comma after the year.

Ⓔ **Specific page number(s).** Give the specific page or pages on which you found the information, unless you are referring to the article as a whole. For numbers 100 and above, give only the last two digits and any other preceding digits if different from the first number (22-24, 409-10, 1437-45, 599-601).

Bibliography Entry

In the bibliography, give the author's last name first, separate the elements by periods, and give inclusive pages for the entire article.

Porter, Michael, and Mark Kramer. "Creating Shared Value." *Harvard Business Review,* January/February 2011, 62.

Sources in Journals, Magazines, and Newspapers

29. Article in a Journal   After the journal title, include the volume number, a comma, and the issue number after the abbreviation "no." Then give the year. In the note, give the specific page number to which you are referring; in the bibliography, give inclusive page numbers of the entire article.

29. Johan Franzen, "Losing Hearts and Minds in Iraq: Britain, Cold War Propaganda and the Challenge of Communism, 1945–58," *Historical Research* 83, no. 222 (2010): 749.

Franzen, Johan. "Losing Hearts and Minds in Iraq: Britain, Cold War Propaganda and the Challenge of Communism, 1945–58." *Historical Research* 83, no. 222 (2010): 747–62.

30. Article in a Monthly Magazine   Magazines are cited by their dates rather than by volume and issue.

30. Joshua Green, "Man Inside," *Atlantic*, May 2010, 39.

Green, Joshua. "Man Inside." *Atlantic*, May 2010, 36–49.

31. Article in a Weekly Magazine   Cite like a monthly magazine, but provide the day of publication.

31. Jane Mayer, "Covert Operations," *New Yorker*, August 30, 2010, 47.

Mayer, Jane. "Covert Operations." *New Yorker*, August 30, 2010, 45–55.

32. Article in a Newspaper   If the name of the newspaper does not include the city, insert the city before the name (and italicize it). If an American city is not well known, name the state as well (in parentheses, abbreviated). Identify newspapers from other countries with the city in parentheses (not italicized) after the name of the newspaper.

Eugene (OR) Register-Guard

Sunday Times (London)

Page numbers may be omitted, since separate editions of the same newspaper may place articles differently. If a paper comes out in more than one edition, identify the edition after the date.

32. Kelly Zito, "Cities Key Source of Toxins in Bay, Study Finds," *San Francisco Chronicle*, October 5, 2010, Bay Area edition.

Zito, Kelly. "Cities Key Source of Toxins in Bay, Study Finds." *San Francisco Chronicle*, October 5, 2010, Bay Area edition.

33. Unsigned Article in a Newspaper or Magazine   If no author is given, begin the note with the title of the article; begin the bibliography entry with the title of the periodical.

33. "NYC May Ban Smoking in Parks, on Beaches," *Boston Globe,* September 16, 2010.

Boston Globe. "NYC May Ban Smoking in Parks, on Beaches." September 16, 2010.

34. Letter to the Editor   Treat as a newspaper article. If no title is provided, place "Letter to the editor" in the title position.

34. Jason Levi, letter to the editor, *Smithsonian,* June 2010.

Levi, Jason. Letter to the editor. *Smithsonian,* June 2010.

35. Review   Give the author of the review, the review title, if any, and then the words "review of" followed by the title and author of the work reviewed and the author or editor (for books) or director or performer (for movies, plays, and similar productions).

35. Stephen Holden, "Students Caught in the School Squeeze," review of *Waiting for Superman,* directed by Davis Guggenheim, *New York Times,* September 23, 2010.

Holden, Stephen. "Students Caught in the School Squeeze." Review of *Waiting for Superman,* directed by Davis Guggenheim. *New York Times,* September 23, 2010.

Print Reference Works

36. Entry in an Encyclopedia, Dictionary, Thesaurus, Handbook, or Almanac   In notes, provide the title of the work (italicized), the edition, the abbreviation "s.v." (for *sub verbo,* or "under the word"), and the title of the entry.

36. *Encyclopaedia Britannica,* 15th ed., s.v. "Lee, Robert E."

Chicago does not recommend including reference works such as encyclopedias or dictionaries in the bibliography.

37. Government Publication   In general, give the issuing body, then the title and any other information (such as report numbers) that would help your readers locate the source. Follow with the publication data and the page numbers if relevant. You may abbreviate "Government Printing Office" as GPO.

37. U.S. Senate, Special Committee on Aging, *Social Security Modernization: Options to Address Solvency and Benefit Adequacy* (Washington, DC: GPO, 2010), 7.

U.S. Senate. Special Committee on Aging. *Social Security Modernization: Options to Address Solvency and Benefit Adequacy.* Washington, DC: GPO, 2010.

38. Pamphlet, Report, or Brochure   Cite it as you would a book (see p. 396).

38. *WIC: Good Food and a Whole Lot More* (Boston: Massachusetts Department of Public Health, 2007).

WIC: Good Food and a Whole Lot More. Boston: Massachusetts Department of Public Health, 2007.

Field Sources

39. Personal Interview   Give the location and date in a note. Do not include unpublished interviews in the bibliography.

39. Rachel Stein, interview by author, Pittsburgh, June 2, 2010.

40. Letter or Other Personal Communication   Do not include personal communications such as letters or phone calls in the bibliography. In a note, give the name of the person with whom you communicated, the form of communication, and the date.

40. Megahn McKennan, conversation with author, March 5, 2010.

41. Sangita Thakore, letter to author, November 12, 2010.

41. Survey   *Chicago* does not specify how to cite unpublished survey results. Cite them in your text as you would a personal communication (see #40 above).

42. Observation Note   *Chicago* does not specify how to cite observation notes. Cite them in your text as you would a personal communication (see #40 above).

43. Lecture or Public Address   Provide the title, the nature of the speech (such as lecture or keynote address), the name of the organization sponsoring the meeting or lecture, and the location and date it was given.

43. Andrew Sullivan, "The Politics of Homosexuality" (lecture, Princeton University, Princeton, NJ, February 18, 2010).

Sullivan, Andrew. "The Politics of Homosexuality." Lecture presented at Princeton University, Princeton, NJ, February 18, 2010.

TUTORIAL

How do I cite articles from databases using Chicago style?

Libraries subscribe to services such as LexisNexis, ProQuest, InfoTrac, and EBSCOhost that provide access to databases of electronic texts. The databases provide publication information, abstracts, and the complete text of documents in a specific subject area, discipline, or profession. (See also Chapter 8.)

This tutorial gives an example of a *Chicago*-style footnote or endnote for a journal article accessed via a database. (An example of the bibliography entry for this source is at the bottom of the page.) To cite magazine and newspaper articles from databases, see also pp. 408–09.

Note

┌──**A**──┐ ┌────────**B**────────┐
3. Bruce Matthews, "The Limits of International Engagement in Human

┌───────**C**───────┐ ┌──**D**──┐
Rights Situations: The Case of Sri Lanka," *Pacific Affairs*, 82, no. 4 (Winter 2009):

┌─────**E**─────┐
577, General OneFile (A216271050).

A **The author.** In the note, give the first name first. Follow the last name with a comma. Separate the names of multiple authors with commas; use the word *and* before the final author's name.

B **The article title.** Give the full title; include the subtitle (if any), preceded by a colon. Put the article title and subtitle in quotes, capitalizing all major words.

C **The journal title.** Italicize the journal title, and capitalize all major words.

D **The publication information.** Insert the volume number followed by a comma, then give the abbreviation *no.*, and the issue number. Include the year in parentheses followed by a colon and the specific page number of the reference. (In the bibliography, give inclusive page numbers.) End with a comma.

E **The DOI number, database, or URL.** Give whatever information is available for the article: a DOI number, the name of the database and the number assigned to the article, or a stable URL for the article.

F **The access date (not shown).** For articles that do not include a publication date, include the word *accessed* and the date of access after the publication information.

Bibliography Entry

Matthews, Bruce. "The Limits of International Engagement in Human Rights Situations: The Case of Sri Lanka." *Pacific Affairs* 82, no. 4 (Winter 2009): 577–97. General OneFile (A216271050).

Chicago

V Documenting Sources

Media Sources

44. Film or Video Recording   Provide the title first, the name of the director, the company, the year it was filmed, and the medium (film, videocassette, DVD).

44. *Michael Jackson's This Is It*, directed by Kenny Ortega (2009; Culver City, CA: Sony Pictures, 2010), DVD.

Michael Jackson's This Is It. Directed by Kenny Ortega. 2009; Culver City, CA: Sony Pictures, 2010. DVD.

45. Television Program   *Chicago* does not specify how to cite a television program. Cite as you would a video recording, identifying the medium as "television program" or "television broadcast."

46. Radio Program   *Chicago* does not specify how to cite a radio program. Cite as you would a video recording, identifying the medium as "radio program" or "radio broadcast."

47. Sound Recording   Give the composer and title of the recording, the performers and conductor, the label, and identifying number.

47. Pyotr Ilyich Tchaikovsky, *Symphony No. 5, Romeo and Juliet Fantasy Overture*, Royal Philharmonic Orchestra, conducted by Daniele Gatti, Harmonia Mundi, MU907381, compact disc.

Tchaikovsky, Pyotr Ilyich. *Symphony No. 5, Romeo and Juliet Fantasy Overture*. Royal Philharmonic Orchestra, conducted by Daniele Gatti. Harmonia Mundi. MU907381. compact disc.

Electronic Sources

All electronic sources should include either a publication date, an access date, or a revision or "last modified" date. After the date, include a DOI or, if source does not have a DOI, a stable URL. For a source accessed through a database, include the name of the database and any number assigned to the source.

48. Article from a Database

48. Michael Lindsay and Robert Wuthnow, "Financing Faith: Religion and Strategic Philanthropy," *Journal for the Scientific Study of Religion* 49, no. 1 (2010): 92, Academic OneFile (A220031117).

Lindsay, Michael, and Robert Wuthnow. "Financing Faith: Religion and Strategic Philanthropy." *Journal for the Scientific Study of Religion* 49, no. 1 (2010): 87-111. Academic OneFile (A220031117).

49. Article in an Electronic Journal

49. Gary Fields, "Palestinian Landscape in a 'Not-too-Distant Mirror,'" *Journal of Historical Sociology* 23, no. 2 (June 2010), doi:10.1111/j.1467-6443.2010.01373.x.

Fields, Gary. "Palestinian Landscape in a 'Not-too-Distant Mirror.'" *Journal of Historical Sociology* 23, no. 2 (June 2010). doi:10.1111/j.1467-6443.2010.01373.x.

50. Article in an Online Magazine

50. Farhad Manjoo, "Don't Worry, the Robot's Driving," *Slate,* October 12, 2010, http://www.slate.com/id/2270815/.

Manjoo, Farhad. "Don't Worry, the Robot's Driving." *Slate,* October 12, 2010. http://www.slate.com/id/2270815/.

51. Nonperiodical Web Site

51. Abdullah Qazi, "The Plight of the Afghan Woman," Afghanistan Online, last modified September 24, 2010, http://www.afghan-web.com/woman.

Qazi, Abdullah. "The Plight of the Afghan Woman." Afghanistan Online. Last modified September 24, 2010. http://www.afghan-web.com/woman.

52. Online Book

52. Martin Jacobsson, Ignas Niemegeers, Sonia Heemstra de Groot, *Personal Networks: Wireless Networking for Personal Devices* (Hoboken, NJ: Wiley, 2010), http://legacy.netlibrary.com/titleselect/home.asp.

Jacobsson, Martin, Ignas Niemegeers, and Sonia Heemstra de Groot. *Personal Networks: Wireless Networking for Personal Devices.* Hoboken, NJ: Wiley, 2010. http://legacy.netlibrary.com/titleselect/home.asp.

53. Article Posted on a Wiki
Cite online postings to Wikis in the text, but not in the bibliography.

Chicago

V Documenting Sources

53. "Popular Culture: Automobiles," *Montana History Wiki*, last modified February 26, 2010, accessed April 5, 2010, http://montanahistorywiki .pbworks.com/w/page/Popular%20Culture#Automobiles.

54. Entire Blog   Put the word "blog" in parentheses following the name of the blog, if it is not already part of the name. If the blog is part of a larger publication, include the name of the publication as well.

54. Michael Lorenzen and Jennie Weber, *American Presidents Blog*, June 14, 2010, http://www.american-presidents.org.

Lorenzen, Michael, and Jennie Weber. *American Presidents Blog*, June 14, 2010. http://www.american-presidents.org.

55. Entry or Comment on a Blog   Put the word "blog" in parentheses following the name of the blog, if it is not already part of the name. If the blog is part of a larger publication, include the name of the publication as well.

55. Noah Snyder-Mackler, "Monkeys with Personality," *Scientist at Work* (blog), *New York Times*, September 30, 2010, http://scientistatwork.blogs .nytimes.com.

Snyder-Mackler, Noah. "Monkeys with Personality." *Scientist at Work* (blog). *New York Times*, September 30, 2010, http://scientistatwork.blogs .nytimes.com.

56. Email Message   *Chicago* recommends that personal communication, including email, not be included in the bibliography, although it can be cited in your text.

56. Brysa H. Levy, e-mail message to author, January 4, 2010.

57. Online Posting to a Discussion Group   Like email, online postings are considered personal communication and are therefore listed in the text only, not the bibliography. Include a URL for archived postings.

57. Alessandro Busà to URBANTH-L discussion group, December 1, 2009, http://lists.cc.ysu.edu/pipermail/urbanth-l/2009-December/002761.html.

TUTORIAL

How do I cite works from Web sites using Chicago style?

You will likely need to search the Web site to find some of the citation information you need. For some sites all of the details may not be available; find as many as you can. Remember that the citation you provide should allow readers to retrace your steps electronically to locate the sources. Consult pp. 408–10 for additional models for citing Web sources.

Note

4. "Kenya's New Constitution Benefits Indigenous Peoples," Cultural Survival

B — title spans
C — name of web site

News, Cultural Survival, August 12, 2010, http://www.culturalsurvival.org/news/

D E F

kenya/kenyas-new-constitution-benefits-indigenous-peoples.

A   **The author (not shown).** In the note, give the first name first. Follow the last name with a comma. Separate the names of multiple authors with commas; use the word *and* before the final author's name. If no specific author is named, as in this case, begin with the title of the work.

B   **The title of the work.** Give the full title; include the subtitle (if any), preceded by a colon. Put the article title and subtitle in quotation marks, capitalizing all major words.

C   **The name of the Web site.** Do not italicize the name of the Web site unless it is the name of a book or periodical.

D   **The name of the sponsoring organization.** If the sponsor's name is not visible on the document page, look at the bottom of the site's home page.

E   **Date of publication or last modified or access date.** If there is no date of publication, include the date the page was last modified or the date on which you accessed the page.

F   **The URL.** Give the URL in full; do not use underlining or angle brackets, and be sure not to introduce any new hyphens or slashes.

Bibliography Entry

"Kenya's New Constitution Benefits Indigenous Peoples." Cultural Survival.
     August 12, 2010. http://www.culturalsurvival.org/news/kenya/kenyas-new-
     constitution-benefits-indigenous-peoples.

Use the bibliography tools at **bedfordresearcher.com** to create notes and a bibliography formatted in *Chicago* style.

Chicago   **V Documenting Sources**

Chicago-Style Research Essay

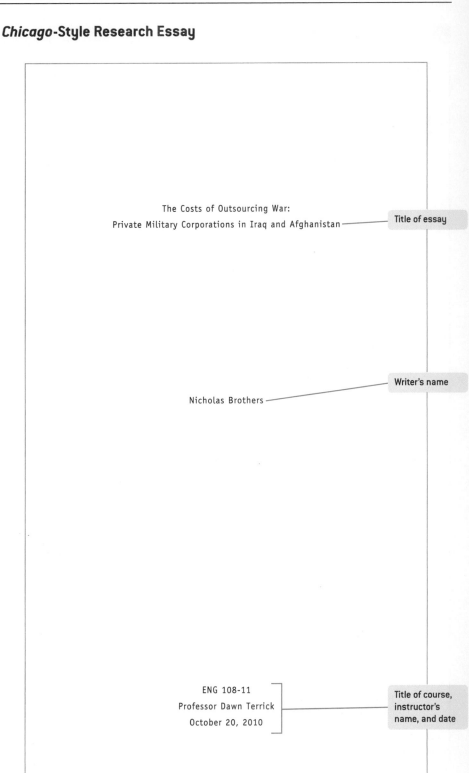

The Costs of Outsourcing War:
Private Military Corporations in Iraq and Afghanistan —————— Title of essay

Writer's name

Nicholas Brothers ——————

ENG 108-11
Professor Dawn Terrick
October 20, 2010

Title of course,
instructor's
name, and date

Brothers 2

The Costs of Outsourcing War:

Private Military Corporations in Iraq and Afghanistan

Title of essay repeated

The United States is considered the preeminent military power of the world. Yet, it is also a military force that today cannot get to the battlefield, feed and house its soldiers, or even protect its bases without the support of a network of nonstate actors. These organizations are sometimes listed on stock exchanges worldwide: they have glossy, professional websites and legions of press agents and lobbyists. They are private military corporations (PMCs). Their duties range from cooking and cleaning to planning and even carrying out covert operations to capture Osama bin Laden. But military privatization comes at a severe price — not just in terms of dollars, but also in terms of national security democratic ideals, and human lives. By relying heavily on PMCs to carry out military operations, the U.S. Department of Defense is undermining its own counterinsurgency efforts in Iraq and Afghanistan.

Thesis states Nicholas's main point.

Our country's reliance on private military corporations did not happen overnight, and although the corporatization of PMCs is relatively new, the idea of privatization is not. From the time of Alexander the Great to the Napoleonic era, private soldiers made up the bulk of military forces. Citizen armies emerged with the invention of cheap, easy-to-use muskets in the early 19th century. Yet as recently as the Cold War, U.S. armed forces were traditionally organized, with conventional army, naval, and air units in combat against similar Soviet units. The idea, of course, was for the military to be self-sufficient. However, as P. W. Singer explains in his book *Corporate Warriors: The Rise of the Privatized Military Industry,* when the Cold War ended in 1991, the Department of Defense began closing bases and dissolving or combining units, setting the stage for the large-scale outsourcing of military operations.[1] Jonathan Euchner, professor of political science at Missouri Western State University, explained that the shift to PMCs must be seen in the context of the overall privatization movement within the U.S. government that began in 1978 under President Jimmy Carter and gained momentum during the 1980s and 1990s.[2] While the role of PMCs remained modest throughout the 1990s, new military engagements after 9/11 provided new opportunities for PMCs. As detailed by investigative journalist Jeremy Scahill in his book *Blackwater: The Rise of the World's Most Powerful Mercenary Army,* the War on Terror as prosecuted by the Bush administration accelerated the privatization of military functions. The new Secretary of Defense Donald Rumsfeld would codify this concept, which became known as the Rumsfeld Doctrine.[3] In this

Interviewee tag indicates the use of field research.

The name of the book identifies the source of the summarized information.

Summarized material

Brothers 3

Doctrine, a highly mobile infantry force supported by airstrikes and by contractors would chase Osama bin Laden and al Qaeda in retaliation for the terrorist attacks on the World Trade Center and the Pentagon. The demand for contractors skyrocketed after the invasion of Iraq, with an overextended military needing more and more support as the repeated deployments dragged on for years. Now, the United States is in the final stages of its involvement in one foreign conflict and intractably embroiled in another. The combat mission in Iraq officially ended on August 31, 2010, but, with an insurgency that's growing stronger rather than weaker in Afghanistan, the planned 2011 withdrawal from that theater of war will likely be scaled back.[4]

Today, companies like DynCorp and Blackwater (now Xe Services) are some of the biggest, most diversified PMCs in a crowded market. In a 2007 online chat with the *Washington Post*, Singer, director of the 21st Century Defense Initiative of the Brookings Institute, asserted that at the time there were about 170 firms doing business in Iraq alone.[5] A July 2010 analysis by the Congressional Research Service reported that "contractors make up 54% of the workforce in Iraq and Afghanistan," meaning that contractors slightly outnumbered U.S. soldiers deployed to those countries. More than 13,000 of these contractors are armed.[6] With so many firms and their contractors in play, the dollar amounts involved are unsurprisingly high. The Congressional Budget Office estimated that the Department of Defense spent $76 billion on contractors in Iraq between 2003 and 2007.[7] The staggering cost raises an important question in the mind of any taxpayer: What are we getting for that money?

As Dr. Euchner pointed out, the civilian and military leadership of the United States is attracted to contractors because they offer streamlined services, with supposedly less bureaucracy and fewer regulations. As Erik Prince, the cofounder and owner of Blackwater/Xe Services, put it, "Our corporate goal is to do for the national security apparatus what FedEx did to the postal service."[8] However, critics of PMCs would say that we're buying the services of mercenaries, since both contractors and mercenaries are essentially hired guns. Throughout his book, Scahill provocatively uses "private military corporation" and "mercenary" as interchangeable terms, underscoring their similarities but failing to provide definitions of either. Yet a look at definitions in Singer's Corporate Warriors reveals that PMCs and traditional mercenaries differ in several key ways. Perhaps the most important difference is that a private military corporation is just that: a legal corporate entity[9] (as opposed to the illegal adventurer or rag-tag squad evoked by the word "mercenary"). Another significant

---

Annotations:

First two paragraphs offer background information and history to orient readers.

Nicholas introduces a government document as the source of the quoted information.

A colon (:) is not used when the quoted text is part of the sentence.

A partial quotation is integrated effectively into the sentence.

Nicholas poses a question that he will answer in his essay.

Speaker tag gives us context for the quotation.

Nicholas points out a disagreement between two of his sources.

Sidebar: Chicago · V Documenting Sources

Brothers 4

distinction is that PMCs offer a wide range of services — "training, logistics, support, operational support post-conflict resolution," according to the head of the PMC Sandline[10] — while mercenaries can rarely do more than engage in combat. However, while PMCs, unlike most mercenaries, are legal, corporate, and diversified in their capabilities, several high-profile abuse cases reveal that it is no wiser to rely on PMCs than on the mercenaries of old.

Numerous examples of abuses, negligence, and outright crimes have taken place since the post-9/11 expansion of the private military industry, and only a handful can be recounted here: A 2002 *Salon.com* feature details the experiences of the whistleblowers who exposed the sex trafficking that DynCorp International employees, under contract to service helicopters during peacekeeping operations, engaged in while stationed in Bosnia.[11] Scahill writes of the largely underreported involvement of contractors from the San Diego–based Titan Corporation and the Virginia-based CACI in the now infamous torture of Iraqi detainees at the Abu Ghraib prison compound in 2004.[12] And in what has become known as the Nisour Square Massacre, Blackwater employees killed 17 Iraqi civilians at a busy intersection in Baghdad.[13] These are, of course, only a small sampling of contractor abuses, but they are clearly criminal actions — incidents that can't be explained away as an errant bullet or malfunctioning "smart" bomb.

It might be argued that these abuses are the actions of the individuals hired by a corporation, not part of corporate policy. And it might be further argued that in some of these cases, regular U.S. troops can and have committed similar crimes (and in the case of Abu Ghraib, were participating right along with the contractors). But a major difference between a contractor and a U.S. soldier is accountability. While there might exist the same opportunity to commit crimes between the private and public sectors, there are clear consequences in place for regular troops, who are subject to the Uniform Code of Military Justice (UCMJ). As of October 2010, 34 U.S. Army soldiers had been court-martialed on charges of murder or manslaughter of civilians in conflict zones in Iraq and Afghanistan, and 22 of those soldiers were convicted.[14] In contrast, it was only in 2006 that the UCMJ was amended so that contractors could be charged with criminal actions under the court-martial system.[15] Unlike regular troops, contractors are backed by strong money: Lobbying groups fight hard and spend millions to make sure the corporations are not held accountable.[16] Although charges were brought against five Blackwater men for the 2007 Nisour Square Massacre, the case

Writer's name is followed by the page number.

The name of the Web site is used to identify the source.

Brothers 5

was dismissed when the judge ruled that the prosecutors could not use statements that the accused had given to State Department investigators on the condition that the information could not be applied as evidence. As reporter James Risen explains in a recent *New York Times* article, "The Blackwater personnel were given a form of immunity from prosecution by the people they were working for and helping to protect."[17] Though the State Department has appealed the Nisour Square case, there have yet to be serious legal consequences for these and other contractors who commit crimes.

The atmosphere of lawlessness inherent in battle zones is compounded by the illegal acts of some of these contractors, which, in a low-intensity conflict, may turn citizens into insurgents. The Army Field Manual states that "people who have been maltreated or have had close friends or relatives killed . . . may strike back at their attackers. Security force abuses . . . can be major escalating factors for insurgencies."[18] And, as the Congressional Research Service report points out, Iraqi and Afghan civilians don't always know the difference between a U.S. soldier and a contractor, meaning that, in the minds of the people, the actions of contractors directly reflect on the U.S. military.[19] However, despite the people's inability to tell them apart, contractors and U.S. soldiers have significantly different motivations. By definition, those in the military are serving their commander-in-chief while those hired as contractors are serving a for-profit company. In regards to PMCs' bottom lines, it would actually be advantageous to shoot first and ask questions later, engendering more fear and insecurity and therefore the need for more contracted security guards. This positive feedback loop should not be considered as some elaborate conspiracy; the situation is merely part of the culture and nature of profit-motivated actors. It's the reason why, until the last couple of decades, defense operations have overwhelmingly been left up to the public, not the private, sector: Ultimately, the motivation of profit is not necessarily in line with the motivation of national security.

Given the potential costs in justice and national security, why hire contractors at all? Ironically, perhaps the most often cited reason for using private contractors is that using these corporations saves the taxpayer money since the government can hire them on an as-need basis and does not have to pay for contractors' training, health care, or pensions.[20] Professor Allison Stanger of Middlebury College challenges this notion in her 2009 book *One Nation Under Contract: The Outsourcing of American Power and the Future of Foreign Policy* when she points out that nearly all private contractors

Tag indicates the source of the paraphrased information.

Source of paraphrased information is provided in a note.

Paraphrased information

Nicholas returns to his original question and asks a more in-depth one.

previously served in the military, meaning that many of them are receiving pension payments anyway. Stanger writes that "the federal government is effectively paying for the training and retirement of the contractors it hires, all appearances to the contrary, as well as paying double or triple the daily rate for their services."[21] Therefore the Department of Defense would actually save taxpayers money by reversing the trend of privatization.

However, reducing the role of PMCs is very difficult because the more money the U.S. government spends hiring these firms, the more these firms can afford to offer in salary, and the more soldiers aspire to leave the military to work for private companies.[22] A brain-drain occurs, sapping the strategic and tactical knowledge of the military, thus creating an increased need for PMCs. Lt. Col. Michael Brothers, who enlisted in 1981, described this process as one that has been emotional for many in the armed forces as men and women in uniform saw their chosen specialties phased out or privatized out from under them.[23] Essentially, PMCs have created a void, filled it, and recreated the void so they can refill it, ad infinitum. This makes it increasingly difficult to reverse the current state of overreliance on PMCs since, according to the Congressional Research Service report, "many analysts now believe that DOD [the Department of Defense] is unable to successfully execute large missions without contractor support."[24] The vicious cycle of paying for help and then becoming more helpless makes it imperative that the United States ends its dependence on PMCs as soon as possible.

U.S. citizens should better understand how our military operations are carried out overseas, since the wars in Iraq and Afghanistan affect our security, our taxes, and our consciences as Americans. But we in the polity have not demanded that contractors paid by the government for military services be held accountable for their actions, and neither have we demanded that our leaders recognize and address the growing threat to national security PMCs represent. A recent bill called the Stop Outsourcing Security Act, submitted to both houses of Congress by Representative Jan Schakowsky (D-Ill.) in the House and Senator Bernie Sanders (I-Ver.), offers one potential route to intervention. The act would "prohibit the use of private contractors for military, security, law enforcement, intelligence, and armed rescue functions unless the President tells Congress why the military is unable to perform those functions."[25] The passage of this Act could be the first step in the process of phasing out the use of private contractors and returning military operations to the public sector. On her website, Schakowsky urges Americans to contact their

Brackets clarify the abbreviation used in the original quotation.

Brothers 7

representatives to cosponsor the legislation and become citizen co-
sponsors of the Stop Outsourcing Security Act themselves. In the end,
we as voters and taxpayers must ask ourselves, who do we want to
carry out U.S. defense missions abroad: those accountable to the U.S.
military, or those beholden to private corporations? Given the costs
in justice and in dollars, it's clear that the U.S. military has come
to overrely on PMCs to a point that is dangerous to national security
and national interests. This reliance must be reduced, perhaps excised
entirely.

Nicholas concludes with a strong, clear statement of his position.

Brothers 8

Notes

Entries listed in order of appearance in the essay

1. P. W. Singer, *Corporate Warriors: The Rise of the Privatized Military Industry* (Ithaca: Cornell University Press, 2003), 15–16.

2. Jonathan Euchner, personal interview, September 25, 2010.

3. Jeremy Scahill, *Blackwater: The Rise of the World's Most Powerful Mercenary Army*, 2nd ed. (New York: Nation Books, 2007), 49–51.

4. C. J. Chivers, Carlotta Gall, Andrew W. Lehren, Mark Mazzetti, Jane Perlez, and Eric Schmitt, with contributions from Jacob Harris and Alan McLean, "View Is Bleaker Than Official Portrayal of War in Afghanistan," *New York Times*, July 25, 2010, http://www.nytimes.com; Eric Schmitt, Helene Cooper, and David E. Sanger, "U.S. Military Seeks Slower Pace to Wrap Up Afghan Role," *New York Times*, August 11, 2010, http://www.nytimes.com.

5. P. W. Singer, "Break the Blackwater Habit: We Can't Fight the War Without the Company — But We Won't Win with It on Our Payroll," *Washington Post*, October 8, 2007, http://www.washingtonpost.com.

6. Moshe Schwartz, *Department of Defense Contractors in Iraq and Afghanistan: Background and Analysis*, Congressional Research Service, July 2, 2010, 18.

7. Ibid., 2.

8. Erik Prince speaking at West 2006 conference, January 11, 2006, quoted in Scahill, *Blackwater*, xix.

9. Singer, *Corporate Warriors*, 46.

10. Andrew Gilligan, "Inside Lt. Col. Spicer's New Model Army," *Sunday Telegraph*, November 24, 1998, quoted in Singer, *Corporate Warriors*, 46.

11. Robert Capps, "Outside the Law," *Salon.com*, June 26, 2002, http://www.salon.com.

12. Scahill, *Blackwater*, 221.

13. Charlie Savage, "Judge Drops Charges from Blackwater Deaths in Iraq," *New York Times*, December 31, 2009, http://www.nytimes.com.

14. Charlie Savage, "Case of Accused Soldiers May Be Worst of 2 Wars," *New York Times*, October 3 2010, http://www.nytimes.com.

15. P. W. Singer, "The Law Catches Up to Private Militaries, Embeds," Brookings Institute, August 25, 2010, http://www.brookings.edu.

16. Barry Yeoman, "Soldiers of Good Fortune," *Mother Jones*, May 2003, http://www.motherjones.com/politics.

17. James Risen, "Efforts to Prosecute Blackwater Are Collapsing," *New York Times*, October 20, 2010, http://www.nytimes.com.

Annotations (margin labels):
- List of notes on a separate page, heading centered
- Field research
- Book with one author
- Semicolon indicates that note 4 includes two distinct sources
- Government report
- Indicates source of material is the same as that for the previous note, but on a different page
- A source quoted within another source
- Abbreviated reference to source identified in note 1
- Article from an online magazine
- Article in a daily newspaper

18. Department of Defense, *Counterinsurgency*, FM 3-24, December 2006, quoted in Schwartz, *Department of Defense*, 16.

19. Schwartz, *Department of Defense*, 16.

20. David Isenberg, "Contractors and Cost Effectiveness," CATO Institute, December 23, 2009, http://www.cato.org.

21. Allison Stanger, *One Nation Under Contract: The Outsourcing of American Power and the Future of Foreign Policy* (New Haven, CT: Yale University Press, 2009), 96–97, quoted in Isenberg, "Contractors and Cost Effectiveness."

22. Robert Young Pelton, *Licensed to Kill: Hired Guns in the War on Terror* (New York: Three Rivers Press, 2007), 58, quoted in Scahill, *Blackwater*, 221.

23. Michael Brothers, phone interview, September 20, 2010.

24. Schwartz, *Department of Defense*, 1.

Nonperiodical Web site — 25. Jan Schakowsky, "Contracting," Congresswoman Jan Schakowsky, last modified October 11, 2010, http://schakowsky .house.gov.

Brothers 10

Bibliography

Capps, Robert. "Outside the Law." *Salon.com*, June 26, 2002. http://
www.salon.com.

Chivers, C. J., Carlotta Gall, Andrew W. Lehren, Mark Mazzetti, Jane Perlez, and Eric Schmitt, with contributions from Jacob Harris and Alan
McLean. "View Is Bleaker Than Official Portrayal of War in Afghanistan." *New York Times*, July 25, 2010. http://www.nytimes.com.

Hemingway, Mark. "Blackwater's Legal Netherworld." *National Review
Online*, September 26, 2007. http://www.nationalreview.com.

Isenberg, David. "Contractors and Cost Effectiveness." CATO Institute.
December 23, 2009. http://www.cato.org.

Pelton, Robert Young. *Licensed to Kill: Hired Guns in the War on Terror*. New
York: Three Rivers Press, 2007. Quoted in Scahill, *Blackwater*, 221.

Risen, James. "Efforts to Prosecute Blackwater Are Collapsing." *New
York Times*, October 20, 2010. http://www.nytimes.com.

Savage, Charlie. "Case of Accused Soldiers May Be Worst of 2 Wars."
New York Times, October 3, 2010. http://www.nytimes.com.

– – –. "Judge Drops Charges from Blackwater Deaths in Iraq." *New York
Times*, December 31, 2009. http://www.nytimes.com.

Scahill, Jeremy. *Blackwater: The Rise of the World's Most Powerful
Mercenary Army*. 2nd ed. New York: Nation Books, 2007.

Schakowsky, Jan. "Contracting." Congresswoman Jan Schakowsky. Last
modified October 11, 2010. http://schakowsky.house.gov.

Schmitt, Eric, Helene Cooper, and David E. Sanger. "U.S. Military
Seeks Slower Pace to Wrap Up Afghan Role." *New York Times*.
August 11, 2010. http://www.nytimes.com.

Schwartz, Moshe. *Department of Defense Contractors in Iraq and
Afghanistan: Background and Analysis*. Congressional Research
Service, July 2, 2010.

Singer, P. W. "Break the Blackwater Habit: We Can't Fight the War Without
the Company — But We Won't Win with It on Our Payroll." *Washington Post*, October 8, 2007. http://www.washingtonpost.com.

– – –. *Corporate Warriors: The Rise of the Privatized Military Industry*.
Ithaca, NY: Cornell University Press, 2003.

– – –. "The Law Catches Up to Private Militaries, Embeds." Brookings
Institute. August 25 2010. http://www.brookings.edu.

Stanger, Allison. *One Nation Under Contract: The Outsourcing of Ameri-
can Power and the Future of Foreign Policy*. New Haven, CT: Yale
University Press, 2009. Quoted in Isenberg, "Contractors and
Cost Effectiveness."

Yeoman, Barry. "Soldiers of Good Fortune." *Mother Jones*, May 2003.
http://www.motherjones.com/politics.

Entries listed alphabetically by author

Article from an online magazine

Article in a daily newspaper

Book with one author

Nonperiodical Web site

Government report

Dashes indicate that these sources are also by Singer

24

Using CSE Style

> **Key Questions**
> **24a. How do I cite sources within the text of my document?**   424
> **24b. How do I prepare the reference list?**   424

In 2000, the Council of Biology Editors (CBE) changed its name to the Council of Science Editors (CSE) to more accurately reflect its expanding membership. In this book, CSE style is based on the seventh edition of *Scientific Style and Format: The CSE Manual for Authors, Editors, and Publishers.*

CSE style, used primarily in the physical sciences, life sciences, and mathematics, recommends two systems:

- a citation-sequence system, which lists sources in the reference list according to the order in which they appear in the document

- a name-year system, which is similar to the author-date system used by the APA (see Chapter 22).

This chapter describes and provides models for the citation-sequence system. For more information on CSE style, visit the Council of Science Editors Web site at councilscienceeditors.org.

CITATIONS WITHIN YOUR TEXT

ENTRIES IN YOUR REFERENCE LIST

Books, Conference Proceedings, and Dissertations

24a

How do I cite sources within the text of my document?

The CSE citation-sequence system uses sequential numbers to refer to sources within a document. These numbers, in turn, correspond to numbered entries in the reference list. This approach to citing sources reduces distraction to the reader and saves space within a document.

1. Format and Placement of the Note   Sources are cited using superscript numbers or numbers placed in parentheses. Superscript numbers should be formatted in a font one or two points smaller than the body text:

> The anomalies in the data [3] call the study's methods into question.

> The anomalies in the data (3) call the study's methods into question.

2. Citing a Previously Mentioned Source   Use the first number assigned to a source when citing the source for the second time. In the following examples, the author is referring to sources earlier numbered 3, 9, and 22:

> The outlying data points [3,9,22] seem to suggest a bias in the methodology.

> The outlying data points (3,9,22) seem to suggest a bias in the methodology.

3. Citing a Source within a Source   When referring to a source cited in another source, use the phrase "cited in":

> The results [12(cited in 8)] collected in the first month of the study . . .

> The results (12 cited in 8) collected in the first month of the study . . .

24b

How do I prepare the reference list?

CSE style specifies that you should create a list of works that are cited in your document or that contributed to your thinking about the document. Sources cited should be identified in a section titled "References," while sources that contributed to your thinking should be given in a section titled "Additional References."

There are, however, two exceptions: personal communication and oral presentations.

Personal communication, such as correspondence and interviews, is cited only in the text of your document, using the term "unreferenced" to indicate that it is not found in the reference list:

> . . . this disease has proven to be resistant to antibiotics under specific conditions (a 2008 letter from Meissner to me; unreferenced, see "Notes").

Typically, information about personal communication is placed in a "Notes" or "Acknowledgments" section. Similarly, oral presentations at conferences that are not available in any form (such as microform, reference database, conference proceedings, or online) should be cited in the text of your document but not included in your reference list.

The *CSE Manual* does not specify the location of the reference list, deferring instead to the formatting guidelines of individual journals in the sciences. In general, however, the reference list appears at the end of print documents and linear documents that are distributed electronically (such as word processing files or newsgroup posts). In the case of longer documents or documents in which sections of a book (such as chapters) are intended to stand on their own, the reference list might appear at the end of each section or chapter. In electronic documents that use links, such as Web sites, the reference list often is a separate page to which other pages are linked.

To see an example of a CSE-style reference list, turn to p. 437.

Books, Conference Proceedings, and Dissertations

4. One Author   Give the author's last name and first initial with no comma. Next, include the title, capitalizing only the first word and proper nouns, followed by publication information. Include the state abbreviation in parentheses after the city. At the end of the citation, add the total number of pages contained in the book, followed by the letter "p" and a period.

4. McKibben B. Eaarth: making a life on a tough new planet. New York (NY): Times Books; 2010. 253 p.

5. Two or More Authors   List the authors in the order in which they appear on the title page, each of them last name first. Note that periods are not used after initials. Separate authors with commas.

5. Ayres RU, Ayres E. Crossing the energy divide: moving from fossil fuel dependence to a clean-energy future. Upper Saddle River (NJ): Wharton School Publishing; 2010. 240 p.

6. Corporate or Group Author   Identify the organization as the author.

6. National Geographic. EarthPulse. 2nd ed. New York (NY): Wiley; 2010. 96 p.

TUTORIAL

How do I cite books using CSE style?

When citing a book, use the information from the title page and the copyright page (on the reverse side of the title page), not from the book's cover or a library catalog. This tutorial gives an example of a citation using the CSE citation-sequence system.

Consult pp. 425–29 for additional models for citing books.

Book cover from BIOLOGY IS TECHNOLOGY: THE PROMISE, PERIL, AND NEW BUSINESS OF ENGINEERING LIFE by Robert H. Carlson, Copyright © 2010 by the Presidents and Fellows of Harvard College, appears courtesy of Harvard University Press.

A **B**

1. Carlson RH. Biology is technology: the promise, peril, and new business of

C **D** **E** **F**

engineering life. Cambridge (MA): Harvard University Press; 2010. 288 p.

A **The author.** Give the last name first, followed by initials for first and middle names. Separate the last name and initials with only a space, not a comma. Do not separate initials. Separate the names of multiple authors with commas (Cobb C, Fetterolf ML). End with a period.

B **The title.** Give the full title; include the subtitle (if any), preceded by a colon. Capitalize only the first word of the title and proper nouns. Do not underline or italicize the title or subtitle. End with a period.

C **The city of publication.** If more than one city is given, use the first one listed. For a city that may be unfamiliar to your readers or confused with another city, add an abbreviation of the state, country, or province in parentheses: Depew (OK). Insert a colon.

D **The publisher.** Give the publisher's name, omitting *The* at the beginning. Insert a semicolon.

E **The date of publication.** Use the publication date if one is given; otherwise use the copyright date. If a month of publication is given, use that as well (2008 Aug).

F **The number of pages.** Give the total number of pages contained in the book, followed by the letter "p" and a period.

Use the bibliography tools at **bedfordresearcher.com** to create a reference list formatted in CSE style.

7. Unknown Author   Begin with the title.

7. The first 100,000 prime numbers. Lenox (MA): Hard Press; 2007. 215 p.

8. Translated Book   Identify the translator after the title, giving last name first.

8. Schoeps KH. Literature and film in the Third Reich. Dell'Orto KM, translator. Columbia (SC): Camden House; 2010. 382 p.

9. Book in an Edition Other Than the First   Note the edition (for instance, "2nd ed." or "New rev. ed.") after the title and with a separating period.

9. Fuller JR. Surgical technology: principles and practice. 5th ed. St. Louis (MO): Saunders Elsevier; 2010. 1128 p.

10. Multivolume Work   Include the total number of volumes if you are making a reference to all volumes in the work, or "Vol." followed by the specific volume number followed by the title of that volume (if that volume is separately titled).

10. Serway RA, Jewett JW. Physics for scientists and engineers. Vol. 5. 8th ed. Pacific Grove (CA): Brooks-Cole; 2010. 368 p.

11. Authored Book with an Editor   Identify the editor(s) before the publication information. Note that CSE style is to abbreviate United Kingdom "GB."

11. Darwin C. Evolution: selected letters 1860-1870. Burkhardt FH, Pearn AM, Evans S, editors. Cambridge (GB): Cambridge University Press; 2008. 336 p.

12. Book in a Series

12. Rosenberg A, Arp B, editors. Philosophy of biology: an anthology. Chichester (GB): Wiley-Blackwell; 2010. (Blackwell philosophy anthologies; 32). 449 p.

13. Anthology or Collection with an Editor   To cite an anthology of essays or a collection of articles, treat the editor's name as you would an author's name but identify with the word "editor."

13. Carlson BM, editor. Stem cell anthology. London (GB): Academic Press; 2010. 402 p.

14. Chapter in an Edited Book or a Work in an Anthology   List the author and title of the section; then include the word "In" followed by a colon, the editor's name (last name first followed by initials) and the word "editor." Include the book title, place, and publisher, and note the inclusive pages of the section rather than the total number of pages in the book.

14. Rothenberg M, Clarke MF. Cancer stem cells. In: Carlson BM, editor. Stem
    cell anthology. London (GB): Academic Press; 2010. p. 221-236.

15. Foreword, Introduction, Preface, or Afterword of a Book   If the part is
written by someone other than the author of the book, treat it as you would a
chapter in an edited book (see #14), identifying the author or editor of the book
before the book title.

15. Groopman J. Introduction. In: Cohen J, editor. The best of The best
    American science writing: ten years of the series. New York (NY): Ecco;
    2010; p. ix-xv.

16. Chapter of a Book   If you wish to refer to a chapter of a book, identify the
chapter of the book after the publication information. End with the inclusive
pages of the chapter.

16. Pendergrast M. Inside the outbreaks: the elite medical detectives of
    the Epidemic Intelligence Service. Boston (MA): Houghton Mifflin
    Harcourt; 2010. Chapter 7, Fighting pox, pandemics, and special
    pathogens; p. 72-90.

17. Published Proceedings of a Conference   List the editors of the proceedings as authors or, if there are no editors, begin with the name and number of the
conference. Then give the title of the publication; the date of the conference; the
place of the conference; and the place of publication, publisher, and date.

17. Berger B, editor. RECOMB 2010. Research in computational molecular
    biology, 14th annual international conference proceedings; 2010
    Apr 25-28; Lisbon, Portugal. Berlin (DE): Springer-Verlag; 2010; 582
    p. (Lecture Notes in Bioinformatics; vol. 6044).

18. Paper Published in the Proceedings of a Conference   Format the citation
as you would a chapter in an edited book.

18. Paten B, Diekhans M, Earl D, St. John J, Ma J, Suh BB, Haussler D.
    Cactus graphs for genome comparisons. In: Berger B, editor. RECOMB
    2010. Research in computational molecular biology, 14th annual
    international conference proceedings; 2010 Apr 25-28; Lisbon,
    Portugal. Berlin (DE): Springer-Verlag; 2010; p. 410-425.

19. Published Dissertation or Thesis   Use the general format for a book,
adding the word "dissertation" or "thesis" in square brackets after the title. Treat
the institution granting the degree as the publisher. Follow with the phrase

"Available from:" or "Located at:" and then list information to aid in locating the source (including any acquisition or database numbers).

19. Prescott JW. Computer-assisted discovery and characterization of imaging biomarkers for disease diagnosis and treatment planning [dissertation]. Columbus (OH): Ohio State University; 2010; 191 p. Available from: http://etd.ohiolink.edu/

20. Unpublished Dissertation or Thesis   Use the general format for a book, adding the word "dissertation" or "thesis" in square brackets as a final element of the title. Treat the institution granting the degree as the publisher.

20. Wagner KP. A generalized acceptance urn model [dissertation]. Tampa (FL): University of South Florida; 2010.

Sources in Journals, Magazines, and Newspapers

21. Article in a Journal   Abbreviate and capitalize all of the major words in a journal's title; omit articles, conjunctions, and prepositions. The CSE manual includes specific guidelines for citing journal titles. A semicolon separates the year and volume number. Give the issue number in parentheses, followed by a colon and the page numbers. There are no spaces between the year, volume number, and page numbers.

21. Seligman HK, Schillinger D. Hunger and socioeconomic disparities in chronic disease. N Engl J Med. 2010;363(1):6-9.

22. Article in a Magazine   Magazines are not identified by volume. Give only the date (year, month, day for weekly magazines; year and month for monthly magazines). Abbreviate all months to their first three letters.

22. Milius S. In field or backyard, frogs face threats. Sci News. 2010 Sep 11:28-29.

23. Article in a Newspaper   Treat newspaper articles as you would magazine articles, identifying their pages by section, page, and column on which they begin (in parentheses).

23. Jalonick MC. Suit says toys in Happy Meals break the law. Boston Globe. 2010 Jun 23;Sect. B:11 (col. 1).

24. Unsigned Article in a Newspaper   Begin the entry with the title of the article. "Anonymous" is not permitted in CSE style.

24. A mouse to save your wrist and hand. Boston Globe. 2010 Nov 29;Sect. B:8 (col. 5).

How do I cite articles from periodicals using CSE style?

Periodicals include journals, magazines, and newspapers. This page gives an example of a citation for a print magazine article. Models for citing articles from journals and newspapers are on p. 429. If you need to cite a periodical article you accessed electronically, follow the guidelines below and see p. 432.

2. Foley J. Boundaries for a healthy planet. Sci Am. 2010 Apr:54-57.

A **The author.** Give the last name first, followed by initials for first and middle names. Separate the last name and initials with only a space, not a comma. Do not separate initials. Separate the names of multiple authors with commas (Cobb C, Fetterolf ML). End with a period.

B **The article title.** Give the full title; include the subtitle (if any), preceded by a colon. Capitalize only the first word of the title and proper nouns. Do not underline or italicize the title or subtitle. End with a period.

C **The periodical title.** Do not underline or italicize the periodical title; abbreviate and capitalize all major words. Omit articles, conjunctions, and prepositions. The CSE manual includes guidelines for abbreviating journal titles. Do not abbreviate one-word titles or one-syllable words in a journal title. End with a period.

D **The date of publication.** For magazines and newspapers, include the month and, if available, the day (2008 Apr 13). Insert a colon.

E **Inclusive page number(s).** Give the page numbers on which the article appears; list the numbers in full (154-177; 1187-1188). Do not add a space between the colon and the page numbers. End with a period.

Use the bibliography tools at **bedfordresearcher.com** to create a reference list formatted in CSE style.

Print Reference Works

25. Encyclopedia, Dictionary, Thesaurus, Handbook, or Almanac   Begin with the title of the reference work and information about the edition. Identify the editor, if listed. Provide publisher and publication date.

25. Encyclopedia of global warming. Dutch SI, editor. Pasadena (CA): Salem
     Press; 2010; 1211 p.

26. Map or Chart   Use the name of the area in place of an author. Follow with the title, type of map in brackets (such as physical map or demographic map), place of publication and publisher, and a description of the map. If the map is part of a larger document, such as an atlas, provide publication information for the document and the page number(s) of the map.

26. Australia and Oceania. Southwest Pacific [physical and political map].
     In: Oxford atlas of the world. 11th ed. London (GB): Oxford University
     Press; 2007. p. 122-123. Color.

27. Pamphlet   Format entries as you would for a book (see also #4 on p. 425).

27. American Academy of Dermatology. Skin cancer. Schaumburg (IL):
     American Academy of Dermatology; 2007.

Media Sources

28. Film or Video Recording   Give the title, then the type of medium identified in square brackets, followed by individuals listed as authors, editors, performers, conductors, and so on. Identify the producer if different from the publisher. Provide publication information, including a physical description of the medium.

28. Great migrations [DVD]. Hamlin D, Serwa C, producers. Washington (DC):
     National Geographic; 2010. 3 DVDs: 200 min., sound, color, 4 3/4 in.

29. Television Program   CSE style does not provide guidance on citing television programs. Cite the title of the program, with the medium designator in brackets, followed by information about the series (if any), including individuals such as the producer, writer, director, and the place and date of broadcast at the end.

29. Mt. St. Helens: back from the dead [television program]. Barrett M,
     executive producer. Nova. New York (NY): Thirteen/WNET; 2010 May 4.

30. Radio Program   CSE style does not provide guidance on citing radio programs. Cite the title of the program, with the medium designator in brackets, followed by information about the series (if any), including individuals such as the producer, writer, director, and the place and date of broadcast at the end.

CSE

V Documenting Sources

30. Mental exercise and dementia [radio program]. Flatow I, host. Talk of the Nation Science Friday. New York (NY): National Public Radio; 2010 Sep 3.

31. Sound Recording   Cite as you would a film or video recording.

31. African safari: Madagascar [sound recording]. Quin D, sound recordist. Glen Ellen (CA): Wild Sanctuary; 2002.

Field Sources

32. Personal Interview   Treat unpublished interviews as personal communication (see p. 424). Cite them in the text only; do not cite them in the reference list.

33. Personal Letter   Cite personal letters as personal communication (see p. 424). Cite them in the text only; do not cite them in the reference list.

34. Lecture or Public Address   Like an unpublished paper presented at a meeting, lectures or public addresses are treated as personal communication and are cited only in the text (see p. 424).

Electronic Sources

35. Material from an Online Database

35. Chen M, Schlief M, Willows RD, Cai Z-L, Neilan BA, Scheer H. A red-shifted chlorophyll. Science. 2010 Sep 10:1318-1319. In: Expanded Academic ASAP [database on the Internet]. Farmington Hills (MI): Gale; 1980-2010 [cited 2010 Nov 24]. Available from: http://infotrac .galegroup.com; doi:10.1126/science.1191127

36. Electronic Book (Monograph)

36. Gliklich RE, Dreyer NA, editors. Registries for evaluating patient outcomes: a user's guide [Internet]. 2nd ed. Rockville (MD): Agency for Healthcare Research and Quality; 2010 [cited 2010 Nov 1]. Available from: http://www.ncbi.nlm.nih.gov/books/NBK49444/

37. Electronic Journal Article

37. Pitaval A, Tseng Q, Bornens M, Thery M. Cell shape and contractility regulate ciliogenesis in cell cycle — arrested cells. J Cell Biol [Internet]. 2010;191(2):303-312. Available from: http://jcb.rupress.org; doi:10.1083/jcb.201004003

TUTORIAL

How do I cite articles from databases using CSE style?

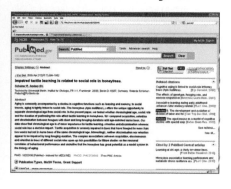

Libraries subscribe to services such as LexisNexis, ProQuest, InfoTrac, and EBSCOhost that provide access to databases of electronic texts. The databases provide publication information, abstracts, and the complete text of documents in a specific subject area, discipline, or profession. (See also Chapter 8.) This page gives an example of a reference in CSE citation-sequence style.

[A] [B]
3. Scheiner R, Amdam GV. Impaired tactile learning is related to social role in

[C] [D] [E] [F]
honeybees. J Exp Biol. 2009 Apr 1;212(7):994-1002. In: PubMed [database on

[G]
the Internet]. Bethdesa (MD): US National Library of Medicine, c2010 [cited 2010

[H]
Aug 4]. Available from: http://www.ncbi.nlm.gov/pmc/articles/PMC2726859/

[A] **The author.** Give the last name first, followed by initials for first and middle names. Separate the last name and initials with only a space, not a comma. Do not separate initials. Separate the names of multiple authors with commas (Cobb C, Fetterolf ML). End with a period.

[B] **The article title.** Give the full title; include the subtitle (if any), preceded by a colon. Capitalize only the first word of the title and proper nouns. Do not underline or italicize the title or subtitle. End with a period.

[C] **The periodical title.** Do not underline or italicize the periodical title; abbreviate and capitalize all major words. Omit articles, conjunctions, and prepositions. The CSE manual includes guidelines for abbreviating journal titles. Do not abbreviate one-word titles or one-syllable words in a journal title. End with a period.

[D] **The date of publication.** For magazines and newspapers, include the month and, if available, the day (2008 Apr 13). Insert a semicolon (for journal articles) or a colon (for magazine and newspaper articles).

[E] **The volume, issue, and inclusive page numbers.** For journal articles, give the volume number and then in parentheses the issue number; do not insert a space between the volume and issue numbers. Then add a colon and give the page numbers on which the article appears; list the numbers in full (154-177; 1187-1188). Do not add a space between the colon and the page numbers. End with a period.

F **Database and publication information.** After the word *In* and a colon, give the name of the database, followed by *database on the Internet* in brackets. Then give the place of publication, the publisher of the database, and the copyright year.

G **Date of access.** Give the access date in brackets and end with a period.

H **The URL.** Give the URL, preceded by *Available from* and a colon. Do not add a period after the URL.

Use the bibliography tools at **bedfordresearcher.com** to create a reference list formatted in CSE style.

38. Electronic Newspaper Article

38. Kolata G. Stem cell biology and its complications. New York Times [Internet]. 2010 Aug 24 [cited 2010 Dec 15]. Available from: http://www.nytimes.com/2010/08/25/health/research/25cell.html

39. Web Site

39. US Geological Survey [Internet]. Washington (DC): US Department of the Interior; [modified 2010 Sep 28; cited 2010 Dec 16]. Available from: http://www.usgs.gov/

40. Document on a Web Site

40. Lavelle M. National Geographic Daily News [Internet]. Washington (DC): National Geographic Society. Forcing gas out of rock with water. 2010 Oct 17 [cited 2010 Dec 16]; [about 9 screens]. Available from: http://news.nationalgeographic.com/news/2010/10/101022-energy-marcellus-shale-gas-science-technology-water/

41. Email Message   Email messages are considered personal communication (see p. 424). Cite them in the text only do not cite them in the reference list.

42. Electronic Discussion List Message

42. Williams JB. Re: Tomato seed question. In: BIONET [discussion list on the Internet]. [London (GB); Medical Research Council]; 2010 Nov 1, 7:57 am [cited 2010 Nov 15]. Available from: http://www.bio.net/bionet/mm/plantbio/2010-November/027780.html

43. Article Posted on a Wiki

43. Epidemic and pandemic spread In: Influenza [wiki on the Internet]; [updated 2011 Jan 22; cited 2010 Jan 25]. Available from: http://en.wikipedia.org/wiki/Influenza#Epidemic_and_pandemic_spread

44. Entire Blog

44. Orth JF. Invasive species weblog [blog on the Internet]. c2002-2010 [updated 2011 Jan 22; cited 2010 Jan 25]. Available from: http://invasivespecies.blogspot.com/

45. Entry or Comment on a Blog

45. Reynolds G. Phys Ed: Brains and Brawn. In: Well [blog on the Internet]. 2011 Jan 19 [cited 2011 Jan 22]. Available from: http://well.blogs.nytimes.com/2011/01/19/phys-ed-brains-and-brawn

TUTORIAL

How do I cite works from Web sites using CSE style?

You will likely need to search the Web site to find some of the citation information you need. For some sites, all of the details may not be available; find as many as you can. Remember that the citation you provide should allow readers to retrace your steps electronically to locate the sources. Consult pp. 432–435 for additional models for citing Web sources.

A

B

4. National Aeronautics and Space Administration [Internet]. Raisin' mountains

C

on Saturn's moon Titan. Pasadena (CA): National Aeronautics and Space

D

E

Administration; 2010 Aug 12 [cited 2011 Feb 3]. Available from: http://

www.nasa.gov/mission_pages/cassini/whycassini/cassini20100812.html

A **The author.** Give the name of the organization or individual author, last name first followed by initials for first and middle names. Separate the last name and initials with only a space, not a comma; separate the names of multiple authors with commas (Cobb C, Fetterolf ML). Include the word *Internet* in brackets. End with a period.

B **The document title.** Give the full title; include the subtitle (if any), preceded by a colon. Capitalize only the first word of the title and proper nouns. Do not underline or italicize the title or subtitle. End with a period.

C **Publisher information.** Give the place of publication followed by a colon, then the publisher or sponsoring organization followed by a semicolon.

D **Publication date and date of access.** Give the date of publication or the copyright date on the Web site; if available, include the date of modification or update in brackets. Then give the date of access in brackets. End with a period.

E **The URL.** Give the URL, preceded by *Available from* and a colon.

Use the bibliography tools at **bedfordresearcher.com** to create a reference list formatted in CSE style.

A Reference List in CSE Citation-Sequence Style

REFERENCES

1. Dodds W. Humanity's footprint: momentum, impact, and our global environment. New York (NY): Columbia University Press; 2007. 283 p.

2. Hall, S. Pandas: Still at risk. San Diego Zoo: conservation and research for endangered species [blog on the Internet]. 2007 Nov 15 [cited 2008 Jan 22]. Available from: http://www.sandiegozoo.org, wordpress/default/pandas-still-at-risk/

3. Bradshaw C. Having your water and drinking it too: resource limitation modifies density regulation. J Anim Ecol. 2007;77(1):1-4.

4. Skidmore AK, Ferwerda JG. Resource distribution and dynamics: mapping herbivore resources. In: Prins HT, van Langevelde F, editors. Resource ecology: spatial and temporal dynamics of foraging. Dordrecht (NL): Springer; 2008. p. 57-78.

5. Animal Ecology Group [Internet]. c2006. Groningen (NL): University of Groningen [updated 2007 Jun 29; cited 2008 Jan 22]. Available from: http://www.rug.nl/biologie/onderzoek/onderzoekgroepen/dieroecologie/index

Acknowledgments (continued from page vi)

Figures 2.6, 2.7, and 2.9: National Renewable Energy Laboratory.

Figures 4.2 and 6.9: Reprinted from *Corporate Warriors*, by P. W. Singer. Copyright © 2003 by Cornell University. Used by permission of the publisher, Cornell University Press.

Figure 4.3: Courtesy of *The Huffington Post* and the Cato Institute.

Page 70: Used with permission of the Associated Press Copyright © 2011. All rights reserved.

Page 90: UMNnews screenshot. "The dope on steroids: Why some athletes take the risk" by Ann Freeman. Published online August 21, 2004. www.umn.edu. © 2004–2007 Regents of the University of Minnesota. Used with permission. All rights reserved.

Figure 6.5: Courtesy of PrivateMilitary.org and courtesy of Microsoft Corporation.

Figure 6.6: Courtesy of the Center for History and New Media.

Figure 6.7: This screenshot is from Zoho Writer, an online word processor. Copyright Zoho Corp. 2011.

Figure 8.2: Courtesy of Bing.com.

Figure 8.15: Copyright 2011 LexisNexis, a division of Reed Elsevier, Inc. All rights reserved. LexisNexis and the Knowledge Burst logo are registered trademarks of Reed Elsevier Properties, Inc., and are used with the permission of LexisNexis.

Figure 8.16: The screen shot is Copyright © 2011 OCLC Online Computer Library Center, Inc., and is used with OCLC's permission. FirstSearch® is a registered trademark of OCLC Online Computer Library Center, Inc.

Figure 8.18: Thomson Reuters Web of Knowledge.

Figure 8.19: Courtesy of the Boston Public Library.

Figure 8.22: Courtesy of Shems Dunkiel Raubvogel & Saunders PLLC.

Figure 8.23: Courtesy of Spezify.com.

Figure 9.1: Reprinted by permission of Randy Paul.

Figure 9.2: Reproduced by kind permission of the Modern Humanities Research Association.

Figure 9.3: Reprinted from *The Readers' Guide to Periodical Literature* © H. W. Wilson Company.

Figure 18.2: From *Newsweek*, January 25, 2010. © 2010 The Newsweek/Daily Beast Company LLC. All rights reserved. Used by permission and protected by the Copyright Laws of the United States. The printing, copying, redistribution, or retransmission of the material without express written permission is prohibited.

Figure 18.5: © 2009, Foundation for National Progress.

Figure 18.6: From *Newsweek*, June 10, 2005. © 2005 The Newsweek/Daily Beast Company LLC. All rights reserved. Used by permission and protected by the Copyright Laws of the United States. The printing, copying, redistribution, or retransmission of the material without express written permission is prohibited. Illustration © Noli Novak.

Figure 18.7: Image courtesy of *Rolling Stone*, issue dated October 14, 2010. © Rolling Stone LLC 2010. All rights reserved. Reprinted by permission. Photos: (top) Dan Monick; (middle) Mick Rock/Retna; (bottom) Dreamworks/courtesy of The Everett Collection.

Page 296: Courtesy of the United Nations Office on Drugs and Crime.

Figures 19.9(a)–19.9(b): The Daily Californian.

Figure 19.16: © Jeremy Horner/CORBIS.

Figure 19.17: (a) AP Photo/Scott Dalton; *(b)* AP Photo/Martin Mejia; *(c)* © Margaret Fenton.

Figure 19.18: (a) © James Leynse/CORBIS; *(b)* George Kashouh/Traveltheworld.com.

Figure 19.19: AP Photo/Juan Karita.

Figure 19.20: (a) John Moore/Getty Images; *(b)* © ALI HAIDER/epa/CORBIS; *(c)* © Bettmann/CORBIS; *(d)* U.S. State Department; *(e)* © Jim Young/Reuters/CORBIS; *(f)* © Laszlo Balogh/Reuters/CORBIS; *(g)* © Bernd Obermann/CORBIS; *(h)* © Larry Downing/Reuters/CORBIS.

Page 338: Book cover from *Confessions of a Young Novelist* by Umberto Eco. Copyright © 2011 by the President and Fellows of Harvard College, appears courtesy of Harvard University Press.

Page 344: Film Quarterly vol. 64, no. 2 (Winter 2010). © 2010 by the Regents of the University of California. Published by the University of California Press.

Page 351: From Gale. Screen shot from Cengage/Galegroup.com Expanded Academic ASAP. © Gale, a part of Cengage Learning, Inc. Reproduced by permission. www.cengage.com/permissions.

Page 353: ZYZZYVA screen shot, used by permission of ZYZZYVA, Inc. Web design by Three Steps Ahead. Portrait of Naomie Kremer by Dennis Letbetter.

Page 369: Book cover from *Women, the Recited Qu'ran, and Islamic Music in Indonesia* by Anne K. Rasmussen. © 2010 by Anne K. Rasmussen. Published by the University of California Press.

Page 373: Courtesy of *Ode Magazine.*

Page 380: National Alliance to End Homelessness screen shot (www.endhomelessness.org/content/article/detail/2570).

Page 397: Book cover from *Urban Agriculture: Ideas and Designs for the New Food Revolution* by David Tracey. Cover design by Diane McIntosh. All photos and illustrations © David Tracey.

Page 403: Reprinted by permission of *Harvard Business Review.* Reprints: http://hbr.org/magazine.

Page 407: From Gale. General OneFile. © Gale, a part of Cengage Learning, Inc. Reproduced by permission. www.cengage.com/permissions.

Page 411: Courtesy of CulturalSurvival.org.

Page 426: Book cover from *Biology is Technology: The Promise, Peril, and New Business of Engineering Life* by Robert H. Carlson. Copyright © 2010 by the President and Fellows of Harvard College, appears courtesy of Harvard University Press.

Page 430: Copyright © 2010 *Scientific American,* a division of Nature America, Inc. All rights reserved.

Page 433: U.S. National Library of Medicine.

Page 436: NASA.

Index

KLAMATH COMMUNITY COLLEGE

Klamath Community College

Directory of Tutorials, Activities, and Checklists